THE VINTAGE

Turgenev

❀❀❀❀❀❀❀❀❀❀❀❀❀❀❀❀❀❀❀❀❀

Volume I

THE VINTAGE

Turgenev

Volume I

❖❖❖❖❖❖❖❖❖❖❖❖❖❖❖❖❖❖❖❖❖❖❖❖❖❖❖❖❖

Translated from the Russian by

HARRY STEVENS

Introduction by AVRAHM YARMOLINSKY

❖❖❖❖❖❖❖❖❖❖❖❖❖❖❖❖❖❖❖❖❖❖❖❖❖❖❖❖❖

VINTAGE BOOKS

A DIVISION OF RANDOM HOUSE

NEW YORK

VINTAGE BOOKS

are published by ALFRED A. KNOPF, INC.

and RANDOM HOUSE, INC.

Reprinted by arrangement with Alfred A. Knopf, Inc.

Introduction

TURGENEV: A REVALUATION

IN his student years Turgenev, who was slow in discovering his true medium, broke into print with some verse. Then he tried his hand at writing for the stage. Although he made at least one permanent contribution to the Russian repertory with *A Month in the Country*, his interest in drama did not persist. He grew to dislike his plays and he kept his poems out of his collected works: a poem, like an oyster, was worthless, he said, if it was less than perfect. The allegories, fantasies, and lyrical pieces that make up the work of his old age, *Poems in Prose*, are examples of a hybrid genre lacking both the form and the substance of poetry.

In his late twenties he published several romantic stories, which passed unnoticed. His work began to attract attention only when he started publishing serially, under the general title *A Hunter's Notes*, better known as *A Sportsman's Sketches*, short pieces ranging from sketches with a factual slant to more formal stories. They are held together by the device of presenting them as accounts of the narrator's experiences during his excursions in pursuit of game. Turgenev wrote many of them abroad, where he had gone to be close to Pauline Viardot, the prima donna with whom, on her first visit to Russia, he had fallen desperately and permanently in love. His great reputation dates from the publication of the *Sketches* in book form in 1852, when he was a man of thirty-four.

The work owed its great initial success in part to the fact that it was taken as an attack on serfdom, the abolition of which was then a burning issue. It is hardly an abolitionist tract, however. Turgenev abominated serfdom, but he was not a crusader by temperament and could no more engage in propaganda than he could walk on his head. In half the pieces the dangerous subject is not touched upon at all. It may be noted that when the book was in the writing the author inherited from that domineering dowager, his mother, fifteen thousand acres and two thousand male "souls," and that un-

Introduction

til the Emancipation he remained the owner — an uneasy one, it is true — of what his friend Herzen called "baptized property." It is certain, nevertheless, that the book did materially help to create an atmosphere hostile to the perpetuation of serfdom and may, indeed, have played a part in disposing the Emperor in favor of the peasant reform.

The movement against Russian serfdom is a battle long ago. Yet after the lapse of a century *A Sportsman's Sketches* still makes uncommonly good reading. It has the evergreen freshness of a classic. An outdoor, wholesome book, it is written out of an intimate knowledge of and sensitiveness to the natural scene, its shapes and colors, its sounds and odors. Felicitously these pages evoke the landscape Turgenev knew best, that of central Russia, where the forest gives way to the grasslands. It is a landscape with figures. The author's main concern here, as in the bulk of his work, is with human beings. In all these respects it represents the lineaments of his later work.

With the publication of *A Sportsman's Sketches* in book form, Turgenev decided that he had come to the close of a period of his life as an author and must strike out in a new direction. "I am done with extracting the triple essence of human character," he wrote to a friend, "pouring it into small bottles: 'Sniff it, please, gentle reader, uncork it and sniff it; it has the Russian bouquet, hasn't it?' Enough, enough!" He must adopt a new manner. He must put his mind to a studied piece of work on a large scale, a novel. But was he capable of "something great and calm"? He knew he couldn't tell until he tried.

In the thirty years that were left him he did produce several long narratives that are usually classed as novels. At the same time he continued to write short pieces. He curbed an inclination to flippancy and a weakness for odd characters, but his manner underwent a less clearly discernible change than his matter. Men and women of the people practically disappeared from his fictions, except as accessory figures, kept well in the background. True, the very year *A Sportsman's Sketches* was published he wrote two peasant tales. One, which Carlyle pronounced the most pathetic story in the world, is the widely anthologized *Moomoo*, an account of the miseries of a gentle giant of a serf, deaf and dumb, almost a symbolical figure. Turgenev never again focused his attention on simple villagers, except to add to *A Sportsman's*

Sketches, many years later, a piece about a peasant woman reduced by an accident to little more than a living corpse, yet accepting her bleak lot with a meekness and fortitude more than human. Henceforth he was to draw his models from the middle class: members of the gentry and people whom education had raised above their unprivileged status.

A distillate of character continues to be the main ingredient of the thirty-odd stories he was to write. In one of his few public addresses Turgenev elaborated a theory of personality, the gist of which was that mankind consists of Hamlets and Don Quixotes, or, more exactly, of persons in whom the hamletic and the quixotic elements are mixed in varying proportions. This view of human nature was useful to him in the construction of his characters, though a healthy instinct kept him from applying the formula with mechanical rigidity. Of course, his best creations refuse to be pigeonholed. Himself a man with a hamletic strain in his make-up, he satisfied his urge to project men and more especially women of the opposite temper. Yet it is significant that even his strong characters are not shown as having realized their ends. Either they die young, with their work undone, or their achievements are merely mentioned as a thing of the future.

A variant of the hamletic type appears in an early narrative that was not included in *A Sportsman's Sketches: The Diary of a Superfluous Man*. This is a characteristic piece of writing, though it does not show the author at his best. Like so many of his tales, it is a story of frustration and failure, enveloped in an atmosphere damp with pathos. Indeed, pathos is the earmark of Turgenev's art. The diarist is defeated in love and, as a victim of consumption, he is defeated in a more elementary, biological sense. Both he and his lucky rival are unworthy of the young heroine. Woman's superiority to man was a belief at which Turgenev arrived early in life. The theme of woman's moral supremacy haunts him as a recurrent dream haunts the mind. It is present in *A Quiet Spot*, which offers in passing a glimpse of the confined, uneventful, leisurely existence of the provincial gentry. It is a tale of unrequited passion, a love story, like nearly all of Turgenev's fictions.

Nothing so fascinates him as does this force welling up from the irrational depths of the soul. Now it floods the heart with "the gay terror" of impending happiness. Now its enchantment creates a new personality. It can clothe the world in glory, it can give a

Introduction

man wings, but it can also act on him like a disease. It "seizes a human being as a hawk does a chick." It may exalt or crush the finer instincts. Be it good or evil, Turgenev's preoccupation with it is not in terms of sensuality but of sentiment. And never does he show fulfillment. He is content to paint the dawn and occasionally the afterglow of love.

His particular delight is to celebrate the secret inception and first stirrings of young love, all compact of expectation and foreboding. Thus in *First Love* he succeeds in capturing the bliss and torment of a schoolboy passion, seen retrospectively in that mood of melting nostalgia to which he not seldom yields. The most striking backdrop for the action here is what Russians call a "sparrow night" — a short summer night tremulous with heat lightning, which is peculiarly appropriate to the mood of the piece. Memories of a dead love are also the substance of *Asya*. This charming story revolves about a rather likable youth who, like so many of Turgenev's male characters, is lacking in ardor and tenacity. At the psychological moment he fails to respond to the feeling he has aroused in the moody, passionate heroine. Fate intervening, their first embrace is also the last — a situation that recurs in Turgenev's work. The youth thus misses his chance of happiness. The story might take as its epigraph the remark of a character in one of Turgenev's later novels: "Man is weak, woman is strong, chance is all-powerful."

The pleasant young man with a fatal flaw in his make-up reappears in that rather mawkish tale, *Torrents of Spring*. He falls in love with an angelic, ravishingly beautiful girl, but ignominiously betrays her by allowing himself to be seduced by a hardly more credible predatory siren. Although his enslavement lasts only a few years, his life is permanently blighted. Like the protagonist of *Asya*, he is doomed to drag out the existence of a lonely old bachelor. It is tempting to relate this emphasis on joyless celibacy to a personal predicament of the novelist's. Because of his lifelong attachment to Pauline Viardot, the exact nature and history of which will probably never be known, he had no family of his own, and, moreover, was an expatriate during the last twenty years of his life. He had an illegitimate daughter by one of his mother's laundresses, but she did not live with him. The situation nourished his self-pity and the sense of unfulfillment that shadows his pages.

Introduction

Other stories of his dwell on the irrationality and the power of love. That it is the most unfathomable of life's mysteries is the conclusion reached by the narrator in *A Hapless Girl*, a somber, melodramatic tale with a tragic finale. The familiar thesis is illustrated more successfully in *The Brigadier*, which, in spite of its meanderings, has the verisimilitude of a case history. In a totally different genre is his last story, *Clara Milich*. An unconventional young actress falls in love with a backward, characterless youth and, when he spurns her, poisons herself. Dead she succeeds, where alive she failed: the ghost takes possession of Aratov. Turgenev was never more emphatic in assigning the active role in the relationship to the woman. Aratov dies (of "a fever complicated by inflammation of the heart") with a blissful smile on his lips, his fingers clutching a strand of his phantom bride's hair. His last words are that love is stronger than death. Turgenev would have been glad to believe this, but his work offers abundant evidence that he did not.

In quite a few of his stories everyday life is invaded by the supernatural. Like Hawthorne, he is careful to leave a loophole for a natural explanation, yet the impression these narratives are apparently intended to leave is that there are more things in heaven and earth than are dreamt of in positivist philosophy. Turgenev kept circling about the occult and peering beyond the gates of the unknown. But he was a man of realistic temper, secular, sober, skeptical. His spectral tales are the nadir of his art. In almost all of them only the creaking machinery of the supernatural is present. An admirable reporter, he could seldom write convincingly about matters outside the range of his experience.

One turns with relief from these apparitions and prophetic dreams, from mesmerism and Oriental magic, to the clear-eyed, bitter realism of *A King Lear of the Steppes*. Equally compelling is that fine character study, *Old Portraits*. One of Turgenev's last stories, it is based on memories of his early years. Indeed, a reminiscential strain pervades many of his shorter narratives. Thus *Old Portraits* evokes the charm of the placid past when the foundations of the ancestral order were still firm, but does not gloss over its horrors. The story ends on a note harsher than any sounded in the peasant tales. A serf, a gay little fellow who is made much of as an accomplished dancer, comes into the possession of a master who goads him cruelly. One day the gentle soul splits his owner's skull with an ax. "Those were good old days — but let's be done with them," are the closing words.

A King Lear of the Steppes may be classed as a novelette, and *Torrents of Spring* comes closer to the proportions of a novel. Turgenev himself dignified by that name only six of his tales, all written between 1855 and 1876: *Rudin, A House of Gentlefolk, On the Eve, Fathers and Sons, Smoke,* and *Virgin Soil.* Henry James, who admired Turgenev this side idolatry and whose work shows traces of his influence, considered his finest novel to be *On the Eve.* There is much to be said for this estimate. *Virgin Soil* is ampler and *Fathers and Sons* has passages of greater depth than those in any other of Turgenev's novels, but structurally it is less satisfactory and the total effect of it does not measure up to that of individual scenes, so that the whole is less than the sum of its parts.

Turgenev's method, generally, is to concentrate on one or more crucial episodes and to report briefly the antecedent and subsequent developments that serve to round out the cycle of the lives involved. As a rule the stories are told by an omniscient narrator, the author or another. Objective though he is, he can never keep himself completely out of the picture. Now and then he offers an obtrusive generalization or puts in a gnomic remark. Rarely, however, does he introduce a character who functions as his mouthpiece. Exceptions are the argumentative Potugin in *Virgin Soil* and Uvar Ivanovich, the penetrating old glutton who acts as a tongue-tied choragus in *On the Eve.* Turgenev practically never explores the sensibilities of his characters through the consciousness of an observer, the author's alert but not all-knowing deputy. The action is usually slight and takes place within a short period of time. There is no concern for suspense. The design is simple, its dominant principle being antithesis: the strong woman versus the weak man, the pure virgin versus the Jezebel, the idealist versus the philistine. Except for *Virgin Soil,* these novels give the impression of expanded short stories. They argue a shortness of breath on the author's part. Can it be that Turgenev's genius, like Chekhov's after him, was most at home with the minor form? He himself seems to have thought so. "Who looks for a novel in the epic sense of the word," he once remarked, "needn't come to me. . . . No matter what I write, it will always be a series of sketches." Fortunately, there is room for novels that are not epic in character.

As might be expected, "the great constringent relation between man and woman" plays an important part in the novels, as it does in the rest of Turgenev's work. Here, as nearly everywhere else, he dwells on the romance of love, rather than passion or durable affection. Even in *Fathers and Sons*, a novel of ideas, it has a prominent role. Arkady's entanglement with the two sisters is delineated with all the delicacy and understanding of which Turgenev was capable in dealing with young lovers. Alone in *Virgin Soil* is the love motif somewhat muted. It is paramount in *A House of Gentlefolk*. Steeped in pathos, the story of Liza and Lavretzky is framed to illustrate the evanescence of happiness, which is no sooner grasped than it escapes. With this theme goes another motif dear to Turgenev's heart: the melancholy wisdom of renunciation. Time was when countless hearts were wrung for the sorrows of this ill-fated pair. In our dry-eyed age few tears are likely to be shed over a heroine who takes the veil to expiate the sin of having fallen in love with another woman's husband, whom she had mistaken for a widower, and over a hero who accepts this decision without protest. Yet though some of these pages have a faded look, it is not difficult to surrender to the art with which the progress of the brief romance is traced in this finely wrought period piece. In *Rudin* the love affair serves as a test of the protagonist, "a man of words, but not of deeds," a test that he ignominiously fails. The involvement here is the familiar one of a high-hearted girl with a weakling of a man.

There are in these novels specimens of conventional girlhood and motherhood, "emancipated" members of the sex, one or two aged harpies and delightful old ladies, and several wicked women: the promiscuous creature who is Lavretzky's wife; the seductive society belle of easy morals who nearly captures Litvinov (in *Smoke*); the unscrupulous wife of Nezhdanov's employer (in *Virgin Soil*). Unique in Turgenev's gallery is the undersexed lady of the beautiful shoulders (in *Fathers and Sons*) through whom Bazarov learns that love is not all a matter of physiology. The center of the stage, however, is usually occupied by a lovely woman of exceptional moral stature, who has the wisdom of the heart as well as of the mind. It is to her that the novels owe their special fragrance and sometimes their meaning. She appears in various guises, all having a family resemblance. These spiritual sisters are idealistic creatures with an intense nature controlled by a firm will. Their stories, which are paralleled in the shorter narratives, form a legend of good women, as true in love as Chaucer's, but with no Cleopatras or Medeas among them.

The most vital example of the type is Yelena (in *On the Eve*). Before our eyes this dreamy girl turns into a woman, single-minded, intransigent, faithful unto death and beyond. She has the bearing of an Antigone. That she should give herself to her lover before their marriage (a bold stroke for so Victorian a novelist) and start with her husband for the hardships and dangers of an alien land might be put down to nothing more unusual than the impulsiveness of a romantic girl deeply in love. But when her husband dies before they reach their destination, the young widow knows neither despair nor confusion. She does not weakly return to her people and her own country. Instead, she resumes her journey to the savage Balkans, resolved to carry on the work to which her husband had dedicated himself: the freeing of his countrymen from the Turkish yoke.

Yelena throws in her lot with a militant Bulgarian nationalist. She plays Ruth to her Insarov's Naomi. For Russia had not bred — not yet — fit mates for her kind: her suitors had been a mercurial artist, a timid pedant, and a soulless bureaucrat. In *A House of Gentlefolk* Liza too is wooed by a young official who is a shallow, self-seeking worldling. But she does meet a Russian who is all but worthy of her. Among philistines and scoundrels, fools and toadies, the author places in a prominent position not only hamletic characters like Rudin and like Nezhdanov (in *Virgin Soil*), but also men of the type of Lavretzky. These members of a gentry that has had its day are honest, well-intentioned, sensitive, and, at least potentially, useful citizens, but they are no towers of strength. Rising head and shoulders above them are only Insarov, the dedicated soul who lives for a cause, Solomin (in *Virgin Soil*), a man of broad social vision and firm purpose, and, of course, Bazarov. The "nihilist" is Turgenev's greatest achievement in portraiture. His impulses and opinions, his crudities and faults, are as unmistakably his own as his long face and green eyes and make him wholly credible. He has a masculinity, a directness and vigor, almost unique in Turgenev's male characters. Rudin, like Lavretzky, can be fully understood only in the context of his age and country. As a projection of the radical temperament, Bazarov, though profoundly Russian and clearly a man of the fifties, has universal validity.

The times favored "engaged" literature; they demanded of the author that he embrace his age and contribute to its self-knowledge. The public looked for guidance to writers of fiction and expected to find in their works an echo of its fears and hopes, a confrontation of the *Zeitgeist*. Though his natural bent was toward the intimate rather than the public theme — he protested that he had no "*politisches Pathos*" and that "to a man of letters politics is poison" — Turgenev tried to live up to these expectations. His novels, unlike his shorter narratives, show a concern for the political questions of the day. The ultimate relevance of the short stories is one of personal morality. They carry no social message, fly no programmatic flag. They have to do with individuals in their private capacity, confronting problems of the inner life and meeting their separate fates. The protagonists of the novels, on the contrary, have a social dimension. These are pages from the history of Russia during the middle decades of the last century, when the country was in the throes of the revolutionary change from a serf economy to one based on free labor.

Thus *Rudin* reflects a phase in the development of the Russian intellectual. The hero's failure on the personal level, in his relationship with Natalia, is seen as symbolic of the inadequacy of the generation to which he, and his creator, belonged: "the idealists of the thirties." Scions of the gentry, nurtured for the most part in a hothouse atmosphere of German romantic literature and philosophy, they were volubly devoted to the good, the true, and the beautiful. But they were apt to be strangers in their own country, rootless men, unfit for action and incapable of feeling, given as they were to an excess of self-analysis. Before the story comes to an end, the author makes a valiant if rather lame attempt to arouse our sympathy for Rudin. The man, he argues, has high moral standards, and his rhetoric, since it can kindle the young with enthusiasm for lofty principles, is a power for good. And the poor devil comes to a quixotic end — an afterthought of Turgenev's, the account of Rudin's death on a barricade in revolutionary Paris appearing only in the second edition of the tale, several years after it was first published.

A man of Rudin's stripe appears in *A House of Gentlefolk*,

which is also set in the forties. This "Poltava Demosthenes," how-ever, is a wholly subsidiary figure. The leading character, Lav-retzky, is not a seedy, declassé intellectual, but the owner of many "souls" and broad acres, an agreeable, cultivated, well-intentioned man. For a few rapt hours he had believed that he would mend his broken life with the aid of Liza's love. We catch our last glimpse of him when, after a lapse of years, he returns, a lonely, aging man, to the scene of his brief bliss. Yet he faces existence with a serenity born of renunciation: he has given up hope of personal happiness and learned to find contentment in useful work. The moral of the tale is not without faint social overtones. Attention is called to the fact that Liza, whose character had been formed by her peasant nurse, talks to a villager without a trace of conde-scension. In managing his estates Lavretzky, whose mother had been a serf, has at heart not only his own interests but also those of his peasants. It is in character that, in an argument with Liza's odious suitor, he should demand reverence for the moral values (*pravda*) cherished by the Russian masses.

On the Eve opens on a summer's day in 1853. Before it closes, the guns have spoken, and Russia is in the midst of a war, the end of which will usher in the period of great reforms. Living up to its title, the novel reflects the anticipatory spirit of the years that opened into the stormy sixties. This is something other than the atmosphere of futility dominating *Rudin* and the aura of nos-talgic melancholy enveloping *A House of Gentlefolk*. Insarov dies without striking a blow in the fight for which his life had been a preparation. Yelena, his widow, goes off to carry on his work and is lost to view. The story ends on a mournfully medi-tative note. Nevertheless this novel breathes the tonic air of promise. To the contemporary reader it was both a reproach ad-dressed to a remiss generation and a pledge that the time was near when Russia would breed men, like the Bulgarian, possessed by the will to fight for the freedom of their own country. It was more than a pledge: Yelena became the model for the young women who in the next generation were to lay down their lives for the revolution.

The promise held out in *On the Eve* is to some extent fulfilled in *Fathers and Sons*. Like not a few youths of the late fifties, Ba-zarov, the young medico on whom the novel turns, holds to the philosophy of "nihilism." This is puerile when it is not brutish, and moreover is at variance with his own thoroughly decent instincts. Like Insarov, a plebeian by birth, he typifies the *razno-chintzy* (commoners) who were beginning to enter the ranks of the intelligentsia, previously limited to members of the privileged classes. What is more essential, he is a rebel, a destroyer, a revolutionary by temperament, with all of a revolutionary's intolerance, all his scorn of finicky sentiments and moral scruples. When he declares: "We mean to fight," it is clear that his kind will pull no punches. Science of the crudely materialistic, utilitarian sort has his fanatical allegiance. Since it cannot offer him a program of social action, he has no political ax to grind and is content to hit out at the modes of thought and behavior associated in his mind with the genteel tradition that he abominates. It may be surmised, however, that the "fight" is to be not only against the "principles" and shams of an aristocratic culture, but against the very foundations of the society that supports it. Not its ostensible theme, the conflict between the generations, but the emergence of democratic radicalism is the heart of the book.

In the novels considered thus far, particularly the last two, the private difficulties of the characters are seen against the larger predicament of the country itself, of this vast, dark, inert Russia. Whence will salvation come? Turgenev's answer in *Smoke* is that of a good European who knew no other remedy for the ills of society than "the homeopathy of science and civilization." Only slow, patient, "pedagogical" activity conducted at the grass-roots level can help. The Russians must learn the rational methods, the habits of industry and efficiency that have produced the civilization of the West. And it behooves them to be humble. The diatribes of Potugin, Turgenev's mouthpiece, against patriotic self-complacency make timely reading in days when Russia, under official stimulus, is indulging in an unparalleled orgy of national pride. For all his European sympathies, Turgenev, as a Russian classic, has not been put on the Index. It is heartening to reflect that his writings, along with those of other Russian authors in the liberal tradition, are exerting their humanizing influence at home.

The message of *Smoke* is underscored by its satire. Gall drips from a pen usually so temperate. Animus is directed against two sets in the Russian summer colony at Baden: on the one hand, the titled aristocrats yearning for the fleshpots of serfdom (the action

Introduction

is laid in the year following the Emancipation), and, on the other, the lunatic fringe of the radical camp. The reactionaries, with their stupidity and illimitable egoism, and the fire-eaters, ridden by a doctrinaire fury, are shown as brothers under the skin, equally alienated from the people. Not that the *mystique* of populism, whether of the Slavophil or the socialist variety, could be acceptable to Turgenev, the least doctrinaire of men. The rights of the individual were paramount with him.

The Westernist credo and the political caricature are dovetailed, with incomplete success, into a love story, a tragic variant of which will appear several years later as *Torrents of Spring*. The satire is heavy-handed, the love story convinces. In spite of its title, which of course refers to Litvinov's meditation on the insubstantiality of all things human, *Smoke* is by no means another monument to futility. And this not only because the novelist allows his hero eventually to rebuild his personal life and engage in honorable, useful work, thus, for once, providing a happy ending. Litvinov is one of those competent, practical, public-spirited men who, being pioneers of civilization, are Russia's hope, and, Turgenev suggests, their number is growing. Finally, there is the boon of Emancipation. Litvinov, at last returning to his estates, finds disorder and confusion. Yet above the troubled waters of Russian life "moved, like the spirit of God, freedom."

Virgin Soil, the last of the novels, is the most explicitly political of the lot. It deals with the inchoate revolutionary movement of the late sixties. The two young people who are the central characters are drawn together by a community of ideals that they mistake for love. Marianna's devotion to the populist cause is depicted with the feeling with which Turgenev usually celebrates the personal relation. She is a virginal creature, pure-hearted and dauntless, ready to die for her convictions. Nezhdanov, on the other hand, is another variation on the hamletic theme, a frustrate and divided soul, involved in revolutionary action only through adventitious circumstances and eventually losing faith in it.

In the end Marianna finds her true mate in Solomin. It is upon the strong plebeian shoulders of men like this hard-headed, hardworking engineer, the author implies, that the future of Russia rests. Like the conspirators who consider him one of their own, he hates the decaying feudal class and the equally predatory bourgeoisie that is bound to supplant it. But he does not share his comrades' belief in the imminence of the agrarian revolution. "A gradualist from below," anticipating the Fabians, he envisages a long, peaceful preparatory process of an essentially educational character. The epigraph to the book speaks of the necessity of tilling virgin soil with a plow that cuts deep. Turgenev meant not violence, but enlightenment. The lesson offered here is the same as that of *Smoke*. And again the beneficiaries of the existing order, whether frankly reactionary or hiding behind a spurious progressivism, are given no quarter. On the other hand, some of the freaks and crackpots who plot peasant uprisings and actually precipitate an ill-starred miniature *Putsch*, are treated with a certain amount of affection. In no other piece of fiction does Turgenev so unmistakably show his democratic sympathies.

The weakness of the novel is apparent when it is contrasted with Dostoevsky's work on virtually the same theme: *The Possessed*. This book, born of fear and wrath, in spite of its distortions gets at the heart of the matter in revealing the possibilities of perversion in the process of revolution. It is clear that the subject is alien to Turgenev. Just as in some of his stories there is the mechanics of the supernatural without its atmosphere, so here we have the apparatus of conspiracy without its animating spirit. Here as elsewhere the fine passages tend to redeem the feebler part of the book. Turgenev properly finds in a sense of injury, inferiority, and failure a mainspring of the revolutionary temper. Paklin, the unhappy fellow traveler, is one of the novelist's most subtly conceived characters. The factual side of the movement is depicted with more accuracy than might be expected, considering that the author was an expatriate who got his information about underground activities at second hand.

Looking back on his novels, Turgenev wrote in 1880, three years before his death: ". . . I strove, within the limits of my power and ability, conscientiously and impartially to represent and incarnate in appropriate types both what Shakspere called 'the body and pressure of the time' and the rapidly changing countenance of educated Russians, who have been the predominant object of my observations." The artist speaks here in the accents of the memoirist or the social historian. Indeed, their procedure was not uncongenial to Turgenev. Some of the pieces in *A Sportsman's Sketches* straddle the borderline between fact and fiction. *The Brigadier* contains the text of a letter that Turgenev had found among his mother's papers. As one reads the long dossier-like digressions in his novels, one feels that a first-rate biographer was lost in him. "Every line I have ever written," he told an American visitor, "has been inspired by something that has actually happened to me or come within my observation." He had the huntsman's eye and ear, as well as a prodigious memory upon which he leaned heavily. He insisted that he discovered rather than invented his characters, drawing them only after they had, in the Russian phrase, "calloused his eyes." George Moore acutely observed that Turgenev's imagination was illuminative rather than creative. Naturally, he transmuted the empirical data with which he worked, and at some point in the process of composition the unconscious put its hand to the wheel. Indeed, he asserted that he wrote *Fathers and Sons* almost in a trance, so that he was sometimes surprised at what came from his pen.

The body of his work is of unquestionable documentary and cognitive value. Within its confines the student will find much that is flesh of the flesh and bone of the bone of "the strangest and most wonderful people in the world," as Turgenev in an expansive moment described his compatriots. To open his books is to enter a lost world under the guidance of one of its inhabitants. Over it hangs a breath of decay. Perhaps for that reason he tends to hark back to his early years, when it was less rickety, and to carry-overs from an even more remote past. *Old Portraits*, as also the eighteenth-century vignette, a miniature masterpiece, in *Virgin Soil*, shows how skillful Turgenev could be in animating amiable fossils. But, for all his nostalgia, nothing was further from his mind than the wish to turn the clock backward. The existing order is doomed, he knows, but a better society lies within man's grasp. All that is needed to obtain the conditions of justice and freedom is persevering work carried on in an atmosphere of enlightenment.

To a generation that has seen what ours has seen there is something unreal about pages that imply the meliorist position dictated by the liberal's faith in reason and science. Turgenev has little to say about the evil in the heart of man. He does, however, convey a sense of Fate's malfeasance in some of his most memorable scenes: that, for instance, of Insarov's end in Venice, and particularly the description of Bazarov's death, one of the cruelest as it is also one of the tenderest things in literature. Characteristically enough, this powerful, ruthlessly veracious passage is not allowed its full force. It ends on a pietistic note that rings hollow. Turgenev has his lapses of taste. Reading *First Love*, for example, one of his best stories, is an experience similar to that of walking along a firm road with a fine view and suddenly stepping into a boggy place.

In a kind of credo that he set down in 1875 at the request of a friend, he wrote: ". . . I am, above all, a realist and chiefly interested in the living truth of the human face." A modern reader is apt to find Turgenev's realism not sufficiently penetrating, a little bloodless, rather timid. He tends to be too explicit. His habit of leaving no loose ends in his narratives gives them a look of spinsterish tidiness. He sees each character in detail, he scans the features, he looks into the heart. The rest of the anatomy is largely neglected. How these men and women came to be what they are is not shown, but reported in factual digressions on which his imagination had not gone to work. He keeps his nose too close to the evidence to permit the vision of far-off things. There is pity in his pages, but no terror. They are the product of an empirical, not a metaphysical mind. Here is an intelligence that does not soar or dive, and if it thus avoids risks, it also misses opportunities for discovery.

One returns to his work for the sake of observing characters sometimes subtly, almost always firmly drawn, against an appropriate background. Here are a few full-length portraits, and any number of neat sketches, intriguing cartoons, and delicate line drawings. One recognizes the nicety of his insights into human feelings and foibles, yields to the moods he creates, senses, too, even when one is strange to them, the beautiful authenticity of his settings. He has the power to conjure up the genius of a place, to give the very breath and being of a moment in a moonlit garden, on a country road, in a room of a dilapidated manor house smelling of kvass, apples, and leather. The scene of practically all his writings is rural or semi-rural. Rusticity is his element. He prefers the diffused light of the outdoors to the theatrical glare of spots. His dramas are played out against a background of earth and sky that has the charm of a Corot and the fine fresh detail of a Constable. What he wrote as a young man remained true to the end: "I should prefer to contemplate the precipitous movements of a duck's wet foot as it scratches the back of its head

Introduction

on the edge of a marsh, or the long and glistening drops of water slowly falling from the muzzle of a motionless cow that has just drunk from a pond in which she stands knee-deep, rather than all that the cherubim can behold in the heavens." Occasionally, however, Turgenev betrays a certain unease in the presence of nature. He asks whether men feel at a loss before her because her completeness mocks their insufficiency. Or he reflects somberly that she maintains her equilibrium in indifference to man's imbalance. But he is not at home with abstractions, is not given to dialectics, and falls back readily into a stasis of resignation or appreciation.

Whatever his attitude, the felicity of Turgenev's style is something that even a mediocre translation must suggest. The dialogue, except in the admirable interchange of his peasants, may be too literary; but the narrative and descriptive passages are couched in a prose never startling, yet both precise and emotional, moving with an ease and grace that has the effect of a cool music. The writing flows along smoothly, and is punctuated by the deliberate simile rather than the flashing metaphor.

Realist though he is, the lyric touch comes naturally to Turgenev. Exploration, analysis, are not his forte. The thinking of this confirmed rationalist is apt to be fraught with feeling. As often as not, he swings between a mild elation and a gentle melancholy. The tone of his fictions is often elegiac. They dwell on "the agitated sadness of expectation in the young, the impassive sadness of regret in the old." When Turgenev touches upon personal annihilation and the transience of all by which the human spirit lives, he strikes the chord of despair, but he does not hold it. If happiness is an illusion, he implies, it is an ineradicable one. Life may be a brief interval between two darknesses, but it admits virtue and beauty. Does the universe care nothing for them? Turgenev cannot contemplate them without an emotion which his art, at its best, renders contagious.

AVRAHM YARMOLINSKY

Contents

THE VINTAGE

Turgenev

❖❖❖❖❖❖❖❖❖❖❖❖❖❖❖❖❖❖❖❖❖❖❖

Smoke

1866

I

At four o'clock in the afternoon of August 10, 1862 very many people were assembled outside the famous Konversationshaus in Baden-Baden. The weather was beautiful; the trees in their leafy green, the light-tinted houses of the cozy little town, the undulating hills — all things were festively arrayed with an overflowing munificence beneath the rays of the benignant sun; all things wore a blind, trustful, and pleasant smile; and the same vague but happy smile roved over the human faces, whether old or young, ugly or handsome. Even the figures of the Parisian *lorettes*, with their blackened eyebrows and powdered faces, did not mar the general impression of obvious complacency and exultation; and the varicolored ribbons, the feathers, the golden and steely sparkles on hats and veils, involuntarily called to mind the vivacious shimmer and gentle play of spring flowers and iridescent wings. Though, truly, the dry, guttural rattle of the French patois, which was to be heard everywhere, could neither replace the twittering of birds nor compare with it.

Everything followed its appointed course, however. The orchestra in the pavilion played a potpourri from *Traviata*, a Strauss waltz, or the Russian ballad *Tell Her*, which the obliging conductor had given an instrumental arrangement. The same well-known figures were crowded round the green baize tables in the Casino, and they all wore the stupid and avaricious, half-amazed, half-indignant, but essentially rapacious expression that is conferred on even the most aristocratic features by the gambling fever. The same rather corpulent and over-fashionably dressed landowner from Tambov, with the same incomprehensible, convulsive haste, goggling his eyes, leaning his chest against the table, and paying no attention even to the croupiers' frigid sneers, scattered the golden louis d'ors with a perspiring hand over all the four corners of the roulette table at the very moment they shouted: "*Rien ne va plus*," and so robbed himself of all hope of winning anything, even if his number did turn up. But that did not prevent his waxing indignant the very same evening as he fawned on Prince Coco, one of the well-known leaders of the court opposition. This was the Prince Coco who in the presence of the Emperor, in Princesse Mathilde's salon at Paris, had remarked so pithily: "*Madame, le principe de la propriété est profondément ébranlé en Russie.*" As usual, our charming compatriots of both sexes gathered at the "Russian tree,"*à l'arbre russe.* They came up with an air of sumptuous, fashionable negligence and greeted one another majestically, with an easy elegance, just as one would expect of creatures who are at the highest level of contemporary culture. But when they met and sat down, they had not the slightest idea what to say to one another, and resorted to empty inanities, or to the hackneyed, highly impudent, and very flat witticisms of a certain Frenchman, a played-out ex-littérateur who wore Jewish shoes on his miserable little feet and had a miserable little beard on his odious face. This buffoon and gasbag passed on to them, *à ces princes russes*, all kinds of filth from old copies of *Charivari* and *Tintamarre;* and they, *ces princes russes*, gurgled with grateful laughter, as though involuntarily admitting both the overwhelming superiority of the foreign wit and their own complete inability to think of anything amusing. And yet here in Baden-Baden was gathered almost all the "*fine fleur*" of our society, "all the nobility and leaders of fashion." Here was our incomparable dilettante Count X, a profoundly musical personality, who was said to "execute" ballads so divinely, but who in reality could not tell one note from another without haphazardly poking his forefinger on the keys, and who sang more like a second-rate gypsy or a Paris barber. Here, too, was our captivating Baron Z, that jack-of-all-trades: writer and administrator, orator and card-sharper. Here, too, was Prince Y, the friend of religion and the people, who once upon a time, in the blessed era of liquor licenses, had made an enormous fortune by selling cheap brandy with thorn-apple juice added; and the brilliant General O. O., who had conquered something or other, had suppressed something or other, but had no idea what to do with himself or even how to introduce himself; and R. R., an amusing fat fellow who regarded himself as a very ailing and a very intelligent man, but who was as healthy as a bull and as stupid as a block. . . . This R. R. was almost the last in our day to preserve the tradition of the lions of the forties, the era of *A Hero of Our Time* [1] and Countess Vorotinskaya. He had preserved the habit of rocking on his heels as he walked, and *"le culte de la pose"* (it is not possible even to write that in Russian), and an unnatural slowness of movement, and a drowsy majesty of expression on his immobile, injured-looking face, and the habit of interrupting someone else's remark with a yawn, of diligently examining his own fingers and toes, laughing through his nose, suddenly pulling his hat from the back of his head down over his eyebrows, and so on. Here were gathered even the statesmen, the diplomats, the aces with European reputations, the men of counsel and intelligence, who thought that the Golden Bull was issued by the Pope, and that the English "poortax" was a tax on the poor.

Here, finally, were the zealous but bashful devotees of the camellia, the young society lions with superb partings down the backs of their heads, with splendid hanging side-whiskers, and dressed in real London clothes; young lions whom, apparently, nothing could prevent being just as vulgar as the notorious French windbag. But our own home produce is not in the vogue, and when the Frenchman was not available the Countess Sh., the well-known arbiter of fashion and the *grand genre*, whom evil tongues nicknamed "Czaritsa of the Wasps" and the "Medusa in a Bonnet," preferred to turn to certain Italians, Moldavians, and American "spiritualists," dashing secretaries of foreign embassies, and Germans with effeminate but prudent faces, etc., who were to be found in the town. The Countess's example was followed by Princess Babette, the same Princess in whose arms Chopin died (it is estimated that in Europe there are a good thousand ladies in whose arms he gave up the ghost). And by Princess Annette, who would captivate everybody but for the fact that occasionally a simple village washerwoman peers through the society mask quite suddenly, like the smell of cabbage amid the subtlest of ambergris. And by Princess Rachette, who had suffered such a terrible misfortune: her husband had been given an important position and suddenly, *Dieu sait pourquoi*, the head of the town had arrived and stolen twenty thousand rubles of government money. And by the risible Princess Zizi and the lachrymose Princess Zozo. All these ladies ignored their fellow countrymen, and treated them

[1] A novel by the poet Lermontov, published in 1840. (Tr.)

rather unkindly. . . . We, in our turn, will take no more notice of them, these charming ladies, and will leave the celebrated tree round which they are sitting in such expensive but tasteless toilets. And may the Lord send them relief from their gnawing boredom!

2

A few steps away from the "Russian tree," at a little table outside the Weber Café, was sitting a handsome man almost thirty years of age, of average height, rather spare and swarthy, with a strong, attractive face. Leaning forward and resting both hands on a cane, he was sitting quietly and unaffectedly, like a man who could not imagine that anyone might notice him or take any interest in him. He slowly gazed about him with large and expressive hazel eyes, shot with yellow, sometimes narrowing them against the sunlight, then suddenly staring after some passing eccentric-looking figure, while a swift, almost childlike smile touched his thin mustaches, lips, and square, prominent chin. He was dressed in a loose coat of German cut, and a gray soft hat was drawn half down over his high forehead. At first glance he gave the impression of being an honest and efficient, rather self-confident young fellow, such as are often met in the world. He appeared to be resting after long continued labors and was all the more artlessly enjoying the picture spread before him because his thoughts were far away, and moreover they circulated, those thoughts, in a world not at all resembling the one surrounding him at that moment. He was Russian; his name was Grigory Mikhailovich Litvinov.

We need to make his acquaintance, and so we shall have to say a few words about his past, which had been quite simple and straightforward.

The son of a retired old-time official of merchant descent, he had been brought up not in a town, as one would have expected, but in the country. His mother was a noblewoman, educated in a "school for young ladies of noble birth," a very kind and very exalted being, yet not without character. She was twenty years younger than her husband, and had re-educated him, so far as she could; she had dragged him out of his official circle into that of a landowner, had tamed and softened his robust, caustic temper. Under her influence he began to dress tidily and behave decently, and gave up swearing; he began to have respect for learning and the learned, although, of course, he never picked up a book, and did his very best not to degrade himself. He even began to walk more quietly and to talk in a languid tone, and more and more about exalted subjects, though this cost him no little effort. "Ah, you ought to be flogged!" he sometimes thought, but aloud he said: "Yes, yes, that is . . . of course; that is the question." Litvinov's mother put her house also on a European basis; she spoke to the servants in the second person plural, and at dinner never allowed anyone to eat so much that he wheezed. As for her estate, neither she nor her husband was able to do anything with it; it suffered from long neglect; but it was of considerable extent, with all kinds of appendages, forests, and a lake. At one time a large factory, founded by the zealous but unmethodical master, had stood beside the lake; in the hands of some swindling merchant it had prospered, but it had gone to utter ruin under the administration of an honest entrepreneur from Germany. Mme Litvinova was satisfied, if only because she did not squander her fortune and did not run into debt. Unfortunately, she could not boast of her health, and she died of consumption in the very year her son entered the Moscow University. He did not complete the course, owing to certain circumstances (the reader will learn about them later), but slipped away into the country, where he lounged about for some time without anything to do, with no connections, almost without acquaintances. Owing to the unfriendliness of the noblemen of his county, who were permeated not so much with the Western theory of the noxious nature of "absentee landlordism" as the homebred conviction that "your own shirt is nearer to your body," in 1855 he was called up for service and all but died of typhus in the Crimea, where he spent six months in a dugout on the shore of the Putrid Sea without seeing a single "Ally." Next he was elected to the local government service for some time, of course not without experiencing some unpleasantness, and, after residing on his estate for a while, developed a taste for farming. He realized that his mother's estate, which was badly and sluggishly managed by his senile old father, did not yield one tenth of the income it could yield, and that in experienced and expert hands it could be transformed into a gold mine. But he also realized that experience and knowledge were precisely what he lacked — and he went abroad to study agronomy and technology, to learn the A B C of farming. He spent more than four years in Mecklenburg, Silesia, and Karlsruhe; he visited Belgium and England, worked conscientiously, and acquired knowledge. All this did not come easily to him, but he endured the ordeal to the end. And now, confident of himself, of his future, of the benefit he would bring to his fellow countrymen, and maybe even to the whole country, he was preparing to return home. For in every letter his father wrote he called him back with desperate adjurations and entreaties; the old man was completely overwhelmed by the emancipation of the peasants, the allocation of the prescriptive rights over the land, the redemption transactions, by all the new order, in a word. . . . But in that case why was he in Baden?

He was in Baden because any day now he was expecting the arrival of his second cousin and fiancée, Tatiana Petrovna Shestova. He had known her almost from childhood and had spent the spring and summer with her in Dresden, where she had taken up residence with her aunt. He sincerely loved, he deeply respected his young kinswoman, and when he had completed his hard, preparatory work and was making ready to enter on a new career, to begin active and not state service, he proposed to her, asking her as the woman he loved, as his comrade and friend, to unite her life with his, for weal and woe, for labor and for repose, "for better, for worse," as the English say. She consented, and he went off to Karlsruhe, where he had left his books, his things, his papers. . . . But then why is he in Baden? you will ask again.

He was in Baden also because the aunt who had brought up Tatiana, Kapitolina Markovna Shestova, an old maid of fifty-five, a very good-natured and honest but eccentric creature, a free spirit, all aglow with the fire of self-sacrifice and self-renunciation, an *esprit fort* (she had read Strauss — truly, in secret from her niece), and a democrat, a mortal opponent of society and the aristocracy, could not resist the temptation of taking at least one look at that very society in such a fashionable place as Baden. . . . Kapitolina Markovna did not wear a crinoline and had her white hair cut short, but luxury and glitter secretly agitated her, and she found it pleasant and sweet to revile and scorn them. . . . So why not give the good old lady that pleasure?

But Litvinov was so tranquil and frank, he looked about him so self-confidently, because his life stretched quite clearly before him, because his destiny was determined. And he was proud of that destiny and rejoiced in it as the work of his own hands.

3

"Well, I never! So there he is!" a squeaky voice suddenly sounded right in his ear, and a puffy hand shook him by the shoulder. He raised his head and saw one of his few Moscow acquaintances, a man named Bambayev, a decent though rather empty sort, no longer young, with cheeks and nose as flabby as though soft-boiled, disheveled, greasy hair, and a flabby, corpulent body. Always without a farthing and always in raptures over something or other, Rostislav Bambayev roamed vehemently but aimlessly over the face of our long-suffering mother earth.

"Now this is what we call a meeting!" he repeated, goggling his bloated little eyes and sticking out his swollen little lips, above which his dyed whiskers bristled absurdly and ineptly. "Hurrah for Baden! They all crawl here like cockroaches. How did you get here?"

(Bambayev addressed Litvinov in the second person singular, as he did absolutely everybody and everything in the world.)

"I arrived three days ago."

"Where from?"

"Why, what do you want to know for?"

"What for? But wait a bit, wait a bit. Perhaps you don't know who else has arrived. Gubariov! Himself, in person! That's who is here! He arrived from Heidelberg yesterday. You know him, of course?"

"I've heard of him."

"Is that all? Really! We'll take you along to see him in a moment, this very minute! Not know such a man! And that reminds me that Voroshilov — But wait, I don't think you know him? I have the honor to introduce you to each other. You are both savants! And he is more, he's a phœnix! Kiss each other!"

At this, Bambayev turned to a handsome young man with a fresh and rosy but already serious face who was standing beside him. Litvinov rose and, of course, did not kiss, but exchanged a slight bow with the "phœnix" who, judging by his standoffish attitude, was not altogether pleased at this unexpected introduction.

"I said 'phœnix,' and I do not withdraw the word," Bambayev went on. "Go to Petersburg, to the —nd corps, and look at the roll of honor: what is the first name you see? Voroshilov, Semion

Yakovlevich! But Gubariov, Gubariov, my boys! That's the man
we must hurry along to, hurry we must! I absolutely worship that
man! And not I alone; everybody without exception worships
him. The work he is writing now, on — on — on —"

"What is it about?" Litvinov asked.

"About everything, my boys, it's a kind of — you know: Buckle
— only more profound, more profound. . . . In it everything will
be settled and clarified once for all."

"But have you read it?"

"No, I haven't, and really it is a secret and shouldn't be made
public; but you can expect everything of Gubariov, everything!
Yes!" Bambayev sighed and folded his arms. "Now if we only had
two, or say three, more heads like his in Russia, ah, if that were
possible! My God! I'll tell you one thing, Grigory Mikhailovich;
no matter what you have been doing recently — and I don't know
what you ever do — no matter what your convictions — and I
don't know them either — in him, in Gubariov, you'll find something to learn from. Unfortunately, he isn't staying here long. We
must profit by the occasion, we must go and see him. Come on,
come on!"

A passing dandy with little red curls and a blue ribbon on his
low hat turned and, smiling sarcastically, stared at Bambayev
through his monocle. Litvinov was vexed.

"What are you shouting for," he said, "as though you were
calling a bloodhound to a trail? I haven't dined yet."

"What does that matter? We can have dinner at once at Weber's
— the three of us. . . . Splendid! Have you enough money to pay
for me?" he added in an undertone.

"I expect I have; only I really don't know —"

"Please don't go on; you'll thank me afterward, and he will be
delighted. Ah, my God!" Bambayev interrupted himself. "They're
playing the finale from *Ernani*. What a joy! . . . '*A som—mo
Carlo* . . .' But that's just like me! In tears in a moment! Well,
Semion Yakovlevich! Voroshilov! Shall we go?"

Voroshilov, who was still standing motionless and stiff, retaining
his rather proud dignity of bearing, significantly dropped his eyes,
knitted his brows, and muttered something between his teeth . . .
but did not refuse. Litvinov thought: "Well, why not? I've got
time for the visit. I've plenty of time." Bambayev took his arm, but
first he beckoned with his finger to Isabella, the well-known

flower-girl of the Jockey Club, thinking he would buy a nosegay from her. But the aristocratic flower-girl did not stir; and indeed why should she for a gentleman whom she had never seen before even in Paris, who was without gloves and was wearing a stained velveteen jacket, a varicolored cravat, and patched boots? Then Voroshilov beckoned to her. For him she came. Choosing a tiny bunch of violets from her basket, he gave her a gulden. He thought such munificence would astonish her, but she did not even raise an eyebrow, and when he turned away she contemptuously writhed her lips to reveal her clenched teeth. Voroshilov was dressed very smartly, even exquisitely, but the Parisian girl's experienced eye at once discerned that his toilet, his figure, even his gait, which bore the signs of premature military training, were lacking in genuine, thoroughbred "chic."

Taking a table in Weber's main hall and ordering dinner, our acquaintances engaged in conversation. Bambayev loudly and fervently expatiated on Gubariov's exalted destiny; but he soon lapsed into silence and, breathing and chewing noisily, tossed off glass after glass. Voroshilov drank and ate little, with a reluctant air, and, after questioning Litvinov concerning the nature of his occupations, began to express his own opinion — not so much about these studies as on various "problems" in general. . . . He suddenly grew animated, and tore along like a mettlesome horse, spiritedly and sharply enunciating every syllable, every letter, like a dashing young cadet at a final examination, and vigorously but awkwardly waving his arms. As no one interrupted him, with every moment he grew more garrulous, more glib; he might have been reading a dissertation or a lecture. The names of the latest scientists, with the addition of the date of birth or death of every one of them, the chapter heads of brochures only just published, and a mass of names, names, names poured rapidly from his tongue, evidently to his own great satisfaction, as could be seen by his flaming eyes. It appeared that Voroshilov was contemptuous of everything old and esteemed only the cream of education, the latest, the foremost viewpoint of science; to mention, even though ineptly, the book of some Dr. Sauerbengel on Pennsylvanian prisons or yesterday's article in the *Asiatic Journal* on the Vedas and Puranas (he pronounced the word *Jernul*, though of course he did not know English) gave him genuine pleasure, amounting to felicity.

Litvinov listened to him and listened, and simply could not make out what was really his special subject. At one moment he was talking about the part the Celtic tribes had played in history; then he was carried back into the ancient world and was discoursing on the Egyptian marbles; he excitedly commented on the sculptor Onatas, who had lived before Phidias, whom, however, he transformed into Jonathan and thus for a moment gave all his argumentation a kind of Biblical or perhaps American tint; now he suddenly jumped to political economy and called Bastiat a fool and blockhead, "as bad as Adam Smith and all the physiocrats." "The physiocrats!" Bambayev whispered after him. "Aristocrats?" In passing, Voroshilov brought an expression of astonishment to Bambayev's face by a perfunctory and parenthetical remark about Macaulay as an out-of-date writer whom knowledge had already superseded. And as for Gneist and Riehl, he announced that they were only worth mentioning, and shrugged his shoulders. Bambayev also shrugged his shoulders. "And all this poured out all at once, without rhyme or reason, in the presence of strangers, in a café," Litvinov meditated, looking at his new acquaintance's fair hair, light eyes, and white teeth (he was especially embarrassed by those large, sugary teeth, and those hands with their awkward movements). "And he never smiles; yet he seems to be quite a good fellow and extremely inexperienced. . . ." Voroshilov quieted down at last; his voice, youthfully ringing and hoarse like a young cock's, broke a little. . . . And then Bambayev began to declaim poetry and again all but burst into tears, which made a scandalous impression on an adjacent table occupied by an English family, who sat giggling at one another. At a second table two *lorettes* were dining with some very old buck in a lilac peruke. The waiter brought the bill; the friends paid.

"Well," Bambayev exclaimed, rising heavily from his seat, "now for a cup of coffee and quick march! And yet there it is, there is our Russia," he added, halting at the door and almost rapturously pointing his soft red hand at Voroshilov and Litvinov. "And what is she like?"

"Yes, Russia!" Litvinov thought; but Voroshilov, who had already restored the concentrated look to his face, smiled condescendingly and clicked his heels a little.

Some five minutes later they were all climbing the stairs of the hotel where Stepan Nikolaevich Gubariov was staying. A tall lady, of graceful figure, wearing a little hat with a short black veil, came briskly down the same staircase and, seeing Litvinov, suddenly turned to him and halted as though struck with astonishment. Her face momentarily flamed and then as swiftly paled beneath the fine net of the lace. But Litvinov did not notice her, and she ran down the broad stairs even more briskly than before.

4

"Let me introduce Litvinov, a very decent fellow, a Russian spirit," Bambayev exclaimed as he led Litvinov up to a man of small size and the appearance of a landowner, with unbuttoned collar, a short jacket, gray morning pantaloons, and slippers, who was standing in the center of the light, well-furnished room. "And this," he added, turning to Litvinov, "this is he, the man himself, d'you understand? I mean Gubariov, in short."

Litvinov fixed inquisitive eyes on "the man himself." At first sight he found nothing unusual in him. He saw a gentleman of respectable and rather stupid exterior, big-browed, big-eyed, with a thick neck and an oblique and downward glance. This gentleman smirked, muttered: "Mmmm — yes — this is a good — very pleasant . . ." raised his hand to his face and, at once turning his back on Litvinov, paced several times up and down the carpet, waddling slowly and queerly, as though moving by stealth. He had the habit of continually walking to and fro, occasionally tugging at and combing his beard with the ends of his long, brittle nails. Besides Gubariov there were two other people in the room. One was a lady about fifty years of age, wearing a shabby silk dress. She had an amazingly mobile face as yellow as a lemon, short black hairs on her upper lip, and swift little eyes that looked ready to dart out of their sockets. The other was a thickset man sitting huddled in a corner.

"Well, my dear Matriona Semionovna," Gubariov began, turning to the lady and evidently not considering it necessary to introduce Litvinov to her, "what was the story you had begun to tell us?"

The lady, who was named Matriona Semionovna Sukhanchikova, was a widow, childless, not at all rich, and for two years now had been wandering from country to country, began to speak at once with a peculiar, vehement enthusiasm:

"Well, and so he calls on the Prince and says to him: 'Your

Excellency, you are in such a rank and in such a position, what would it cost you to alleviate my lot? You cannot but respect the purity of my convictions! And in our day is it possible to persecute anyone for his convictions?' And what do you think the Prince, that educated, highly placed dignitary, did?"

"Well, what did he do?" Gubariov said, meditatively lighting a cigarette.

The lady drew herself up and stretched her bony right hand before her with the index finger extended:

"He summoned his lackey and told him: 'Take that coat off this man at once and keep it for yourself. I give it to you.' "

"And the lackey took it off?" Bambayev asked, with a gesture of astonishment.

"He took it and kept it. And that was done by Prince Barnaulov, a well-known plutocrat, a magnate, entrusted with special authority, a representative of the government! And what else may we expect after that?"

All Mme Sukhanchikova's puny body shook with indignation, her face was contorted with spasms, her consumptive breasts heaved convulsively beneath her shapeless corset; of her eyes one may not even speak, they darted from side to side so rapidly. But they were always darting, no matter what she talked about.

"A scandal, a crying scandal!" Bambayev exclaimed. "There is no punishment fit for it!"

"Mmm — mmm. . . . Rotten from top to toe," Gubariov remarked, even now not raising his voice. "It isn't punishment — here a different measure — is necessary."

"But really, is it true?" Litvinov asked.

"Is it true?" she retorted. "Why, one may not even think of doubting it, n-n-n-not even think —" She pronounced the last word with such force that she writhed. "I was told the story by a most trustworthy man. Why, you know him, Stepan Nikolaevich — Yelistratov Kapiton. He himself heard it from eyewitnesses, from eyewitnesses of this disgusting scene."

"Which Yelistratov?" Gubariov asked. "The one that was in Kazan?"

"That's the one. I know somebody spread a story about him that he had taken money from some contractor or distiller or something. But who spread the story? Pelikanov! And can anyone believe Pelikanov, when everybody knows he's nothing but a spy?"

"But pardon me, Matriona Semionovna," Bambayev intervened, "I am a friend of Pelikanov. Why do you call him a spy?"

"Because that's what he is — a spy!"

"But wait, pardon —"

"He's a spy, a spy!" the lady shouted.

"But he isn't, he isn't; wait a bit; I'll tell you something," Bambayev shouted in his turn.

"A spy, a spy!" she declared.

"No, no! Now, Tenteleev, he's another story!" Bambayev bawled at the top of his voice.

Mme Sukhanchikova was momentarily silent.

"I have authentic information," he went on in his ordinary tone, "that when the Third Department [1] sent for that man, he crawled at the feet of Countess Blazenkrampf and whined and whined: 'Save me, speak for me!' But Pelikanov never let himself descend to such turpitude."

"Mmm — Tenteleev . . ." Gubariov muttered, "that — that needs to be noted."

She contemptuously shrugged her shoulders.

"They're both excellent!" she said. "But I know an even better story about Tenteleev. As everybody knows, he was a terrible tyrant to his people, though he also pretended to be an emancipator. And one day he was sitting with acquaintances in Paris, and suddenly Madame Beecher Stowe walked in — you know her, *Uncle Tom's Cabin*. Tenteleev is a terribly conceited man, and he asked the host to introduce him. But as soon as she heard his name: 'What?' she said, 'he dares to make the acquaintance of the author of *Uncle Tom*?' And she slaps his cheek! 'Get out!' she says, 'this minute!' And what do you think? He picked up his hat, tucked in his tail, and slipped off."

"Well, I think that's exaggerated," Bambayev remarked. "She certainly did say 'Get out!' to him, that's a fact; but she didn't slap his face."

"She did slap his face, she did slap his face!" she repeated with convulsive intensity. "I don't talk rubbish. And you're a friend of people like that!"

[1] The Czarist secret police. (Tr.)

"Excuse me, excuse me, Matriona Semionovna, I never claimed that Tenteleev was any friend of mine; I was talking about Pelikanov."

"Well, if it isn't Tenteleev, it's someone else; Mikhniov, for instance."

"And what has he done?" Bambayev asked, already feeling intimidated.

"What? Do you say you don't know? On the Voznesensky Avenue he shouted for all the world to hear that all the liberals ought to be put in prison. And then some old colleague of his high-school days, poor of course, goes up to him and says: 'Can I have dinner with you?' And he answers: 'No, you can't; I've got two counts coming to dinner today — clear off!'"

"But that's a slander, I tell you!" Bambayev began to howl.

"A slander — a slander? To begin with, Prince Vakhrushkin, who also had dinner with your Mikhniov —"

"Prince Vakhrushkin," Gubariov sternly intervened, "is my cousin. But I don't allow him to call on me. . . . There's no need even to mention him."

"Secondly," Sukhanchikova continued, humbly bowing her head in Gubariov's direction, "Praskovia Yakovlevna told me herself."

"Now you've found someone to appeal to! She and that Sarkizov, they're the biggest fabricators of all."

"Well, you'll pardon me!" she retorted. "Sarkizov's a liar, I agree; he took the brocade pall off his dead father, I shall never stop to argue about him. But Praskovia Yakovlevna — what a comparison! Remember how nobly she parted from her husband! But you, I know you're always ready —"

"Now, enough, enough, Matriona Semionovna," Bambayev interrupted her. "Let's drop this filthy gossip, and we'll soar to the empyrean. I'm a man of the old school. Have you read *Mlle de la Quintinie*? It's really delightful! And it just fits your principles."

"I no longer read novels," she replied dryly and curtly.

"Why not?"

"Because this is not the time for them. I've only one thing in my head now: sewing-machines."

"What machines?" Litvinov asked.

"Sewing, sewing; we must provide all women, every one of them, with sewing-machines, and form a society. Then they will all earn their own bread, and in an instant they'll become independent. Otherwise they will never achieve their emancipation. That is an important, a very important social problem. We had an argument about it with Boleslav Stadnitsky. Boleslav Stadnitsky is a wonderful character, but he has a terribly frivolous outlook on these matters. He always laughs — the fool!"

"In due time they will all be called to account, from each will it be exacted," Gubariov declared slowly, in an admonitory or maybe prophetic tone.

"Yes, yes," Bambayev reiterated, "it will be exacted; precisely, it will be exacted. But tell me, Stepan Nikolaich," he added, lowering his voice, "is the work moving?"

"I am collecting the materials," Gubariov replied, knitting his brows. Turning to Litvinov, whose head was beginning to spin with this collection of unknown names, this frenzy of slander, he asked: "What are you engaged in?"

Litvinov satisfied his curiosity.

"Ah! natural sciences, in other words. That is useful, as training; as training, not as an aim. The aim now should be — mm — should be — different. Pardon me for asking, but what opinions do you hold?"

"What opinions?"

"Yes. I mean, to be precise, what are your political convictions?"

Litvinov smiled.

"To be precise, I haven't any political convictions."

At these words the thickset man sitting in the corner suddenly raised his head and stared at Litvinov attentively.

"How do you mean?" Gubariov said with strange moderation. "You haven't yet thought about it, or you've already grown tired?"

"How can I put it? It seems to me that it is still early for us Russians to have political convictions or to imagine we have them. Note that I give the word 'political' the meaning that belongs to it by right, and that — "

"Aha! One of the immature," Gubariov interrupted him in the same mild tone. Going up to Voroshilov, he asked him: "Have you read the brochure I gave you?"

Voroshilov, who, to Litvinov's surprise, had not said a word since his arrival, but had only wrinkled his brows and rolled his eyes significantly (it was his custom either to make a speech or to be silent), Voroshilov threw out his chest in military fashion and, clicking his heels, nodded affirmatively.

"Well, and what do you think? Were you satisfied?"

"So far as the main bases are concerned, I am. But I don't agree with the conclusions."

"Mmm. . . . But Andrei Ivanich recommended that brochure to me. You must expound your doubts to me later."

"Would you like them in writing?"

Gubariov was obviously surprised; he had not expected this question. But after a moment's thought he said:

"Yes, in writing. And, by the way, I ask you also to state your conceptions — in regard to — in regard to the association."

"Would you like me to do so according to Lassalle's method or that of Schulze-Delitzsch?"

"Mmm — according to both. The point is, you understand, that for us Russians the financial aspect is particularly important. And, of course, the co-operative working gang — as the core. . . . All that will have to be taken into account. It needs to be gone into thoroughly. And so, too, with the question of the peasants' allocation of land."

"But tell me, Stepan Nikolaich, what is your view of the amount of land each peasant should have?" Voroshilov asked in a tone of respectful delicacy.

"Mmm. . . . But what of the peasant community?" Gubariov remarked profoundly. Nibbling at a tuft of beard, he fixed his eyes on a table leg. "The community — d'you understand? That is a great word! And then what do those conflagrations mean — those — those governmental measures against secular Sunday schools, reading-rooms, periodicals? And the peasants' refusal to sign the statutory documents? And finally, all that's happening in Poland? Don't you see where all this is leading to? Don't you see that — mm —that we — we need now to fuse with the people, to find out — find out their opinion?" He was suddenly possessed by an oppressive, almost malevolent agitation; he turned livid and breathed heavily, but even now he did not raise his eyes and continued to chew his beard. "Don't you see . . ."

"Yevseev is a scoundrel!" Mme Sukhanchikova suddenly let fly, as Bambayev told her something, speaking in an undertone in deference to his host. Gubariov turned sharply on his heels and again waddled about the room.

Smoke

More visitors began to arrive; toward the end of the evening quite a number of people had gathered. Among them was the Mr. Yevseev whom Sukhanchikova had referred to so harshly; she talked very amicably with him and asked him to see her home. And there was a man named Pishchalkin, who made an ideal arbitrator, one of those men of whom, perhaps, Russia has particular need: to wit, narrow-minded, with little knowledge and no talent, but conscientious, patient, and honest. The peasants of his patrimony all but prayed for him, and he treated himself very deferentially, as though he were someone worthy of respect. Other arrivals included several young officers, who had dashed into Europe on short leave and were delighted at having the opportunity, of course with all prudence and always bearing the regimental commander in mind, to play with fire in the form of intelligent and even rather dangerous people. Two scraggy little students from Heidelberg came hurrying in; one of them did nothing but look about him contemptuously, the other laughed spasmodically — both felt very awkward. Immediately after them a little Frenchman, one of the so-called *"p'tites gens,"* insinuated himself; he was rather dirty, rather badly off, and rather stupid. He was renowned among his colleagues, the *commis voyageurs,* because Russian countesses fell in love with him; but he himself was more concerned with the possibility of getting a free dinner. The last to appear was Tit Bindasov, who was a turbulent *Bursch* to look at, but who in reality was a hard-headed wealthy peasant and a skinflint, in his speech a terrorist, a policeman by vocation, and the friend of Russian merchants' wives and Parisian *lorettes;* he was bald, toothless, and drunk. He arrived very flushed in the face and unhappy, declaring that he had paid his last kopek to that "scoundrel Benazet," though in reality he had won sixteen guldens. . . .

In a word, quite a crowd of people assembled. Very remarkable was the respect with which all the visitors turned to Gubariov as their mentor or head; they laid their doubts before him, submitted them to his judgment. And he replied — with bellows, with tugs at his beard, rolling his eyes or uttering desultory, insignificant remarks, which were at once caught up as pronouncements of the very highest wisdom. He himself rarely intervened in the discussions; on the other hand, all the others zealously exercised their lungs. More than once three or four were shouting together for

ten minutes on end, and they were all satisfied and they all understood. The talk went on till past midnight and was distinguished,
as usual, by the abundance and variety of subjects discussed. Mme
Sukhanchikova talked about Garibaldi, about someone named
Karl Ivanovich, who had whipped his servants, about Napoleon III,
about female labor, about the merchant Pleskachev, who was
known to have worn out twelve working women and in return
had received a medal with the inscription "For service," about the
proletariat, about the Georgian Prince Chukcheulidzeve, who had
shot his wife out of a cannon, and about the future of Russia. Pishchalkin also talked about the future of Russia, about the licensing
system, about the meaning of nationality, and how most of all he
hated the mean and base. Voroshilov was suddenly carried away:
in one breath, almost choking, he mentioned Draper, Firkhov, Mr.
Shelgunov, Bische, Helmgoltz, Star, Stour, Reymont, John Miller
the physiologist and John Miller the historian (obviously confus-
ing them), Taine, Renan, Mr. Shchapov, and then Thomas Nash,
Peel, and Green.

"And what birds are they?" Bambayev muttered in astonishment. "Predecessors of Shakspere, bearing the same relationship
to him as the foothills of the Alps to Mont Blanc!" Voroshilov
answered trenchantly. And he, too, touched on the future of
Russia.

Bambayev also talked about the future of Russia, and even described it in iridescent colors, but he was especially transported at
the thought of Russian music, in which he saw something "ah,
tremendous!" In proof of this he struck up a ballad by Varlamov,
but was soon interrupted by a general shout that "He is really
singing the '*Miserere*' from *Il Trovatore*, and making a horrible
mess of it."

Under cover of the tumult one of the officers abused Russian
literature, another quoted some moderate verse from the periodical
Iskra. But Tit Bindasov put things even more simply: he declared
that all these rogues and swindlers ought to have their teeth
knocked out and be done with it, not, however, defining who
"these rogues and swindlers" were. The smoke of the cigars grew
asphyxiating; everybody was hot and uncomfortable, they all
went hoarse, all eyes were bleary, the sweat poured down like rain
from every face. Bottles of cold beer appeared and were emptied
in a moment. "What was it I was just saying?" said one. "But

whom was I arguing with just now, and what were we arguing about?" asked another. Amid all this hubbub and smoke Gubariov strolled about indefatigably, still waddling, and muttering in his beard, now listening to somebody's remark with one ear thrust forward, now putting in a word of his own. And everybody involuntarily felt that he, Gubariov, was indeed the mother of them all, that here he was the host and the leading figure. . . .

Toward ten o'clock Litvinov developed a severe headache and left quietly and unnoticed, taking advantage of a sudden outburst of general shouting. Mme Sukhanchikova had recalled some further injustice committed by Prince Barnaulov: he had all but ordered someone's ear to be bitten off.

The fresh night air nestled gently against Litvinov's inflamed face, flowed in a perfumed stream between his parched lips. "What is all this?" he thought as he walked along the dark avenue. "What have I just been present at? Why have they come together? What were they shouting for, cursing for, letting themselves go for? What is the point of it all?" He shrugged his shoulders and made his way to Weber's, obtained a newspaper, and asked for an ice. The newspaper contained a great deal about the Roman problem,[1] and the ice was not at all nice. He was on the point of going home when a stranger in a hat with a broad brim came up to him and, saying in Russian: "I hope I'm not disturbing you?" sat down at his table. Only then did Litvinov, looking more closely at the man, recognize him as the stolid gentleman who had skulked in one corner of Gubariov's room and had looked at him so attentively when the talk turned to political convictions. This gentleman had not opened his mouth all the evening. Now, as he sat down opposite Litvinov and removed his hat, he gave him a friendly and rather embarrassed look.

5

"Mr. Gubariov, in whose room I had the pleasure of seeing you this evening," he began, "did not introduce me to you; and so, if you will allow me, I shall introduce myself: I am Potugin, a retired court councilor;[2] I served in the Ministry of Finance, in St. Petersburg. I hope you will not consider it strange — I don't usually

[1] The question of the inclusion of Rome (held by the Vatican) in the newly born Kingdom of Italy. (Tr.)

[2] Seventh class in the Czarist civil-service hierarchy. (Tr.)

make a habit of striking up such a sudden acquaintance — but in your case — "

At this point he stopped short and asked the waiter to bring him a glass of kirschwasser. "To give me courage," he added with a smile.

Litvinov looked more closely at this last of all the new faces whom he had had to meet during the day, and at once thought: "He's not the same as the others."

Certainly he was not the same. Opposite Litvinov, fingering the edge of the table with thin, small hands, sat a broad-shouldered man, with a bulky body on short legs, a drooping, curly head, very intelligent and very sad little eyes beneath thick eyebrows, a large, well-proportioned mouth, bad teeth, and that purely Russian nose which has been nicknamed "potato-nose"; a man awkward and even a little uncouth to look at, but certainly out of the ordinary. He was dressed negligently; an old-fashioned type of coat hung about him like a sack, and his cravat had slipped to one side. His sudden trustfulness not only did not seem intrusive; on the contrary, secretly Litvinov was flattered by it: it was quite obvious that this man was not in the habit of forcing himself on strangers. He made a queer impression on Litvinov: he aroused a feeling of respect, and sympathy, and an involuntary feeling of compassion.

"I really am not disturbing you?" he repeated in a soft, rather hoarse and weak voice, which could not have better accorded with his whole figure.

"Of course not," Litvinov protested. "Indeed, I am very glad."

"Really? Well, and I'm glad too. I have heard a great deal about you; I know what you are studying and what your intentions are. It's a good purpose. But you didn't talk at all this evening."

"Well, you, too, said very little, I think," Litvinov remarked.

Potugin sighed.

"Others talked rather a lot. I listened. Well, what do you think?" he added after a little silence, amusingly raising his eyebrows. "Did you like our Tower of Babel?"

"That's just the word: Babel. You've put it perfectly. I continually felt like asking them what they were making such a hubbub about."

Potugin sighed again.

"That's just the point, they themselves don't know. In the old days people would have said: 'They are blind instruments of higher purposes'; but these days we use rather more pungent epithets. And note that really I have no intention whatever of condemning them; I would go farther and say they are all — or at any rate almost all — splendid people. Concerning Madame Sukhanchikova, for instance, I certainly know a great deal that is to her credit: she gave her last farthing to two poor nieces. Even if we assume that a desire to show off a little, to pose a little, had its part in that deed, still you must agree that it is a remarkable self-sacrifice for a woman who herself is not rich! And about Mr. Pishchalkin there is no need to speak: the peasants of his estate will undoubtedly present him with a silver bowl shaped like a watermelon some time or other, and possibly an icon with a representation of his particular angel. And even if in his speech of thanks he tells them that he does not deserve such honor, he will be telling an untruth: he does deserve it. Your friend, Mr. Bambayev, has a marvelous heart. Truly, like the poet Yazikov, who, they say, sang the praises of debauchery while sitting over a book and drinking water, he possesses an enthusiasm that is not really directed toward anything; but all the same it is enthusiasm. And Mr. Voroshilov is also one of the best. He, and all the people of his school, the people of the roll of honor, are, so to speak, assigned as orderlies to science, to civilization, and even their silences are eloquently phrased; but he is still so young! Yes, yes, they are all splendid people, but in the last resort they all amount to nothing; the victuals are of the finest quality, but for goodness' sake don't taste the dish!"

Litvinov listened to Potugin with growing astonishment; all the style, all the turns of his unhurried yet self-confident speech revealed both an ability and a desire to talk.

And truly Potugin both liked and knew how to talk; but he talked as a man whom life had succeeded in robbing of some of his self-esteem; he waited with philosophic calm for the right opportunity, for a kindred spirit.

"Yes, yes," he began again, with the queer, not painful, but despondent humor peculiar to him, "it is all very strange. And there's something else I ask you to note. When ten Englishmen, for example, come together, they at once begin to talk about the submarine telegraph, about the paper-tax, about a method of dressing rats' skins — in other words, about something positive, definite. If ten Germans come together, well, of course, then

Schleswig-Holstein and the unity of Germany are the subject of conversation. If ten Frenchmen come together, the talk inevitably touches on cultivated strawberries, no matter how they begin. But if ten Russians meet, the question that at once arises — you have had an opportunity to be convinced of this today — is that of the meaning, the future, of Russia, and it is all discussed in very general outline, beginning with Leda's egg, inconclusively, hopelessly. They chew and chew over that unfortunate problem like children chewing indiarubber; there's no taste in it, nor object. And, of course, they always have a smack at the rotten West. It's very queer, you know, it beats us in every respect, does the West — yet it's rotten! And it wouldn't be so bad if we really did despise it, but that is all talk and lies. We swear at it and abuse it, but its opinion is the only one we value, and fundamentally it is the opinion of Parisian idiots. I have an acquaintance, a decent fellow, seemingly, the father of a family, and no longer young; he was depressed for several days because in a Paris restaurant he asked for *une portion de bifteck aux pommes de terre*, and a genuine Frenchman at once shouted: '*Garçon, bifteck pommes!*' My friend burned with shame; and he's been shouting '*Bifteck pommes*' and instructing others to do the same ever since. Even the *lorettes* are amazed at the reverential tremor with which our young steppe creatures enter their shameful drawing-rooms. . . . My God! our youngsters think, but where am I? With Anna Deslions herself!"

"Please tell me," Litvinov asked, "what do you think is the reason for Gubariov's undoubted influence on all those who surround him? Not his talents, not his abilities, surely?"

"Oh no, oh no! He hasn't anything of that sort. . . ."

"Then is it his character?"

"He hasn't any character either, but he has considerable willpower. As is well known, we Slavs generally are not rich in that quality and we call 'Pass' to it. Mr. Gubariov wanted to be the head, and they have all recognized him as the head. What else would you expect? The government has freed us of feudal dependence, for which we have to thank it; but the habits of serfdom are too deeply ingrained in us: we shan't get rid of them so quickly. Always and everywhere we need a master; usually that master is a living thing, but sometimes it is some so-called tendency that takes possession of us. . . . Now, for instance, we have all entered into a conspiracy in regard to natural sciences. . . . Why and by force of what arguments we subscribe to the conspiracy is obscure; evidently it is just our nature. But the main thing is that we must have a master. Well, and now we have got one; and that means it is ours, and we spit on all the rest! We're perfect slaves! With both slavish pride and slavish humiliation. A new master has been born — down with the old! It was Yakov, and now it is Sidor; knock Yakov down and throw yourselves at Sidor's feet! Remember how many escapades we have indulged in along those lines! We talk of negation as our distinguishing quality; but we do not negate as a free man would, smiting with his sword, but like a lackey hitting with his fist; and besides, in all probability he even uses his fists on the master's orders. Well, but we are a soft people too: it isn't difficult to take charge of us. And that is how Mr. Gubariov has become the master; he has pecked and pecked at one point and pecked his way through. People see a man with a good opinion of himself, believing in himself, and giving orders — that's the main thing, that he gives orders; so he must be right, and he must be obeyed. All our schisms, our Onufriev movement and Akulinov movement, were based on this very principle. The man with the stick is the man to pick."

Potugin's cheeks flushed and his eyes filmed, but, strange to say, his speech, bitter and even malevolent, did not sound splenetic, but rather sorrowful — with a true, sincere sorrow.

"How did you come to know Gubariov?" Litvinov asked.

"I've known him a long time. And note one other strange feature about us: a certain writer, say, who all his life in prose and verse had denounced drunkenness and decried the licensing system, suddenly bought not one but a couple of wineries and rented a hundred taverns — and that's quite all right! Anyone else would be wiped off the face of the earth, but no one even reproaches him. And so with Mr. Gubariov: he's a Slavophil, and a democrat, and a socialist, and anything you like, but his estate was and still is run by his brother, a master of the old breed, the kind that used to be called '*dentistes*.'[1] And the same Madame Sukhanchikova who makes Madame Beecher Stowe slap Tenteleev on the face all but crawls to Gubariov. Yet the only thing in his favor is that he reads sensible books and is always trying to achieve profundity. What

[1] A jocular term for advocates of a hard-fist policy in regard to the peasants. (Tr.)

gift of speech he has you were able to judge for yourself this evening; and we have to thank God that he talks little and only shrivels up. For when he is in the mood and opens his heart, then even I, a patient man enough, cannot stand it. He begins to banter and to tell dirty stories — yes, yes, our great Mr. Gubariov tells dirty stories and laughs filthily as he tells them. . . ."

"Are you so patient?" Litvinov said. "I assumed the contrary. . . . But may I ask your name and patronymic?"

Potugin sipped a little of the kirschwasser.

"My name is Sozont — Sozont Ivanich. They gave me that beautiful name in honor of a relative who was an archimandrite, and that is all I owe to him. I, if I may dare to express myself so, am of a priestly generation. And as for your doubts in regard to my patience, they are beside the mark: I am patient. I served twenty years under my own blood uncle, the active state councilor Irinarkh Potugin. You don't happen to know him?"

"No."

"On which I congratulate you. Yes, I am patient. But 'let us return to the beginning,' as my worthy spiritual brother, the martyred archpriest Avvakum, says. I am amazed at my compatriots, my dear sir. They are all in a state of gloom, they all go about with long faces, and at the same time they are all filled with hope, and at the least thing they go into a rage. Take the Slavophils, for example, among whom Mr. Gubariov reckons himself; very fine people, but all the selfsame mixture of despair and enthusiasm; they all live for some undefined future. Everything will be, will be. There is nothing to show yet; and for a whole ten centuries Russia has produced nothing of her own, either in administration, or in law, or in science, or in art, or even in crafts. . . . But wait, be patient: everything will be. But why will it be, you may be inquisitive to know. Because we, you know, we educated people — are trash; but the people — oh, it's a great people! You see that peasant overcoat? That's where everything will come from! All other idols are destroyed, so let us believe in the peasant coat. Well, but supposing the coat betrays us? No, it will not betray us; you read Kokhanovskaya and then you'll see! Really, if I were a painter I would paint this picture: an educated man standing before a peasant and bowing low to him. 'Cure me,' he is saying, 'little father peasant, I am perishing with disease.' And the peasant, in his turn, bows low to the educated man. 'Teach me,' he is saying, 'little father and master, I am perishing of ignorance.' And of course neither of them gets anywhere. But it would only be necessary to effect a real reconciliation — not only in words — and to learn a little from our elder brothers, to see what they have invented, better than we could and before we could! *Kellner, noch ein Gläschen Kirsch!* Don't think I am drunk, but alcohol loosens my tongue."

"After what you have just said," Litvinov remarked with a smile, "there is no point in my asking to what party you belong, and what is your opinion of Europe. But allow me to make one comment. You have just said that we ought to study and borrow from our elder brothers. But how is it possible to borrow without taking into account the climatic conditions, the soil, the local and national peculiarities? My father, I remember, ordered an iron winnowing-machine that was particularly recommended. It was in fact a very good machine, but what happened? For a full five years it stood in a shed without being used, until it was replaced by a wooden American one, which was much more suited to our way of existence and to our habits, as all the American machines are generally. You mustn't take over things haphazardly, Sozont Ivanovich."

Potugin raised his head.

"I didn't expect such an objection from you, my dear Grigory Mikhailovich," he began after a moment. "Who is forcing you to take things over haphazardly? Why, you borrow other people's ideas not because they are other people's, but because they are of use to you. Accordingly, you think it over and you choose. And as for results — you need not be so anxious; they will have their own peculiarity as the result of those same local, climatic, and other conditions you have mentioned. You just offer good food, and the national stomach will digest it in its own fashion; and with time, when the organism has grown strong, it will provide 'its own' juice. Take our language just as an example. Peter the Great flooded it with thousands of foreign words — Dutch, French, and German. These words expressed conceptions that it was necessary for the Russian nation to become acquainted with. Without philosophizing or standing on ceremony, Peter poured these words *en masse*, tubs and barrels of them, into our belly. Certainly, at first the result was something monstrous, but then that very process of digestion which I have just explained to you began. The conceptions were grafted on and assimilated; the foreign forms

27

were gradually sweated out, the language found something to replace them within its own womb. And now your humble servant, quite a mediocre stylist, undertakes to translate any page you like from Hegel — yes, yes, from Hegel — without using a single non-Slavonic word. What happened with the language will happen, we are entitled to hope, in other things also. The whole question is whether the nature is strong. And our nature is all right, it will stand it: that wasn't the cause of all the trouble. Only people suffering from nervous ailments, and nations that are weak, need be afraid for their health, for their independence; just as only the empty-minded can exult till they foam at the mouth because we, you see, are Russian. I take a lot of care for my health, but I never go into raptures over it; I'd feel ashamed."

"All that is true, Sozont Ivanich," Litvinov began in his turn; "but why must we necessarily be subjected to such tests? You yourself admit that at first something rather monstrous came of it! Well, but supposing that monstrosity were to remain? And besides, it has remained, you know that yourself."

"Only not in the language — and that means a great deal! But I didn't make our people; it is not my fault that it is condemned to pass through such a school. 'The Germans have developed on right lines,' the Slavophils shout; 'give us, too, a sound development!' But where are you to get it, when the very first historical step taken by our tribe, of inviting a prince from overseas to rule them, was already an unsound step, an abnormality, and that same abnormality is repeated in every one of us right down to this day? Every one of us, at least once in his life, has indubitably said to something foreign, not Russian: 'Come and rule and lord it over me!'

"I am ready, perhaps, to agree that if we deposit a foreign substance in our own body, we can never know for certain in advance what it is we are depositing; a piece of bread or a piece of poison! But then it is a well-known fact that you never go from worse to good through the better, but always through the worse — and in medicine poison can be beneficial. Only blockheads and foxes consider it decent to point triumphantly to the poverty of the peasants after their emancipation, to their increased drunkenness since the abolition of the private liquor licenses. Through the worse to the better!"

Potugin passed his hand over his face.

"You asked me my opinion of Europe," he began again. "I am amazed at her and extremely devoted to her elements, and don't in the least think it necessary to conceal the fact. Long since — no, recently — for some time now, I have ceased to be afraid to express my convictions — just as you didn't have any misgivings about telling Mr. Gubariov your manner of thought. I, thank God, have ceased to reckon with the conceptions, views, and habits of the person with whom I am talking. I know nothing fundamentally worse than that unnecessary cowardice, that contemptible complaisance, which makes some important official of ours ingratiate himself with some poor little student who is quite insignificant in his eyes, and almost play with him, and fuss around him like a little dog. Well, presumably that sort of official behaves like that out of a desire for popularity, but why should the likes of us, independent and educated, twist and prevaricate? Yes, yes, I am a Westerner, I am devoted to Europe. I mean, to put it more exactly, I am devoted to its cultured standards, to those same cultured standards at which our people poke such delightful fun these days — its civilization — yes, yes, that word is still better. And I love it with all my heart, and I believe in it, and I have and will have no other belief. That word: civ-i-li-za-tion" (Potugin distinctly and emphatically pronounced every syllable), "is both comprehensible, and clean, and sacred; but all the rest, the nationality, say, and the glory, stinks of blood. . . . Let them go."

"Yes, but Russia, Sozont Ivanich, your country — do you love her?"

Potugin passed his hand over his face.

"I love her passionately, and I hate her passionately."

Litvinov shrugged his shoulders.

"That is an old song, Sozont Ivanich, that is a platitude."

"Well, and what of it? Is it the worse for that? Fancy being frightened of that! A platitude! I know many good platitudes. For instance: freedom and order — that is a well-known platitude. Why, do you think it is better as we have it: hierarchy and disorder? And besides, aren't all those phrases which intoxicate the young heads so much — the contemptible bourgeoisie, the *souveraineté du peuple*, the right to work — aren't they all platitudes too? And as for love, inseparable from hate —"

"That's Byronism," Litvinov interrupted him, "the romanticism of the thirties."

"Pardon me, you are mistaken; the first to point to such a mingling of feelings was Catullus, the Roman poet Catullus,[1] two thousand years ago. I quoted it from him, because I know a little Latin as the result of my spiritual origin, if I may venture to put it in that way. Yes, I both love and hate my Russia, my strange, dear, rotten, precious country. Now I have abandoned her: I had to give myself a bit of an airing after sitting for twenty years in an official chair, in an official building. I have abandoned Russia, and here I am very comfortable and happy; but I shall go back soon, I feel that. Garden soil is good, but you can't grow cloudberries on it!"

"You're happy, you're comfortable, and I, too, like being here," said Litvinov, "and I came here to study; but that doesn't prevent my seeing such things as that, for instance." He pointed to two passing *lorettes*, with several members of the Jockey Club grimacing and lisping around them, and to the Casino, packed to its doors, despite the lateness of the hour.

"But who told you that I'm blind to it?" Potugin caught him up. "You'll excuse me, but your remark reminds me of the triumphant way in which our unfortunate little periodicals pointed to the defects of the British military administration, as shown up by the *Times*, during the Crimean War. I myself am not an optimist, and I do not take any rosy view of everything human, of all our life, of all this comedy with a tragic ending. But why ascribe solely to the West something that maybe is rooted in our very human nature? That Casino is repulsive, I agree; but our own home-grown swindling, is it any more attractive? No, my dear Grigory Mikhailovich, let us be more humble and more quiet. A good pupil sees his teacher's mistakes, but is respectfully silent about them; for those very mistakes act to his benefit and set him on the right road. But if you really do want to wag your tongue about the rotten West, there's Prince Coco jogging along over there; I expect that in fifteen minutes at the green table he has lost the hard-won, extorted rents of a hundred and fifty families; his nerves are all in rags. And yet I saw him in Marx's today turning over the pages of a brochure by Veuillot. . . . He will make an excellent conversational companion for you!"

[1] "*Odi et amo. Quare id faciam, fortasse requiris.*
    Nescio: sed fieri sentio et excrucior."
                                        Catullus, Book LXXXVI.

"But one minute, one minute," Litvinov said hurriedly, seeing that Potugin was rising from his seat. "I know Prince Coco very little, and of course I prefer to talk with you —"

"I am very grateful to you," Potugin interrupted him, rising and bowing, "but I have already had a rather long conversation with you, or rather I have done all the talking, while of course you have mentally noted that a man always feels awkward and conscience-stricken when he does all the talking. Especially when it is their first conversation: 'Behold and see what manner of man I am,' so to speak. To our next pleasant meeting. . . . But, I repeat, I am very glad to have made your acquaintance."

"But wait a moment, Sozont Ivanich, tell me at any rate where you live and whether you intend to stay here long?"

Potugin seemed to shrink a little.

"I am remaining in Baden another week or so, but in any case we can meet here at Weber's, or at Marx's. Or if not, then I'll call on you."

"All the same, I ought to have your address."

"Yes, but there's one difficulty: I'm not alone."

"Are you married?" Litvinov asked abruptly.

"No, for goodness' sake — why ask such absurdities? . . . But I have a girl with me."

"Ah!" Litvinov said with a courteous twist of the lips, as though apologizing; and he looked down.

"She's only six years old," Potugin went on. "She's an orphan, the daughter of a certain lady — a very good acquaintance of mine. It would be better for us to meet here. Good-by."

He clapped his hat on his curly head and walked away swiftly; his figure showed up more clearly once or twice as he passed beneath the bracket gas lamps that dimly lit the road leading to the Lichtentaler Allee.

6

"A strange fellow!" thought Litvinov as he walked back to his hotel. "A strange fellow! I shall have to look him up!" He entered his room; a letter lying on the table caught his eyes. "From Tania!" he thought, and rejoiced prematurely: it was from his father in Russia. He broke the heavy, crested seal and began to read. . . . A strong, very pleasant and familiar scent caught his attention. He looked round and saw a large bouquet of fresh heliotrope in a glass

31

of water at the window. He bent over them in some astonishment, touched them, breathed in their perfume. . . . Something seemed to quicken in his memory, something very remote . . . but he could not think exactly what it was. He rang for the boots and asked him where the flowers had come from. The man replied that they had been brought by a lady who didn't wish to give her name, but said that he, "Herr Zluitenhoff," would certainly guess who she was by these flowers. Again Litvinov had a vague recollection of something. . . . He asked what the lady looked like. The man explained that she was tall and beautifully dressed, but had a veil over her face.

"Probably a Russian countess," he added.

"Why do you think so?" Litvinov asked.

"She gave me two guldens," the man replied, and smirked.

Litvinov dismissed him and stood for a long time in a reverie before the window. But at last he gave it up and turned back to the letter from his father. It contained all his usual complaints; he declared that no one would take the grain even as a gift, that the servants had got completely out of hand, and that in all probability the end of the world would come before long. "Would you believe it," he wrote, "they cast the evil eye on my last coachman, the little Kalmuck — d'you remember him? — and the man would surely have been done for, and I had no one to drive me, but, thank goodness, some decent people gave me some advice and suggested sending the patient to Ryazan, to a priest well known for his cures of the evil eye and spells; and the treatment certainly couldn't have been a greater success, in confirmation of which I enclose a letter from the priest himself, as a document." Litvinov read this "document" with interest. It stated that:

"The yardman Nikanor Dmitriev succumbed to an illness not susceptible to medical science, as it was due to evil people; but the real cause of it was the man Nikanor himself, because he had not kept his promise to a certain maiden, and so through certain people she had made him good for nothing, and if in these circumstances I, the priest, had not announced that I would help him, he would have perished completely, like a cabbage caterpillar; but I, trusting in the All-Seeing Eye, became the support of his life, though how I accomplished this is a secret; but I ask Your Excellency to see that in future this maiden does not resort any more to such evil elements, and it will do no harm even to threaten her, otherwise she may again have an evil influence upon him."

Litvinov was lost in thought over this document; it brought to him a breath of the remote and isolated steppe, the impenetrable gloom of a life moldered and fusty, and it seemed remarkable that he had read this letter in Baden of all places. Meanwhile midnight had long passed; he got into bed and blew out the candle. But he could not sleep; the faces he had seen, the speeches he had heard, kept turning and circling, strangely interweaving and jumbling in his burning head, which ached terribly from the tobacco smoke. Now he thought he heard Gubariov's bellow and saw his downcast eyes with their dull and obstinate gaze; now suddenly those same eyes flamed and danced, and he recognized Mme Sukhanchikova, heard her crackling voice and involuntarily repeated softly after her: "She slapped his face, she slapped his face"; now Potugin's awkward figure rose before him, and for the tenth, the twentieth time he recalled every word he had said; now, like a jack-in-the-box, Voroshilov sprang up in his close-fitting coat, which enveloped him like a new uniform; and Pishchalkin sagely and gravely nodded his perfectly trimmed and undoubtedly well-intentioned head; and Bindasov shouted and cursed, and Bambayev exulted lachrymosely. . . .

But, above all, that perfume, that persistent, importunate, sweet, heavy perfume did not give him any rest, but pervaded the room more and more strongly in the darkness, and more and more insistently reminded him of something that he simply could not define. . . . It occurred to him that the scent of flowers in a bedroom at night is detrimental to the health, and he rose, groped his way to the bouquet, and carried it into the other room; but even then the exhausting perfume penetrated to him on his pillow, under the blanket, and he turned over fretfully from side to side. Now a fever was beginning to steal upon him; a priest, "a master against enchantments," ran twice across his head, in the form of a very lively hare with a beard and pigtail, and Voroshilov, sitting in the enormous plume of a general's helmet, as though in a bush, began to twitter like a nightingale in front of him . . . when suddenly he raised himself in the bed and, throwing up his hands, exclaimed: "Surely it isn't *she*? It can't be!"

But in order to explain this exclamation we have to ask the indulgent reader to go back with us several years. . . .

7

At the beginning of the fifties the numerous members of a family belonging to the princely Osinin line were living at Moscow in very straitened circumstances, almost in poverty. They were true, not Tatar-Georgian, but pure-blooded princes, descendants of Rurik; their name is often mentioned in Russian annals during the times of the first grand dukes of Moscow, who consolidated the Russian lands. They owned very extensive patrimonies and many estates, were paid more than once for their "labors and blood and injuries," they sat in the boyars' Duma, one of them was even granted the right to the honorable title of "vich." But they fell into disgrace for a hostile plot in "sorcery and calumny," they were ruined "terribly and endlessly," they were stripped of their honors, they were exiled to remote spots. The Osinins crashed and never recovered, never regained their power; in the course of time their disgrace was removed and even their "little palace at Moscow" and their "chattels" were returned to them, but all to no avail. Their line grew poor and "impoverished," it did not recover either under Peter or under Catherine, and, continually declining and growing more petty, it now included estate administrators, wineshop-owners, and district police officers among its members. The Osinin family to which we have referred consisted of a husband, a wife, and five children. They resided near Sobaka Square, in a one-story wooden house with a small boarded front porch facing the street, green lions at the gate, and other noble devices, and only just managed to make ends meet, owing money to the grocer and quite often without wood or candles in the winter. The Prince himself was a sluggish and rather stupid man, at one time handsome and a fop, but now completely gone to pieces. Not so much out of respect for his name as a mark of attention to his wife, who had been a maid of honor, he had been given one of the Moscow traditional stewardships with a small salary, a queer name, and nothing to do; he never interfered in anything, and did nothing but smoke from morning till evening, never changing out of his dressing-gown, and always groaning. His wife was a sickly and bad-tempered woman, continually worried over domestic troubles, the placing of the children in state educational institutions, and the maintenance of her Petersburg connections; she simply could not get used to her position and her retirement from the court.

During his residence in Moscow, Litvinov's father had made Osinin's acquaintance, had had occasion to do him certain services, and once had made him a loan of three hundred rubles. Litvinov himself, while a student, often called on the Osinins; it happened that his apartment was not far from their house. But it was not their proximity that attracted him, not the poor comforts of their mode of life that allured him; he began to call on the Osinins regularly when he fell in love with their eldest daughter, Irena.

She was then a little past her seventeenth birthday; she had only just left the young ladies' institute, from which her mother had withdrawn her after some unpleasantness with the headmistress. The unpleasantness arose over the circumstance that at the public graduation celebration Irena was to have addressed the patron with some verses of welcome in French, but immediately before the function she was set aside in favor of another girl, the daughter of a very rich liquor licensee. The Princess could not stomach this affront, and even Irena did not forgive the headmistress her injustice; she had been dreaming of how, with all eyes on her, the center of attraction, she would rise and say her verses, and how Moscow would talk about her afterward. . . .

And she was right, Moscow would certainly have talked about Irena. She was a tall and graceful girl, with virgin breasts and angular shoulders, a pale, velvety complexion unusual for her age and as clear and smooth as porcelain, and thick, fair hair with very distinctive mingled darker and lighter strands. Her features were exquisitely, almost artificially regular and had not entirely lost the artless expression of early youth. But the deliberate movements of her beautiful neck, and her smile, a rather abstracted or rather weary smile, suggested that she was a highly strung young lady; and the very outlines of her fine, faintly smiling lips and her small, aquiline, rather firm nose expressed a self-willed and passionate quality — a quality dangerous both for others and for herself. Astonishing, truly astonishing were her eyes, which were a very dark gray shot with green, with a languishing look, and unusally long, like those of Egyptian goddesses, with radiating lashes and boldly sweeping brows. There was a strange expression in those eyes: they seemed to be attentively and thoughtfully looking out from an infinite depth and distance. At the institute Irena had had the reputation of being one of its most intelligent and capable pupils, but also of possessing an uncertain, ambitious character and a mischievous head. One class mistress prophesied of her that her passions would ruin her — *"vos passions vous perdront"* — whereas another class mistress chided her for her coldness and insensibility and called her *"une jeune fille sans cœur."* Her friends found her proud and secretive, her brothers and sisters were afraid of her, her mother did not trust her, and her father felt awkward when she fixed her mysterious eyes on him; but in both father and mother she inspired a feeling of involuntary respect, not because of her qualities, but because of the peculiar, vague expectations that she aroused in them, for no obvious reason.

"You'll see, Praskovia Danilovna," the old Prince said to his wife one day, removing his pipestem from his mouth; "our Irinka will yet mend over fortunes."

The Princess grew angry and told her husband that he had *"des expressions insupportables,"* but then she was lost in thought and repeated through her set teeth:

"Yes, and she should mend them well!"

Irena enjoyed almost unlimited freedom in her parents' house. She was not spoilt, the rest of the family even felt rather hostile to her; but they did not thwart her, and that was all that mattered to her. . . . At times, during some unusually humiliating scene — a shopkeeper arriving and shouting, for all the world to hear, that he had grown tired of calling for his money, or their own servants turning to swear at their masters to their face: "What sort of princes are you when you yourselves are tightening your belts with hunger?" — Irena would not even stir an eyebrow and would sit motionless, with an unpleasant smile on her moody face. But her parents found that very smile more painful than any reproaches, and they had a feeling of guilt, of innocent guilt, toward this creature, who from the very day of her birth had seemed to have a right to wealth, to luxury, to devotion.

Litvinov fell in love with Irena as soon as he saw her (he was only three years older than she), but for a long time he could not gain even her attention, still less any return of his feelings. Her conduct toward him was stamped with hostility, as if he had done her some injury, and though she would not reveal the reason, she could not forgive him. He was then too inexperienced and young to realize what might be hidden beneath this hostile, almost contemptuous harshness. There were times when, forgetting his lessons and exercise books, he would sit in the cheerless reception room of Osinin's house and would take surreptitious looks at Irena, while his heart slowly and mournfully sank, grew heavy with its load. But she seemed to be angry, or bored; she would rise and walk about the room, would gaze at him coldly, as if at a table or chair, would shrug her shoulders and fold her arms. Or, even when talking to him, she would deliberately avoid looking at him all the evening, as though refusing him even that charity. Or, finally, she would pick up a book and fix her eyes on it, without reading it, while she knitted her brows and bit her lips, or would suddenly ask her father or brother in a loud voice: "What is the German for 'patience'?" He attempted to break free of the enchantment in which he was tormented, and struggled incessantly like a bird caught in a snare. He left Moscow for a week. . . .

He all but went out of his mind with yearning and ennui and was quite thin and ill when he called on the Osinins again. . . . Strange to relate, Irena also had grown perceptibly thinner during those few days, her face had gone yellow, her cheeks were hollow . . . but she greeted him with even greater chilliness, with almost malevolent unconcern, as though he had even added to the secret injury he had done her. . . .

She tormented him thus for a couple of months. Then everything changed in a single day. As though it had flamed up in a conflagration, or had sped like a thunder cloud, love took possession of her. One day — he remembered that day for long after — he was sitting by the window in the Osinins' reception room and gazing unthinkingly out into the street, and he felt chagrin and ennui and contempt for himself, and he could not stir. . . . He felt that if a river had been flowing just beneath the window he would have thrown himself into it with horror, but without regret. Irena seated herself not far away and was strangely silent and very still. For some days now she had not spoken to him at all, nor, for that matter, did she speak to anybody. She sat all the time with her head in her hands, as though bewildered, and only occasionally gazed slowly about her.

At last this chilly languor grew too much for Litvinov: without taking his leave of her, he rose and began to look for his hat. "Stay!" he suddenly heard a quiet whisper. His heart trembled.

He did not recognize Irena's voice at once: there was an unusual note in that single word. He raised his head and was petrified: she was looking at him graciously, yes, graciously. "Stay," she repeated, "don't go. I want to be with you." She lowered her voice still more. "Don't go — I ask you." Completely at a loss, not fully realizing what he was doing, he went to her and held out his hands. . . . She at once gave him both hers, then smiled, and her face flamed. She turned away and, still smiling, left the room. . . .

A few minutes later she returned with her younger sister, looked at him once more with that long and gentle gaze, and made him sit beside her. . . . At first she could not say a word: she only sighed and blushed. Then she began shyly to question him concerning his studies, a thing she had never done before. During the evening she apologized to him again and again for failing to appreciate him before and assured him that now she was completely changed; she astonished him by displaying an unexpected tendency toward republicanism (at this period of his life he worshipped Robespierre and would not have dreamed of censuring Marat), and within a week he knew that she loved him. Yes, he remembered that first day for long after. . . .

Nor did he forget those that followed — those days when, still striving to doubt and fearing to believe, with a sinking feeling of rapture, almost of fear, he realized how his unexpected happiness had sprung to birth, had grown and, invincibly sweeping away everything before it, had come flooding at last. Now they experienced those luminous moments of first love, moments that are not fated to be repeated, and that, indeed, should not be repeated in one and the same life. Irena suddenly became as obedient as a lamb, as soft as silk, and endlessly kind. She began to give her younger sisters lessons — not on the piano, she was not a musician, but in French and English. She went through their schoolbooks with them and took her share in running the home. Everything amused her, everything interested her; she would chatter away without cease, or would be sunk in a speechless tenderness. She made various plans, gave herself over to endless speculation about what she would do when she married Litvinov (they had not the least doubt that they would be married), how together they would begin — "To toil?" Litvinov suggested. "Yes, to toil," she repeated, "to read . . . but most of all to travel." She particularly wanted to leave Moscow as soon as possible, and when he pointed out that he had not yet finished his university studies, she always, after thinking a little, replied that he could finish in Berlin or — somewhere abroad. She made little attempt to moderate the expression of her feelings, and so her attitude to Litvinov did not remain a secret from the Prince and Princess. They were not exactly delighted, but, taking all the circumstances into account, they did not consider it necessary to impose their veto at once. Litvinov's fortune was considerable.

"But his family, his family! . . ." the Princess remarked.

"Well, of course, there's the question of family," the Prince answered. "But, after all, he is not entirely outside the nobility; and the main thing is that in any case Irena will not listen to us. Have you ever known her not to do what she wished? *Vous connaissez sa violence!* And besides there is nothing definite yet." So the Prince reasoned, but he at once mentally added: "Madame Litvinova — is that all? I expected more."

Irena took complete possession of her future bridegroom, and he readily delivered himself into her hands. It was as though he had fallen into a whirlpool, as though he had lost himself. . . . It was both frightening to him and sweet; and he did not regret anything, and did not spare anything. To ponder on the meaning, on the duties of married life, on whether he, so irrevocably subjugated, could be a good husband, and what kind of wife Irena would make, and whether their mutual relations were sound — these were questions he could not enter into. His blood began to burn, and he knew one thing only: that he must follow her, must go with her, henceforth and without end, and then come what come may!

But despite his complete lack of resistance and her excess of impulsive tenderness, none the less the affair did not proceed without certain misunderstandings and upsets. One day he hurried to her straight from the university, in an old coat and with ink-stained hands. She rushed to meet him with her usual endearing welcome, but stopped short.

"You haven't any gloves," she pronounced deliberately, at once adding: "Pah! What a — student you are!"

"You're too sensitive, Irena," he remarked.

"You're — a real student," she repeated, "*vous n'êtes pas distingué.*"

Turning her back on him, she left the room.

Truly, an hour later she implored him to forgive her . . . In general she readily punished and reproached herself in his presence. But, strange to say, often, all but weeping, she reproached herself with evil motives that she did not possess, and obstinately denied her real defects. Another time he found her in tears, with her head resting on her hand, her curls fallen over her back. When, thoroughly alarmed, he asked the reason for her sorrow, she silently pointed her finger to her breast. He involuntarily shivered. "Consumption!" the thought flashed through his head, and he seized her hand.

"Are you ill?" he asked in a quivering voice (they had already begun to use the intimate second person singular to each other on serious occasions). "If so I'll go at once for a doctor —"

But Irena did not allow him to finish. She stamped her foot with vexation.

"I am quite well — but this dress — don't you really understand?"

"What's the matter — that dress — ?" he said in perplexity.

"What is the matter? Why, that I haven't any other, and it is old and disgusting; and I am forced to put on this same dress every day — even when you — even when you" (here she corrected the pronoun to the plural) "come. . . . In the end you will cease to love me, seeing me in such a slovenly state!"

"Really, Irena, what are you saying! That dress is very nice! . . . I am particularly fond of it because you were wearing it the first time I saw you!"

She flushed.

"Please, Grigory Mikhailovich, don't remind me that I hadn't another dress even then."

"But I assure you, Irena Pavlovna, that it suits you charmingly."

"No, it is disgusting, disgusting," she declared, pulling nervously at her long, soft curls. "Oh, this poverty, poverty, this darkness! How can one escape from this poverty! How emerge, how emerge from the darkness!"

He did not know what to say and half turned away.

Suddenly she jumped up from her chair and put both hands on his shoulders.

"But you do love me, don't you? You love me?" she uttered, bringing her face close to his; and her eyes, though still filled with tears, began to sparkle with the gaiety of happiness. "You love me even in this disgusting dress?"

He flung himself down on his knees before her.

"Ah, love me, love me, my dear, my savior!" she whispered, bending down to him.

So the days passed, the weeks went by, and although no formal explanations had been entered into, although Litvinov still delayed with his formal request, not, of course, by his own desire, but in expectation of Irena's command (she remarked one day that they were both absurdly young, they must add at least a few more weeks to their age), yet everything was moving toward the denouement, and the immediate future was being delineated more and more clearly. When suddenly an event occurred that dissipated all these presumptions and plans like dust on a road.

8

During that winter the court visited Moscow. One function followed another; the time came for the usual great ball in the Palace of the Nobility. The news of this ball, though in the form of an announcement in the *Police Gazette*, reached the little house on Sobaka Square. The Prince was the first to raise the alarm; he at once decided that he must go in any case and must take Irena with him, that it would be unforgivable to lose the opportunity to see Their Majesties, that the blue-blooded nobility was even under a kind of obligation to do so. He maintained his opinion with a degree of fervor that was quite foreign to him; the Princess agreed with him to some extent and only sighed over the expenses; but Irena was resolutely opposed to the idea.

"It's quite unnecessary, I shall not go," she replied to all her parents' arguments. She grew so vehement under obduracy that the old Prince decided to ask Litvinov to try to persuade her and to point out to her, among other "reasons," that it was not seemly for a young lady to be unsociable, that she ought "to have this experience too," that, as matters stood, no one ever saw her. Litvinov undertook to put these "reasons" to her. Irena gazed at him fixedly and attentively, so fixedly and so attentively that he was embarrassed. Playing with the ends of her belt, she calmly said:

"Do you desire this? You?"

"Yes—I think so," he replied hesitantly. "I agree with your father. . . . And besides why shouldn't you go—to see people and to be seen?" he added with a little laugh.

"To be seen," she slowly repeated. "Well, good, I'll go. Only, remember that you yourself desired this."

41

"That is, I — " Litvinov began.

"You yourself desired it," she interrupted him. "And I have one other condition: you must promise me that you will not be present at the ball."

"But why not?"

"It is my wish."

He flung out his hands.

"I submit. . . . But, I confess, it would be very delightful for me to see you in all your magnificence, to be a witness of the impression you will surely make. . . . How proud I would be of you!" he added with a sigh.

Irena smiled. "All my magnificence will consist of a white gown; and as for the impression — well, in a word, that is how I want it to be."

"Irena, you seem to be angry."

She smiled again.

"Oh no! I am not angry. Only you — " (she fixed her eyes on him, and it seemed to him that never before had he seen such an expression in them). "Perhaps it is necessary," she added in an undertone.

"But, Irena, you do love me?"

"I love you," she replied with almost a solemn seriousness, and gave his hand a strong, vigorous squeeze.

All the following days Irena was diligently occupied with her toilet, her coiffure. On the eve of the ball she felt unwell; she could not sit still, and she shed a tear or two in solitude. So long as Litvinov was present she seemed to wear a fixed smile . . . for that matter, though she was as affectionate to him as ever, she was abstracted, and looked at herself in the mirror from time to time. On the actual day of the ball she was very taciturn and pale, but calm. At nine in the evening Litvinov arrived to take a look at her. When she came out to him in a white tarlatan gown, with a chaplet of small blue flowers in her slightly fluffed-up hair, he gasped, so beautiful and majestic, even beyond her years, did she seem to him. "Yes, she has grown since this morning," he thought. "And what a carriage! What a lot birth does mean, after all!" She stood with arms hanging loosely, without a smile and without affectation, looking resolutely, almost boldly, not at him, but into the distance, straight before her.

"You are just like a legendary princess," he said at last. "But no; you are like a general before the battle, before victory. . . . You would not permit me to attend this ball," he continued, while she still stood motionless, apparently not listening to him, but following some other, inner voice. "But you will not refuse to accept these flowers from me and take them with you?"

He gave her a bouquet of heliotrope.

She threw him a swift glance, raised her hand, and, suddenly seizing one end of the chaplet adorning her head, she said:

"Would you like me to? Say only the word and I will tear off all this and remain at home."

Litvinov's heart beat madly. Her hand was already pulling at the chaplet. . . .

"No, no, why should you?" He restrained her hurriedly, in an outburst of grateful and generous feelings. "I am not an egotist. Why restrict your freedom — when I know that your heart —"

"Well, then, don't come near me, you'll crease my gown," she said hastily.

He was disconcerted.

"But you'll take the bouquet?" he asked.

"Of course. It is very nice, and I am very fond of that perfume. *Merci*. . . . I shall keep it in memory —"

"Of your first coming out," Litvinov remarked; "of your first triumph."

Irena looked across her shoulder at herself in the mirror, slightly bending her figure.

"And am I really so very beautiful? You're not prejudiced?"

He broke into enthusiastic praises. But she was no longer listening to him. Raising the bouquet to her face, she again gazed into the distance with her strange, seemingly deepened and dilated eyes. Sent fluttering by a gentle breath of air, the ends of the fine ribbons lifted a little from her shoulders, like wings.

The Prince appeared, wearing a crimped peruke, a white cravat, a faded black frock coat, and with the ribbon of the order of St. Vladimir in his buttonhole. He was followed by the Princess in a silk figured gown of old-fashioned cut. With that fussy severity which mothers resort to in the attempt to conceal their agitation, she arranged her daughter's dress at the back: in other words, she quite unnecessarily shook out the folds of her gown. A four-seated hired coach, harnessed to two shaggy nags, crawled up to the porch, with its wheels squeaking and scrunching through the drifts of unswept snow, and a conceited lackey in an incredible livery jumped down from the box and reported with a swagger that the carriage was ready. . . . After blessing the children who were to be left for the night, and wrapping themselves in their furs, the Prince and the Princess went to the door: Irena, in a thin, short mantle — how she hated that mantle already! — silently followed them. Litvinov, who saw them off, hoped to receive one farewell glance from her; but she seated herself in the carriage without turning her head.

About midnight he walked past the windows of the Palace of the Nobility. The innumerable candles of the enormous chandeliers shone like points of light through the crimson curtains, and all the square, which was crowded with equipages, was filled with the dashing, festive, challenging sounds of a Strauss waltz.

Next day Litvinov called on the Osinins about one o'clock. He found only the Prince at home, and was at once informed that Irena had a headache, that she was in bed and would not get up until evening, and that, after all, such an upset was not in the least surprising after her first ball.

"*C'est très naturel, vous savez, dans les jeunes filles,*" the Prince added in French, which somewhat astonished Litvinov, who at the same moment noticed that he was not in his dressing-gown as usual, but in a coat. "And besides," Osinin continued, "how could she avoid being unwell after yesterday's occurrences?"

"Occurrences?" Litvinov murmured.

"Yes, yes, occurrences, occurrences, *de vrais événements.* You cannot imagine, Grigory Mikhailovich, *quel succès elle a eu!* All the court noticed her. Prince Alexandr Fiodorovich said that her place was not here, and that she reminded him of the Duchess of Devonshire — you know, that — well-known — And old Blazenkrampf declared for all to hear that Irena was *la reine du bal* and expressed the desire to be introduced to her. He introduced himself to me, too; I mean, he told me he remembered me as a hussar and asked where I was serving now. He's highly amusing, is the Count, and such an *adorateur du beau sexe!* But what was I saying? My Princess — she, too, was not given any peace; Natalia Nikitishna herself talked with her — and what else? Irena danced *avec tous les meilleurs cavaliers;* they even put me in an awkward position — awkward. I even lost count. Will you believe it? — they all walked round us in crowds; during the mazurka they all wanted to dance only with her. When he learned that she was a Muscovite, one foreign diplomat said to His Majesty: 'Sire!' he said, '*décidément c'est Moscou qui est le centre de votre empire!*' And another diplomat added: '*C'est une vraie révolution, Sire*'; *révélation* or *révolution* — something of that sort. Yes — yes — it — it — I tell you, it was something extraordinary."

"Yes, but how about Irena Pavlovna herself?" asked Litvinov, whose hands and feet had been going colder and colder all the time the Prince was speaking. "Did she enjoy herself, did she seem satisfied?"

"Of course she enjoyed herself, and as if she wouldn't be satisfied! And, by the way, you know you never can understand her all at once. Everybody said to me yesterday how amazing it was, *jamais on ne dirait que mademoiselle votre fille est à son premier bal.* Among other things Count Reizenbach — of course you know him — "

"No, I don't know him at all and never have."

"He's my wife's first cousin — "

"I don't know him."

"He's wealthy, a court chamberlain, he lives in Petersburg, he's a man of affairs, he has everybody dancing attendance on him in Livonia. Hitherto he has ignored us — and I'm not the sort to chase after people. *J'ai l'humeur facile, comme vous savez.* Well, to get back to him. He sat down with Irena, talked to her for a quarter of an hour, no more, and afterward said to my Princess: '*Ma cousine*,' he said, '*votre fille est une perle; c'est une perfection;* everybody is congratulating me on having such a niece. . . .' And then I saw him go up to — an important personage and speak to her, while he went on gazing at Irena . . . and the personage looked, too. . . ."

"And so Irena Pavlovna will not leave her room all day?" Litvinov asked.

"No; she has a bad headache. She asked us to greet you on her behalf and to thank you for your bouquet, *qu'on a trouvé charmant.* She needs the rest. . . . My Princess has gone to pay some visits . . . and I myself am, as you see — "

The Prince began to cough and fidget, as though he had difficulty in finding anything further to say. Litvinov picked up his hat, said that he had no intention of hindering him and would call later to inquire about Irena's health, and withdrew.

A few paces from the Osinins' house he saw an elegant two-seated carriage standing close to a policeman. With a negligent air a liveried footman, as elegant as the carriage, bent down from the box and asked the policeman, a local Finn, where Prince Pavel Vasilievich Osinin lived. Litvinov glanced into the carriage: inside it was a middle-aged man wrapped in sables, with a lined and arrogant face of florid complexion, a Grecian nose, and evil lips: by all the signs an important dignitary.

9

Litvinov did not keep his promise to call later; he realized that it would be better to postpone his visit till the following day. When, about twelve o'clock, he entered the only too well-known reception hall, he saw the younger princesses, Victorina and Cleopatrina. He greeted them, then asked whether Irena Pavlovna was better and could he see her.

"Dear Irena has driven somewhere with Mamma," Victorina replied; though she lisped, she was less bashful than her sister.

"What do you mean — driven somewhere?" he repeated after her, and something quietly began to quiver in the very depths of his breast. "Surely — surely — surely at this time of day she ought to be occupied with you, giving you your lessons?"

"Dear Irena will not be giving us lessons any more," Victorina replied. "Not any more," Cleopatrina repeated after her.

"But is your papa at home?" Litvinov asked.

"Papa is not at home either," Victorina said. "But Irena isn't well: she cried all night, all night."

"Cried?"

"Yes, cried — so Yegorovna told me, and her eyes were so red, and they were so swollen — "

Litvinov paced the room once or twice, shivering a little as though with the cold, then returned to his apartment. He experienced a sensation similar to that which takes possession of a man when he looks down from a lofty tower: all his internals sank, and his head swam slowly and sickeningly. He felt a dull bewilderment, though his thoughts went scurrying like mice; he was conscious of a vague horror and mute expectation and a peculiar, almost malevolent curiosity; there was the bitterness of unshed tears in his choking throat, an attempt at a vacuous smile on his lips, and in his heart a meaningless, aimless supplication. . . . Oh, how cruelly and humiliatingly infamous it all was! "Irena doesn't want to see me," the thought persistently recurred to his mind; "that is quite clear. But why doesn't she? What could have happened at that unfortunate ball? And how could such a sudden change be possible? So abruptly —" (Human beings are constantly witnessing the fact that death comes abruptly, but they can never get accustomed to this abruptness, and think it senseless.) "She does not give them any message for me, she does not wish to give me any explanation. . . ."

"Grigory Mikhailich!" a tense voice sounded right by his ear.

He started, and saw his man with a note in his hand. He recognized Irena's writing. . . . Even before he unsealed the note he had a presentiment of disaster and sank his head on his chest and hunched his shoulders, as though protecting himself against a blow.

At last he plucked up courage and tore the envelope open. On the small sheet of paper inside were the following words:

Forgive me, Grigory Mikhailich! Everything is over between us; I am going to Petersburg. It is terribly hard for me, but the deed is done. Evidently, it is my fate — but no, I have no wish to justify myself. My presentiments have come true. Forgive me, forget me; I am not worthy of you.

Irena

Be magnanimous: do not try to see me.

Litvinov read these six lines and sank slowly onto the sofa as though someone were pushing him in the chest. He dropped the note, picked it up, read it again, whispered: "To Petersburg," dropped it again, and let it lie. He was even possessed by a feeling of tranquillity; with hands flung behind him he even adjusted the cushion to his head. "People crushed to death don't struggle," he thought; "as it came, so it has gone again. . . . It is all quite natural, I always expected it. . . ." (He was lying to himself; he had never expected anything of the sort.) "Wept? . . . She wept? . . . What did she weep for? After all, she didn't love me! However, it is all understandable and in keeping with her character. She, she is not worthy of me. . . . You don't say so!" (He smiled bitterly.) "She herself did not know what power lurked within her, and once she had been convinced of its effect at the ball, how could she be satisfied with an insignificant student? . . . That is all quite understandable."

But then he remembered her tender words, her smiles, and those eyes, those unforgettable eyes, which he would never see again, eyes that lit up and melted if they happened to meet his eyes; he remembered her swift, timid, burning kiss — and he suddenly burst into sobbing. He sobbed convulsively, frenziedly, rancorously, with his face turned to the sofa, and so sobbing and panting, with frantic satisfaction, as though seeking to tear himself and everything around him to pieces, he beat his inflamed face against the cushion, chewed the material. . . .

Alas! the gentleman whom Litvinov had seen in the carriage the previous day was Princess Osinin's cousin, the court chamberlain and man of fortune Count Reizenbach. Observing the impression Irena made on highly placed personages, and at once realizing *"mit etwas Accuratesse"* what advantages could be derived from this circumstance, the Count, being an energetic man as well as a toady, at once formulated his plan. He decided to act swiftly, in Napoleonic fashion. "I'll take that remarkable young lady into my home at Petersburg," he deliberated. "I'll make her my heiress, damn it, though not to all my fortune. It so happens that I haven't any children, and she is my niece, and my Countess is bored with being alone. . . . Life is always more pleasant when there's a pretty face in the reception hall. . . . Yes, yes; that's it; *es ist eine Idee, es ist eine Idee!"* He would have to dazzle, to bemuse, to astound her parents. . . . "They haven't anything," he continued his meditations as he sat in the carriage on his way to Sobaka Square, "so I don't expect them to be obstinate. They're not so sensitive as all that. I could give them a lump sum, for that matter. But how about her? She will agree too. Honey is sweet — she had a taste of it yesterday. Granted that this is a whim on my part; well, let them have the benefit of it — the fools. I shall tell them my conditions, and they must decide. And if not, I'll take another; an orphan — still more convenient. Yes or no, twenty-four hours to decide, *und damit Punctum."*

When the Count presented himself to the Prince, he used these very words; he had advised him the night before, at the ball, of his intention to call. It does not seem worth while enlarging to any extent on the consequences of this visit. The Count was not mistaken in his calculations: the Prince and Princess were not obstinate and accepted a sum of money, and Irena did agree before the time limit had expired. It was not easy for her to break off her relations with Litvinov; she loved him and, having sent him the note, she all but took to her bed, and wept incessantly, went thin and yellow. . . . But, none the less, a month later the Princess carried her off to Petersburg and installed her with the Count, entrusting her to the protection of the Countess, who was a very good woman, but had the mentality of a hen and looked like a hen.

Litvinov threw up his studies at the university and went to live with his father in the country. Little by little his wound healed. At first he had no news whatever of Irena, and indeed he avoided all talk of Petersburg and Petersburg society. Then gradually rumors began to circulate concerning her: not evil rumors, but strange; she was the subject of common gossip. The name of Princess Osinina, was surrounded with an aureole of general report, was remarked upon with peculiar emphasis, and began to be mentioned more and more even in provincial circles. It was mentioned with curiosity, with respect, with envy, as the name of Countess Vorotinskaya had once been mentioned. Finally the news was spread that she had married. But Litvinov paid hardly any attention to this latest report: by then he was betrothed to Tatiana.

Now the reader probably understands exactly what he recalled when he exclaimed: "Surely not?" And so we return to Baden and take up the thread of our interrupted story.

10

Litvinov fell asleep very late and did not sleep long; the sun had only just risen when he got out of bed. Visible from his windows, the crests of the shadowed hills showed humidly blood-red against the clear sky. "It ought to be fresh beneath the trees," he thought. He hurriedly dressed, glanced abstractedly at the bouquet, which had opened still more exuberantly during the night, took his stick, and set off to walk beyond the Old Castle to the well-known Cliffs. The morning clasped him in its strong and quiet caress. Bravely he breathed, bravely he moved; the health of youth played in his every tiny vein; the earth itself seemed to be conferring more resilience on his lightly striding legs. With every step he grew more free, more gay; he walked in the dewy shade, over the coarse sand of the paths, by the firs, all the tips of which were edged with the brilliant green of the vernal shoots. "How glorious it is!" he told himself from time to time. Suddenly he heard familiar voices: he looked up and saw Voroshilov and Bambayev coming toward him. The sight was so jarring that, like a pupil escaping from a teacher, he started to one side and hid behind a bush. . . . "Creator!" he implored, "carry my compatriots past!" One can only assume that at that moment he would have given any sum to ensure that they did not see him. . . . And in fact they did not see him. The Creator carried his compatriots past. Voroshilov, talking in a voice as self-satisfied as any cadet's, was explaining to Bambayev the various "phases" of Gothic architecture, while Bambayev only mooed approvingly. Evidently Voroshilov's lecture on the "phases" had already lasted a long time, and the good-natured enthusiast was beginning to be bored. Biting his lip and stretching his neck, Litvinov listened to the retreating footsteps for quite a while; the guttural and nasal tones of the edifying speech continued to reach him for a long time; at last all sounds died away. He sighed, emerged from his ambush, and walked on.

For some three hours he wandered about the hills. Sometimes he left the path and went leaping from stone to stone, occasionally slipping on the smooth moss. Sometimes he sat down on a piece of rock beneath an oak or beech and thought pleasant thoughts, to the unceasing whisper of the little streams overgrown with bracken, the reassuring rustle of the leaves, the ringing song of a solitary black thrush. A light and pleasant drowsiness stole over him, seemed to envelop him from behind, and he dozed off. . . . But suddenly he smiled and looked about him; the gold and green of the forest, the forest air, were borne gently to his eyes — and he smiled again and closed them again. He felt that he would like some breakfast, and he made his way to the Old Castle, where for a few kreutzers one can get a glass of good milk and coffee. But he had not even had time to seat himself at one of the small white tables scattered about the platform before the castle when he heard the heavy snorting of horses, and three carriages appeared and discharged quite a large company of ladies and gentlemen.

Though they were all talking French, Litvinov at once recognized them as Russian — just because they were talking French. The ladies' toilets were distinguished by an artificial elegance; the gentlemen were wearing morning coats — spick and span morning coats, but tight-fitting and with fitted waists, which is not exactly usual in our day — shot gray pantaloons, and very glossy town

50

hats. Each of these gentlemen had a low-hanging black tie, which tightly clasped his neck, and there was a military quality in the bearing of all. They were, in fact, military men; Litvinov had lighted upon a picnic of young generals, members of high society and of considerable weight. Their importance was indicated in all their mannerisms: their air of restrained jauntiness, their pleasantly dignified smiles, the tense abstraction of their gaze, the effeminate shrug of their shoulders, the way they swayed their bodies and bent their knees; it was indicated by the very tone of their voices, such a tone as they might have used to express their affable and loathsome thanks to a crowd of underlings. All these officers were superlatively washed, shaved, and saturated with a perfume peculiar to the genuine courtier and guardsman, a blend of finest cigar smoke and subtle patchouli. And every one of them had courtiers' hands, white and large, with nails as strong as ivory; they all had gleaming mustaches and sparkling teeth, and their fine skin was flushed with crimson on their cheeks and was bluish at the chin. Some of these young generals were playful, others thoughtful; but they all bore the stamp of exquisite propriety. Each one seemed to be profoundly conscious of his own worth, of the importance of his future role in the state, and bore himself both easily and with stern restraint, with just a touch of that mettle, that "damn it all" which so naturally develops during travels abroad.

After seating themselves noisily and elegantly, the company summoned the bustling waiters. Litvinov hastened to finish his glass of milk, paid his bill, and, clapping on his hat, was just slipping past the generals' picnic. . . .

"Grigory Mikhailich," came a woman's voice. "Don't you recognize me?"

He involuntarily halted. That voice — that voice in past days had made his heart beat all too rapidly. . . . He turned and saw Irena.

She was sitting with her arms folded over the back of a chair that she had drawn away from a table. Smiling, with her head cocked a little to one side, she gazed at him with a welcoming, almost joyous look.

He recognized her at once, though she had changed since he had last seen her, ten years ago, and though the girl he had known was transformed into a woman. Her slender figure had developed

51

and blossomed, the contours of her once angular shoulders now recalled those of the goddesses depicted on the ceilings of ancient Italian palaces. But her eyes had remained the same, and it seemed to Litvinov that they looked at him just as they had in that long past time in that small Moscow house.

"Irena Pavlovna —" he said uncertainly.

"So you recognized me? How glad I am, how glad —" She stopped, reddened slightly and drew herself up. "This is a very pleasant meeting," she continued in French. "Let me introduce you to my husband. Valérien, this is M'sieur Litvinov, *un ami d'enfance;* and this is Valerian Vladimirovich Ratmirov, my husband."

One of the young generals, perhaps the most exquisite of them all, rose from the table and bowed to Litvinov with unusual courtesy. But his colleagues knitted their brows a little, or rather not so much knitted their brows as withdrew for a moment each into himself, as though protesting in advance against any rapprochement with some civilian outsider; while the other ladies present deemed it necessary to narrow their eyes a little and to smile, and even to adopt a look of astonishment.

"You — have you been long in Baden?" General Ratmirov asked, attitudinizing in rather an un-Russian fashion and obviously not knowing what to talk about to a friend of his wife's childhood.

"Not long," Litvinov answered.

"And are you intending to stay for long?" the courteous general continued.

"I haven't yet decided."

"Ah! That is very pleasant — very."

The general was silent. Litvinov also said nothing. They both held their hats in their hands and, smirking and bending their bodies forward, looked at each other's eyebrows.

"*Deux gendarmes, un beau dimanche,*" a shortsighted and rather yellow-faced general began to sing, of course in a falsetto voice — we have never yet come across a Russian nobleman who did not sing falsetto. This general wore an expression of permanent irritability, as though he could not forgive himself his own exterior. Among them all, he alone had no resemblance whatever to a rose.

"But why don't you sit down, Grigory Mikhailich?" Irena said at last.

Litvinov complied and sat down.

"I say, Valérien, give me some fire," [1] said another general, also young, but already corpulent, with immobile eyes looking as though fixed on space, and thick, silky whiskers, in which he slowly buried his snow-white fingers.

Ratmirov handed him a silver match-box.

"*Avez-vous de papiros?*" one of the ladies asked; she could not roll her "r's" properly.

"*De vrais papelitos, Comtesse.*"

"*Deux gendarmes un beau dimanche,*" the shortsighted general again struck up, all but grinding his teeth.

"You simply must call on us," Irena was saying to Litvinov meanwhile. "We are staying at the Hôtel de l'Europe. I am always at home from four to six. It's such a long time since we saw each other."

Litvinov glanced at Irena; she did not lower her eyes.

"Yes, Irena Pavlovna, it is a long time. Not since Moscow."

"Since Moscow, since Moscow," she said slowly. "Come and see me; we'll have a talk and recall the old times. But you know, Grigory Mikhailich, you haven't changed much."

"Really? But you have changed, Irena Pavlovna."

"I've grown older."

"No. That's not what I wanted to say —"

"Irène?" a lady who was wearing a yellow hat on her yellow hair said interrogatively, after a preliminary whisper and giggle with the gentleman sitting beside her. "Irène?"

"I have grown older," Irena continued without answering her, "but I have not changed. No, no, I haven't changed in the least."

"*Deux gendarmes un beau dimanche!*" was now heard again. The irritable general could remember only the first line of the well-known ballad.

"It still stings, Your Excellency," the corpulent general with the whiskers said in a loud voice, probably alluding to some amusing story known to all the beau monde. Laughing a curt, wooden laugh, he again fixed his eyes on space. All the rest of the company also laughed.

"What a sad dog you are, Boris!" Ratmirov remarked in an undertone. He spoke in English and pronounced the name Boris in the English fashion.

[1] In English in the original. (Tr.)

"*Irène?*" the lady in the yellow hat called a third time. Irena turned swiftly to her.

"*Eh bien, quoi? Que me voulez-vous?*"

"*Je vous le dirai plus tard,*" the lady replied in a finicky tone. Despite her quite unattractive appearance, she continually minced her words and grimaced. Some wit had said of her that she "*minaudait dans le vide.*"

Irena knitted her brows and impatiently shrugged her shoulders.

"*Mais que fait donc Monsieur Verdier? Pourquoi ne vient-il pas?*" one lady exclaimed with that drawling emphasis which is a peculiarity of the Great Russian accent, but which the French find unbearable.

"*Ah, voui, ah voui, Msie Verdie, Msie Verdie,*" groaned another lady, who obviously originated directly from Arzamas.[1]

"*Tranquillisez-vous, mesdames,*" Ratmirov intervened. "*Monsieur Verdier m'a promis de venir se mettre à vos pieds.*"

"He-he-he!" The ladies began to play with their fans.

A waiter brought several glasses of beer.

"*Bayrisch bier?*" asked the general with the whiskers, deliberately speaking in a deep tone and pretending to surprised. "*Guten Morgen.*"

"Tell me! Is Count Pavel still there?" one young general coldly and languidly asked another.

"Yes," the other replied as coldly. "*Mais c'est provisoire.* Serge is in his place, they say."

"Aha!" the first general muttered through set teeth.

"M'yes!" the second hissed through his teeth.

"I cannot understand," began the general who had struck up the song, "I cannot understand what made Pavel attempt to justify himself, to make all kinds of excuses. . . . After all, he had squeezed the merchant a bit, *il lui a vait rendre gorge.* . . . But what of it? He may have had his reasons."

"He was afraid — of charges in the press," someone snorted.

The irritable general flared up.

"Well, that's the last word! The press! Charges! If it depended on me, I'd allow that press of yours to print only the taxes on meat or bread, and advertisements for the sale of furs or boots."

"And noblemen's estates for auction," Ratmirov put in.

---

[1] A small provincial town of central Russia, famous for its geese. (Tr.)

"Maybe, in the present circumstances . . . But what a conversation for Baden, *au Vieux Château!*"

"*Mais pas du tout! Pas du tout!*" the lady in the yellow hat lisped. "*J'adore les questions politiques.*"

"*Madame a raison,*" another general with an extremely pleasant and rather girlish face intervened. "Why should we avoid these questions — even in Baden?" With these words he looked at Litvinov courteously and gave him a condescending smile. "An honest man should never and in no circumstances betray his convictions. Isn't that so?"

"Of course," the irritable general replied, also throwing a look at Litvinov and, it seemed, obliquely rebuking him. "But I don't see the necessity — "

"No, no," the condescending general interrupted in his previous mild manner. "Our friend Valerian Vladimirovich just mentioned the sale of noblemen's estates. Well, and isn't that a fact?"

"But in any case it is impossible even to sell them now, no one wants them!" the irritable general exclaimed.

"Maybe — maybe. And for that very reason it is necessary to proclaim the fact — that mournful fact — at every step. We are ruined — excellent; we are impoverished, that is not to be disputed; but we, the large landowners, all the same we represent an element — *un principe.* It is our duty to maintain that principle. *Pardon, madame,* I think you have dropped your handkerchief. When a certain obscurity, so to speak, dominates even the highest minds, we must point, must with humility point" (the general extended his finger), "point out to the citizen with our finger the bottomless pit into which everything is rushing. We must warn him, we must say with respectful firmness: 'Turn, turn back. . . .' That is what we ought to say."

"But it isn't possible to go right back," Ratmirov remarked thoughtfully.

The condescending general only smirked.

"Right back; right back, *mon très cher.* The farther back, the better."

The general again glanced politely at Litvinov. Litvinov could stand no more.

"But surely we haven't to go right back to the days of state anarchy, Your Excellency?"

"Yes, even so far! I express my opinion without ambiguity; everything that has been done must be redone — yes — redone."

"And the 19th of February?"[1]

"And the 19th of February, in so far as that is possible. *On est patriote ou on n' l'est pas.* 'But how about freedom?' they say to me. Do you think the people find this freedom sweet? You ask them —"

"You try," Litvinov retorted, "you try to take that freedom from him —"

"*Comment nommez-vous ce monsieur?*" the general whispered to Ratmirov.

"But what are you talking about?" The corpulent general, who evidently played the role of the spoilt child in this society, suddenly began to speak. "Still about the press? About the quill-drivers? Allow me, I'll tell you an incident I had with a quill-driver — it was extraordinary! I was told that *un folliculaire* had written a pasquil about me. Well, of course, I immediately put him under arrest. They brought the fellow along. 'My friend,' I said, 'how do you dare, you *folliculaire*, to write pasquils about me? I suppose your patriotism conquered you?' 'It did,' he said. 'Well,' I said, 'and do you like money, *folliculaire*?' 'I do,' he said. Then, my dear sirs, I gave him the knob of my stick to smell. 'And do you like that, my angel?' 'No,' he says, 'I don't like that.' 'But you take a good smell of it!' I said; 'my hands are quite clean.' 'I don't like it,' he said, 'and that's sufficient.' 'But I, my soul,' I said, 'I like it very much, only not for myself. Do you understand this allegory, my treasure?' 'I understand,' he said. 'Well, now you be a good boy in the future, and here's a silver ruble for you; clear out and bless me day and night.' And the *folliculaire* departed."

The general laughed, and everybody again laughed after him, all except Irena, who did not even smile, but gazed at the narrator moodily.

The condescending general shook Boris by the shoulder.

"You invented all that story, my dear friend. I should like to see you threatening anybody with a stick. Why, you don't even own a stick. *C'est pour faire rire ces dames.* Just for the sake of talking! But that is not the point. I have just said that we need to

[1] Emancipation of the serfs, February 19 (old style), 1861. (Tr.)

56

go right back. Understand me aright. I am not an enemy of so-called progress; but all these universities and seminaries and elementary schools, these students, these priests' sons, these independent educated classes, all this small fry, *tout ce fond du sac, la petite propriété, pire que le prolétariat*" (the general spoke with an effeminate, almost debilitated voice), "*voilà ce qui m'effraie —* that is where it is necessary to come to a stop — and to stop them." (He gave Litvinov another gracious look.) "Yes, it is necessary to come to a stop. Don't forget that no one ever wants anything, or asks for anything, in our country. Local government, for instance — does anyone ask for it? Do you indeed ask for it? Or you? Or you? Or you, *mesdames*? As it is, you already govern not only yourselves, but all the rest of us" (the general's handsome face lit up with a diverting smile). "My dear friends, why run like a hare? Democracy is glad of you, it flatters you, it is ready to serve your ends . . . but remember it is a two-edged sword. Then surely it is better the old way, the former way — that is far more reliable. Don't allow the rabble to show off their intelligence, but trust in the aristocracy, in which alone is strength. . . . Really, it will be better so. But progress — I myself have nothing against progress. Only don't give us just lawyers, and barristers, and a crowd of officials from the zemstvos,[1] and then there's the question of discipline; above all, don't touch the discipline. But you can build bridges, and embankments, and hospitals, and why not light the streets with gas?"

"Set fire to Petersburg on all four sides, there's your progress!" the irritable general hissed.

"Ah, I see you're in a bad temper," the corpulent general said, lazily swaying. "It would be a good idea to make you attorney general. But in my view, *avec Orphée aux enfers le progrès a dit son dernier mot.*"

"*Vous dites toujours des bêtises,*" the lady from Arzamas giggled.

The general assumed a dignified look.

"*Je ne suis jamais plus sérieux, madame, que quand je dis des bêtises.*"

"M'sieur Verdie has already made that same remark more than once," Irena observed in an undertone.

"*De la poigne et des formes!*" exclaimed the corpulent general.

---

[1] Provincial local government organizations. (Tr.)

"*De la poigne surtout.* And that can be translated: politely, but with the first in the teeth!"

"Ah, you're a joker, an incorrigible joker!" the condescending general took him up. "Mesdames, please do not listen to him. He would not hurt a fly. He is content to devastate hearts."

"But, all the same, you're wrong, Boris," Ratmirov began, exchanging glances with his wife. "A joke's a joke, but that's exaggeration. Progress is a manifestation of social life, that is what we mustn't forget; it is a symptom. We must follow it, must watch it."

"Why, yes," the corpulent general retorted, and wrinkled his nose. "We understood that you are aiming at the statesmen!"

"Not at all at the statesmen. What have the statesmen to do with it? But the truth has to be admitted."

Boris again thrust his fingers into his whiskers and fixed his eyes on space.

"The social life is very important, because in the development of the nation, in the destinies, so to speak, of the fatherland —"

"Valérien," Boris interrupted authoritatively, "*il y a des dames ici.* I hadn't expected this of you. Or do you want to be elected to a committee?"

"They're all dissolved now, thank God!" the irritable general observed, and once more began to sing: "*Deux gendarmes, un beau dimanche. . . .*"

Ratmirov raised his batiste handkerchief to his nose and gracefully said no more; the condescending general repeated: "A joker, a joker!" But Boris turned to the lady who was grimacing at empty space and, without lowering his voice, not even changing the expression on his face, began to ask her when she would "crown his flame," because he loved her madly and was suffering extraordinarily.

As this conversation proceeded, Litvinov had felt more and more awkward. His pride, his honest, plebeian pride, rose in indignant revolt. What was there in common between him, the son of a petty official, and these military Petersburg aristocrats? He loved everything that they hated, he hated everything they loved; he saw that all too clearly, he felt it with all his being. He thought their jokes flat, their tone intolerable, their every movement false; in the very gentility of their speech he sensed a revolting contempt — and yet he seemed abashed by them, by these people, these enemies. . . . "Pah! How beastly! I am a constraint on them, they think me funny!" the thought went through his head. "So why am I staying here? I'll go, I'll go at once!" Irena's presence could not detain him; she, too, awakened unhappy feelings in him. He rose from his chair and began to take his leave.

"You're going already?" Irena said. But after a moment's thought she made no attempt to insist on his staying and only persuaded him to promise that he would certainly call on her. General Ratmirov bowed to him with his previous exquisite courtesy, shook his hand, accompanied him to the edge of the platform. . . .

But Litvinov had hardly turned the first bend in the road when a sudden burst of laughter broke out behind him. This laughter had no connection with him, but was aroused by the long expected M'sieur Verdier, who unexpectedly came onto the platform in a Tyrolean hat and a blue blouse, and riding an ass. But the blood rushed to Litvinov's cheeks, and he felt bitter: as though wormwood were gluing his compressed lips together. "Contemptible, ignoble people," he muttered, not realizing that the few moments he had spent in their company gave him no cause to express himself so strongly. And it was into this world that Irena, she who had been his Irena, had fallen! In it she circled, she lived, she reigned, for it she had sacrificed her own dignity, the finest feelings of her heart. . . . Evidently that was as it should be; evidently she was not worthy of a better fate! How he rejoiced that she had not thought of questioning him on his intentions! He would have had to tell her in front of "them," in "their" presence. . . . "Not for anything! Never!" he whispered, taking a deep breath of the fresh air and all but running down the road leading to Baden. He thought of his fiancée, of the dear, kind, good Tatiana; and how pure, how noble and true she seemed to him! With what unfeigned tenderness he recalled her features, her words, her very habits . . . with what impatience he awaited her arrival!

The swift walk soothed his nerves. When he returned to his hotel he sat down at a table and picked up a book, but abruptly dropped it, even shivered. . . . What had happened to him? Nothing had happened to him, but Irena — Irena — his meeting with her suddenly seemed astonishing, strange, extraordinary. Was it possible? Had he met and talked with that same Irena? . . . And why was it that the repulsive, worldly impress that was so firmly stamped on all those others was not noticeable in her? Why did he imagine that she seemed to be bored, or sad, or oppressed with her position? She was in their company, but she was not an enemy. And what could have made her turn to him and so cordially invite him to see her?

Litvinov gave a start. "Oh, Tania, Tania!" he exclaimed passionately; "you alone are my angel, my good genius, you alone do I love and will love forever. I shall not call on her. She can do what she likes! Let her amuse herself with her generals!"

He turned again to his book.

11

He turned to his book, but he did not read. He left the hotel, strolled about for a while, listened to the music, watched the gaming in the Casino for a time, then returned to his room and again attempted to read — all quite aimlessly. The time seemed to drag past very sluggishly. Pishchalkin, the well-intentioned arbitrator, dropped in and sat on for a good three hours. He talked, he explained, he posed problems, expatiated in turn first on exalted subjects, then on practical subjects, and finally spread such an air of boredom around him that poor Litvinov all but howled. Even among people of the highest morality, who are well known as experts in this regard, Pishchalkin had no rivals in the art of inducing boredom, a yearning, chilly, hopeless, and endless boredom. The very sight of his close-cropped and sleekly greased hair, his light and devitalized eyes, his genteel nose, aroused an involuntary feeling of despondency, while his deliberate, sleepy, baritone voice seemed a chosen instrument for giving persuasive and lucid expression to such platitudes as that two and two are four, and not five or three; that water is wet, and virtue laudable; that a private individual needs credit for financial operations just as much as the state, and the state just as much as a private individual. And with all this he was an excellent man! But then, that is in the very nature of human destiny in Russia: our excellent people are such bores! Pishchalkin departed; he was replaced by Bindasov, who immediately, with great impudence, demanded a loan of a hundred guldens. Litvinov gave it to him, though he was far from interested in Bindasov, and really loathed him and knew perfectly well that he would never get his money back; and yet he had need of it himself. "Then why did he give it to him?"

the reader will ask. The devil knows why! The Russians are great fellows for that sort of thing too. Let the reader set his hand on his heart and recall how many of his own actions have had no other reason whatever. But Bindasov did not even thank Litvinov: he asked for a glass of Affentaler (the red wine of Baden) and left without wiping his lips, and brazenly clattering with his boots. And how vexed Litvinov was with himself, as he stared after the departing peasant miser's golden mane!

Late in the afternoon he received a letter from Tatiana, informing him that she could not arrive in Baden for another five or six days as her aunt was not well. This news had an unpleasant effect on Litvinov: it added to his mortification. And he went to bed early, feeling very down in the mouth.

The following day proved to be no better than its predecessor, and perhaps was even a little worse. From early morning Litvinov's room was inundated with his compatriots; Bambayev, Voroshilov, Pishchalkin, the two officers, the two Heidelberg students, all arrived at once and somehow or other did not depart till dinnertime, though they soon said all they had to say and were obviously bored. They simply did not know what to do with themselves, and, once in Litvinov's room, they were "stranded" there, as one says. At first they discussed the fact that Gubariov had gone back to Heidelberg, and declared that everybody ought to go and visit him there. Then they philosophized a little and touched on the Polish question. Then they turned to the discussion of gaming, of *lorettes*, then to telling scandalous stories. Finally the conversation meandered into consideration of athletes, fat men, and gluttons. The time-worn stories about Lukin, the deacon who ate thirty-three herring at one sitting, the Uhlan Colonel Izyedinov, famous for his corpulence, and the soldier who broke a bullock's bone against his forehead were all brought out into the light of God's day, and of course they were followed by out-and-out lies. Pishchalkin himself told with a yawn of how he had known a woman in Malorussia who on her death had been found to weigh nearly a thousand pounds, and of a landowner who ate three geese and a sturgeon for breakfast. Bambayev suddenly went into ecstasies and announced that he himself felt that he could devour a whole sheep, "of course with the trimmings," while Voroshilov retailed some story concerning a comrade of his, a cadet athlete, so utterly absurd that they were all struck dumb, sat in silence, stared at one another, then reached for their hats and departed. Left alone, Litvinov thought he would devote some time to study. But it was just as though his brains were addled; he could not do anything sensible, and the evening also was wasted.

He was getting ready for breakfast next morning when someone knocked at his door. "Lord," he thought, "some of yesterday's friends again," and called, not without a shiver:

"*Herein!*"

The door was quietly opened, and Potugin entered the room. Litvinov was extremely delighted to see him.

"Now, this is really pleasant," he said, vigorously shaking his unexpected guest's hand. "Thank you indeed! I would have called on you without fail, but you wouldn't tell me where you are staying. Please sit down and put your hat somewhere. Do sit down."

Potugin made no answer to Litvinov's warm remarks, but stood shifting from foot to foot in the middle of the room and only smiled and shook his head. Litvinov's cordial welcome obviously moved him, but his face had a rather embarrassed expression.

"There's — a little misunderstanding —" he began, not without some hesitation. "Of course, I am always pleased . . . but as a matter of fact I — I have been sent to you."

"That is, you mean," Litvinov said in a mournful tone, "that you wouldn't have called on me of your own choice?"

"Oh no, please don't think that! . . . But I — I don't think I would have ventured to trouble you today if I had not been asked to call on you. In a word, I have a message for you."

"May I ask from whom?"

"From someone you know, from Irena Pavlovna Ratmirova. You promised to call on her two days ago, and you haven't been."

Litvinov stared at him in bewilderment.

"Are you acquainted with Madame Ratmirova?" he asked.

"As you see."

"And well acquainted?"

"I am her friend to some extent."

Litvinov made no comment.

"May I ask you," he said at last, "whether you know why Irena Pavlovna would like to see me?"

Potugin went across to the window.

"Up to a point I do. So far as I can judge, she was very glad to meet you, and, well, she desires to renew her previous relationship."

"Renew," Litvinov repeated. "Excuse me if I seem lacking in modesty, but may I further ask you whether you are aware of the nature of that relationship?"

"No, as a matter of fact, I am not. But I assume," Potugin added, suddenly turning to Litvinov and smiling at him amiably, "I must assume that it was a very good relationship. Irena Pavlovna was full of your praises, and I had to give her my word that I would bring you to her. Will you go?"

"When?"

"Now — this minute."

Litvinov only threw out his hands.

"Irena Pavlovna," Potugin continued, "thinks that that — how can I put it? — that milieu, perhaps, in which you saw her two days ago could hardly have been particularly agreeable to you. But she told me to say that the devil is not so black as he is painted."

"Hm. . . . Does that saying apply expressly to that — milieu?"

"Yes — and more generally."

"Hm. . . . Well, but how about you, Sozont Ivanich? What is your opinion of the devil?"

"I think, Grigory Mikhailich, that in any case he is not what he is made out to be."

"Is he better?"

"Whether better or worse is difficult to decide, but he is not what people think. Well, shall we go, then?"

"But first sit down for a little while. I confess that it seems somewhat strange to me — "

"What does, I dare to ask."

"That you, you in particular, have become a friend of Irena Pavlovna's."

Potugin ran his eyes over himself.

"In view of my figure, and my position in society, it is truly difficult to believe. But, you know, Shakspere said: 'There are more things in heaven and earth, Horatio — ' and so on. And besides, life is not fond of joking. Here is a comparison for you: you are looking at a tree, and there is no wind; how can a leaf on a lower branch manage to touch a leaf on an upper branch? It simply cannot. But then a storm arises, everything is shifted from its place, and the two leaves touch."

"Aha! So there was a storm!"

"Of course! Can you get through life without them? But away with philosophy! It's time we were going."

Even now Litvinov hesitated.

"Oh, Lord!" Potugin exclaimed with a comical grimace. "What is wrong with the young people these days! A very charming lady invites them to call on her, sends express couriers for them, and yet they stand on ceremony! Here's your hat. Take it, and *'vor-wärts!'* as our friends the passionate Germans say."

For a moment or two longer Litvinov stood irresolutely, but he ended by picking up his hat and leaving with Potugin.

12

They went to one of the finest hotels in Baden and asked for Mme Ratmirova, the general's wife. The porter first asked their names, then at once replied: *"Die Frau Fürstin ist zu Hause."* He himself conducted them through the hotel, knocked at the door of the suite, and reported their arrival. *"Die Frau Fürstin"* received them at once. She was alone; her husband had gone to Karlsruhe to see a highly placed dignitary, a man of "influence," who was passing through that town.

Irena was sitting at a small table, doing some frame embroidery, when Potugin and Litvinov entered the room. She briskly threw the needle aside, pushed away the table, and rose; her face wore an expression of unfeigned satisfaction. She was wearing a morning gown that fitted closely to the neck; the beautiful contours of her shoulders and arms were revealed through the light material; her carelessly braided hair had come undone and had fallen low over her slender neck. She threw a swift glance at Potugin, whispered: *"Merci,"* and, holding out her hand to Litvinov, gently reproached him for his forgetfulness. "And an old friend, too," she added.

He began to apologize. "*C'est bien, c'est bien,*" she said hurriedly. With gentle force she took his hat from him and made him sit down. Potugin also sat down, but at once got up again, saying that he had urgent business to attend to and that he would drop in after dinner. He began to bow his way out. Irena threw him another swift glance and nodded to him cordially, but did not detain him. As soon as he had disappeared behind the portiere, she turned to Litvinov with impatient vivacity.

"Grigory Mikhailich," she began in Russian in her soft and musical voice, "we're alone at last, and I can tell you that I am very glad of our meeting, because it — it enables me — " (she looked straight into his face) "to ask your forgiveness."

Litvinov involuntarily started. He had not expected such a rapid onslaught. He had not expected that she herself would turn the conversation to talk of the old times.

"Forgiveness — for what?" he muttered.

Irena crimsoned.

"For what? . . . You know for what," she said, and turned a little away from him. "I did you a wrong, Grigory Mikhailich — although, of course, it was my fate" (he recalled her letter) "and I do not repent . . . it would be too late in any case. But, meeting you so unexpectedly, I said to myself that we simply must become friends, simply must . . . and I would be greatly upset if that did not come about. . . . And I think that in order to achieve that friendship I must explain everything to you without delay and once for all, so that there will not afterward be any — *gêne*, any awkwardness; once for all, Grigory Mikhailich. And you must tell me you forgive me; otherwise I shall presume that you are feeling — *de la rancune. Voilà!* Perhaps it is a great deal for me to ask, because you've probably forgotten it all long ago; but all the same, do tell me you forgive me."

She said all this speech without taking breath, and he noticed that tears, real tears, were glittering in her eyes.

"But really, Irena Pavlovna," he hurriedly began, "aren't you ashamed to apologize, to ask forgiveness? . . . It is all a thing of the past, it is gone like a stone into water, and I can only wonder that you, amid all the splendor that surrounds you, could still retain a memory of the obscure companion of your first youth. . . ."

"Does that surprise you?" Irena said quietly.

"It moves me," he retorted, "because I simply could not imagine — "

"But even now you haven't told me you forgive me," she interrupted.

"I am sincerely glad that you are happy, Irena Pavlovna, and with all my heart I wish you all the best that the world can give. . . ."

"And you don't remember the wrong I did you?"

"I remember only those wonderful moments that I once owed to you."

She held out both hands to him. He squeezed them strongly and did not let them go at once. . . . At that gentle touch something that for long had been nonexistent secretly stirred in his heart. Once more she looked straight into his face; but this time she smiled. . . . And he for the first time looked directly and fixedly at her. He again recognized features once so dear, those deep eyes with their extraordinary lashes, and the mole on the cheek, and the special way the hair lay above the brow, and her habit of pleasantly and amusingly twisting her lips and very slightly twitching her eyebrows; he recognized them all — all. . . . But how beautiful she had grown! What enchantment, what strength there was in the youthful femininity of her body! And no rouge, no cerise, nor pencil, nor powder, nothing artificial at all on the fresh, clean face. . . . Yes, she certainly was beautiful!

He fell into a reverie. . . . He was still gazing at her, but his thoughts were far away — she noticed it.

"Well, that's splendid," she said in a loud voice. "Now my conscience is at rest, and I can satisfy my curiosity."

"Curiosity?" he repeated, as though he did not understand.

"Yes, yes — I simply must know what you have been doing all this time, and what your plans are. I want to know everything — what, when, how — everything, everything. And you must tell me the truth, because I warn you I have never lost sight of you — so far as was possible. . . ."

"You did not lose sight of me — there — in Petersburg?"

"Amid all the splendor that surrounded me, as you put it just now. Yes, exactly; I did not lose sight of you. We'll talk later about that splendor, but now you must tell me all that has happened to you, a full story, a long story. No one will interrupt us. Ah, how marvelous it will be!" she added, gaily sitting down and attitudinizing a little in an armchair. "Well, now begin."

"Before I start to tell my story, I must thank you," Litvinov began.

"What for?"

"For the bouquet of flowers I found in my room."

"What bouquet? I don't know anything about it."

"What?"

"I tell you I don't know anything about it. . . . But I'm waiting — waiting for your story. . . . Ah, how clever Potugin was to bring you!"

Litvinov pricked up his ears.

"Have you been acquainted with Mr. Potugin long?" he asked.

"Quite a long time . . . but begin your story."

"And do you know him well?"

"Oh, yes!" Irena sighed. "There are particular reasons. . . . You have heard of Eliza Belskaya, of course — the one that died such a terrible death two years ago? . . . Ah, of course, I had forgotten that you do not know our stories. . . . It is fortunate, fortunate that you do not. Oh, *quelle chance!* At last, at last I have met one man, a living man, who doesn't know anything about us. And one can talk to him in Russian, and though it is a stupid language, still it is Russian and not that everlasting, cloying, repellent Petersburg French!"

"And Potugin, you say, was in contact with — "

"It is very painful for me even to recall it," she interrupted. "Eliza was my best friend in the institute; and later, in Petersburg, we were always seeing each other. She confided all her secrets to me; she was very unhappy, she suffered a great deal. Potugin behaved perfectly in the affair, like a true knight! He sacrificed himself. Only then did I appreciate his true worth. But we've gone off at a tangent again. I am waiting for your story, Grigory Mikhailich."

"But my story cannot interest you in the least, Irena Pavlovna."

"That is not for you to decide."

"Remember, Irena Pavlovna, it is ten years since we saw each other, a whole ten years. How much water has flowed under the bridges since then!"

"Not only water, not only water!" she repeated, with a peculiar, bitter expression. "That is just why I want to hear about you."

"And besides, to tell the truth, I cannot imagine where to begin."

"At the beginning. From that very moment when you — when I went off to Petersburg. You left Moscow then. . . . Do you know, I have never been back to Moscow since."

"Really?"

"At first it was quite impossible. And later, when I married —"

"Have you been married long?"

"Four years."

"Haven't you any children?"

"No," she answered curtly.

Litvinov was silent for a moment.

"And until you were married you lived all the time with, what was his name, Count Reizenbach?"

She looked at him fixedly, as though wishing to discover why he had asked this question.

"No —" she said at last.

"So your parents — By the way, I haven't even asked you about them. How are they?"

"They are both well."

"And still living in Moscow?"

"Still living in Moscow."

"And your brothers and sisters?"

"They're all doing well; I have provided for them all."

"Ah!" He glanced at her from under knitted brows. "In reality, Irena Pavlovna, it is not I but you who should tell the story, if only —"

He suddenly pulled himself up and was silent.

Irena raised her hands to her face and twisted her engagement ring on her finger.

"And why not? I do not refuse to," she said at last. "Some day — perhaps. . . . But first you — because, you see, although I watched you, I know almost nothing about you, but as for me — well, you have certainly heard enough about me. Isn't that so? For you have heard about me, haven't you?"

"Irena Pavlovna, you have occupied too prominent a position in the world not to cause some talk — especially in the provinces, where I was, and where every rumor is believed."

"But did you believe those rumors? And what did they say?"

"I have to admit, Irena Pavlovna, that very few of them came to my ears. I lived a very solitary life."

"Why do you say that? You were in the Crimea, in the general levy, weren't you?"

"Do you know even that?"

"As you see. I told you I have watched you."

Litvinov could not help being astonished again.

"But why should I bother to tell you what you know already?" he said in an undertone.

"In order — in order to do what I ask. For I do ask you, Grigory Mikhailich."

He bowed his head and began. . . . He began a little incoherently, in general outlines, to tell her his simple adventures. He often stopped and looked at her interrogatively: perhaps she had heard enough? But she insistently demanded that he should continue and, throwing her hair back behind her ears, propping her head on the chair arm, seemed to be listening to every word with the utmost attention. An outsider looking at her and following the expression of her face might, perhaps, have thought that she was not listening at all to what Litvinov said, but was only buried in contemplation. . . . But it was not Litvinov she was contemplating, though he grew embarrassed, and reddened beneath her persistent gaze. Before her arose a whole life, another life — not his, but her own.

He did not finish, but lapsed into silence, constrained by an unpleasant feeling of increasing awkwardness. This time Irena did not say anything to him, did not ask him to go on. Pressing her palm to her eyes as though tired, she slowly leaned back against the chair and was still. He waited a little; then, realizing that his visit had already lasted more than two hours, he reached for his hat. Suddenly the swift stride of thin patent-leather boots sounded in the next room; preceded by the same exquisite perfume, blended of nobility and the guards, Valerian Vladimirovich Ratmirov entered.

Litvinov rose from his chair and exchanged bows with the handsome general. But Irena unhurriedly took her hand from her face and, looking coldly at her husband, said in French: "Ah! So you're back already! But what is the time, then?"

"It will soon be four o'clock, *ma chère amie*, and you're not dressed yet. The Princess will be waiting for us," the general replied. Elegantly inclining his tightly clothed figure toward Litvinov, he added with the almost effeminately playful tone peculiar to him: "Evidently your kindly guest has helped you to kill the time."

At this point the reader will allow us to impart some information concerning General Ratmirov. His father was the natural —

What are you thinking? You are not mistaken, but that is not what I wanted to say — the natural son of an aristocratic magnate of the Alexandrine period and a pretty little French actress. The magnate introduced his son into society, but did not leave him any fortune, and this son (the father of our hero) also failed to achieve a fortune: he died with the rank of colonel and the status of chief of police. A year before his death he married a beautiful young widow who had had to resort to his protection. Valerian Alexandrovich, his son by the widow, was appointed through patronage to the *corps des pages*. He attracted the attention of the authorities, not so much by his successes in study as by his splendid bearing, excellent manners, and good conduct (though he was subjected to everything that students in state military institutions were subjected to at that time), and entered the guards. He made a brilliant career, thanks to the modest cheerfulness of his disposition, his grace in dancing, his masterly horsemanship as orderly at parades — usually on a horse he had never ridden before — and, finally, to some special gift for establishing familiarly respectful relations with higher officers, for a pensively endearing, almost forlorn subservience, with an admixture of vague liberalism, as light as gossamer. . . . This liberalism, however, did not prevent his flogging fifty peasants in a rebellious Byelorussian village to which he was sent to suppress a revolt. He had an attractive and unusually youthful appearance; sleek, ruddy, lithe, and clinging, he enjoyed amazing success with the ladies; the aristocratic old women simply raved about him. Prudent by habit, taciturn by calculation, like an industrious bee extracting the juice from even the meanest of flowers, General Ratmirov continually moved in the highest circles. He was without morals, had the reputation of being efficient though there was no evidence of it, had a nose for people and an understanding of circumstances, but most of all he possessed an unswervingly firm desire for his own good; and at last he saw all roads open before him. . . .

Litvinov smiled forcedly, but Irena only shrugged her shoulders.

"Well," she said in the same cold tone, "did you see the Count?"

"Of course I saw him. He commanded me to convey his greetings to you."

"Ah! And is he just as stupid as ever, your patron?"

General Ratmirov did not answer and only laughed a little in his nose, as though indulgent to the temerity of feminine judgment. Kindly adults respond to children's absurd tricks with exactly the same laugh.

"Yes," Irena added, "the stupidity of your Count is only too obvious; and I think I have seen enough in my time."

"You sent me to him yourself," the general snarled. Turning to Litvinov, he asked him in Russian: "Are you taking the Baden waters?"

"I enjoy good health, thank God," Litvinov answered.

"That is much the best," the general continued, smiling amiably. "And besides, nobody comes to Baden for the cure. But the waters here are very effective, *je veux dire, efficaces;* and anyone who suffers, as I do for instance, from a nervous cough — "

Irena rose swiftly to her feet. "We shall see you again, Grigory Mikhailich, and soon, I hope," she said in French, contemptuously interrupting her husband's speech; "but now I must go and dress. That old Princess is unbearable with her everlasting *parties de plaisir,* where there is nothing whatever to do except get bored."

"You are very disparaging today," her husband muttered, and he slipped into the other room.

Litvinov went toward the door. . . . Irena stopped him.

"You have told me all the story," she said, "but have kept the chief thing a secret."

"What are you referring to?"

"They say you are engaged?"

He flushed to his ears. He had in fact deliberately said nothing about Tania; but now he felt terribly vexed, first that Irena knew about his forthcoming marriage, and secondly that she seemed to be charging him with a desire to conceal that marriage from her. He simply did not know what to say, and she did not remove her eyes from him.

"Yes, I am getting married," he said at last, and went at once.

Ratmirov returned to the room.

"Well, why aren't you dressing?" he asked.

"Go by yourself; I have a headache."

"But the Princess — "

Irena measured her husband with a look from head to foot, turned her back on him, and went to her room.

13

Litvinov was far from satisfied with himself; he felt as though he had lost at roulette or had broken his word. An inner voice told him that as a fiancé, as a man with a sense of responsibility and no longer a boy, he should not have yielded either to the prick of curiosity or to the seduction of memories. "Much need I had to go!" he deliberated. "On her part it is only coquetry, a whim, caprice. . . . She's bored, she's sick of everything, she's clutched at me . . . a gourmet suddenly has a fancy for some black bread . . . well, and very nice too. But what did I go for? Is it possible that I — do not feel contempt for her?" It cost him some effort to pronounce the word "contempt," even mentally. "Of course, there is no danger whatever in it, nor can there be," he continued his deliberations. "After all, I know whom I'm dealing with. But, all the same, one shouldn't play with fire. . . . I shan't set foot in her place again." He did not dare to think or else he was not yet conscious of how beautiful she had seemed to him and how strongly she had moved him.

That day also dragged by idiotically and interminably. At dinner he found himself sitting next to a portly *belle-homme* with dyed whiskers, who sat without speaking and only puffed and goggled his eyes. . . . He suddenly hiccuped, however, and proved to be a fellow countryman, for he remarked angrily in Russian: "But I said it wasn't wise to eat the melon!" Nor did anything of a consoling nature happen during the evening. Under Litvinov's very eyes Bindasov won a sum four times as large as the amount he had borrowed, yet he not only did not return his debt, but he even stared threateningly right into Litvinov's face, as though to penalize him even more just because he had seen him win.

Next morning another horde of compatriots poured into his room. He managed at last to get away from them and, setting off into the hills, first ran into Irena — he pretended not to recognize her and walked swiftly past — then into Potugin. He would have stopped to talk, but Potugin did not give him any encouragement. He was holding the hand of a smartly dressed little girl with fluffy, lint-white curls, large black eyes in a pale, sickly little face, and that peculiar, imperative, and impatient expression that spoilt children wear. Litvinov spent a couple of hours in the hills and returned home along the Lichtentaler Allee. . . . A lady in a blue veil, who was sitting on a bench, briskly rose and came up to him. . . . He recognized Irena.

"Why are you avoiding me, Grigory Mikhailovich?" she said in the uncertain tone that indicates a heart in turmoil.

He was embarrassed. "I avoid you, Irena Pavlovna?"

"Yes, you — you. . . ."

She seemed agitated, almost angry.

"You are mistaken, I assure you."

"No, I am not mistaken. This morning — when we met — do you think I didn't see that you recognized me? Will you say you didn't recognize me? Will you?"

"Really I — Irena Pavlovna —"

"Grigory Mikhailovich, you are not a deceitful man, you always told the truth; tell me, tell me, you did recognize me, didn't you? You deliberately turned away, didn't you?"

He glanced at her. Her eyes were glittering with a peculiar glitter, but behind the fine mesh of her veil her cheeks and lips were of a deathly pallor. The expression of her face, the very sound of her impetuous whisper, was so invincibly mournful, imploring. . . . He could not keep up the pretense any longer.

"Yes — I recognized you," he said, not without effort.

She gently shivered and gently dropped her hands.

"Why didn't you come and speak to me?" she whispered.

"Why didn't I — why?" He turned off the path; she silently followed him. "Why?" he repeated yet again, and his face suddenly flamed, and a feeling akin to anger clutched at his chest and throat. "You — you ask that, after all that has happened between us? Not now, of course, not now, but there — there — in Moscow."

"But you see we decided, but you promised —" Irena began.

"I promised nothing. You must forgive the harshness of my words, but you ask the truth, so judge for yourself: to what can I ascribe your — I do not know what to call it — your persistence if not to coquetry — which I admit I find incomprehensible — or a desire to see how far you still have power over me? Our roads have parted so completely! I had forgotten it all, I had got beyond all that pain long since, I had become quite a different man; and you are married, are happy, at least superficially, you enjoy an enviable position in the world; then what is the purpose, what is the object of this new approach? What am I to you, or you to me? We cannot even understand each other now, we have nothing whatever in common now, neither in the past nor in the present! Especially — especially in the past!"

He uttered all this speech hurriedly, jerkily, without looking at her. She did not stir and only held out her hands a little toward him from time to time. She seemed to be imploring him to halt and listen to her. But at his last words she slightly bit her lower lip, as though suppressing a feeling of acute and sudden pique.

"Grigory Mikhailich . . ." she began at last in a more composed voice, and she walked still farther away from the path, to avoid occasional strollers.

He followed her.

"Grigory Mikhailich, believe me: if I imagined that I still had the least power over you, I would rather avoid you. If I did not do that, if I decided, despite — despite my former guilt, to renew my acquaintance with you, it is because — because — "

"Why?" he asked almost roughly.

"Because," Irena replied with sudden strength, "it has now become too intolerably, unbearably stifling for me in that world, in that enviable position you have spoken of. Because, having met you, a living man, after all those dead dolls — you saw specimens of them three days ago, at the *Vieux Château* — I rejoiced as though I had found a spring in the desert. But you call me a coquette and are suspicious of me, and repulse me under the pretext that I really was to blame in regard to you, and even more in regard to myself."

"You chose your own lot, Irena Pavlovna," he said moodily, still not looking at her.

"I did, I did — nor do I complain, I have no right to complain," she said hurriedly, and apparently his very harshness gave her secret comfort. "I know that you must condemn me, nor do I attempt to justify myself. I only want to explain my feeling to you, I want to convince you that I am far from coquetry now. . . . I behave like a coquette with you! Why, there's no sense in it. . . . When I saw you, all the good, the youthful in me was awakened . . . the time when I had not yet chosen my lot, all that lies back in that happy period, beyond the past ten years."

"But now you really must forgive me, Irena Pavlovna! So far

as I know, the happy period of your life began from the very moment when we parted. . . ."

She raised her handkerchief to her lips.

"That is a very cruel thing to say, Grigory Mikhailich; but I cannot be angry with you. Oh no, that time was not happy, not for happiness did I leave Moscow; not one minute, not one second of happiness have I known — believe me, no matter what others may tell you. If I had been happy, could I talk to you as I am talking now? . . . I repeat, you do not know what those people are. . . . You see, they understand nothing, they have no feeling for anything, they haven't even any mind, *ni esprit, ni intelligence,* but only cunning, and a certain flair. Why, fundamentally music, and poetry, and art are all equally alien to them. . . . You will say that I myself was rather indifferent to all that; but not to such an extent, Grigory Mikhailich — not to such an extent! It is not a woman of society that stands before you now — you have only to glance at me — no lioness — that is what I think they call us — but a poor, poor creature, who, in very truth, is deserving of pity. Don't be astonished at my words — I am not concerned about pride now! I extend my hand to you as a beggar — do realize that clearly — as a beggar. . . . I ask for alms," she added suddenly with an involuntary, irresistible outburst. "I ask for alms, but you — "

Her voice betrayed her. He raised his head and looked at her. She was breathing rapidly, her lips were quivering. His heart suddenly began to pound, and his feeling of anger disappeared.

"You say our roads have separated," she went on. "I know you are marrying according to your inclination, and you have now drawn up a plan to cover all your life. Yes, that is all true, but we haven't grown alien to each other, Grigory Mikhailich, we can still understand each other. Or do you suppose that I have grown quite unfeeling, that I have sunk completely into that mud? Ah, no, please don't think that! Let me unburden my soul, I ask you, if only in the name of those former days, if you do not want to forget them. Let your response be such that our meeting shall not have been in vain: that would be very bitter; as it is, it will not last long. . . . I do not know how to say what I want to say, but you will understand me, because I ask little, very little — only a little sympathy, only that you will not repulse me, but will let me unburden my soul. . . ."

She was silent; tears had sounded in her voice. She sighed, and timidly, with a sidelong, questioning gaze, looked at him, held out her hand to him. . . .

He slowly took that hand and feebly squeezed it.

"Let us be friends," Irena whispered.

"Friends," he repeated thoughtfully.

"Yes, friends . . . but if that is too great a demand, then let us at least be good acquaintances. . . . Let us be simply as if nothing had ever happened."

"As if nothing had ever happened . . ." he again repeated her words. "You just told me, Irena Pavlovna, that I do not want to forget the former days. . . . Ah, but supposing I cannot forget them?"

A blissful smile flickered across Irena's face and at once vanished, to be replaced by an anxious, almost frightened expression.

"Be like me, Grigory Mikhailich, remember only the good. But, above all, give me your word now — your word of honor —"

"What for?"

"Not to avoid me — not to grieve me unnecessarily. . . . You promise? Tell me!"

"I promise."

"And you will drive all unpleasant thoughts out of your head?"

"Yes. . . . But all the same I give up trying to understand you."

"It isn't even necessary to understand — yet wait a little and you will understand me. But you promise?"

"I have already said yes."

"Well, thank you. But beware, I am accustomed to believing you. I shall expect you today, or tomorrow; I shall not leave the hotel. But now I must leave you. The Duchess is coming along the avenue. . . . She has seen me, and I cannot avoid speaking to her. . . . *Au revoir.* . . . But give me your hand, *vite, vite. Au revoir.*"

Giving his hand a strong squeeze, Irena went toward a woman of middle age and majestic appearance who was walking heavily along the sandy path, accompanied by two other ladies and a liveried, extremely good-looking lackey.

"*Eh bonjour, chère madame,*" the lady said as Irena respectfully curtsied to her. "*Comment allez-vouz aujourd'hui? Venez un peu avec moi.*"

"Votre Altesse a trop de bonté," Litvinov heard Irena's ingratiating voice.

14

He allowed the Duchess and all her suite to proceed for some distance; then he, too, emerged into the avenue. He could not be quite certain of his feelings: he felt ashamed, and even afraid, and his self-esteem was flattered. . . . The unexpected explanation with Irena had taken him by surprise; her burning, hurried words had passed over him like a threatening shower. "All these society women are queer," he thought; "they've got no sense of logic . . . and how they are perverted by the milieu in which they live, and the infamy that they themselves are conscious of! . . ." To be exact, he did not think this at all, but only mechanically repeated these hackneyed phrases, as if by doing so he hoped to rid himself of other, more frightening thoughts. He realized that it was not advisable to indulge in serious reflection at the moment, that if he did in all probability he would be bound to upbraid himself, and he walked along with loitering steps, almost forcing himself to pay attention to whatever he met. . . . He suddenly noticed that he was level with a bench, noticed someone's legs, ran his eyes upward over them. . . . The legs belonged to a man sitting on the bench and reading a newspaper. The man was Potugin. Litvinov let fall a muffled exclamation. Potugin laid the newspaper on his knees and gazed at him fixedly, without a smile; and Litvinov gazed at Potugin also fixedly and also without a smile.

"May I sit down beside you?" he asked at last.

"Certainly; I shall be delighted. Only I warn you: if you want to carry on conversation with me now, don't get angry; at present I am in a very misanthropic mood, and I have an exaggeratedly unpleasant view of everything."

"I don't mind, Sozont Ivanich," Litvinov said, dropping on the bench; "in fact, it is very much how I feel. . . . But why are you in this mood?"

"In reality I have no right to be annoyed," Potugin began. "I've just been reading in this newspaper about the draft bill for the transformation of the judicial system in Russia, and I note with genuine satisfaction that we, too, have at last got some sense and intelligence and are no longer intending to attach a home-grown tail to pure and clear European logic, under the pretext of our independence, nationality, or originality. On the contrary, we are taking a good foreign thing in its entirety. No more making isolated concessions to the peasantry. . . . Now we are to settle the general question of landownership! Truly, truly, I ought not to be annoyed; but, unfortunately for me, I ran into one of our Russian natural prodigies and had a talk with him; and these natural prodigies and self-educated people will give me cause for anxiety even in the grave!"

"Who was this natural prodigy?" Litvinov asked.

"Why, there's some gentleman running about Baden who regards himself as a musical genius. 'I,' he says, 'of course, am nothing, I am a cipher, for I haven't studied; but I have incomparably more melodies and more ideas than Meyerbeer.' To begin with, I ask, and why didn't he study? And secondly, even without mentioning Meyerbeer, the most insignificant German flautist who modestly whistles his part in the worst of German orchestras has twenty times as many ideas as all our rough diamonds; only the flautist keeps these ideas to himself and doesn't brag about them in the land of Mozarts and Haydns. But our rough diamond strums a little waltz or a ballad, and then you see him with his hands in his pantaloons and his mouth twisted contemptuously; 'I,' he says, 'am a genius!' And it's just the same in painting, and in everything else. Oh, these natural prodigies — I've had enough of them! And everybody knows that they are boasted of only in those countries where there is neither genuine science, something that has passed into the people's flesh and blood, nor genuine art. Surely it is time to put an end to all this bragging, this common lumber, together with all the well-known phrases to the effect that in Russia no one ever dies of hunger, and road travel is the fastest in the world, and that we can do everything better than anyone else? They sicken me with their impudent talk about the ability of the Russian character, with their 'instinctive genius,' with their Kulibin. . . . But where is that ability, for goodness' sake, gentlemen? It's nothing but the fuddled talk of a man half asleep, or else it's a bestial cunning. Instinct! There they've found something to boast about! Catch an ant in the forest and carry it a mile from its nest, and it will find its own way home. Man cannot do anything like that, but does that mean that he is lower than an ant? Instinct, even if it be of the highest genius, is unworthy of man. Reason — simple, healthy, everyday reason — that is our clear achievement, our pride; reason never plays such tricks, and that is why everything is guided by it. But as for Kulibin, who, without knowing anything about mechanics, constructed some perfectly monstrous clock — I'd order that clock to be exhibited on a pillory. Look, good people, I'd say, and see how things should not be done. In this case Kulibin himself is not to blame, but all the same his work is rubbish. People praise Telushkin for his daring and agility because he climbed the Admiralty Needle [1] — let them; why not praise him? But that doesn't justify us in shouting: 'Look how he has shown up the German architects! And what good are they? All they do is take our money. . . .' He didn't show them up at all; but afterward a forest of timber had to be raised round the Needle for it to be mended in quite an ordinary manner. For God's sake, don't encourage us Russians to think that anything can be achieved without study! No; you can have as much brains as you like, but study, study from the A B C up! Otherwise be quiet and sit still with your tail tucked under you! Pfooh, it's made me go quite hot!"

Potugin took off his hat and fanned himself with his handkerchief.

"Russian art," he began again, "Russian art! . . . I know the Russian resilience, and I know the Russian impotence too; but I'm sorry, I've never come across Russian art. For twenty years continuously they did homage to that inflated nullity Briullov, [2] and imagined that we, too, had developed a school, and that it would be even purer than all others. . . . Russian art, ha-ha-ha! ho-ho!"

"But all the same, pardon me, Sozont Ivanich," Litvinov remarked, "so you don't accept Glinka?"

Potugin scratched himself behind his ear.

"You know, exceptions only prove the rule; but even in this case we couldn't refrain from bragging! Nobody would bother to deny that, for instance, Glinka was certainly a remarkable musician, whom only circumstances, both internal and external, prevented from being the founder of Russian opera. But no, how can one stop there! Now he must be raised to the rank of *général en chef*, the *Oberhofmarschall* in the musical field; and not only

---

[1] An architectural feature of the Admiralty in Petersburg. (Tr.)
[2] Famous eighteenth-century Russian painter. (Tr.)

that, but other nations have got to be depreciated: they've got nothing in the least like it, and then they ask us to admire some 'mighty' home-grown genius whose works are nothing but a miserable imitation of second-rate foreign composers — and the second-rate especially, for it is easier to imitate them. Nothing in the least like it! Oh, beggarly idiot barbarians, for whom there is no such thing as succession in art, and artists are something on the lines of Rappot: the foreigner can lift two hundredweight with one hand, but our man can lift four hundredweight! Nothing in the least like it? But I venture to tell you that the following memory is always with me: Last spring I was visiting the Crystal Palace near London. As you know, this palace contains a kind of exhibition of everything human inventiveness has achieved, it is an encyclopedia of humanity, that has to be admitted. Well, I walked, I walked past all these machines and weapons, and the statues of great men; and I thought then: if an order were to be issued that when any nation disappears from the face of the earth everything that that nation has invented must disappear from the Crystal Palace — our Little Mother, the true-believing Russia, could sink into the bottomless pit, and the darling's disappearance would not disturb a single little nail, not a single little pin. Everything would remain quite undisturbed in its place, because even the samovars, and the bast shoes, and the yoke, and the knout — all those celebrated products of ours — were not of our invention. It would be impossible to make such an experiment even with the Sandwich Islands; their inhabitants have invented boats and spears, and the visitors to the exhibition would notice their absence. That is a slander, that is too harsh, you may say. . . . But I say, to begin with, that I don't know how to censure with a smile; and secondly, that evidently it is impossible for anyone to look not only the devil, but even himself straight in the eye; and in Russia it isn't only the children that like lullabies. Our old fables reached us from the East, our new ones we have taken over from the West, but we still go on talking about independent Russian art! Other brave fellows have even discovered a Russian science: why, twice two are four in Russia too, and for some reason it is more clever there."

"But wait a moment, Sozont Ivanich," Litvinov exclaimed, "wait a moment! After all, we, too, are sending something to the universal exhibitions, and surely Europe is acquiring something from us?"

"Yes, raw stuff, raw materials. And note, my dear sir: to a large extent that raw material of ours is good only because it is conditioned by other wretched circumstances. Our bristles, for instance, are long and hard because our pigs are of poor quality; our hides are solid and thick because the cows are miserable specimens; the lard is rich because it is rendered down half with the meat. . . . For that matter, why should I expatiate to you on that subject? You're studying technology, you ought to know it all better than I. Inventiveness, they tell me! Russian inventiveness! Our landowner gentry complain bitterly and suffer losses because we haven't any satisfactory grain-driers which would save them the necessity of putting the shocks in drying-barns, just as they did in the time of Rurik.[1] Those drying-barns are terribly unprofitable, just like bast shoes and bast matting, and they're always catching fire. The landowners complain, but we're still without grain-driers. And why are we? Because the Germans don't need them; they thresh their grain damp, and so they don't worry about inventing them, while we — are unable to! Unable to — and that's the end of it. No matter how much you need them! From this day onward I promise myself that whenever some rough diamond or self-taught specimen is exposed to me, I shall say to him: 'Stop, my worthy sir, but where is the grain-drier? Let us have it!' But how can he? Now, if it's a case of picking up some old, well-patched shoe that has long since dropped off the foot of a Saint-Simon or a Fourier and of reverentially setting it on our head, treating it as a sacred relic — that we can do; or of scribbling a little article on the historical and modern significance of the proletariat in the chief cities of France — that, too, we can do. But I once suggested to some writer and political economist like your Mr. Voroshilov that he should name me twenty towns in that same France, and do you know what came of it? The result was that in his despair the political economist finally mentioned Mont-Fermelle, probably remembering Paul de Kock's novel. And now I have just remembered the following story. I was making my way through a forest with a gun and a dog one day — "

"Are you a hunter, then?" Litvinov asked.

[1] Varangian founder of Novgorod principality, died A.D. 873.

"I shoot a bit. I was making my way to a marsh after snipe; some other hunters had told me about this marsh. I looked and saw a fellow as fresh and pithy as a shelled nut, sitting in a glade outside a small hut. There he was sitting and smirking, what at, goodness knows. And I asked him: 'Where's the marsh around here, and are there any snipe in it?' 'Certainly, certainly'; he began to sing immediately, looking just as if I had given him a ruble. 'With great pleasure; the marsh is first-class, and as for all kinds of wild birds — my God, there is an excellent abundance.' I set off, but not only did I not find any wild birds, but even the marsh had long since dried up. Well, tell me for mercy's sake, why does the Russian tell lies? Why should a political economist lie, and about a wild bird, too?"

Litvinov did not answer and only sighed sympathetically.

"But you start talking to that same political economist," Potugin went on, "about the most difficult tasks of social science, only in generalities, without adducing any facts — whir! he soars like a bird, like an eagle. But on one occasion I managed to catch one such bird: as you will see, the decoy I used was well and truly visible. I was talking with one of our present-day 'young hopefuls' about various questions, as they put it. Well, he was very angry, as usual; and among other things he rejected marriage with a simply childish obstinacy. I put forward various arguments . . . but it was like beating your head against a wall! I could see there was no way of getting at him at all. And then I had a happy thought! 'Permit me to say,' I began — you always have to talk respectfully to young hopefuls — 'that I am amazed at you, my dear sir; you are interested in natural sciences, yet so far you have given not the slightest consideration to the fact that all the carnivorous animals and beasts of prey, all animals and birds that have to go out to catch their prey, work hard to supply living food for themselves and their children . . . but you include man among such creatures, don't you?' 'Of course I do,' the young hopeful retorted, 'man generally is nothing but a carnivorous animal.' 'And a beast of prey,' I added. 'And a beast of prey,' he confirmed. 'Well said!' I declared. 'Well then, I am surprised you haven't noticed that all such creatures live in monogamy?' The young hopeful started. 'What's that?' 'Why, it's quite true. Think of the lion, the wolf, the fox, the hawk, the kite; and besides, what else could they do? You try to think. It's difficult enough even for the two of them to feed the children.' My young hopeful was lost in thought. 'Well,' he said, 'in that case man must not copy the animals.' At that I called him an idealist, and then he was annoyed! He all but wept. I had to comfort him and promise that I would not betray him to his comrades. To earn the name of idealist — is that easy to bear? That's the whole point, that our young people of today have gone wrong in their calculations. They imagine that the time of the former, obscure underground work has passed, that it was all right for their old fathers to burrow like moles, but that for us such a role is humiliating, we shall act aboveground, we shall act — My dear fellows! Not even your children will act. But wouldn't it be as well for you to go on burrowing, burrowing in the tracks of your fathers?"

There was a brief silence.

"I, dear sir, am of the opinion," Potugin began once more, "that we are not obliged to civilization only for knowledge, art, and laws, but that the very feeling of beauty and poetry develops and comes into force under the influence of that same civilization, and that so-called popular, naïve, unconscious creation is absurd rubbish. Even in Homer one can already perceive the traces of a refined and rich civilization; even love is ennobled by it. The Slavophils would willingly hang me for such a heresy if they were not such tender-hearted creatures; but, all the same, I stand by my guns, and no matter how much they regale me with Madame Kokhanovskaya [1] and 'swarm in peace,' I shan't take even a sniff at that *triple extrait de moujik russe*, because I don't belong to higher society. From time to time that society has to reassure itself that it is not in the least Frenchified, and in fact this literature *en cuir de Russie* is specially written for it. You try reading the most trenchant, the most 'popular' parts of *Swarm* to one of the common people — the real sort — he'll think you're informing him of a new attack upon fraud or hard drinking. I repeat, without civilization there is no poetry. Do you want to get a clear idea of the poetic ideal of the uncivilized Russian? Glance through our folk poems, our legends. I won't adduce the fact that in them love is always the result of magic, of a love-potion, is produced by a 'philter' and is even called a spell, an enchantment. Nor do I adduce the fact that among all the European and Asiatic literatures our

[1] Pseudonym of Nadezhda Stepanova Sokhansky (1825–84), Russian writer of stories of the provincial gentry. (Tr.)

so-called epic literature alone (alone, mark you) failed to produce (if we leave Ivan and Tania out of account) any typical loving couple; not that the Holy Russian hero always opens his acquaintance with his 'destined future' by beating her on her white body 'mercilessly,' and as the result 'the female sex lives as a hireling.' I shall not stop to discuss all that, but I do take the liberty of drawing your attention to the magnificent specimen of youth, the *jeune-premier*, as he was delineated in the imagination of the primitive, uncivilized Slav. Here he comes, the *jeune-premier;* he has made himself a fur coat of marten skins stitched down all the seams; his belt is fastened right up under his armpits; his fingers are covered with gloves; the fur collar is turned up above his head, you can't see his ruddy face from the front, nor his white neck from the back; his little cap rides over one ear, and on his feet are morocco-leather boots, with toes like awls, and pointed heels — round the point of the toe you can roll an egg, under the heels a sparrow can flutter and fly. And this youngster walks with mincing little steps, that celebrated 'elegant' gait with which our Russian Alcibiades, Churilo Plenkovich, produced such an astonishing, almost medicinal effect on the old women and young girls; the very same gait with which that cream, that flower of Russian elegance, that *nec plus ultra* of Russian taste, our native waiter, even today minces so inimitably with all his joints loose. I am not joking when I say that our artistic ideal is a baggy jauntiness. A fine picture, isn't it? With plenty of material in it for painting, for sculpture? And what of the beauty who captivates the youth, and who has 'as much blood in her face as if she were a hare'? However, I rather think you are not listening to me?"

Litvinov started. It was true that he had not been listening to Potugin; he was thinking, persistently thinking about Irena, about his last meeting with her. . . .

"Excuse me, Sozont Ivanich," he began, "but I want to ask you again my previous question about . . . about Madame Ratmirova."

Potugin folded his newspaper and thrust it into his pocket.

"You want to know again how I made her acquaintance?"

"No, not that; I should like to have your opinion — of the role she played in Petersburg. What was that role really?"

"To tell the truth, I don't know what to say, Grigory Mikhailich. I became quite friendly with Madame Ratmirova — but quite by accident and not for any length of time. I did not even look into her world, and what went on there remained unknown to me. Certain things were talked about in my hearing, and, as you know, in Russia slander is prevalent not only in democratic circles. For that matter, I was not curious. I see, however," he added after a brief silence, "that you are interested in her."

"Yes; we have had a couple of very frank talks. But I still ask myself: is she sincere?"

Potugin looked down. "When she is interested she is sincere, like all passionate women. Her pride also sometimes prevents her telling lies."

"But is she proud? I rather would say she is capricious."

"As proud as a demon; but that is nothing."

"It seems to me she exaggerates sometimes . . ."

"That, too, is nothing; she is still sincere. But, in any case, whom would you go to for truth? The very finest of these ladies is depraved to the marrow of her bones."

"But, Sozont Ivanich, remember, didn't you yourself say you were her friend? Wasn't it you yourself who took me to her almost by force?"

"And what of it? She asked me to bring you; and I thought: 'Well, why not?' But I really am her friend. She isn't lacking in some good qualities: she is very kind, I mean generous; I really mean that she gives others what she herself has no absolute need of. But, after all, you should know her just as well as I do."

"I knew Irena Pavlovna ten years ago; but since then —"

"Ah, Grigory Mikhailich, what are you suggesting? Does the human character change? What we are in the cradle, we are in the grave. Or, perhaps —" at this point Potugin huddled into himself still more — "perhaps you are afraid of falling into her hands? That certainly — But then, you can't avoid falling into someone's hands."

Litvinov smiled forcedly. "Do you think so?"

"You just can't. Man is weak, woman is strong, chance is all-powerful, to reconcile oneself to a colorless existence is difficult, completely to forget oneself is impossible . . . and then come beauty and sympathy, and warmth and light — how can you resist? And you run like a child to its nurse. Well, and afterward, of course, come cold and gloom, and emptiness — as usual. And it ends with your getting unaccustomed to everything, you cease to understand anything. In the beginning you will not understand how anyone can love; but afterward you will not understand how it is possible to live."

Litvinov stared at Potugin and thought that he had never met a man more lonely, more friendless — more unhappy. On this occasion he was not diffident, he was not formal; utterly morose and pale, with his head on his chest and his hands on his knees, he sat motionless and only smiled a despondent smile. Litvinov felt sorry for this poor, splenetic eccentric.

"Among other matters," he began in an undertone, "Irena Pavlovna mentioned a certain close acquaintance of hers, whose name was, I think, Belskaya or Dolskaya —"

Potugin glanced at Litvinov.

"Ah!" he said gruffly. "She mentioned her — well, and what of it? However," he added, yawning unnaturally, "it's time I was getting home, to dinner. I must ask your pardon."

He jumped up from the bench and strode away briskly before Litvinov had time to utter a word. . . . His pity was replaced by a feeling of vexation, with himself, of course. Immodesty of any kind was not natural to him; he had simply wanted to express his sympathy. But the result had been rather like an inept innuendo. With secret discontent in his heart he returned to his hotel.

"Depraved to the marrow of her bones," he thought a little later . . . "but as proud as a demon! She, this woman who all but goes down on her knees to me — proud? Proud, and not capricious?"

He tried to drive Irena's picture out of his head, but he could not. And so he did not even attempt to think of his fiancée; he felt sure that that picture would not give way today. He decided that, without worrying himself any more, he would await the denouement of all this "strange history." The denouement could not be delayed, and he had not the least doubt that it would be quite harmless and natural. So he thought, but meanwhile it was not only Irena's picture that would not leave him: all her words passed successively through his memory.

A waiter brought him a note; it, too, was from Irena.

"If you are doing nothing this evening, come and see me. I shall not be alone; I shall have guests, and you will see our circle, our society, at even closer quarters. I very much want you to see them, I think they will display themselves in all their glory. And

86

it is important that you should know the kind of air I breathe. Do come; I shall be glad to see you, and you will not be bored" (she had wanted to write: "bored with me"). "Prove to me that our talk today has once for all made any misunderstanding between us impossible. Your devoted, I."

Litvinov put on his frock coat and made his way to Irena's hotel. "It is all very trivial," he mentally repeated as he went, "and I can take a look at them — why shouldn't I? It will be interesting." A few days previously these same people had aroused a different feeling in him: they had aroused a feeling of indignation.

He walked at a rapid pace, with his hat pulled down over his eyes, with a tense smile on his lips. And Bambayev, who was sitting outside Weber's café, pointed him out in the distance to Voroshilov and Pishchalkin and exclaimed enthusiastically: "D'you see that man? He's a stone! He's a rock! He's granite!"

15

He found quite a large number of guests already arrived. Three of the generals at the picnic — the fat, the irritable, and the condescending one — were sitting at a card-table in a corner. They were playing dummy whist, and no words in any human language could convey the seriousness with which they dealt, took tricks, led with clubs, led with diamonds . . . they were true statesmen! Leaving it to the independent professions, to the bourgeoisie, to indulge in the stories and facetious remarks customary at cards, the generals uttered only the most indispensable words. The stout general did, however, allow himself to roll out energetically between two deals: "Ce satané as de pique!" Among the visitors Litvinov recognized ladies who had been present at the picnic; but there were others he had not previously seen. One of them was so old that she looked as though she would fall to pieces at any moment; she wriggled her bare, horrible, dark-gray shoulders and, covering her mouth with her fan, gave Ratmirov languid looks with her already quite dead eyes. He danced attendance on her: in high society she was greatly respected as the last surviving lady in waiting of the Empress Catherine. By the window, dressed as a shepherdess, sat Countess Sh., "the Princess Wasp," surrounded with young people; among them was the celebrated, rich, handsome Finikov, distinguished from the rest by his haughty bearing, perfectly flat cranium, and his soullessly animal facial expression, worthy of a khan of Bokhara or a Roman Heliogabalus. Another lady, also a countess, known by the brief name of Lise, was talking to a long fair-haired pale-faced "spiritualist"; beside them stood a gentleman, also pale and long-haired, who laughed meaningly. This gentleman also believed in spiritualism, but in addition he engaged in prophecy and on the basis of the Apocalypse and the Talmud foretold all kinds of amazing events. None of these events ever came to pass, yet he was never disconcerted, but continued to prophesy. At the piano was that same natural prodigy who had moved Potugin to such indignation; he played chords with an abstracted hand, *d'une main distraite*, and looked about him. Irena was sitting on a divan between Prince Coco and Mme X, a once well-known beauty and all-Russian wit, who had long since been transformed into a worthless toadstool and gave off a scent of vegetable oil and stale poison. When Irena saw Litvinov she flushed, rose, and, when he went across to her, squeezed his hand firmly. She was wearing a black crepe gown with hardly perceptible gold ornamentation; her shoulders were of an unpolished marble whiteness, and her face, also white beneath the momentary crimson wave that flooded over it, breathed with the exultation of beauty, and not only of beauty: a repressed, almost a mocking joy shone in her half-closed eyes, fluttered round her lips and nostrils. . . .

Ratmirov came up to Litvinov and, after exchanging the customary greetings, which were not, however, accompanied by his usual playfulness, introduced him to two or three ladies, including the old ruin, the Princess Wasp, and Countess Lise. . . . They received him quite favorably. He did not belong to their little circle . . . but he was quite, in fact very handsome, and the expressive features of his youthful face aroused their interest. He was not capable of retaining that interest, however; he was not accustomed to society and felt embarrassed; and now the stout general also fixed his eyes on him. "Aha! the partridge, the freethinker!" that immobile, heavy gaze seemed to be saying, "so he's come crawling into our circle, with a 'give me your hand.' " Irena came to Litvinov's rescue. She arranged matters so neatly that he found himself in a corner by the door, a little behind her. Whenever she spoke to him she had to turn round, and each time she turned he delighted in the beautiful curve of her gleaming neck,

he drank in the subtle scent of her hair. The expression of gratitude, profound and still, did not pass from her face; he could not
but recognize that it was indeed gratitude that those smiles, those
glances expressed, and he himself was seething with the same feeling, and he felt conscience-stricken, and blissful, and horrified.
. . . And at the same time she seemed continually to be saying:
"Well, what do you think of them? What are they like?" Litvinov caught that unspoken question even more clearly whenever
one of the company said or committed some banality; and that
happened more than once during the evening. On one occasion
even she could not restrain herself, and she laughed outright.

Countess Lise, a highly superstitious lady who was drawn toward all things supernatural, talked to her heart's content with
the fair-haired spiritualist about Home,[1] turning tables, self-
playing concertinas, and so on, and ended by asking him whether
any living creatures were affected by magnetism.

"Certainly, one such creature does exist," Prince Coco joined
in from some distance away. "You know Milvanovsky, of course.
He was put to sleep in my presence, and he even snored. Dear,
dear!"

"You are very naughty, *mon prince;* I am talking about real
animals, *je parle des bêtes.*"

"*Mais moi aussi, madame, je parle d'une bête. . . .*"

"Real animals are affected, too," the spiritualist intervened. "For
instance, crabs; they are very nervous and easily go into a catalepsy."

The Countess was amazed.

"What? Crabs? Really? Ah, now, that is extraordinarily interesting! I'd like to see that! M'sieur Luzhin," she added, turning to
a young man with a face as stony as that of a new doll and wearing a stony collar (he boasted that he had irrigated that same
face and that same collar with sprinkles of water from Niagara
and the Nubian Nile, but he could never remember anything of
all his travels and was fond only of Russian puns). "M'sieur Luzhin, be so kind as to get us a crab."

M'sieur Luzhin smirked. "Quick or only quickly?" he asked.

The Countess did not understand him. "*Mais oui,* a crab," she
repeated, "*une écrevisse.*"

"What? What's that? A crab, a crab?" Countess Sh. sternly

[1] D. D. Home (1833–86), a well-known medium of the period. (Tr.)

intervened. She was vexed by the fact that M'sieur Verdier was absent; she could not understand why Irena had not invited that most charming of Frenchmen. The ruin, who had long since lost all understanding of anything — and besides, she was very deaf — only tossed her head.

"*Oui, oui, vous allez voir.* M'sieur Luzhin, please — "

The young traveler bowed, went out, and returned very quickly. He was followed by a waiter who, smiling all over his face, was carrying a dish on which a large black crab was visible.

"*Voici, madame,*" exclaimed Luzhin; "now we can proceed to the 'cancer' operation. Ha-ha-ha!" (Russians are always the first to laugh at their own witticisms.)

"He-he-he!" Prince Coco responded in the capacity of patriot and patron of all native products.

(We ask the reader not to be astonished and not to be indignant; who can vouch for himself that if he were sitting in the parterre of the Alexandrinsky Theater in Petersburg and carried away by its atmosphere, he would not clap an even feebler pun?)

"*Merci, merci,*" the Countess said. "*Allons, allons, Monsieur Fox, montrez-nous ça.*"

The waiter placed the dish on a small round table. The guests started into gentle movement; several necks were craned; only the generals at the card-table preserved an imperturbable solemnity of attitude. The spiritualist tousled his hair, knitted his brows, and, approaching the table, began to make passes; the crab raised itself, fell back, and extended its claws. The spiritualist repeated and accelerated his movements; the crab continued to raise itself.

"*Mais que doit-elle donc faire?*" asked the Countess.

"*Elle doit rester immobile et se dresser sur sa queue,*" Mr. Fox replied with a strong American accent, convulsively shaking his fingers over the dish. But the magnetism did not act, the crab continued its movements. The spiritualist announced that he was not in a good mood and moved away from the table with a dissatisfied air. The Countess began to console him, assuring him that similar failures had sometimes occurred even with Mr. Home. . . . Prince Coco confirmed her words. The expert on the Apocalypse and the Talmud surreptitiously went across to the table and, swiftly but vigorously jabbing his fingers toward the crab, also tried his luck, but unsuccessfully: no signs of catalepsy appeared. Then the waiter was summoned, and he was ordered to carry out the crab, which he did with his former broad smile; his snorts as he shut the door behind him were audible in the room. . . . When he told the story in the kitchen, there was a good deal of laughter *über diese Russen*. The natural prodigy, who during the experiments on the crab had continued to play chords, keeping to minor tones, as after all it was impossible to know what effect anything would have — the natural prodigy played his invariable waltz and, of course, received the most flattering approbation.

Carried away by a feeling of rivalry, Count X, our incomparable dilettante (see Chapter 1), "sang" a chansonette of his own invention, entirely stolen from Offenbach. Its playful refrain, consisting of the words *"Quel bœuf? Quel bœuf?"* sent almost all the ladies' heads swaying to right and left; one even began to groan faintly, and the irresistible, inevitable word *"Charmant," "Charmant!"* flew from mouth to mouth. Irena exchanged glances with Litvinov, and once more that repressed, derisive expression flickered round her lips. . . .

But it began to play even more definitely a little later, it even acquired a malicious nuance, when Prince Coco, that representative and defender of the nobility's interests, took it into his head to expound his views to the spiritualist and, naturally, at once brought into action his celebrated phrase about the profound disturbance of the principle of property in Russia, during which, of course, the democrats also received a basting. The spiritualist's American blood was aroused; he began to argue. The Prince, as is proper, at once started to shout at the top of his voice, and instead of providing any proofs incessantly repeated: *"C'est absurde, cela n'a pas le sens commun!"* The wealthy Finikov took to making audacious remarks, without regard for persons; the Talmudist began to scream, even Countess Sh. grated. . . . In a word, there was almost as much idiotic hubbub as there had been at Gubariov's; perhaps the only difference being that here there was no beer and tobacco smoke, and everybody was wearing better clothes. Ratmirov tried to restore silence (the generals expressed their dissatisfaction, and Boris was heard to exclaim: *"Encore cette satanée politique!"*), but the attempt was a failure. A dignitary who was present, one of the gently persuasive kind, took it on himself to present *le résumé de la question en peu de mots*, and suffered defeat. To tell the truth, he mumbled and repeated himself so much, he was so obviously incapable of either listening to or understanding objections, and so obviously did not really know what *la question* was, that it was impossible to expect any other result. And then, to make matters worse, Irena stealthily instigated and poisoned the disputants against one another, looking round at Litvinov occasionally and nodding slightly to him. . . . But he sat as though enchanted, heard nothing, and only waited for those splendid eyes to glitter again before him, and for that pale, delicate, evil, delightful neck to gleam once more. . . . It all ended with the ladies rising in revolt and demanding that the quarrel should end. . . . Ratmirov asked the dilettante to repeat his chansonette, and the natural prodigy played his waltz. . . .

Litvinov remained till past midnight and was the last to leave. During the evening the conversation had touched upon many subjects, diligently avoiding anything in the least interesting. Having ended their majestic game, the generals majestically joined in the conversation; the influence of these statesmen was felt at once. The talk turned to the Parisian demimonde celebrities, whose names and talents appeared to be very well known to all the company, to Sardou's latest play, About's novel, and Patti in *Traviata*. Someone suggested a game of *"au secrétaire,"* but it was not a success. The answers were insipid and not without grammatical errors; the stout general related how he had once answered the question *"qu'est ce que l'amour?"* by saying it was *"une colique remontée au cœur,"* and immediately burst into his wooden laugh; the ruin gave him a swinging tap on the hand with her fan; this violent movement caused a lump of cerise to fall from her brow. The withered toadstool began to recall the Slavonic dukedoms and the necessity for Russian Orthodox propaganda beyond the Danube, but, obtaining no response, she spluttered and faded out. Most of the conversation was about Home; even the "Princess Wasp" told of how hands had slipped over her, and how she had seen them and put her own ring on one of them.

Irena certainly had cause for exultation: if Litvinov had paid even more attention than he did to all the talk, he would not have carried away a single sincere word, a single useful thought, a single new fact from all its incoherent and lifeless babble. No enthusiasm was to be detected even in the shouts and exclamations; even in the denials no passion was to be felt; only from time to time, behind the mask of pseudo-civic indignation, or pseudo-contemptuous indifference, a tearfully whimpering fear of every possible kind of privation was to be detected, and several names that posterity will not forget were uttered with a grinding of teeth. . . . And beneath all this lumber and rubbish there was not one drop from a living stream! What outworn, what unnecessary nonsense, what empty trifles occupied all these heads, these souls; and not only during this one evening, not only in society, but at home also, during every hour of every day, throughout all the breadth and depth of their existence. And, in the last resort, what boorishness! What inability to understand everything on which human life is based, everything with which it is adorned!

As she said good-by to Litvinov, Irena again squeezed his hand and significantly whispered: "Well, what do you think? Are you satisfied? Have you seen enough? Is it good?" He did not answer and only made a low, calm bow.

Left alone with her husband, Irena was about to go to her bedroom. . . . He halted her.

"*Je vous ai beaucoup admirée ce soir, madame,*" he said, lighting a cigarette and leaning on the mantelpiece. "*Vous vous êtes parfaitement moquée de nous tous.*"

"*Pas plus cette fois-ci que les autres,*" she replied unconcernedly.

"How do you wish that to be understood?" he asked.

"As you like."

"Hm. *C'est clair.*" Cautiously, with a catlike movement, he brushed off the ash of his cigarette with the long nail of his index finger. "Yes, that reminds me! That new acquaintance of yours — what is his name? — Mr. Litvinov should have the reputation of being a very intelligent man."

At the mention of Litvinov, Irena turned sharply.

"What are you trying to say?"

The general smiled.

"He never says a word — evidently he's afraid of compromising himself."

Irena also smiled, only not at all like her husband.

"Better to be silent than to talk — as others talk."

"*Attrapé*" he said with feigned humility. "Joking apart, he has a very interesting face. Such a — concentrated expression . . . and his bearing generally — yes." The general adjusted his tie and with head thrown back gazed at his own mustaches. "I should think he is a republican, like that other friend of yours, Mr. Potugin. Now, there's another of your speechless sages."

Irena slowly raised her eyebrows above her dilated, gleaming eyes, while she compressed and very slightly twisted her lips. "What is the point of your saying all this, Valerian Vladimirich?" she remarked in a sympathetic tone. "You're only firing into the air. . . . We're not in Russia, and nobody is listening."

He shuddered.

"That is not only my opinion, Irena Pavlovna," he began with a suddenly guttural voice. "Others also consider that this gentleman looks like a *Carbonero*." [1]

"Really? And who are these others?"

"Why, Boris, for instance."

"What? And did he have to express his opinion?"

Irena wriggled her shoulders as though flinching from the cold and gently ran the tips of her fingers over them.

"He — yes, he — he too. Allow me to put it to you, Irena Pavlovna, that apparently you are angry. And you know yourself that anyone who gets angry — "

"I am angry? What about?"

"I don't know; perhaps you were unpleasantly affected by the remark I permitted myself to make just now concerning — "

He hesitated.

"Concerning?" she repeated interrogatively. "Ah, please, without irony, and quickly! I'm tired, I want to get to bed." She picked up a candle from the table. "Concerning — ?"

"Why, again concerning that same Mr. Litvinov. As there is now no doubt that you are greatly interested in him . . ."

Irena raised the hand holding the candlestick, so that the flame was level with her husband's face, and gazing into his eyes attentively, almost with curiosity, suddenly burst into laughter.

"What's the matter with you?" he asked, frowning.

She did not stop laughing.

"But what is all this?" he repeated, and he stamped his foot.

He felt that he was insulted, cut to the quick, yet at the same time the beauty of this woman who was confronting him so easily and boldly involuntarily dumbfounded him — she tormented him.

---

[1] Originally, a member of an early nineteenth-century Italian secret society of democratic and republican principles; later used as a label for any subversive or even progressive movement. (Tr.)

He beheld all her charm; even the rosy gleam of her shapely nails on the slender fingers firmly gripping the dark bronze of the heavy candlestick — even that gleam did not escape his notice . . . and the feeling of injury ate even more deeply into his heart. But Irena went on laughing.

"What? You? You're jealous?" she said at last. Turning her back on her husband, she left the room. "He's jealous," he heard her say through the door, and she laughed again.

Ratmirov stared morosely after his wife — even at that moment he could not but observe the enchanting harmonious grace of her figure, of her movements — and, putting out his cigarette with a vigorous blow on the marble mantelshelf, he flung it far from him. His cheeks suddenly turned pale, his chin quivered convulsively, and his eyes dumbly and bestially wandered over the floor, as though looking for something. . . . All semblance of refinement vanished from his face. It must have worn a similar expression when he slaughtered the Byelorussian peasants.

But Litvinov went home to his room and, sitting on a chair before the table, took his head in both hands and remained so, motionless, for a long time. He got up at last, opened the table drawer, and, picking up his document case, took Tatiana's portrait out of an inner pocket. Her face, distorted and, as is usual, aged by the photograph, gazed at him mournfully. Litvinov's fiancée was a girl of Great Russian blood, fair, rather full, and with somewhat heavy features, but with an amazing expression of good nature and modesty in her intelligent, light-brown eyes, and with a delicate white brow on which a ray of sunlight seemed to lie permanently. For long he did not remove his eyes from the portrait; then he gently put it away and once more clutched his head with both hands. "It's all over!" he whispered at last. "Irena! Irena!"

Only now, only at that moment did he realize that he was irrevocably and insanely in love with her, had loved her from the day of that first meeting with her in the Old Castle, that he had never ceased to love her. But how astonished he would have been, how utterly incredulous, how he would even have laughed, perhaps, if anyone had told him so a few hours ago!

"But Tania, Tania! My God! Tania! Tania!" he repeated remorsefully; yet even then Irena's picture rose before him in her black, almost mourning clothes, with the radiant silence of victory on her white marble face.

16

Litvinov did not sleep all night and did not undress. He felt greatly oppressed. As an honest and just man, he realized all the meaning of obligation, of sacred duty, and would have considered it shameful to be casuistic with himself, with his weakness, with his delinquency. At first a torpor took possession of him; for a long time he could not rid himself of the obsessive oppression of one invariable, half-conscious, vague sensation. Then he was seized with horror at the thought that the future, his almost conquered future, was again enveloped in gloom, that his house, his solidly built, only just erected house had suddenly rocked. . . . He began to upbraid himself mercilessly, but at once put a stop to his outbursts. "What pusillanimity!" he thought. "This is not the moment for reproaches; now I must act. Tania is my fiancée, she believed in my love, my honor; we are united forever, and we cannot, we must not be parted." He vividly recalled all Tatiana's virtues, he mentally turned them over and catalogued them; he tried to quicken in himself a feeling of fondness and tenderness. "There is only one thing left for me to do," he thought again, "I must hurry, hurry at once, not waiting for her arrival, must hurry to meet her; even if I suffer, even if I am tortured with Tania — that is incredible — but in any case even to consider it, even to take it into consideration, is out of the question. I must do my duty, even if I die after!" "But you haven't any right to deceive her," another voice whispered to him, "you haven't any right to conceal from her the change that has occurred in your feelings. Perhaps when she learns that you have fallen in love with another, she will not wish to become your wife." "Rubbish! Rubbish!" he objected; "that's just sophistry, contemptible cunning, false scruples. I have no right not to keep my plighted word, that's the point. Well, excellent. . . . Then I must go away from Baden without seeing Irena. . . ."

But at this his heart sank, he turned cold, physically cold; a momentary shiver ran over his body, his teeth chattered quietly. He stretched himself and yawned, as though in a fever. Not pondering further on that last thought, smothering that thought, turning from it, he began to be astonished and wonder how he could again—again have fallen in love with that perverted, worldly creature, in all her repellent, inimical milieu. He attempted to ask himself: "But wait, are you sure you have fallen in love with her?" and only dismissed the very question. He was still feeling amazement and incomprehension when before him, as though out of a soft, scented mist, emerged an enchanting face; radiant lashes were raised; gently, and irresistibly, bewitching eyes pierced into his heart, and a voice sounded sweetly, and gleaming shoulders, the shoulders of a young princess, enveloped him in their freshness and voluptuous fire. . . .

Toward morning a decision matured at last in Litvinov's soul. He proposed to travel that same day to meet Tatiana; he would see Irena for the last time, would tell her—if there were no other way out—all the truth, and then part from her forever.

He put his things in order and packed them, waited till twelve o'clock, then went to her. But at the sight of her half-curtained windows his heart sank—he could not summon up sufficient spirit to enter the hotel. He walked up and down the Lichtentaler Allee several times.

"Our respects to Mr. Litvinov!" a derisive voice suddenly sounded behind him from the height of a swiftly moving dog-cart. He raised his eyes and saw General Ratmirov sitting beside Prince M., a well-known sportsman and amateur of English equipages and horses. The Prince was driving, and the general leaned over the side and bared his teeth, raising his hat high above his head. Litvinov bowed to him, and at the same moment, as though submitting to a secret command, went at a run to Irena.

She was at home. He sent a messenger to report his arrival; he was received at once. When he entered, she was standing in the middle of the room. She was wearing a morning blouse with broad, open sleeves; her face, as pale as yesterday, but not as fresh as yesterday, showed signs of weariness; the languid smile with which she welcomed her guest defined this expression even more clearly. She held out her hand to him and gave him a kindly but abstracted look.

"Thank you for coming," she said in a mournful voice, and dropped into a chair. "I am not quite well today; I spent a bad night. Well, what have you to say about yesterday evening? Wasn't I right?"

97

He sat down.

"I've come to you, Irena Pavlovna—" he began.

She momentarily straightened up and turned to him; she fixed her eyes on him.

"What is the matter with you?" she exclaimed. "You're as pale as a corpse, you are ill. What is wrong?"

He was disconcerted.

"With me, Irena Pavlovna?"

"Have you had some bad news? Some misfortune has occurred, tell me, tell me. . . ."

He in turn stared at her.

"I haven't had any bad news," he said, not without effort, "but a misfortune has indeed occurred, a great misfortune—and it is that which has brought me here."

"A misfortune? What is it?"

"Why—that—"

He tried to go on—and could not. He only clenched his hands until the fingers cracked. Irena leaned forward and seemed to turn to stone.

"Ah! I love you!" the words burst at last in a muffled groan from his breast, and he turned away, as though wishing to hide his face.

"What, Grigory Mikhailich, you—" She, too, could not finish her sentence. Leaning against the back of the chair, she raised both hands to her eyes. "You—love me?"

"Yes—yes—yes . . ." he repeated harshly, turning his face more and more away from her.

There was complete silence in the room; a butterfly that had flown in beat its wings and struggled between the curtain and the window.

He was the first to speak.

"There, Irena Pavlovna," he began, "there is the misfortune that has—struck me, that I should have foreseen and avoided if I hadn't fallen at once into the whirlpool just as I did in that former Moscow time. Evidently it pleased fate once more to compel me, and once more through you, to endure torments that, one would have thought, should never have been repeated. . . . Not without reason did I resist—try to resist; but there, what is to be will be. . . . But I tell you all now in order to put an end more quickly to this — this tragicomedy," he added with a new outburst of ruthlessness and shame.

He was silent again; the butterfly was still beating and fluttering. Irena did not take her hands from her face.

"And you are not deluding yourself?" her whisper came from behind those white, apparently bloodless hands.

"I am not deluding myself," he replied in a toneless voice. "I love you as I have never loved anyone but you. I do not intend to upbraid you: that would be too absurd. I do not intend to emphasize that perhaps none of this would have happened if you yourself had behaved differently with me. . . . Of course, I alone am to blame, my self-reliance has been my undoing. I am justly punished, and you could not expect this in the least. Of course, you did not realize that it would have been far safer for me if you had not been so ardently conscious of your guilt — your ostensible guilt toward me, and had not wished to expunge it . . . but what is done cannot be undone. I only wanted to explain my situation to you: it is difficult enough as it is. . . . At least, there will not be any misunderstanding, as you say; and the frankness of my confession, I hope, will diminish the feeling of offense that you cannot but have."

He spoke without raising his eyes; but even if he had glanced at Irena he could not have seen what was occurring in her face, for she did not remove her hands. Meanwhile, if he could have seen he certainly would have been astonished: fear and joy were expressed in that face, and a blissful exhaustion, and alarm; the eyes hardly glittered beneath the drooping lids, and a deep, spasmodic breathing chilled the parted, apparently thirsting lips. . . .

He waited a moment, in expectation of some response, some sound. . . . Nothing!

"There is only one thing left to me," he began again. "I must go away; I have come to say good-by."

Irena slowly dropped her hands to her knees.

"But I remember, Grigory Mikhailich," she began, "that — that person of whom you spoke to me, she should be coming here? Aren't you expecting her?"

"Yes; but I shall write to her . . . she will stop somewhere on the road — at Heidelberg, for instance."

"Ah! At Heidelberg — yes — that is a good place. . . . But all this must derange your plans. Are you sure, Grigory Mikhailich, that you are not exaggerating, *et que ce n'est pas une fausse alarme?*"

She spoke quietly, almost coldly, with brief pauses, and looking away to the window. He did not answer her last question.

"Only why did you say something about my being offended?" she continued. "I am not offended – oh, no! And if either of us is to blame, then in any case it is not you; not you alone. . . . Recall our last conversation, and you will be convinced that not you are to blame."

"I never had any doubt of your magnanimity," Litvinov said through set teeth. "But I wish to know: do you approve of my intention?"

"To go away?"

"Yes."

She continued to look away from him.

"For one moment I thought your intention premature . . . but now I have thought over what you have just said . . . and if you are sure you are not mistaken, then I think you should go away. That will be better — better for us both."

Her voice grew softer and softer, and her very speech grew slower and slower.

"Certainly, General Ratmirov might notice — " he began.

Her eyes dropped again, and a strange expression flickered round her lips — flickered and faded.

"No. You haven't understood me aright," she interrupted him. "I was not thinking of my husband. Why should I? There would be nothing for him to notice. But I repeat: separation is necessary for both of us."

Litvinov picked up his hat, which had fallen to the floor.

"It's all over," he was thinking, "I must go." "And so now I have only to say good-by to you, Irena Pavlovna," he said aloud; and he suddenly felt afraid, as though he were about to pronounce sentence on himself. "It remains only for me to hope that you will not think badly of me — and that if at any time we — "

She again interrupted him:

"Wait, Grigory Mikhailich, don't say good-by to me yet. That would be too hasty."

Something quivered inside him; but at once, and with re-doubled force, a corrosive bitterness took possession of his heart.

"But I cannot remain!" he exclaimed. "What for? Why continue this exhausting ordeal?"

"Don't say good-by to me yet," Irena repeated. "I must see you once more — another dreary parting like that one in Moscow? No, I do not want that! You may go now; but you must promise me, must give me your word of honor, that you will not go away without seeing me once more."

"Do you wish that?"

"I demand it. If you go away without saying good-by to me I shall never, never forgive you; do you hear? Never! It is strange!" she added, as though to herself; "I simply cannot realize that I am in Baden — I continually have the feeling that I am in Moscow. . . . Go!"

He rose.

"Irena Pavlovna," he said, "give me your hand."

Irena shook her head.

"I told you I do not wish to say good-by to you . . ."

"I am not asking it in farewell. . . ."

She was about to hold out her hand, but for the first time since his confession she glanced at him — and drew her hand back.

"No, no," she whispered, "I will not give you my hand. No — no. Go!"

He bowed and went. He had no idea why she had refused him that last friendly handshake. . . . He could not know what she feared.

He went; but she dropped back into the chair and again covered her face with her hands.

17

He did not return home; he went off into the hills and, plunging into the heart of the forest, flung himself face-downward on the earth and lay there for about an hour. He did not suffer, did not weep; he simply went oppressively and exhaustingly numb. Never before had he felt anything like it: he had an unbearably nagging and gnawing sensation of emptiness, emptiness in himself, in everything around him, everywhere. . . . Neither of Irena nor of Tatiana did he think. He felt only one thing: the blow had fallen, and life was severed like a cable, and he was being dragged forward and caught up by something unknown, yet cold. At times he felt that a whirlwind had swept him away, and he was conscious of the rapid beating and disorderly blows of its somber wings. . . . But his resolution did not waver. To remain in Baden — that was unthinkable. Mentally he had already left; he was already sitting in the thundering and smoky carriage and fleeing, fleeing into the mute, dead distance.

He raised himself at last and, leaning his head against a tree, remained still; only with one hand, himself not noticing what he was doing, did he seize the upper frond of some bracken and swing it measuredly. The sound of approaching steps brought him out of his torpor; two charcoal-burners with great sacks over their shoulders were making their way along the steep track. "Time to go!" he whispered, and followed the charcoal-burners down into the town, then turned aside to the railway station and sent a telegram to Tatiana's aunt, Kapitolina Markovna. In this telegram he informed her of his plan for immediate departure from Baden and proposed to meet her at the Schrader Hotel in Heidelberg. "To end, to end it at once," he thought; "there's no point in postponing it till tomorrow."

Then he went into the Casino. With dull curiosity he stared two or three players in the face, noted Bindasov's odious nape and Pishchalkin's irreproachable features in the distance, and, after standing a few moments under the colonnade, went, unhurriedly, to Irena. Not in the grip of a sudden, involuntary attraction did he go to her: having decided to leave, he also decided to keep his given word and to see her once more. Unnoticed by the porter, he entered the hotel, went up the stairs without meeting anyone, and did not knock at the door, but mechanically pushed at it and entered the room. Irena was sitting in the room, in the same chair, in the same dress, in exactly the same position as three hours before. . . . It was obvious that all that time she had not moved from her seat, had not even stirred. She slowly raised her head and, seeing Litvinov, shuddered from head to foot and clutched at the chair arm.

"You frightened me," she whispered.

He gazed at her in speechless amazement. The expression of her face, of her faded eyes, astounded him.

She smiled forcedly and tidied her fallen hair. "It's nothing — to tell the truth, I don't know — I think I must have fallen asleep here in my chair."

"Excuse me, Irena Pavlovna," he began, "I came in without warning. . . . I have called to do that which you insisted I should do. As I am leaving today —"

"Today? But I think you told me you first wanted to write a letter —"

"I have sent a telegram."

"Ah! You found it necessary to hurry. And when are you leaving? At what time, I mean?"

"At seven in the evening."

"Ah! At seven o'clock! And you've come to say good-by?"

"Yes, Irena Pavlovna, to say good-by."

She was silent.

"I must thank you, Grigory Mikhailich. It must have been far from easy for you to come."

"Yes, Irena Pavlovna, it was very far from easy."

"Life generally is far from easy, Grigory Mikhailich; what do you think?"

"It depends on who it is, Irena Pavlovna."

She was again silent, as though in a reverie.

"You have proved your friendship by coming," she said at last. "I thank you. And I must say I approve of your intention to put an end to everything as quickly as possible — because any delay — because — because I, that same I, whom you accused of coquetry, whom you called a comedienne — that, I think, is what you called me — ?"

She swiftly rose and, seating herself in another chair, huddled and pressed her face and hands against the edge of the table. . . .

"Because I love you . . ." she whispered through her clenched fingers.

He fell back as though someone had struck him in the chest. She grievously turned her head away, as though wishing in turn to hide her face from him, and rested it on the table.

"Yes, I am in love with you — I love you — and you know it."

"I? I know it?" Litvinov said at last. "I?"

"Well, but now you see," she continued, "that you really must go, that you must not delay — both for us and for me there must be no delay. That is dangerous, that is fearful. . . . Good-by," she added, starting impetuously out of her chair. "Good-by!"

She took a few steps in the direction of the door of her room and, stretching out her hand behind her, hurriedly passed it through the air, as though wishing to meet and squeeze Litvinov's hand. But he stood as though rooted to the floor, far off. . . . She once more said: "Good-by, forget!" and rushed out without looking back.

He was left alone, but he could not come to his senses. He collected himself at last, went swiftly to her room door, called her name once, twice, thrice. . . . He already had his fingers on the handle . . . Ratmirov's ringing voice floated up from the hotel veranda.

Litvinov pulled his hat down over his eyes and went down the stairs. The elegant general was standing in front of the porter's box and explaining to him in bad German that he wished to hire a carriage for all the following day. Seeing Litvinov, he again raised his hat unnaturally high and again expressed his "respects." He was obviously making fun of him, but Litvinov was not concerned with that. He hardly replied to Ratmirov's bow. On reaching his room, he halted before his trunk, which was already packed and locked. His head was whirling, his heart was quivering like a violin string. What was he to do now? And could he have foreseen this?

Yes, he had foreseen it, no matter how incredible it seemed. It had stunned him like a thunderclap, but he had foreseen it, though he did not dare to admit it. He had known nothing for certain, however. Everything inside him was tangled and confused; he had lost the thread of his own thoughts. He remembered Moscow, he remembered how then, too, "it" had come upon him like a sudden storm. He panted; exultation, yet an exultation that was joyless and hopeless, tore and burdened his breast. Not for anything in the world would he have agreed that the words Irena had said should not have been uttered. . . . But what of it? Even so, those words could not change the decision he had made. He did not vacillate any more than before, and he held firmly, like an anchor dropped overboard. He had lost the thread of his own thoughts . . . truly; but his will was still for the moment his, and he disposed of himself as though he were some other, subordinated person.

He rang for the waiter, ordered him to bring his account, reserved a seat in the evening omnibus; he deliberately cut off all his ways of retreat. "And then afterward you can die if you like," he declared, as he had during the past sleepless night; he particularly liked that phrase. "And then afterward you can die if you like," he repeated, slowly pacing backward and forward about the room. And only occasionally did he involuntarily close his eyes and cease to breathe, when those words, those words of Irena's, burst into his soul and scorched it with fire. "Evidently you don't fall in love twice," he thought. "Another life has entered into yours, you have let it in — and never shall you rid yourself of that poison until the end, never shall you snap those threads! True; but what does that prove? Happiness. . . . As if that is possible? You love her, let us assume — and she — she loves you. . . ."

But now he again had to take himself in hand. Like a traveler on a dark night who sees before him a tiny light and, afraid of losing his road, does not remove his gaze from that light for a moment, so Litvinov continually concentrated all the strength of his attention on one point, on one end. To present himself to his fiancée, and not even, strictly speaking, to his fiancée (he tried not to think of her), in that room of the Heidelberg hotel — that was what faced him steadfastly, like a guiding light. What would happen after he did not know, nor did he want to know. . . . One thing was beyond doubt: he would not come back. "After that you can die if you like," he repeated for the tenth time, and glanced at his watch.

Six fifteen! How long he still had to wait! He again took to pacing backward and forward. The sun declined to its setting, the sky flushed above the trees, and a crimson half-light streamed through the narrow windows into his darkened room. Suddenly he had the feeling that a door was opened behind him quietly and swiftly, and was as swiftly closed again. . . . He turned; at the door stood a woman, wrapped in a black mantilla. . . .

"Irena," he exclaimed, and opened his arms wide. . . .

She looked at him and fell into his arms.

Two hours later he was sitting on the sofa in his room. The trunk was standing in one corner, open and empty, and on the table, among things scattered untidily, lay a letter from Tatiana, which he had only just received. She wrote that as her aunt's health was completely restored, she had decided to hasten her departure from Dresden, and that, apart from unforeseen obstacles, they would both arrive at Baden at twelve o'clock next day, and they hoped he would come and meet them at the railway station. He had already reserved an apartment for them in his hotel.

He sent a note to Irena that same evening, and her answer came the next morning. "Whether a day later, or a day earlier," she wrote, "it was inevitable. But I repeat to you what I said yesterday: my life is in your hands, do with me as you wish. I do not desire to constrain your freedom, but you must know that if necessary I will abandon everything and follow you to the ends of the earth. We shall see each other tomorrow, shall we not? Your Irena."

The last two words were written in a large and bold, resolute hand.

18

Among the people who gathered on the railway-station platform just before twelve o'clock of August 18 was Litvinov. A few minutes previously he had seen Irena: she was sitting in an open carriage with her husband and another, elderly gentleman. She caught sight of Litvinov, and he noticed that she saw him; her eyes momentarily darkened, but she at once hid from him behind her parasol.

Since yesterday a strange transformation had occurred in him: in all his appearance, in his movements, in the expression of his face; and he himself felt that he was a different man. His self-confidence had vanished, his calm had vanished also, and his respect for himself; nothing was left of his previous mental poise. His recent ineffaceable impressions had veiled all else. An unprecedented feeling, strong, sweet — and evil, had taken charge of him; a mysterious guest had made his way into the sanctuary and occupied it, and had lain down in it silently, but throughout all its extent, like the master of a new house. Litvinov was no longer ashamed, he was afraid — and at the same time a desperate audacity had flamed up within him. The captured and the conquered are acquainted with that blend of antagonistic feelings; nor is it unknown to the thief, after his first robbery. Litvinov too was conquered, conquered suddenly . . . and what had become of his integrity?

The train was several minutes late. His weariness passed into a tormenting yearning; he could not stand still and, quite pale, he pushed and rubbed shoulders with the crowd. "My God," he thought, "if only another twenty-four hours . . ." His first glance at Tania, Tania's first glance — that was what was terrifying him, that was what he had to face, and the sooner the better. . . . And afterward? But afterward — let come what may! . . . He no longer made any decision, he no longer answered for himself. Yesterday's phrase morbidly flickered through his head. . . . And this was how he was meeting Tania. . . .

At last there was a long-drawn-out whistle, a heavy, steadily rising roar was heard, and the locomotive appeared, slowly steaming round a bend in the track. The crowd rushed to meet it, and Litvinov followed the crowd, dragging his feet like a man condemned. Faces, ladies' hats began to emerge from the cars, a white handkerchief fluttered at one window — Kapitolina Markovna was waving to him. . . . It was the end: she had seen Litvinov, and he recognized her. The train came to a halt. He rushed to the door and opened it; Tatiana was standing beside her aunt; smiling brightly, she held out her hand.

He helped them both to alight, said a few words of greeting, unfinished and vague, and at once began to fuss about, began to collect their tickets, their traveling bags, their rugs, ran to find a porter, called a carriage; other people fussed all around him, and he was glad of their presence, their hubbub and shouts. Tatiana stepped a little aside and, not ceasing to smile, calmly waited for him to complete his hurried arrangements. Kapitolina Markovna, on the contrary, could not stand still; even now she could not believe that at last she had reached Baden. She suddenly cried: "But how about the parasols? Tania, where are the parasols?" not noticing that she had them firmly tucked under her arm. Then she began to take a loud and prolonged farewell of another lady, with whom she had made acquaintance during the journey from Heidelberg to Baden. This lady was none other than the Mme Sukhanchikova already known to us. She had been to Heidelberg for the adulation of Gubariov, and had returned with "instructions." Kapitolina Markovna was wearing a rather queer, varicolored mantelet and a round traveling hat shaped like a mushroom, beneath which her close-cut white hair was breaking loose untidily; short and gaunt, she was flushed with the journey and talked in Russian with a penetrating singsong voice. . . . She at once attracted everybody's attention.

At last Litvinov seated her and Tatiana in the carriage and placed himself opposite them. The horses set off. Now questions began to be asked, hands were again shaken, there were mutual smiles, greetings. . . . He breathed more easily: the first moments had passed without event. Evidently Tania had not been disturbed by anything unusual in him; she looked at him just as openly and trustfully, blushed just as pleasantly, laughed just as good-naturedly. At last he himself decided to look, not sidelong and fleetingly, but directly and fixedly at her; hitherto his eyes had not been under his command. An involuntary tenderness took possession of his heart: the unperturbed expression of that honest, open face reacted on him like a bitter reproach. "So you have come here, poor girl," he thought, "you whom I have so long awaited and called, with whom I wanted to pass all my life to the end; you have arrived, you believed me . . . but I—but I—I—" He bowed his head. But Kapitolina Markovna would give him no opportunity for meditation; she plied him with questions.

"What is that building with the columns? Where is the gambling casino? Who is that coming? Tania, Tania, look, what crinolines! But now who is that? I should think most of them are Frenchwomen from Paris, aren't they? Lord, what a hat! Can you find everything here, as in Paris? Only I suppose everything is terribly dear? Ah, what an excellent, intelligent woman I have met! You know her, Grigory Mikhailich; she told me she had met you when visiting a certain Russian, who also is extremely intelligent. She has promised to call on us. The way she disposes of all these aristocrats—it's simply marvelous! Who is that gentleman with gray whiskers? The King of Prussia? Tania, Tania, look, that's the King of Prussia. No? It isn't the King of Prussia? The Dutch Ambassador? I can't hear, the wheels are making so much noise. Ah, what marvelous trees!"

"Yes, auntie, they are marvelous," Tania agreed; "and how green and cheerful everything is here! Isn't it, Grigory Mikhailich? . . ."

"Very cheerful," he replied through set teeth.

The carriage drew up outside the hotel. Litvinov led the two travelers to the suite reserved for them, promised to come back in an hour, and returned to his room. The enchantment, which had momentarily lost its power, possessed him again immediately he entered. Here, in this room, since yesterday Irena reigned;

everything spoke of her visit. . . . He again felt himself her slave. He took out her handkerchief, which he had hidden at his breast, and pressed his lips to it; and oppressively burning memories spread through his veins in a subtle poison. He realized that this time there was no return, no alternative; the mournful fondness Tatiana aroused in him melted like snow in fire, and his contrition died away — died away so completely that even the agitation within him was lulled, and the possibility of dissimulation, which occurred to his mind, did not arouse his indignation. . . . Love, Irena's love — that was now his right, his law, his conscience. . . . The prudent, common-sense Litvinov did not even think of how he was to extricate himself from his position, of which he felt even the horror and infamy quite lightly and almost, as it were, objectively.

Before an hour had passed, a waiter called at his room with a message from the newly arrived ladies: they asked him to join them in the hall. He followed the messenger down and found them already dressed in outdoor clothes and hats. They both expressed the desire to go out and see Baden at once; fortunately the weather was excellent. Kapitolina Markovna especially was burning with impatience; she was even a little downcast when she learned that it was not yet the hour for the fashionable parade outside the Konversationshaus. Litvinov took her by the arm, and an official promenade began.

Tatiana walked at her aunt's side and looked about her with tranquil curiosity; Kapitolina Markovna continued her interrogations. The sight of the roulette tables, the stately croupiers, whom, if she had met them in another place, she would certainly have taken for ministers of state, the sight of their nimble rakes, the gold and silver piles on the green cloth, the gambling old women and the painted *lorettes* reduced Kapitolina Markovna to a state of impotent frenzy; she quite forgot that she ought to be indignant and only stared, stared her eyes out of her head, shuddering occasionally at some new exclamation. . . . The whir of the ivory ball in the roulette bowl penetrated to her very marrow — and only when she found herself in the fresh air did she summon up sufficient strength, after emitting a profound sigh, to call the game of chance an immoral invention of aristocratism. A fixed, unpleasant smile appeared on Litvinov's lips; he spoke spasmodically and sluggishly, as though he were angry or bored. . . . But now he turned to Tatiana and was inwardly disconcerted: she was looking at him attentively, with an expression that suggested she was asking herself what impression he was making on her. He hastened to nod to her; she answered with a nod and again stared at him interrogatively, with some straining of her gaze, as though he were standing much farther from her than he was in reality. Litvinov conducted his ladies away from the Konversationshaus and, avoiding the "Russian tree," beneath which his compatriots were already in session, led them toward the Lichtentaler Allee. Even before he entered the avenue he saw Irena in the distance.

Accompanied by her husband and Potugin, she was coming toward him. He turned as white as a sheet; but he did not slacken his pace, and as he drew level with her he silently made a low bow. She also bowed to him pleasantly, but coldly; she ran her eyes swiftly over Tatiana as she glided past. . . . Ratmirov raised his hat high in the air, Potugin muttered something.

"Who is that lady?" Tatiana suddenly asked. Until that moment she had hardly opened her lips.

"That lady?" Litvinov repeated. "That lady? She is Madame Ratmirova."

"Russian?"

"Yes."

"Did you make her acquaintance here?"

"No; I've known her a long time."

"How beautiful she is!"

"Did you notice her toilet?" Kapitolina Markovna intervened. "Ten families could be fed for a whole year on the money her laces alone must have cost. Was that her husband walking with her?" She turned to Litvinov.

"Yes."

"He must be terribly rich?"

"I really don't know; I don't think so."

"And what is his rank?"

"He's a general."

"What eyes she has!" Tatiana said. "There is a strange expression in them: thoughtful, and piercing — I have never seen such eyes before."

Litvinov did not reply; he imagined that he again felt Tatiana's interrogative gaze fixed on his face. But he was wrong; she was looking down at her feet, at the sand of the path.

"My goodness! Who is that monster?" Kapitolina Markovna suddenly exclaimed, pointing to a low gig in which a red-haired and snub-nosed woman in unusually sumptuous finery and lilac stockings was insolently sprawling.

"That monster! Why, that is the well-known Mam'selle Cora."

"Who?"

"Mam'selle Cora — a Parisian — celebrity."

"What? That pug dog? But she's hideously ugly."

"Evidently that doesn't matter."

Kapitolina Markovna only gave it up.

"Well, your Baden!" she said at last. "But can we sit here on this bench? I'm feeling rather tired."

"Of course we can, Kapitolina Markovna — that is what the benches are put there for."

"The Lord knows! They say there are benches on the Paris boulevards too, but it isn't proper to sit on them."

Litvinov made no reply to her; only now did he realize that two paces away was the very spot where he and Irena had held that fateful, decisive conversation. Then he remembered that he had noticed a small rose-colored patch on her cheek as she passed. . . .

Kapitolina Markovna dropped on the bench. Tatiana sat down beside her. Litvinov remained standing on the path; between him and Tatiana — or did he only imagine it? — something was being accomplished . . . unconsciously and gradually.

"Ah, she's a buffoon, a buffoon," Kapitolina Markovna declared, commiserately shaking her head. "Now, if *her* toilet were to be sold, one could feed not ten, but a hundred families. Did you see the diamonds beneath her hat, on that red hair of hers? Diamonds in daytime, what d'you think of that!"

"Her hair isn't really red," Litvinov remarked. "She dyes it red; that's the fashion now."

Kapitolina Markovna again gave it up and was even lost in thought.

"Well," she said at last, "we haven't reached such a scandalous state of affairs at Dresden yet. For, after all, it is farther from Paris. You're of the same opinion, aren't you, Grigory Mikhailich?"

"I?" he answered, and wondered: "What is she talking about?" "I? of course — of course. . . ."

But at that moment unhurrying steps were heard, and Potugin approached.

"Good day, Grigory Mikhailich," he said, smiling and nodding.

Litvinov at once seized him by the arm.

"Good day, good day, Sozont Ivanich. I, I think I saw you here just now with — just now, in the avenue."

"Yes, it was I."

Potugin bowed respectfully to the seated ladies.

"Let me introduce you, Sozont Ivanich. My very good friends, relatives, only just arrived in Baden. Ladies, this is Potugin — Sozont Ivanich, a fellow countryman of ours, also visiting Baden."

Both ladies rose a little from their seats. Potugin repeated his bows.

"This is a real *rout*," Kapitolina Markovna began in a faint voice. The good-natured old maid felt a little diffident, but above all she tried to preserve her dignity. "Everybody regards it as a pleasant duty to visit Baden."

"Baden is certainly a pleasant place," Potugin replied, looking sidelong at Tatiana. "A very pleasant place is Baden."

"Yes, only it is too aristocratic, so far as I can judge. I and my niece have been living in Dresden all this time — Dresden's a very interesting town; but here it is a real *rout*."

"She likes that word," thought Potugin.

"You are absolutely right in that remark," he said aloud; "but then, the surrounding country is very striking, and the situation of the town is almost incomparable. Your companion especially should appreciate that. Don't you think so, madame?" he added, turning to speak directly to Tatiana.

Tatiana raised her large, clear eyes to him. She seemed to be puzzled to know what he wanted of her and why Litvinov had introduced her, on the very day of their arrival, to this stranger, who, however, had an intelligent and kindly face and looked at her with a welcoming and friendly air.

"Yes," she said at last, "it is very good here."

"You must visit the Old Castle," Potugin went on. "I advise you particularly to make an excursion to the Yburg."

"The Saxon Switzerland —" Kapitolina began.

A sudden burst of trumpets echoed along the avenue; the Prussian military band from Rastatt (in 1862 Rastatt was still a fortress of the German Confederation) had begun its weekly concert in the pavilion. Kapitolina Markovna rose at once.

"Music!" she said. "*Music à la Conversation!* . . . We must go there. It's four o'clock now, isn't it? I suppose society is beginning to assemble?"

"Yes," Potugin replied, "this is the most fashionable hour for society, and the music is excellent."

"Then there's no point in waiting — come, Tania!"

"Will you permit me to accompany you?" Potugin asked, to Litvinov's no little astonishment; it did not occur to him that Irena had sent him.

Kapitolina Markovna simpered.

"With the greatest of pleasure, M'sieur — M'sieur — "

"Potugin," he himself prompted her, and offered her his arm.

Litvinov gave his arm to Tatiana, and the two couples made their way toward the Konversationshaus.

Potugin continued to discuss various questions with Kapitolina Markovna. But Litvinov walked along without uttering a word, and only smiled a couple of times without cause and feebly pressed Tatiana's arm. There was falsity in those squeezes, to which she made no response, and he was conscious of that falsity. They did not convey any reciprocal assurance of the close union of two mutually devoted souls, as in the past; they only temporarily took the place of the words that he could not find. This taciturnity which had developed between them increased and was established firmly. Tatiana again looked at him attentively, almost fixedly.

The same relationship was continued outside the Konversationshaus, around the little table at which they all seated themselves, with the sole difference that because of the bustle of the crowd and the thunder and crash of the music, Litvinov's silence seemed more understandable. Kapitolina Markovna let herself go completely, as one says; Potugin could hardly keep pace with her in his attempts to satisfy her curiosity. Fortunately for him, among the mass of passers-by appeared the gaunt figure of Su-khanchikova, with her everlastingly darting, glittering eyes, Kapitolina Markovna at once recognized her, called her over to the table, and asked her to sit with them. And then a verbal storm set in.

Potugin turned to Tatiana and began to talk to her in a low, soft voice, with a kindly expression on his face, slightly inclined toward her. And she, to her own astonishment, answered him easily and freely. She found it pleasant talking to this casual acquaintance, this stranger, whereas Litvinov continued to sit motionless, with the same fixed and unpleasant smile on his lips.

Dinnertime arrived at last. The music died away, the crowd began to thin. Kapitolina Markovna took a tender farewell of Sukhanchikova. Immense was the respect she had conceived for her, though she afterward told her niece that "that person" was very malicious, but that on the other hand she knew everything about everybody. And certainly sewing-machines ought to be introduced as soon as the wedding had been celebrated. Potugin bowed his good-by to them all; Litvinov saw his ladies home.

At the entrance to the hotel he was handed a note; he stepped aside and hurriedly tore open the envelope. On a small scrap of vellum paper were the following words, written in pencil: "Come this evening at seven o'clock for one minute, I implore you. Irena." He thrust the note into his pocket and, turning round, smiled again — at whom? And why? Tatiana was standing with her back to him.

They had dinner at the general table. Litvinov sat between Kapitolina Markovna and Tatiana and strangely came to life, talked a great deal, told stories, poured out wine for himself and the ladies. He behaved in such a free and easy manner that a French infantry officer from Strasbourg, with an imperial and mustaches *à la* Napoleon III, who was sitting opposite them, was able to intervene in the conversation and even ended with a toast *à la santé des belles Moscovites!* Dinner over, Litvinov conducted both the ladies to their rooms and, after standing a moment with knitted brows at the window, abruptly announced that he must leave them for a short time to attend to a business matter, but would certainly return by the evening. Tatiana said nothing, turned pale, and lowered her eyes. Kapitolina Markovna was in the habit of sleeping after dinner. Tatiana knew that Litvinov was aware of her aunt's habit, and she had expected that he would take advantage of it, that he would remain, as he had not had a minute alone with her since her arrival, had not had any intimate talk with her. And now he was going out! How was she to take that? And altogether his behavior all day . . . .

He hurriedly withdrew without waiting for objections. Kapitolina Markovna lay down on the sofa and, after groaning and sighing once or twice, went off into a tranquil sleep; but Tatiana retired to a corner and sat down in an armchair, her hands firmly folded over her breast.

19

Litvinov walked briskly up the stairs of the Hôtel de l'Europe. . . . A girl about thirteen years old, with a crafty little Kalmuck face, who evidently was on the lookout for him, stopped him, saying in Russian: "This way, please; Irena Pavlovna will come in a minute." He stared at her in astonishment. She smiled, repeated: "Please, please," and led him into a small room opposite Irena's bedroom, a boxroom filled with traveling bags and trunks. Then she disappeared, quietly shutting the door. Before Litvinov had time to look about him the same door was swiftly flung open and Irena appeared in a rose-colored evening gown, with amber in her hair and at her neck. She rushed to him, seized both his hands, and stood for several moments speechless; her eyes sparkled and her breast heaved, as though she had been running uphill.

"I could not receive — you there," she began in a hurried whisper. "We're just going to a dinner engagement; but I simply had to see you. . . . That was your fiancée, wasn't it, whom I saw you with today?"

"Yes, that was my fiancée," he said, emphasizing the word "was."

"Well, then, I wanted to see you for one minute, in order to tell you that you should consider yourself absolutely free, that all that happened yesterday should not change your decisions in the least. . . ."

"Irena!" he exclaimed, "why are you saying this?"

He said these words in a loud voice. They throbbed with supreme passion. She involuntarily closed her eyes for a moment.

"Oh, my dear!" she continued in a still quieter whisper, but with uncontrollable fervor, "you don't know how much I love you; but yesterday I only paid my debt, I effaced my former guilt. . . . Ah! I could not give you my youth, much as I wished to; but I imposed no obligations on you, and so there was no promise from which I had to absolve you, my dear! Do as you wish; you are as free as the air, you are bound in no way, understand that; you must understand that!"

"But I cannot live without you, Irena," he interrupted her in a whisper. "Since yesterday I am yours forever and always. . . . Only at your feet can I breathe. . . ."

He tremulously pressed his face against her hands. Irena gazed at his bowed head.

"Well, then know also," she said, "that I, too, am ready for anything, that I, too, shall spare no one and nothing. As you decide, so will it be. I, too, am forever yours — yours."

Someone knocked cautiously at the door. She bent over him and whispered yet again: "Yours. . . . Good-by!" Litvinov felt her breath on his hair, the touch of her lips. When he straightened up she was no longer in the room; but her gown rustled in the corridor, and in the distance he heard Ratmirov's voice: "*Eh bien? Vous ne venez pas?*"

Litvinov sat down on a large trunk and hid his face in his hands. A feminine scent, fine and fresh, enveloped him . . . Irena was holding his hands in her hands. "This is too much — too much," he was thinking. The girl entered the room; smiling again in response to his anxious glance, she told him:

"Please go, while . . ."

He rose and left the hotel. There could be no thought of his returning to his own hotel at once: he must recover his tranquillity. His heart was beating protractedly and unevenly inside him; the earth seemed to be gently stirring beneath his feet. He made his way once more to the Lichtentaler Allee. He realized that the decisive moment had come, that it had become impossible to procrastinate any longer, to dissemble, to avert his face, and that he must clear up the position with Tatiana. He imagined how she was sitting there and not stirring, and waiting for him . . . he had a presentiment of what he would tell her. But how to set about it, how to begin? He dismissed all his sound, well-arranged, well-ordered future; he knew that he was flinging himself head over heels into depths into which he should not even have glanced . . . but that did not disturb him. That question was settled. But how to go before his judge? And if it had been indeed a judge that awaited him — an angel with a flaming sword — it would have been easier for his sinful heart . . . but as it was, he himself must plunge the knife. . . . Infamous! But to turn back, to renounce the other, to take advantage of the freedom he was offered, which was recognized to be his — No! Rather die! No, he did not want that gelid freedom, but preferred to be flung down into the dust, so long as those eyes beamed with love over him. . . .

"Grigory Mikhailich," someone's mournful voice called, and someone's hand lay heavily on him.

He looked round, not without alarm, and recognized Potugin.

"Excuse me, Grigory Mikhailich," Potugin began with his usual grimace. "Perhaps I disturbed you. But seeing you in the distance, I thought — But if you don't want me — "

"On the contrary, I am very glad," Litvinov said through set teeth.

Potugin walked along at his side.

"A beautiful evening," he began; "so warm! Have you been out long?"

"No, not long."

"But there, why do I ask? I saw you come out of the Hôtel de l'Europe."

"So you followed me?"

"Yes."

"Have you something to say to me?'

"Yes," Potugin repeated almost inaudibly.

Litvinov halted and looked at his uninvited companion. Potugin's face was pale, the eyes absent; a former, ancient sorrow seemed to be revealed in his distorted features.

"And what exactly is it you wish to say to me?" Litvinov said slowly, and again walked on.

"Well, if you don't mind — one minute. If it's all the same to you, let's sit on this bench. It will be more convenient here."

"This is all rather mysterious," Litvinov said, sitting down beside him. "You don't seem to be yourself, Sozont Ivanich."

"No, I'm all right; and there's nothing mysterious about it, either. I simply wanted to communicate to you — the impression your fiancée made on me. She is your fiancée, isn't she? Well, in a word, the young lady to whom you introduced me today. I must say that in all my life I have never met a creature of a more pleasant temperament. She has a golden heart, and a truly angelic soul."

He said all this with the same bitter and afflicted air, so that even Litvinov could not help noting the strange contradiction between the expression on his face and the words he was saying.

"You are quite right in your estimate of Tatiana Petrovna," Litvinov began; "though I have to express my astonishment, first that you know my relations with her, and secondly that you have divined her character so quickly. She has, indeed, an angelic soul. But permit me to ask whether that is what you wanted to talk to me about."

"It is impossible not to recognize her character immediately," Potugin replied, and he seemed to be evading the last question. "You have only to take one look into her eyes. She is deserving of every possible happiness on earth, and enviable is the lot of the man who is destined to give her that happiness! One must hope that he will prove worthy of such a part."

Litvinov frowned a little.

"Excuse me, Sozont Ivanich," he said; "I must admit I find our conversation decidedly unusual. . . . I should like to know: do your words refer to me?"

Potugin did not answer at once; evidently he was struggling with himself.

"Grigory Mikhailich," he began at last, "either I have been completely mistaken in you or you are capable of listening to the truth, no matter whence it comes and beneath no matter what opaque integument it is presented. I said just now that I saw where you had come from."

"Why, yes, from the Hôtel de l'Europe. And what of it?"

"But I know whom you saw there!"

"What?"

"You saw Madame Ratmirova."

"Well, yes, I called on her. And what further?"

"What further? You, the fiancé of Tatiana Petrovna, you have been meeting Madame Ratmirova, whom you love—and who loves you."

Litvinov momentarily rose from the bench; the blood rushed to his head.

"What is this?" he said at last in an exasperated, choking voice. "A bad joke? Spying? Please explain."

Potugin gave him a despondent look.

"Ah! Don't be offended at my words, Grigory Mikhailich; and you certainly cannot offend me. That was not my object in wanting this talk with you, and joking is far from me at this moment."

"Maybe, maybe. I am prepared to believe in the purity of your intentions; none the less I take the liberty of asking you by what right you interfere in the domestic affairs, in the private life, of another man, and on what basis you so self-confidently put forward your—invention as the truth."

"My invention! If I had invented it, you would not have been angry. And as for the truth, I have never yet heard of anyone asking himself whether he has any right to stretch out a hand to a drowning man."

"I humbly thank you for your solicitude," Litvinov fierily retorted. "Only I have no need of it whatever, and all those phrases about the ruin prepared by society ladies for inexperienced youths, about the immorality of high society, and so on, I regard simply as phrases, and even in a sense I feel contempt for them. And so I ask you not to lift your saving hand, but calmly to let me drown."

Potugin again raised his eyes to Litvinov. He was breathing with difficulty, his lips were quivering.

"But look at me, young man," the words at last burst from him, and he beat himself on the chest. "Do I really look like a commonplace, self-satisfied moralist, like a sermonizer? Don't you really understand that I would not let fall one word, would not give you any right to reproach me with something that is absolutely repellent to me, with immodesty, with impertinence, simply out of commiseration for you, no matter how strongly I felt you deserved it? Don't you really see that this is quite a different question, that the man talking to you has been shattered, destroyed, completely annihilated by the very same feeling, that he wants to save you from the consequences of that feeling, which you have—for—for the very same woman?"

Litvinov fell back a pace.

"Is it possible? What did you say? You—you—Sozont Ivanich? But Madame Belskaya—that child . . ."

"Ah, don't question me—believe me! It is a dark, a terrible story, and I shall not stop to tell it to you. I hardly knew Madame Belskaya. That child is not mine, but I took everything on myself—because—because *she* wished it, because it was vital to *her*. Why should I be here, in this loathsome Baden of yours? And, finally, do you really assume, could you even for one minute imagine, that I decided to warn you out of sympathy for you? I am sorry for that good, kind girl, your fiancée; but really, what is your future, what does either of you matter to me? . . . No, I am afraid for her — for her."

"That does you honor, Mr. Potugin," Litvinov began, "but as, in your words, we are both in the same position, why don't you read similar admonitions to yourself, and why shouldn't I attribute your fears to another feeling?"

"In other words, to jealousy, you wish to say? Ah, young man, young man, shame on you to shuffle and palter, shame on you not to understand what bitter woe is now being spoken through my lips! No, you and I are not in the same position! I, I am an old, ludicrous, completely harmless eccentric. . . . And you? But why talk about it? Not for one second would you agree to take on yourself the role that I play, and play with gratitude! And jealousy? A man does not feel jealousy who has not even the least hope, and this would not have been the first time I had been forced to experience that feeling! I am only afraid — afraid for her, understand that. Could I have expected, when she sent me to you, that the feeling of guilt that she admitted she possessed would carry her so far?"

"Pardon me, Sozont Ivanich, you seem to know —"

"I know nothing, and I know all. I know," he added and turned away, "I know where she was yesterday. But there is no restraining her now: like a thrown stone, she must roll down to the bottom. I would be an even greater madman if I imagined that my words would halt you at once — you, whom such a woman — But enough of that. I could not compel myself to do otherwise, that is my only excuse. And besides, how is one to know, and why not try? Perhaps you will think better of it, perhaps some word of mine will penetrate into your soul; you do not wish to ruin both her and yourself and that innocent, noble creature. . . . Oh, don't get angry, don't stamp your foot! What have I to fear? Why should I stand on ceremony? It is not jealousy that speaks in me now, not chagrin. I am ready to fall at your feet, to implore you — But in any case, good-by. Don't be afraid, this will all remain a secret. I wish you well."

Potugin strode off along the avenue and quickly disappeared in the oncoming dusk. . . . Litvinov did not detain him.

Smoke

"A terrible, a dark story . . . " Potugin had said to Litvinov, and had not been willing to tell him that story. . . . We, too, shall touch on it in only a few words.

Some eight years previously Potugin's ministry had temporarily posted him to assist Count Reizenbach. It was summertime. Potugin traveled with documents to the Count's summer residence outside the town and spent days on end in this fashion. At that time Irena was living in the Count's house. She had never felt any contempt for people of lowly position; at any rate, she was not hostile to them, and the Countess more than once remonstrated with her because of her excessive Moscow familiarity. Irena soon recognized that this modest official, enveloped in a tightly buttoned, uniform frock coat, was an intelligent man. She frequently and readily talked to him . . . and he — he fell in love with her passionately, deeply, secretly. . . . Secretly! So *he* thought. The summer passed; the Count ceased to have need of outside help. Potugin lost sight of Irena, but he could not forget her. Some three years later he quite unexpectedly received an invitation from a certain lady of medium quality, whom he knew only slightly. At first this lady had difficulty in saying what she had in mind, but after making him swear to keep everything he heard a profound secret, she proposed to him that — he should marry a certain young lady who occupied a prominent position in the world and for whom marriage had become a necessity. The lady hardly dared to hint at the chief figure in the drama, and she at once promised him money — much money. Potugin did not take offense, his astonishment mastered his feeling of indignation, but, needless to say, he flatly refused. Then the lady handed him a note addressed to him — from Irena. "You are a noble and kind man," she wrote, "and I know you will do anything for me; I ask this sacrifice of you. You will save a creature who is dear to me. Saving her, you will save me too. . . . Don't ask: 'How?' I would not venture to address myself to anyone else with such a request, but to you I stretch out my hand and say: 'Do this for me.'" Potugin thought it over, and said that for Irena Pavlovna he was certainly ready to do a great deal, but he would like to hear her ask him with her own lips. The interview took place that same evening; it did not last long, and no one else knew of it except the lady who acted as intermediary. Irena was now no longer living with Count Reizenbach.

"Why did you think of me in particular?" Potugin asked her. She was about to expatiate on his good qualities; but she suddenly stopped.

"No," she said, "I must speak the truth to you. I knew, I know, that you love me; and that is why I ventured . . ." And she told him everything.

Eliza Belskaya was an orphan; her relations disliked her and hoped to gain her inheritance . . . she was faced with ruin. In saving her, Irena was in reality doing a service to the one who had been the cause of it all, and who now himself had become very dear to her, to Irena. . . . Potugin, not saying a word, gazed long at Irena, and agreed. She burst into tears and, streaming with tears, flung herself round his neck. He, too, broke into tears; but their tears were for different reasons. Now everything was prepared for a secret marriage, a powerful hand removed all the obstacles. . . . But an illness supervened . . . and during it a daughter was born, and during it the mother — took poison. What was to be done with the child? From the same hands, from the hands of Irena, Potugin took her into his charge.

A terrible, dark story. . . . Pass on, reader, pass on!

More than an hour elapsed before Litvinov could bring himself to return to his hotel. He was quite close to it when he suddenly heard steps behind him. It seemed that someone was persistently following him, walking more quickly when he accelerated his pace. As he passed beneath a street lamp he looked back and recognized General Ratmirov. In a white cravat and a dandyish unbuttoned topcoat, with a string of stars and crosses on a gold chain dangling from the buttonhole of his frock coat, the general was returning from the dinner, alone. His gaze, directly and arrogantly fixed on Litvinov, expressed such contempt and such hatred, all his bearing conveyed such a resolute challenge, that Litvinov considered it his duty to turn, reluctantly, to meet him, to turn and face a "scene." But as the general drew level with Litvinov his face changed in a moment: he adopted his customary look of playful elegance, and one hand in a pale lilac glove raised his gleaming hat high above his head. Litvinov silently raised his hat, and each went his way.

"He must have noticed something," Litvinov thought. "If it had been someone else," the general thought.

Smoke

Tatiana was playing piquet with her aunt when Litvinov entered their room.

"But I must say you're a fine specimen, my boy!" Kapitolina Markovna exclaimed, flinging her cards on the table. "Our very first day, and you vanish for the whole evening! We waited for you, and waited, we swore and swore — "

"I didn't say anything, aunt," Tatiana remarked.

"Well, we all know your meekness! Shame on you, my dear sir, and a fiancé, too!"

Litvinov awkwardly made his apologies and sat down at the table.

"Why have you stopped playing?" he asked after a brief silence.

"There's a fine thing! She and I are playing cards because we're bored, because we've nothing else to do. . . . But now you've arrived."

"If you would like to listen to the evening music," he said, "I will take you with the greatest of pleasure."

Kapitolina Markovna looked at her niece.

"If you'd like to go, auntie, I'm ready," Tatiana said. "But wouldn't it be better to stay at home?"

"That's an idea! We'll drink tea in our fashion, Moscow fashion, with a samovar; and we'll have a good talk. We haven't had a proper chat yet."

Litvinov gave orders for tea to be brought, but the good talk failed to develop. He felt a continual pricking of conscience; no matter what he said, he felt continually that he was playing the hypocrite and that Tatiana guessed. Yet no change was to be observed in her; she behaved just as unconstrainedly . . . only, not once did her gaze rest on Litvinov; it rather seemed to slip over him condescendingly and timorously. And she was paler than usual.

Kapitolina Markovna asked her if her head ached.

At first she was about to reply that it did not, but, thinking better of it, she said: "Yes, a little."

"It's the journey," Litvinov remarked, and he even went red with shame.

"The journey," Tatiana repeated, and her gaze again slipped over him.

"You must have a rest, Tania dear."

"In any case, I'll be going to bed soon, auntie."

On the table lay a copy of the *Guide des voyageurs*. Litvinov began to read aloud a description of the environs of Baden.

"That's all very well," Kapitolina Markovna interrupted him, "but one thing we mustn't forget. They say that linen is very cheap here, and it would be as well to buy some for the dowry."

Tatiana looked down.

"We've plenty of time, auntie. You never think of yourself; but you simply must get yourself a dress. Look what fine clothes everybody wears here."

"Oh, my soul, why should I? I'm not one of the smart set. That would be all right if I were as beautiful as that acquaintance of yours, Grigory Mikhailich — what is her name?"

"What acquaintance?"

"Why, the one we met today."

"Ah, that one!" Litvinov said with hypocritical indifference, and he again felt loathing and shame for himself. "No!" he thought; "it is impossible to go on like this."

He was sitting close to his fiancée; and only a few inches away from her, in his side pocket, was Irena's handkerchief.

Kapitolina Markovna went into the other room for a minute.

"Tania —" he said with an effort. It was the first time he had used that affectionate name all day.

She turned to him.

"I — have something very important to say to you."

"Ah! Have you really? When? Now?"

"No, tomorrow."

"Ah! Tomorrow. Well, all right."

An infinite pity momentarily filled his soul. He took Tatiana's hand and kissed it humbly, like a guilty child. Her heart stood still for a moment, and that kiss did not give her any joy.

That night, about two o'clock, Kapitolina Markovna, who was sleeping in the same room as her niece, suddenly raised her head and listened.

"Tania!" she called, "are you crying?"

Tatiana did not answer at once.

"No, auntie," her gentle voice called back at last. "I've got a touch of catarrh."

"Why did I say that to her?" Litvinov thought next morning as he sat in his room, by the window. He shrugged his shoulders irritably; he had made that remark to Tatiana precisely in order to cut off all his ways of retreat. On the windowsill lay a note from Irena: she summoned him to visit her at twelve o'clock. Potugin's words came to his mind again and again; they sounded like an ominous, though feeble, underground rumble. He grew angry, but simply could not rid himself of them. Someone knocked at the door.

"*Wer da?*" Litvinov asked.

"Ah, so you're at home! Open the door!" he heard Bindasov's deep, hoarse voice.

The door handle was shaken.

Litvinov went pale with fury.

"I'm not at home," he said sharply.

"What d'you mean, not at home? What sort of game is this?"

"I tell you I'm not at home; clear off!"

"What a pleasant reception! And I'd come to borrow a little money," Bindasov snorted.

None the less he departed, clattering his heels as usual.

Litvinov all but rushed out after him, so strong was his desire to twist the brazen-faced fellow's neck. The events of the last few days had played on his nerves; a little more and he would burst into tears. He drank a glass of cold water, locked all the drawers of the furniture without knowing why, and went to see Tatiana.

He found her alone. Kapitolina Markovna had gone out to do some shopping. Tatiana was sitting on the sofa and holding a book in both hands; she was not reading it, and hardly even knew what it was about. She did not stir, but her heart beat violently in her breast, and the white collar round her neck quivered visibly and measuredly.

Litvinov was embarrassed. . . . None the less he sat down beside her, greeted her, and smiled; and she silently smiled back at him. She had inclined her head to him when he entered, nodding politely, but not with warmth — and had not looked at him. He held out his hand to her; she gave him her chilly fingers, at once released them, and turned back to her book. Litvinov felt that to begin the conversation with trivialities would only be insulting her. She, as usual, was demanding nothing, but all her attitude was saying: "I am waiting, I am waiting. . . ." He must keep his promise. But — though he had thought of nothing else almost all night — he had not prepared even the first, preliminary remarks and had no idea at all how to break this cruel silence.

"Tania," he began at last, "I told you yesterday that I have something important to tell you" (when alone with her at Dresden he had begun to talk to her in the second person singular, but now such intimacy was quite unthinkable). "I am ready, only I ask you in advance not to make a scene and to rest assured that my feelings for you — "

He stopped. His breath failed him. Even now she did not stir and did not look at him; she only gripped the book more firmly than before.

"Between us," he went on without finishing the previous sentence, "between us there has always been complete frankness. I respect you too much to palter with you. I want to prove to you that I can appreciate the loftiness and freedom of your soul, and although I — although of course — "

"Grigory Mikhailich," Tatiana began in an even voice, and all her face was suffused with a deathly pallor. "I will come to your aid. You have ceased to love me, and you don't know how to tell me so."

He involuntarily started.

"But why — ?" he said almost inaudibly, "how could you think — ? I really don't understand — "

"Well, isn't it true? Isn't it true? Tell me! Tell me!"

She turned all her body toward him; her face, with the hair flung back, drew near to his face, and her eyes, which for so long had not looked at him, were now fixed on his eyes.

"Isn't it true?" she repeated.

He did not say a word, did not utter a sound. He could not have lied at that moment, even if he had known that she would believe him and that his lie would save her. He was not even able to endure her gaze. He did not say a word, but now she no longer had need of an answer. She read that answer in his very silence, in those guilty, downcast eyes — and she threw herself back and dropped the book. . . . Even until that moment she had had doubts, and Litvinov realized that; he realized that she had still doubted, and realized how infamous, how utterly infamous was all that he had done!

He flung himself down on his knees before her.

"Tania," he exclaimed, "if only you knew how hard it is for me to see you in this situation, how terrible it is for me to think that it is I—I! My heart is torn asunder; I don't recognize myself. I have lost myself and you, and all. . . . Everything has been shattered, Tania, everything! Could I ever have expected that I—I would strike such a blow at you, my best friend, my guardian angel? . . . Could I ever have expected that you and I would see each other in such circumstances, would spend together such a day as was yesterday?"

Tatiana tried to rise and leave the room. He restrained her by the hem of her dress.

"No, listen to me just one more minute. See, I am down on my knees before you. But it is not for pardon that I have come to ask—you cannot and you should not pardon me. I have come to tell you that your friend is lost, that he is falling into an abyss and does not wish to drag you down with him. . . . But as for saving me—no, not even you can save me. I myself would thrust you away. . . . I am lost, I am lost irrevocably."

She gazed at him.

"You are lost?" she said, as though she did not fully understand him. "You are lost?"

"Yes, Tania, I am lost. All the past, everything that is precious, everything for which I have lived hitherto, is lost to me. Everything is destroyed, everything is wrested from me, and I know not what awaits me in the future. You have just said that I have ceased to love you. . . . No, Tania, I have not ceased to love you; but another, a terrible, irresistible feeling has come upon, has come over me. I resisted as long as I could. . . ."

Tatiana rose; her brows drew together; her pale face darkened. Litvinov also got up.

"You have fallen in love with another woman," she began, "and I guess who it is. We met her yesterday, didn't we? . . . Well, then! I know what is left for me to do now. As you yourself say that this feeling in you is immutable." (She paused for a moment: perhaps she still hoped that he would not let that last word pass without protest; but he said nothing.) "It remains for me to return you—your word."

He bowed his head, as though humbly receiving a well-deserved blow.

"You have every right to be indignant with me," he said. "You have every right to reproach me with pusillanimity — with deceit."

She looked at him again.

"I have not reproached you, Litvinov, I do not accuse you. I agree with you: the most bitter truth is better than what occurred yesterday. What sort of life would ours be now!"

"What sort of life will mine be now!" came a mournful response in Litvinov's soul.

Tatiana went toward the door of the bedroom.

"I ask you to leave me alone for a little while, Grigory Mikhailich. We shall see each other again, we shall talk more about it. It has all been so unexpected. I must gather a little strength . . . leave me . . . spare my pride. We shall see each other again."

And, having said these words, she swiftly retreated and locked the door behind her.

He went out into the street like a man in a fog, as though stunned; an obscure and oppressive feeling was implanted in the very depths of his heart; a man who has committed a murder must feel a similar sensation. Yet at the same time he felt lighter, as though he had at last thrown off a hateful burden. Tatiana's magnanimity had shattered him, he was vividly conscious of all he had lost . . . and what of it? His contrition was mingled with chagrin; he was passionately drawn to Irena, as to his sole remaining refuge — and he was annoyed with her. For some time past and with every day his feelings had grown continually stronger and more confused; this confusion tormented, irritated him; in this chaos he was lost. He desired just one thing: to come out at last on a road, no matter what; anything rather than go on circling in this meaningless twilight. Positive minds like Litvinov's should not be carried away by passion; it violates the very meaning of their life. . . . But nature does not concern herself with logic, with our human logic; she has her own, which we do not understand and do not recognize until it passes over us, like a wheel.

When he parted from Tatiana, Litvinov had only one thought in mind: to see Irena; and he went to her hotel. But the general was at home—so, at least, the porter told him—and he did not want to go up, did not feel capable of dissimulation; and he wandered off to the Konversationshaus. On this occasion Litvinov's inability to dissemble was felt personally by both Voroshilov and Pishchalkin, who happened to fall in with him; in an outburst of candor he told the one that he was as empty as a drum, the other that he bored him stiff. It was a good thing that Bindasov did not turn up, for then there would certainly have been a *"grosser Skandal!"* Both the young men were dumbfounded; Voroshilov even asked himself whether an officer's honor did not call for satisfaction—but, like Gogol's Lieutenant Pirogov, he appeased himself with *Butterbrot* in a café. In the distance Litvinov saw Kapitolina Markovna fussily running in her motley mantle from shop to shop. . . . He felt conscience-stricken at the sight of the good, funny, noble old lady. Then he remembered Potugin and yesterday's conversation. . . . But now something breathed on him, something intangible, yet indubitable; the waft could not have been more elusive if it had come from a falling shadow, yet he felt at once that it was Irena approaching. In very deed, she appeared a few paces away, arm in arm with another lady; their eyes met immediately. She must have noticed something unusual in Litvinov's expression: she halted before a shop selling innumerable tiny wooden clocks of Black Forest manufacture and summoned him to her with a movement of the head. Pointing to one of these little clocks, inviting him to admire the attractive clockface with a painted cuckoo above it, she said, not in a whisper, but in her usual voice, as though continuing a phrase she had begun—it was less likely to attract others' attention:

"Come in an hour's time, I shall be at home alone."

But now the well-known ladies' man M'sieur Verdier flew up to her and went into raptures over the *feuille morte* color of her gown, and her low-fitting Spanish hat, drawn right over her brows. . . . Litvinov vanished in the crowd.

21

"Grigory," Irena said to him two hours later as she sat beside him on the sofa with both her hands on his shoulder, "what is the matter with you? Tell me now, quickly, while we're alone."

"The matter with me?" Litvinov said. "I am happy, happy, that is what is the matter with me."

She looked down, smiled, and sighed.

"That is not an answer to my question, my dear."

He was lost in thought.

"Well, then, you must know—since you absolutely demand it" (she opened her eyes wide and started back a little), "today I have told my fiancée everything."

"Everything? Did you mention my name?"

Litvinov was decidedly astonished.

"Irena, for goodness' sake, how could you ever think that I—"

"Well, forgive me—forgive me. But what did you say?"

"I told her I didn't love her any more."

"Did she ask why?"

"I did not conceal from her that I had fallen in love with another woman and that we must part."

"Well—and what did she say? Did she agree?"

"Ah, Irena! What a wonderful woman she is! She is all self-sacrifice, all magnanimity!"

"I believe it, I believe it. . . . In any case, there was nothing else she could do."

"And not a single reproach, not a single bitter word did she say to me, to a man who has spoiled all her life, deceived her, deserted her pitilessly. . . ."

Irena examined her nails.

"Tell me, Grigory—did she love you?"

"Yes, Irena, she loved me."

She was silent for a moment, adjusting her dress.

"I admit," she began, "that I don't quite understand why you took it into your head to tell her."

"You don't understand why, Irena? Surely you didn't want me to lie, to dissemble to her, to that pure soul? Or did you suppose—"

"I didn't suppose anything," she interrupted. "I have to admit I thought little about her—I haven't the capacity to think of two people at once."

"That is, you mean to say—"

"Well, and what next? Is she going away, this pure soul?" she interrupted him a second time.

"I haven't the least idea," he replied. "I have to see her again. But she will not remain here."

"Ah! Pleasant journey!"

"No, she will not remain. For that matter, I, too, am not thinking of her now. I am thinking of what *you* said to me, of what *you* promised me."

Irena looked at him with knitted brows.

"Ingrate! Aren't you satisfied yet?"

"No, Irena, I am not satisfied. You have made me happy, but I am not satisfied, and you understand why."

"You mean, I —"

"Yes, you understand why. Remember your words, remember what you wrote to me. I cannot share you with another; no, no, I cannot agree to the miserable role of a secret lover. I have thrown not only my own life, but another life, too, at your feet, remorselessly and irrevocably. But on the other hand I believe, I am firmly convinced, that you, too, will keep your promise and unite your fate with me forever. . . ."

"You want me to run away with you? I am ready" (he exultantly pressed his lips to her hands), "I am ready, I do not go back on my word. But have you yourself thought about the difficulties — have you prepared the means?"

"I? I haven't had time to think of anything yet, or to prepare anything. But say only the word, give me permission to act, and before a month has passed —"

"A month! In a fortnight we are traveling to Italy."

"Even a fortnight is sufficient for me. Oh, Irena! You seem to be receiving my proposal coldly, perhaps to you it seems only a dream. But I am not a boy, I am not accustomed to comforting myself with dreams; I know what a terrible step it is, I know what responsibility I am taking on myself. But I do not see any other way out. Think: to do this I have to sever all connections with the past forever, so that I shall not become notorious as a contemptible liar in the eyes of that girl whom I have sacrificed to you!"

Irena abruptly drew herself up, and her eyes began to glitter.

"Well, you must forgive me, Grigory Mikhailich! If I make the decision, if I run away, then I run away with a man who has done this for me, just for me, and not in order to prevent

131

his lowering himself in the opinion of a phlegmatic young lady who hasn't blood, but water and milk, *du lait coupé*, in her veins! And one other thing I tell you: I have to confess this is the first time I have been told that the man whom I favor is worthy of commiseration, is playing a miserable role. I know a still more miserable role: the role of a man who does not know what is occurring in his own soul!"

Litvinov drew himself up in his turn.

"Irena —" he began.

But she suddenly pressed both her palms to her brow and, vehemently flinging herself on his chest, embraced him with unwomanly strength.

"Forgive me, forgive me," she said in a quivering voice, "forgive me, Grigory! You see how spoilt I am, how loathsome, how jealous, how evil! You see how much I need your help, your indulgence! Yes, save me, wrest me out of this abyss, before I have completely perished! Yes, let us flee, let us flee from these people, from this world, into some distant, beautiful, free country! Maybe your Irena will at last become more worthy of those sacrifices you are making for her! Don't be angry with me, forgive me, my dear — and know that I will do all you order, I will go wherever you lead me!"

Litvinov's heart leaped up. She clung to him more strongly than ever with all her young and supple body. He bent over her perfumed, disordered hair, and in his intoxication of gratitude and exultation he hardly dared to caress it with his hand, hardly touched it with his lips.

"Irena, Irena," he declared, "my angel . . ."

She suddenly raised her head and listened. . . .

"That's my husband's steps — he's gone into his room," she whispered. She promptly moved away and seated herself in a chair. Litvinov was about to rise. "But where are you going?" she continued in the same whisper. "Stay! As it is, he suspects you. Or are you afraid of him?" She did not take her eyes off the door. "Yes, it is he; he will be coming in here in a minute. Tell me some story, be talking to me." Litvinov could not think of anything at once and remained silent. "You're not going to the theater tomorrow, are you?" she said aloud. "They're playing *Le Verre d'eau*; it's an old-fashioned play, and Plessis grimaces terribly. . . . It's just as though we're in a fever," she added, lowering her voice. "We can't go on like this; we must think it over thoroughly. I must warn you that all my money is in his hands; *mais j'ai mes bijoux*. We'll go to Spain, would you like that?" She raised her voice again. "Why do actresses always get so stout? Look at Madeleine Brohan, for instance. . . . Oh, do say something, don't sit there silent. My head is swimming. But you must not have any doubt of me. . . . I shall let you know when to come tomorrow. Only there was no need for you to have told that young lady — Ah, *mais c'est charmant!*" she exclaimed suddenly and, laughing nervously, tore the flounce of her dress.

"May I come in?" Ratmirov asked from the other room.

"Of course — of course."

The door opened, and the general appeared on the threshold. He frowned when he saw Litvinov, but he bowed to him; in other words, he swayed the upper part of his body.

"I didn't know you had a visitor," he said. "*Je vous demande pardon de mon indiscrétion.* So you're still finding amusement in Baden, M'sieur — Litvinov?"

Ratmirov always pronounced Litvinov's name with a slight pause, as though he always forgot, but immediately recalled it. He thought that this trick, and that of exaggeratedly raising his hat on meeting Litvinov, would sting him.

"I am not bored here, *M'sieur le général.*"

"Really? But I'm terribly tired of Baden. We're leaving here soon, aren't we, Irena Pavlovna? *Assez de Bade comme ça.* By the way, I won five hundred francs for you today."

Irena coquettishly held out her hand.

"Then where is it? Give it to me. For pin-money."

"It's mine, it's mine. . . . But are you going, M'sieur — Litvinov?"

"Yes, I am going, as you can see."

Ratmirov again swayed his body.

"To our next pleasant meeting!"

"Good-by, Grigory Mikhailich," Irena said. "But I shall keep my promise."

"What promise? May I be so inquisitive?" her husband asked. She smiled.

"No, it's something — between us. *C'est à propos du voyage — où il vous plaira.* Do you know Stahl's compositions?"

"Ah! Of course, of course, I know them. Very nice drawings."

Ratmirov seemed to be on good terms with his wife: he spoke to her in the second person singular.

22

"It is better not to think, really it is!" Litvinov assured himself as he strode along the street and felt that a tumult was again rising within him. "The question's decided. She will keep her promise, and now all I have to do is to take all the necessary steps. . . . But she seems to have doubts. . . ." He shook his head. Even to himself his own intentions were presented in a strange light; they looked strained and improbable. It is impossible to worry for long over one and the same thought: it gradually shifts its position, like the little pieces of glass in a kaleidoscope; as you watch, the pictures you see change completely. Litvinov was mastered by a feeling of profound weariness. . . . If he could only rest for a little hour. . . . But Tania? He shook himself and, no longer stopping to deliberate, humbly wandered home, with the sole thought that today he was being tossed like a ball from one to the other. . . . No matter; he must put an end to it. He returned to the hotel and just as humbly, almost senselessly, without hesitation or delay, went to Tatiana.

Kapitolina Markovna came forward to meet him. As soon as he looked at her he realized that she knew everything: the poor old maid's eyes were swollen with tears, and her reddened face, framed in fluffy white hair, expressed fear and anxious indignation, grief, and unbounded astonishment. She was on the point of rushing to him, but she stopped at once and, biting her quivering lips, looked at him as though she wanted to plead with him, and kill him, and assure herself that it was all a dream, a lunacy, an impossible business, wasn't it?

"And so you — you've come, you've come," she began. . . . That same moment the door from the next room was flung wide open, and Tatiana, translucently pale, but calm, entered with a light step.

She quietly put one arm round her aunt and seated her beside herself.

"And you sit down too, Grigory Mikhailich," she said to Litvinov, who had remained standing at the door, as though lost. "I am very glad to have this further meeting with you. I have told auntie your decision, our joint decision; she completely shares it and approves it. . . . Without mutual love there cannot be happiness; mutual respect alone is insufficient" (at the word "respect" Litvinov involuntarily cast down his eyes), "and it is better to part earlier than to repent later. Isn't that so, auntie?"

"Yes, of course," Kapitolina Markovna began; "of course, my dear Tania, anyone who does not know how to appreciate you — who has decided — "

"Auntie, auntie," Tatiana interrupted her, "remember what you promised me. You yourself have always told me: 'the truth, Tatiana, the truth above all — and freedom.' Well, but the truth isn't always pleasant, nor is freedom; otherwise what merit would we possess?"

She gently kissed Kapitolina Markovna on her white hair and, turning to Litvinov, continued:

"Auntie and I have decided to leave Baden — I think it will be easier so for all of us."

"When are you thinking of going?" he asked thickly. He recalled that Irena had only recently used these very same words.

Kapitolina Markovna was about to speak first, but Tatiana restrained her with a gentle touch on the shoulder.

"Probably soon, very soon."

"And may I ask where you are intending to go?" he said in the same tone.

"First to Dresden, and then probably to Russia."

"But what do you need to know for now, Grigory Mikhailich?" Kapitolina Markovna exclaimed.

"Auntie, auntie!" Tatiana again intervened. There was a brief silence.

"Tatiana Petrovna," he began, "you can understand what painfully difficult and mournful feelings I must be experiencing at this moment. . . ."

Tatiana rose.

"Grigory Mikhailich," she said, "don't let us talk about that. Please! I ask you, if not for your sake, then for mine. I knew you before yesterday, and I can well imagine what you must be feeling now. But what is the point of talking, why make things worse?" (She stopped; it was obvious that she was waiting to master the agitation rising within her, to choke back the tears starting to her eyes; and she succeeded.) "Why aggravate a wound that cannot be healed? Let us leave it to time. But now I have one request of you, Grigory Mikhailich; if you will be so good, I'll give you a letter in a moment. Take this letter to the post yourself, it is rather important, and auntie and I haven't the time now. . . . I shall be very grateful to you. Wait just a minute —I'll be back."

At the door Tatiana turned and looked anxiously at Kapitolina Markovna; but her aunt was sitting so seriously and sedately, with such a stern expression in her knitted brows and tightly pressed lips, that she only nodded to her and went out.

The door had hardly closed behind her, however, when all the look of seriousness and sternness vanished from Kapitolina Markovna's face. She rose, ran across to Litvinov on tiptoe, and, crouching down and trying to look into his eyes, began to speak in a quivering, tearful whisper.

"My God!" she said, "Grigory Mikhailich, what is this? Surely it's a dream? *You* are rejecting Tatiana, you have ceased to love her, you are betraying your word! You are doing this, Grigory Mikhailich, you, in whom we all put our hopes as in a rock! You? You? You? You, our dear Grigory? . . ." She paused. "Why, you'll kill her, Grigory Mikhailich," she continued without waiting for an answer, and the tears rolled in tiny drops down her cheeks. "Don't take any notice of the fact that she is putting a good face on it; you know her character, she never complains. She is not sparing herself, and so others should spare her! She has just been telling me: 'Auntie, we must preserve our dignity!' But what has dignity to do with it when I know she will die, will die. . . ." Tatiana made a noise with a chair in the other room. "Yes, I know she will die," the old woman hurried on even more quietly. "And what could have happened? Someone has bewitched you, surely? Only the other day you were writing her the tenderest of letters, weren't you? And, in the last resort, can an honest man behave like this? You know I am a woman without any prejudices, *un esprit fort*, and I have given Tania a similar upbringing; she, too, has a free soul. . . ."

"Auntie!" Tatiana's voice sounded from the other room.

"But one's word of honor — that is a duty, Grigory Mikhailich. Especially for people with your, with our rules of conduct! If we are not going to recognize our duty, what is left to us? That may not be repudiated just out of personal caprice, without any regard for what it means to someone else! It is disgraceful — yes, it is a crime. What sort of freedom is that?"

"Auntie, come here, please," they heard again.

"One minute, my dear, one minute." Kapitolina Markovna seized Litvinov by the hand. "I see you are angry, Grigory Mikhailich." ("I? I angry!" he wanted to exclaim, but he was tongue-tied.) "I don't want to make you angry, oh, my goodness, no! How could I? On the contrary, I want to ask you: come to your senses while there is still time, don't ruin her, don't ruin your own happiness, she will still believe in you. Grigory dear, she will believe you, nothing is lost yet; you see, she loves you as no one else ever will love you! Leave this hateful Baden-Baden, we'll go away together; only free yourself of this magic, and, above all, have pity, have pity. . . ."

"Now, auntie," Tatiana called with a hint of impatience in her tone.

But Kapitolina Markovna did not hear her.

"Say only yes," she said to Litvinov, "and I'll manage the rest. . . . Well then, at least nod your head! Nod just one little once, like this!"

It seems that Litvinov would gladly have died at that moment, but he did not utter the word "yes," nor did he nod his head.

Tatiana appeared, with the letter in her hand. Kapitolina Markovna at once started back from Litvinov and, turning her face away, bent low over the table as though examining the accounts and papers lying on it.

Tatiana went to Litvinov.

"Here is the letter I mentioned to you," she said. "You will go to the post at once, won't you?"

He raised his eyes. Before him, in very deed, stood his judge. Tatiana seemed taller, more harmoniously proportioned; the face that had beamed with unusual beauty was set majestically, statuesquely; her breast did not stir, and her gown, of one color and as close-fitting as a chiton, fell in straight, long, marble folds to her feet, which it concealed. She gazed directly before her, at Litvinov alone; and even her gaze, level and cold, was the gaze of a statue. In it he read his sentence. He bowed, took the letter from the hand rigidly extended toward him, and left without saying a word.

Kapitolina Markovna rushed to Tatiana, but she avoided her

embrace and lowered her eyes; a flush spread over her face, and with the words: "Well, now quickly!" she returned to the bedroom. Kapitolina Markovna followed her, hanging her head.

The letter that Tatiana had entrusted to Litvinov was addressed to one of her Dresden friends, a German woman who had small furnished apartments to let. He dropped the letter in the box, and had the feeling that with that little scrap of paper he had dropped all his past, all his life, into a grave. He walked out of the town and wandered a long time over the narrow tracks running between the vineyards; as though it were the buzzing of an importunate summer fly, he could not rid himself of a constant feeling of self-contempt: he had played a very unenviable role in this last meeting. . . .

But when he returned to the hotel and, some little time later, inquired after his ladies, he was informed that the moment he went out they gave orders for a carriage to take them to the station and left by the post train for an unknown destination. Their things had been packed and their accounts paid since morning. It was obvious that Tatiana had asked Litvinov to take the letter to the post in order to get rid of him. He tried to find out from the porter whether the ladies had left any note for him, but the man replied in the negative and was even astonished; it was obvious that he, too, thought there was something strange and suspicious in this sudden departure from a suite taken for a week. Litvinov turned his back on the man and locked himself in his room.

He did not leave it till the following day. A large part of the night he spent at his table, writing and tearing up what he wrote. . . . Dawn was coming when he finished his labor: it was a letter to Irena.

23

Here is what he wrote in his letter to Irena:

My fiancée left yesterday; we shall never see her again. . . . I don't even know for certain where she will reside. With her she has taken all that hitherto has seemed desirable and precious to me; all my assumptions, my plans, my intentions have vanished with her; even my labors have gone by the board, my prolonged work has been reduced to nothingness, all my studies are without sense and purpose; that is dead; since yesterday my I, my former I, is dead and buried. I clearly feel that, see it, know it. . . . And I do not regret it in the least. Not for the sake of complaining have I written of this to you. . . . Is it for me to complain when you love me, Irena? I only wanted to tell you that of all that dead past, of all those enterprises and hopes — turned to smoke and dust — just one has remained living and inviolable: my love for you. Apart from that love I have nothing and am left with nothing; to call it my sole treasure would be inadequate; I am entirely in this love, that love is all I; in it is my future, my calling, my holy of holies, my country! You know me, Irena, you know that all phrase-mongering is alien and repellent to me, and no matter how strong the words in which I attempt to express my feelings, you will not suspect their sincerity, you will not think them exaggerated. It is not a boy who is stammering unconsidered vows to you, in an outburst of momentary rapture, but a man tested by the years — who simply and straightforwardly, all but with horror, is expressing that which he has recognized to be the undoubted truth. Yes, your love has changed everything for me — everything, everything!

Judge for yourself; can I leave this everything in another man's hands? Can I allow him to have the disposal of you? You, you will belong to him; all my being, the blood of my heart will belong to him — but I myself — where am I, what am I? To one side, a spectator — a spectator of my own life! No, that is impossible, impossible! To share, to share clandestinely in something without which my life has no reason for existence, or even possibility of existence — that is falsehood and death.

I know what a great sacrifice I am demanding of you, without any right to do so; and besides, what can confer any right to a sacrifice? But not out of egotism am I acting so: it would be easier and lighter for an egotist not to raise this question at all. Yes, my demands are heavy, and I shall not be surprised if they frighten you. You hate the people with whom you have to live, you are oppressed by society; but have you strength enough to throw aside that society, to trample on the crown with which it has crowned you, to arouse social opinion, the opinion of those hateful people, against you? Question yourself, Irena; do not undertake a burden you cannot carry. I do not want to reproach you, but remember: already once you have been unable to resist the temptation. I can give you so little in exchange for what you will lose! So listen to my final words: if you do not feel capable even tomorrow, even today, of leaving all and following me — you see how boldly I speak, how I do not spare myself — if you are frightened by the unknown of the future, by alienation, and loneliness, and human censure, if, in a word, you do not have confidence in yourself: then tell me so frankly and without procrastination, and I will go. I shall go with tormented soul, but I shall bless you for your truth. But if you, my beautiful, radiant empress, have really fallen in love with such a petty and obscure man as I, and are really ready to share his destiny — well, then give me your hand, and we shall set out together on our difficult road! Only, do realize that my decision is beyond doubt: all or nothing! That is mad — but I can do no other; I cannot, Irena! I love you too much.

Your
G. L.

Litvinov himself was not much pleased with this letter; it did not quite accurately and exactly express what he wanted to say; clumsy expressions, bombast, bookish turns had found their way into it, and of course it was no better than many other letters that he had torn up. But it happened to be the last he wrote, and in any case the main thing was said; and tired, tormented as he was, he did not feel capable of writing anything more. In addition, he did not possess the gift of expounding his thoughts in a literary fashion, and, as always in such cases, he fussed over every syllable. His very first letter was probably the best of all: it poured more fervently from his heart. Whether this was so or not, Litvinov sent his missive to Irena.

She replied in a brief note:

Come to me today [she wrote]; *he will be away all day. Your letter has greatly agitated me. I think and think — and my head swims with thoughts. Things are very difficult for me, but you love me, and I am happy. Come.*

Your
I.

She was sitting in her room when Litvinov entered. He was shown in by the same thirteen-year-old girl who had watched for him at the stairs on a previous occasion. On the table before Irena lay an open semicircular box containing lace; with one hand she was abstractedly turning the lace over; in the other she held his letter. She had only just ceased weeping: her eyelashes were wet and her eyelids swollen; on her cheeks were the traces of unwiped tears. He halted at the door; she did not notice his arrival.

"Are you crying?" he said in astonishment.

She started, passed her hand over her hair, and smiled.

"Why are you crying?" he repeated. She silently pointed to his letter. "Is that how it —" he said slowly.

"Come here and sit down," she said; "give me your hand. Why, yes, I have been crying. Why are you surprised? Is *this* so easy?" She again pointed to the letter.

Litvinov sat down.

"I know that it is not easy, Irena. I myself said so in my letter. . . . I understand your position. But if you believe in the meaning of your love for me, if my words have convinced you, you must also understand what I feel now at the sight of your tears. I have come like a man awaiting sentence, and I wait: what shall I be told? Death or life? Your answer decides all. Only don't look at me with such eyes. They remind me of your former, Moscow eyes."

She suddenly flushed and turned away, as though she herself felt something awkward in her gaze.

"What made you say that, Grigory? Aren't you ashamed? You wish to know my answer — but can you have any doubt of it? You are embarrassed by my tears — but you haven't understood them. Your letter, my friend, sent me into a reverie. In it you write that my love for you has changed everything, that even your former studies must now remain without application; but I ask myself, can a man live only by love? Won't it bore him in the end, won't he desire activity, and won't he upbraid the thing that has lured him away from it? That is the thought that frightens me, that is what I am afraid of, and not what you assumed."

Litvinov looked at her closely, and Irena looked closely at him, as though each of them wanted to penetrate farther and more deeply into the soul of the other, farther and more deeply than can be achieved or than can be revealed by words.

"There is no reason for you to be afraid of that," he began; "I must have expressed myself stupidly. Boredom? Inactivity? In face of the new powers that your love gives me? Oh, Irena, believe me, in your love is all my world, and I myself cannot yet foresee all that may develop out of it!"

She grew thoughtful.

"And where shall we go?" she whispered.

"Where? We can talk about that later. But so — so you agree, you agree, Irena?"

She gazed at him. "And you will be happy, Grigory?"

"Oh, Irena!"

"You will never regret anything? Never?"

She bent over the box of laces and began to turn them over again.

"Don't be angry with me, my dear, for occupying myself with this rubbish at such a moment. I have to go to a ball a certain lady is giving. I have been sent these pieces of rag, and I must choose today. Ah, it is terribly hard for me!" she suddenly exclaimed, and she set her face against the edge of the box. The tears once more began to well from her eyes. . . . She turned away; otherwise the tears might have fallen on the lace.

"Irena, you're crying again," he said anxiously.

"Why yes, again," Irena replied. "Ah, Grigory, don't torture me, don't torture yourself! . . . We shall be free! What matters it that I am crying! Why, I myself, do I understand why I am crying? You know, you have heard my decision, you are sure that it will not be changed, that I agree to — how did you put it? — to all or nothing. . . . What else do you want? We shall be free! What is the point of these mutual chains? You and I are one now, you love me, I love you; have we nothing else to do but cross-examine each other for our opinions? Look at me; I didn't want to vaunt myself before you; not by a single word have I hinted that perhaps it is not so easy for me to trample on my duties as a wife . . . and I do not delude myself, I know that I am a criminal, and that *he* would be entitled to kill me. Well, and what of it? We shall be free, say I. Today is ours, all eternity is ours."

She rose from her chair and looked Litvinov up and down, faintly smiling and narrowing her eyes, and with her arm, bare to the elbow, brushing back from her face a long tress on which two or three tears were glittering. A rich lace neckerchief slipped from the table and fell to the floor, beneath her feet. She scornfully trod on it.

"Or do I not please you today? Have I grown more ugly since yesterday? Tell me, have you often seen a more beautiful hand? And this hair? Tell me, do you love me?"

She caught him with both hands, pressed his head to her breast; her comb jingled and dropped out, and her falling hair enveloped him in a perfumed and gentle wave.

24

Litvinov walked up and down his room in the hotel, his head sunk thoughtfully on his breast. Now he was faced with the transition from theory to practice, with seeking the means and ways for the flight, for removal to unknown countries. . . . But, strange to say, he was thinking not so much about these means and ways as whether the decision on which he had so obstinately insisted had actually, indubitably been taken. Was the final, irrevocable word spoken? But, after all, Irena had said to him at their parting: "Act, act, and when everything is ready, only let me know in advance." It was settled! Away with all doubts. . . . He must set to work. And he set to work — for the time being — to cogitate.

First and foremost the question of money. He found that in cash he had 1,328 guldens and 2,855 French francs; not a considerable sum, but sufficient for immediate needs. And when they arrived he must write at once to his father to send as much as possible; he could sell a forest, part of the estate. . . . But on what pretext? . . . Well, a pretext would be found. True, Irena had spoken of her *bijoux*, but they must not be taken into consideration at all; they would be of service, who knows, for a rainy day. In addition he had a good Genevan semi-chronometer, for which he could get — well, at least four hundred francs. He went to his banker and inquired in ambiguous terms whether it would be possible to have a loan, if necessary. But the bankers in Baden are a badgered and cautious lot, and in response to such circumlocutions they immediately adopt an evasive and drooping look, for all the world like a field flower that has had its stalk cut by a scythe; though some of them laugh bravely and boldly in your face, as if enjoying your innocent little jest. To his own shame, Litvinov even tried his fortune at roulette, and even (oh, ignominy!) put a taler on number thirty, which corresponded to his age. He did this with a view to enlarging and rounding off his capital; and certainly, though he did not enlarge it, he rounded it off by getting rid of the surplus twenty-eight guldens.

The second question, also of no little importance, was that of a passport. But for a woman a passport is not so obligatory, and there are countries where they are not required at all. Belgium, for instance, or England. In the last resort one can even get a non-Russian passport. He gave very serious thought to all this; his resolution was strong, and without the least vacillation. But meanwhile, against his will, despite his will, thoughts anything but serious, almost comic, emerged and tinged his meditations, just as though his very enterprise were a joking matter, and no one had ever run away with anybody in real life, but only in comedies and novels, and perhaps somewhere in the provinces, in some Chukhlom or Sizran province, where, according to one traveler's statements, the people even vomit to relieve their boredom. Here he called to mind how one of his friends, the retired cornet Batsov, carried off a merchant's daughter in a hired carriage with bells, first making the parents drunk, and his bride-to-be too; and how afterward it transpired that it was they who had tricked him and all but caught him into the bargain. Litvinov grew extremely angry with himself for having such inept reminiscences; and as he recalled Tatiana, her abrupt departure, all that sorrow and suffering and shame, he at once felt all too deeply that what he had brought about was by no means a joking matter, and that he was profoundly right when he told Irena that for his own very honor there was no other way out. . . . And again at her very name something corrosive momentarily, with a pleasurable pain, entwined itself round his heart and was still.

He heard the sound of horses' hoofs behind him. He stepped aside. . . . Irena, on horseback, overtook him; the corpulent general was riding with her. She recognized Litvinov, nodded to him, and, striking her horse's flank with the whip, put it into a gallop, then suddenly shook loose the reins and gave the animal its head. Her dark veil streamed in the wind. . . .

"*Pas si vite! Nom de Dieu! Pas si vite!*" the general shouted, and galloped after her.

Smoke

25

Next morning Litvinov had only just returned from his banker, with whom he had had another talk about the playful inconstancy of the Russian rate of exchange and the best means of sending money abroad, when the porter handed him a letter. He recognized Irena's writing and, not breaking the seal at once — for some reason an unpleasant presentiment awoke within him — he went to his room. This is what he read (the letter was written in French):

My dear! I have thought all night about your proposal. . . . I shall not try to temporize with you. You were frank with me, and I shall be frank. I cannot flee with you, I haven't the strength to do it. I feel how guilty I am in regard to you; my second guilt is even greater than my first — I despise myself, my pusillanimity, I burden myself with reproaches; but I cannot transform myself. In vain do I tell myself that I have destroyed your happiness, that you are now quite justified in regarding me as only a frivolous coquette, that I myself offered, I myself gave you solemn promises. . . . I am horrified, I hate myself; but I cannot behave otherwise; I cannot, I cannot. I do not wish to justify myself, I shall not try to persuade you that I was carried away — all that means just nothing. But I want to tell you and to repeat, and repeat yet again: I am yours, yours forever; dispose of me as you wish, when you wish; unconditionally and unreservedly I am yours. . . .
But to run away, to leave everything — No! No! No! I implored you to save me, I myself hoped to blot out everything, to burn up everything as in a fire. . . . But evidently there is no salvation for me; evidently the poison has penetrated too deeply into me; evidently one cannot breathe this air for many years without having to pay for it! I long hesitated whether to write this letter to you, it is terrible to think of the decision you may make, my only hope is in your love for me. But I considered that it would be dishonest on my part not to tell you the truth — the more so as you may already have begun to take the first steps toward the fulfillment of our plan. Ah! It was beautiful, but unrealizable. Oh, my friend, regard me as an empty, feeble woman, despise me, but do not abandon me, do not abandon your Irena! . . .

I am not strong enough to give up this world, but neither can I live in it without you. Soon we shall be returning to Petersburg; come there, live there, we shall find you an occupation, your past labors will not be wasted, you will find a useful application for them. . . . Only live near me, only love me as I am, with all my weaknesses and defects, and know that no other heart will ever be so tenderly devoted to you as the heart of your Irena. Come quickly to me, I shall not have a moment's rest until I see you.

Your, your, your
I.

The blood struck at Litvinov's head like a hammer, then slowly and heavily sank into his heart; and there it petrified like a stone. He reread the letter and then, completely exhausted, as on that previous occasion in Moscow he fell on the sofa and lay still. A dark abyss suddenly enveloped him on all sides, and he gazed into that abyss senselessly and desperately. And so, once more, deceit — no, worse than deceit — falsehood and vulgarity. . . . And life shattered, everything torn up by the roots, from its very depths, and that sole thing at which it was still possible to clutch — that last support — also in fragments!

"Follow us to Petersburg," he repeated with bitter inward laughter; "we'll find you an occupation there." . . . "I suppose they would appoint me as a clerk in charge of an office section. And who are these 'we'? That was her past speaking. There we have that secret, that hideous thing of which I have no knowledge, but which she had attempted to blot out and to burn up as if in fire! There we have that world of intrigues, secret connections, the story of the Belskayas, the Dolskayas. . . . And what a future, what a beautiful role awaits me! To live near her, to visit her, to share with her the depraved melancholy of a fashionable lady who is oppressed and bored by society, but cannot exist outside its circle; to be a domestic friend of her and, of course, His Excellency . . . until — until the whim has passed, and the plebeian friend loses his piquancy, and that fat general or some Mr. Finikov replaces him — now, that is possible and pleasant and perhaps useful . . . she herself speaks of a useful application of my talents, doesn't she? — but our design is unrealizable! Unrealizable! . . ."

Smoke

Sudden gusts of frenzy swept over Litvinov's soul like the momentary gusts of wind before a storm. . . . Every expression in Irena's letter aroused his indignation, her very assurances of the immutability of her feelings affronted him. "It cannot be left like this," he exclaimed at last. "I shall not allow her to play so pitilessly with my life. . . ."

He jumped up and seized his hat. But what could he do? Rush to her? Answer her letter? He stopped and let his hands drop.

Yes: what was to be done?

Had he not himself presented her with this fatal choice? It had fallen otherwise than as he wished — any choice is liable to that misfortune. She had changed her decision, truly; she herself had been the first to declare that she would abandon everything and follow him, that also was true. Yet she did not deny her guilt: she openly called herself a weak woman. She did not wish to deceive him, she had been deceived in herself. . . . What could he object to in that? At the least she was not dissembling, was not temporizing . . . she was frank with him, ruthlessly frank. Nothing had compelled her to reveal her attitude at this moment, nothing had prevented her lulling him with promises, and procrastinating, and leaving everything in uncertainty right down to the departure — the departure with her husband for Italy! But she had ruined his life, she had ruined two lives! . . . Little was lacking, surely!

But in regard to Tatiana it was not Irena who was guilty; he was guilty, he alone, and he had no right to wash his hands of the responsibility that his guilt had laid on him like an iron yoke. . . . That was all true; but now what was there left to do?

He again flung himself on the sofa; and again the moments fled by dark and dull and traceless, with a consuming speed.

"But why not submit to her?" the thought flashed through his head. "She loves me, she is mine, and in our very attraction for each other, in that passion which, after so many years, has forced its way to the surface with such power, is there not something inevitable, irresistible, like a law of nature? To live in Petersburg — why, shall I be the first to have been placed in such a situation? And besides, where could she and I find shelter? . . ."

He was sunk in thought, and Irena's image quietly rose before him as it had been impressed forever in his latest memories. . . .

147

But not for long. He aroused himself and with a new outburst of indignation thrust away even those memories, even that enchanting image.

"You are giving me to drink from a golden goblet," he exclaimed; "but there is poison in your drink, and your white wings are soiled with filth. . . . Away! To remain here with you, after I — have driven away, driven away my future bride — that would be dishonorable, dishonorable!" He clenched his fists bitterly, and another face, with the imprint of suffering on its set features, with unspoken reproach in its farewell gaze, emerged from the depths. . . .

For long did he continue to torture himself; for long, like a difficult patient, his lacerated mind tossed restlessly. . . . He quieted down at last; at last he came to a decision. From the very first moment he had had a presentiment of that decision; it had appeared to him first as a distant, hardly perceptible point amid the whirlwind and gloom of his inward struggle; then it had begun to draw ever nearer and nearer, and it ended by driving like an icy steel blade into his heart.

Once more he dragged his trunk from the corner, once more, unhurrying, and even with a dull, meticulous care, he packed all his things, rang for the waiter, settled his account, and sent a note in Russian to Irena. It read as follows:

I don't know whether your guilt is greater toward me than before; but I do know that this blow is far stronger. . . . This is the end. You tell me: "I cannot," and I also repeat to you: I cannot do — what you desire. I cannot and I do not wish to. Don't answer this. You are not capable of giving me the only answer I would accept. I am leaving tomorrow morning by the first train. Good-by, be happy. . . . I don't suppose we shall ever see each other again.

All that day Litvinov remained in his room. Was he waiting for anything? God knows! About seven in the evening a lady in a black mantle, with a veil over her face, twice approached the entrance to his hotel. She drew back a little to one side and gazed into the distance, then she suddenly made a resolute gesture and went to the entrance yet a third time. . . .

"Where are you going, Irena Pavlovna?" A tense voice sounded behind her.

She turned round with a convulsive, hasty movement. Potugin ran up to her.

She halted, thought a moment, then rushed to him, took him by the arm, and drew him aside.

"Take me away, take me away," she demanded, panting.

"What is the matter with you, Irena Pavlovna?" he muttered in bewilderment.

"Take me away," she repeated with redoubled strength, "if you don't want me to remain forever — there!"

He humbly bowed his head, and they both hurried away.

Early next morning Litvinov was all ready for his journey when into his room walked Potugin himself.

He came up to him without speaking and squeezed his hand without speaking. Litvinov also said nothing. They both had long faces, and they both vainly tried to smile.

"I have come to wish you a good journey," Potugin said at last.

"But how do you know that I am going away today?" Litvinov asked.

Potugin looked round him at the floor. "It has become known to me — as you see. Our last conversation has now had such a strange result — I did not wish you to depart without expressing my sincere sympathy."

"You sympathize with me now — when I am going away?"

Potugin looked at Litvinov mournfully. "Ah, Grigory Mikhailich, Grigory Mikhailich," he began with a brief sigh, "this is not the time for that sort of thing, for such subtleties and hairsplittings. You, so far as I have been able to observe, are rather indifferent to our native literature, and so perhaps you have never heard of Vaska Buslaev?"

"Of whom?"

"Vaska Buslaev, a Novgorod hero — in Kirsh Danilov's anthology."

"What Buslaev?" Litvinov said, somewhat puzzled by such an unexpected turn in the conversation. "I've never heard of him."

"Well, it doesn't matter. But this is what I wished to draw your attention to. Vaska Buslaev took his Novgorod people on a pilgrimage to Jerusalem, and there, to their horror, bathed his naked body in the sacred waters of the river Jordan, because he believed 'neither in sneeze, nor in dream, nor in any feathered fowl,' and then this logical Vaska Buslaev climbed Mount Tabor, and on top of this mountain lay a large stone, over which all sorts of people had vainly attempted to jump. Vaska also wanted to try his fortune. And on the way he came across a skull, a human head; he kicked it with his foot. Well, and the head said to him: 'What are you kicking for? I knew how to live, I know how to roll in the dust — and the same will happen to you.' And it was right: Vaska jumped over the stone, and would have jumped clean over it, but he caught his heel and broke his head. And here I may remark that it would not be a bad thing if my friends the Slavophils, who are so fond of kicking all kinds of dead heads and rotten nations, were to pause to reflect over that legend."

"But what is the point of all this?" Litvinov at last interrupted him impatiently. "It's time I was off, you must excuse me."

"Why, just this," Potugin answered, and his eyes lit up with such a friendly feeling as Litvinov had not even expected of him; "just this, that you have not kicked aside a dead human head, and so, perhaps, because of your goodness, you may succeed in jumping over the fatal stone. I shall not keep you any longer, only permit me to embrace you in farewell."

"I shall not even try to jump," Litvinov said, as he and Potugin kissed three times; and with the dreary feelings that overfilled his soul was mingled a fleeting commiseration for this lonely wretch. "But I must go, I must go. . . ." He flung himself about the room.

"Would you like me to carry something?" Potugin offered his services.

"No, thank you very much; don't trouble, I can manage. . . ." He put on his cap and picked up his bag. "And so, you say," he asked, even as he stood at the door, "you have seen her?"

"Yes, I have."

"Well — and how is she?"

Potugin was silent for a moment. "She waited for you yesterday — and she will be waiting for you today."

"Indeed! Well, then tell her — No, there's no need, no need to say anything. Good-by — good-by!"

"Good-by, Grigory Mikhailich. . . . Let me say one more word to you. You still have time to listen: you have over half an hour before your train leaves. You will return to Russia. There you will — in the course of time — be active. . . . So allow an old chatterbox — for I, alas, am a chatterbox and nothing more — to give you some parting advice. Every time you have to turn to a task, ask yourself: are you serving civilization — in the exact and strict meaning of the word — are you carrying through one of its ideas, has your labor that educative, European character which alone is beneficial and fruitful in our day, in our country? If so, then go boldly forward: you are on the right road, and your work is blessed! God be thanked! You are not alone now. You will not be a 'sower of the wilderness'; laborers — pioneers — have come into being now in our country too. . . . But you have no time for this at the moment. Good-by, do not forget me!"

Litvinov went down the stairs at a run, flung himself into the carriage, and drove to the station without looking back once at the town where so much of his personal life was left. . . . He seemed to yield himself to a wave: it caught him up, carried him off, and he firmly decided not to resist its tow . . . he renounced all other manifestation of will.

He was already entering the car.

"Grigory Mikhailich — Grigory — " he heard an imploring whisper behind him.

He shuddered. Surely not Irena? Yes, it was she. Wrapped in her maid's shawl, with a traveling hat on her untended hair, she was standing on the platform and looking at him with faded eyes. "Turn back, turn back, I have come for you," said those eyes. And how much, how much they promised! She did not stir, she had no strength to add a word; everything in her, even the disorder of her dress, everything seemed to be pleading for mercy. . . .

Litvinov could hardly keep his feet, he all but rushed to her. . . . But the wave to which he had surrendered had its way. . . . He jumped into the car and, turning, pointed Irena to the seat beside him. She understood him. The time had not yet passed. Only one step, one movement, and two forever united lives would be tearing into an unknown distance. . . . While she hesitated, there was a loud whistle, and the train began to move.

Litvinov threw himself back in his seat. But Irena went with staggering steps to a bench and fell on it, to the great amazement of a petty diplomat who had happened to wander into the station. He did not know Irena well, but he was deeply interested in her and, seeing her lying apparently unconscious, he thought that she had suffered "*une attaque de nerfs.*" And so he considered it his duty, the duty *d'un galant chevalier,* to go to her aid. But his amazement grew far greater when, at the first word he said to her, she suddenly rose, thrust away the proffered hand, and, running into the street, in a few seconds disappeared in the milky mist that is so common in the Black Forest climate during the first days of autumn.

26

We happened one day to go into the hut of a peasant woman who had only just lost her only, deeply loved son, and, to our no little surprise, found her absolutely tranquil, all but cheerful. "Don't trouble her," said her husband, who evidently noticed my surprise; "she is 'ossified' now." And Litvinov also was "ossified." During the first few hours of his journey a similar tranquillity came upon him. Completely annihilated and hopelessly unhappy, none the less he rested, rested after the alarms and torments of the past week, after all the blows that one after another had fallen on his head. They had shaken him all the more strongly because he was not created for such storms. Now it was as though he hoped for nothing and tried not to remember, most of all not to remember; he was traveling to Russia — he had to go somewhere! But he now made no assumptions concerning himself. He did not recognize himself; he did not understand his conduct, it was as though he had lost his real "I," and altogether he had little part at all in that "I." Sometimes it seemed to him that he was carrying his own corpse, and only the rare bitter spasms of irremediable spiritual pain that fled through him reminded him that he was still concerned with life. At times it seemed to him incomprehensible that a man — a man! — could allow a woman, and love, to have such influence over him. . . . "Shameful weakness!" he whispered; and brushed his greatcoat and settled himself more comfortably into his seat, as though saying: "Now the old is ended, we begin a new — minute"; and he only smiled bitterly and was amazed at himself.

He turned to looking out of the window. The day was gray and raw; it was not raining, but the mist still held, and low clouds veiled all the sky. The wind was blowing to meet the train; whitish billows of steam, sometimes singly, sometimes mingled with other, darker billows of smoke, tore in an endless string past the window beside which he was sitting. He began to watch that steam, to watch that smoke. Winding incessantly, rising and falling, whirling and clinging to the grass, to the bushes, as though grimacing, lengthening and melting, cloud after cloud was carried past . . . it unceasingly changed and remained the same . . . a monotonous, hurrying, boring game! Sometimes the wind changed, the road curved — the whole mass suddenly disappeared and immediately after was to be seen through the opposite window; then once more the enormous tail was flung across, and once more it veiled his view of the broad Rhineland plain. He watched and watched, and a strange reverie came upon him. . . . He was sitting alone in the car; no one disturbed him. "Smoke, smoke," he repeated several times; and abruptly everything seemed to be smoke — everything, his own life, Russian life, everything human, but especially everything Russian. "It is all smoke and vapor," he thought. "Everything seems to be incessantly changing, everywhere there are new pictures, phenomena speed after phenomena, but in essence everything is the same and still the same; everything is hurrying, hastening somewhere — and everything vanishes without a trace, without achieving anything; another wind blows — and everything is flung to the opposite side, and there too the same incessant, anxious, and unnecessary game goes on." He recalled much that had been accomplished before his eyes, with thunders and tumults, of recent years . . . "smoke," he whispered, "smoke." He remembered the burning arguments, the jostles and shouts in Gubariov's room, in other people's rooms, of people highly and lowly placed, foremost and rearmost, old and young people . . . "smoke," he repeated, "smoke and vapor." He recalled, finally, that celebrated picnic, he recalled other judgments and speeches of other statesmen, and even everything that Potugin had preached . . . smoke, smoke, and nothing more. But his own strivings and feelings, and struggles, and dreams? He only shrugged his shoulders.

But meanwhile the train was speeding and speeding; already Rastatt, and Karlsruhe, and Bruchsal had been left behind; the hills on the right-hand side of the track first turned away, retreated into the distance, then drew near again, but now not so lofty, and more rarely covered with forest. . . . The train swung sharply to one side . . . and now they were at Heidelberg. The cars drew under the roof of the station; he heard the shouts of newsboys selling all kinds of periodicals, and even Russian papers. The travelers fidgeted in their seats or went out on the platform. But Litvinov did not leave his corner and continued to sit with his head sunk on his chest. Suddenly someone called him by name. He raised his eyes: Bindasov's face was thrust through the window, and behind him — or did he only imagine it? No, it was so: all the familiar faces from Baden: Mme Sukhanchikova, Voroshilov, and even Bambayev; they all moved toward him, and Bindasov bawled:

"But where's Pishchalkin? We were expecting him. But it doesn't matter; out you get, lazybones, we're all going to see Gubariov."

"Yes, brother, yes, Gubariov's waiting for us." Bambayev confirmed, pushing forward. "Out you get!"

Litvinov would have been angry but for the dead burden that lay on his heart. He glanced at Bindasov and turned away without speaking.

"I tell you Gubariov's here," Mme Sukhanchikova exclaimed, and her eyes all but popped out.

Litvinov did not stir.

"Now listen, Litvinov," Bambayev said at last, "there's not only Gubariov here; there's a whole phalanx of very outstanding, very intelligent young people, Russians, and they are all studying natural science, and they all have the finest of convictions. You might remain at least for their sake. For instance, here we've got a certain — oh dear! I've forgotten his name. But he's an absolute genius!"

"Oh, let him go, let him go, Rostislav Ardalionich," Mme Sukhanchikova intervened. "Let him go! You see the sort of man he is; and all his family are the same. He's got an aunt who I thought at first was traveling our road; but I came here with her two days ago — she had only just arrived in Baden and back she was flying again — and as we came along I began to question her. . . . Would you believe it, I couldn't get a word out of her arrogance! The loathsome aristocrat!"

Poor Kapitolina Markovna, an aristocrat! Had she ever expected such a disgrace?

But Litvinov still said nothing, and turned away and pulled his cap down over his eyes. The train started off at last.

Smoke

"But do say something at least in parting, you lifeless stone!" Bambayev shouted. "You can't go off like that!"

"You scum, you dolt!" Bindasov howled. The cars were moving faster and faster, and he could swear with impunity. "You curmudgeon! You slug! You beer-glass licker!"

Whether Bindasov had invented this last nickname on the spot or whether he had got it from others is not known; but evidently it delighted two of the very noble young men studying natural sciences who were standing beside him; for several days later it was printed in the Russian periodical sheet then being published in Heidelberg, under the headline: "*A tout venant je crache!*" or: "God does not give. A swine is never full." [1]

But Litvinov again repeated the word he had previously been uttering: smoke, smoke, smoke! "For instance," he thought, "there are more than a hundred Russian students in Heidelberg at present; they're all studying chemistry, physics, physiology — and don't want to hear of anything else. . . . But in five or six years' time there won't be fifteen students attending the courses given by the same celebrated professors. . . . The wind will change, the smoke will shift to the other side . . . smoke . . . smoke . . . smoke!" [2]

Toward nightfall he passed through Kassel. Together with the darkness, an unendurable yearning dropped like a kite on him, and he burst into tears, huddling into the corner of the car. Long his tears flowed without lightening his heart, corrosively and grievously lacerating him. But at that very moment Tatiana was in bed with a fever in one of the Kassel hotels, and Kapitolina Markovna was seated beside her.

"Tania," she said, "for God's sake let me send a telegram to Grigory Mikhailovich. Do let me, Tania!"

"No, auntie," she said, "there's no need, don't be alarmed. Give me some water; it will soon pass."

And she was right; a week later she was restored to health, and the two friends continued their journey.

---

[1] A historical fact. (Author's note.)

[2] Litvinov's presentiments were justified. In 1866 there were thirteen Russian students attending Heidelberg University during the summer term, and twelve during the winter term. (Author's note.)

27

Stopping neither in Petersburg nor in Moscow, Litvinov returned to his estate. He was alarmed when he saw his father, so
feeble and decrepit had the old man grown. Old Litvinov was
delighted to see his son, in so far as a man who has finished
with life can delight in anything; he immediately handed over
to him all his badly disorganized affairs, and, after creaking in
the joints for a few more weeks, he departed this earthly course.
Litvinov was left alone in the dilapidated wing of his house and,
with a heavy heart, without hopes, without zeal, and without
money, began to manage the estate. Husbandry in Russia is not a
cheerful occupation, as all too many know; we shall not stop
to enlarge on how bitter it proved to Litvinov. Of course
there could be no thought of transformations and innovations;
the application of the knowledge he had gained abroad was
postponed for an indefinite period; necessity compelled him to
live from day to day, to agree to all kinds of concessions, both
material and moral. The new was accepted reluctantly, the old
had lost all its strength;[1] the bungler clashed with the unscrupulous; all the shaken life was quaking like a marsh, and only the
one great word "freedom" hovered like the Divine Spirit above
the waters. Patience was required most of all, and patience not
passive, but active, insistent, not without some knack, not without
cunning for the moment. . . . In his mental and psychological
state Litvinov found it doubly hard. Little desire to live was left
in him. . . . So where was he to find desire for troubles and
labors?

But a year passed, and after it another; a third began. The great
idea was realized little by little, was transformed into flesh and
blood; sprouts emerged from the scattered seed, and now no
enemy — either open or secret — could trample it down. Litvinov
himself, though he ended by giving a large part of his land to
peasants on a fifty-fifty basis — in other words, reverting to impoverished, primitive husbandry — did manage to achieve something: he restored the factory, ran a tiny farm with five hired
laborers, and from time to time had as many as forty working
for him. He paid off the largest of the private debts. . . . And

[1] All the following passage refers to the emancipation of the peasants in
1861, and the consequent transference of land to them. (Tr.)

his spirit grew strong within him; he again began to resemble the former Litvinov. True, a sorrowful, deeply hidden feeling never left him, and he grew quiet beyond his years, shut himself up in his narrow circle, severed all his former relations. . . . But his deathly indifference disappeared, and among the living he again moved and acted like the living. And the last traces of the enchantment that had possessed him also disappeared; all that had occurred in Baden seemed like something seen in a dream. . . .

But Irena? She, too, faded and disappeared, and Litvinov had only a vague sense of something dangerous beneath the mist that gradually enveloped her image. He had news of Tatiana from time to time; he knew that she had settled with her aunt on her small property, some hundred and fifty miles away, and lived quietly, rarely left home, and hardly ever had guests. But she was quiet and well. And one day, one beautiful day of May, he was sitting in his study and indifferently turning over the pages of the latest number of a Petersburg periodical when a servant entered and reported the arrival of his old uncle. This uncle was Kapitolina Markovna's cousin, and he had recently visited her. He had bought a property adjacent to Litvinov's and was transferring to it. He stayed with his nephew for days on end and told him a great deal about the life Tatiana was living.

The day after his departure Litvinov sent a letter to her, the first since their parting. He asked permission to renew their acquaintance at least in writing, and also wished to know whether he must forever abandon the thought of seeing her again. Not without anxiety he awaited the answer . . . it arrived at last. Tatiana responded favorably to his question. "If it occurs to you to visit us," she ended, "by all means, come; they say that even sick people find things easier together than separately." Kapitolina Markovna joined in greeting him. Litvinov was as delighted as a child; not for long nor for anything else had his heart beat so merrily. And suddenly everything seemed light and clear. . . . Just as, when the sun rises and disperses the darkness of night, a little breeze speeds with the sun's rays over the face of the resurrected earth. All that day Litvinov smiled and smiled, even when he went round his farm and gave orders. He at once began to prepare for the journey, and two weeks later he was on his way to Tatiana.

He drove quite slowly, along byroads, without any particular adventures except that the tire of one back wheel broke. A smith welded it and welded it, swore both at it and at himself, but gave it up in the end. Fortunately it transpired that even with a broken tire one can travel quite comfortably in Russia, especially over the "soft" — in other words, through the mud. On the other hand, he had two or three quite interesting meetings. At one postal station he came upon an arbitration congress,[1] and in the chair was Pishchalkin, who impressed him as being a Solon or Solomon, with such exalted wisdom were his speeches filled, with such unbounded respect did the landowners and the peasants regard him. . . . Even in appearance Pishchalkin had begun to look like an ancient sage; the hair had gone from his temples, but his face had filled out and had frozen into a kind of majestic jelly of quite unbridled virtue. He greeted Litvinov on his arrival "in my — if I may use such an ambitious expression — my own country," but at once went into a spate of well-intentioned feelings. But he did manage to communicate one piece of news — namely, concerning Voroshilov. The knight of the roll of honor had again entered the military service and had already found time to read a lecture to the officers of his regiment on "Buddhism" or "dynamism" or something of that sort — Pishchalkin did not well remember what.

At the next postal station some long time elapsed before fresh horses were harnessed into Litvinov's carriage — it was at dawn — and he dozed off as he sat in his seat. He was aroused by a voice that seemed familiar; he opened his eyes. . . .

Lord! Surely it wasn't Mr. Gubariov in a gray jacket and baggy pajama trousers, standing and swearing on the balcony of the postal house? . . . No, it was not Mr. Gubariov. . . . But what a striking resemblance! . . . Except that this gentleman had a mouth still wider and toothier, and the look of his gloomy eyes was still more ferocious, and the nose was bigger, and the beard thicker, and all the features even more heavy and repellent.

"The scou-oundrels! The scou-oundrels!" he said slowly and malevolently, opening wide his wolfish mouth. "The filthy little

[1] Part of the machinery for settling land disputes between landowners and their peasants, after 1861. (Tr.)

peasants! . . . There you have it — your boasted freedom . . .
and you can't get horses! . . . The scou-oundrels!"

"The scou-oundrels! Scou-oundrels!" came a second voice
through the door, and on to the balcony walked another — also
in a gray jacket and baggy pajamas — and this time it was genuinely, undoubtedly, the real Mr. Gubariov himself, Stepan Nikolaevich Gubariov in person.

"The filthy peasants!" he went on in imitation of his brother
(it transpired that the first gentleman was his elder brother, the
"*dentiste*" [1] of the old school, who ran his estate). "They deserve
a good hiding, that's what; a few punches in the face; that's the
freedom they need . . . in their teeth. . . . How they talk! . . .
The local head man . . . I'd show them. . . . And where is that
M'sieur Roston? . . . Why doesn't he see to it? . . . It's his
business, the drone . . . he never troubles himself. . . ."

"But I have told you again and again, brother," said Gubariov
senior, "that he is good for nothing, he's just a drone, as you
say! Only you would, for old time's sake . . . M'sieur Roston,
M'sieur Roston! . . . Where have you got to?"

"Roston! Roston!" shouted the younger, the great Gubariov.
"Give him a good shout, brother Dorimedont Nikolaich!"

"That's what I am doing, brother Stepan Nikolaich. M'sieur
Roston!"

"Here I am, here I am, here I am!" came a hurried voice, and
out of the house flew Bambayev.

Litvinov gasped. A well-worn Hungarian coat with holes in
the sleeves flapped miserably about the unfortunate enthusiast;
his features had not so much changed as twisted and drawn together; his terrified little eyes expressed servile fear and hungry
subservience; but his dyed whiskers still bristled above his downy
lips. From the height of the balcony the brothers Gubariov immediately and violently began to berate him. He halted below,
in the mud, before them and, humbly bowing his back, attempted
to appease them with a timid little smile, and crumpled his peaked
cap in his crimson fingers, and fidgeted with his feet, and muttered that the horses would be coming in a minute. . . . But the
brothers did not stop nagging until at last the younger man
happened to cast a glance at Litvinov. Whether he recognized
him, or whether he was shamed in the presence of a stranger, one

[1] See note, p. 25. (Tr.)

cannot say; he suddenly turned on his heels, like a bear, and, chewing his beard, waddled into the post station. The other brother at once lapsed into silence and, also turning like a bear, followed him. Evidently the great Gubariov had not lost his influence even in his native land.

Bambayev was about to wander in after the brothers. . . . Litvinov called him by name. He looked round, stared, and, recognizing Litvinov, rushed to him with outstretched hands. But on reaching the carriage he clutched at the door leaned his chest against it, and broke into a flood of tears.

"Enough, enough of that, Bambayev!" Litvinov said, bending over him and touching him on the shoulder.

But he went on sobbing. "You see — you see — you see what I've come to . . ." he muttered as he sobbed.

"Bambayev!" the brothers thundered from the house.

Bambayev raised his head and hurriedly wiped away his tears.

"Greetings, my dear fellow!" he whispered, "greetings and good-by! . . . Do you hear? They're calling me."

"Yes, but what fate has brought you here?" Litvinov asked. "And what does all this mean? I thought they were calling a Frenchman — "

"I'm their — domestic manager, their steward," Bambayev answered, cocking his finger at the house. "And I've become a Frenchman by way of a joke. What is one to do, brother! I've nothing to eat, I've spent my last farthing, and so willy-nilly you slip your head through the collar. And not through ambition."

"But has *he* been long in Russia? And how did he part from his former comrades?"

"Ah, brother! That's all put away now. . . . You see, the weather's changed. . . He simply threw out Matriona Sukhanchikova on her neck. In her grief she went to Portugal."

"Why to Portugal? What an idiotic idea!"

"Yes, brother, to Portugal, with the two Matrionovites."

"With whom?"

"With the Matrionovites: that's what the members of her party call themselves."

"Has Matriona Kuzminishna formed a party, then? And is it very numerous?"

"Why, it consists of just those two. But soon it will be six months since *he* returned here. Others were placed under surveillance, but not he. He is living in the country with his brother, and you should hear now —"

"Bambayev!"

"Coming, Stepan Nikolaich, coming! But you're flourishing and enjoying life, my boy! Well, and God be thanked! Where are you off to now? . . . I never thought, I never guessed — Do you remember Baden? Ah, that was a life! And, by the way, do you remember Bindasov too? Just imagine, he's dead. He became an excise official. And one day he began to quarrel in a pub, and they gave him one with a stick and split his head open. Yes, yes, difficult times have arrived! But I still say: Russia — ah, this Russia! Look even at that couple of geese: in all Europe you won't see anything like them! Real Arzamas geese!"

And after paying this last tribute to his incorrigible necessity to rhapsodize, Bambayev ran to the postal station, where his name had been shouted again, and not without some banging of fists.

Toward the end of that same day Litvinov drove into Tatiana's village. The small house in which his former fiancée lived stood on a hillock above a little river, in the midst of a recently laid-out garden. The house also was new, only recently built, and could be seen for a long distance across the river and fields. It was revealed to Litvinov's eyes nearly a couple of miles away, with its steep-roofed mezzanine floor, and a row of windows glowing crimson in the evening sun. Ever since the last posthouse he had felt a secret anxiety; but now he was simply filled with embarrassment, an embarrassment joyous but not without a touch of fear. "How will they welcome me?" he thought; "how shall I present myself? . . ." To occupy himself with something he fell to talking with his driver, a sedate peasant with a gray beard, who, however, had charged him for eighteen miles, whereas the distance was not fifteen. He asked him whether he knew the landowners named Shestovy.

"The Shestovys? Of course I know them! They're good ladies, there's no denying! They give us peasants medical treatment. It's the truth I'm telling. They're doctors! People go to them from all the district round. It's true. They even crawl. When someone falls ill, for instance, or has cut himself, or something, they go to them at once, and they at once give them fomentations, powders, or plasters, and it's of great help. And you can't imagine how the people show their gratitude; but they say they can't agree to taking anything; they don't do it for money. And they've started a school. . . . But that's a waste of time!"

All the time the driver was talking, Litvinov did not take his eyes off the house. . . . Now a woman in white came out on the balcony, stood there awhile, stood and then vanished. . . . "Surely it isn't she?" His heart leaped within him. "Hurry! Hurry!" he shouted to the driver; the man whipped up his horses. A few more seconds . . . and the carriage rolled through the open gates. . . . And Kapitolina Markovna was standing on the veranda and, quite beside herself, clapping her hands, was shouting: "I recognized him, I was the first to recognize him! It's he! It's he! . . . I recognized him!"

Litvinov jumped out of the carriage before the page who ran up could open the door, and hurriedly embraced Kapitolina Markovna, then rushed into the house, through the vestibule, into the hall. . . . Before him stood Tatiana, all blushes. She looked at him with her kindly, gracious eyes (she was a little thinner, but that suited her) and gave him her hand. But he did not take the hand; once more he fell on his knees before her. She had not expected that in the least and she did not know what to say, what to do. . . . The tears started to her eyes. She was alarmed, but all her face lit up with joy. . . . "Grigory Mikhailich, what are you doing, Grigory Mikhailich?" she said. . . . But he went on kissing the hem of her dress . . . and he remembered with emotion how he had gone down on his knees before her at Baden also. . . . But then — and now!

"Tania," he repeated, "Tania, have you forgiven me, Tania?"

"Auntie, auntie, what does this mean?" Tatiana turned to Kapitolina Markovna as she entered.

"Don't stop him, don't stop him, Tania," the good old woman answered. "You see: he has brought a contrite heart."

However, it is time to end. Besides, there is nothing to add; the reader will guess for himself. . . . But what of Irena?

She is just as charming as ever, despite her thirty years; young men without number fall in love with her, and even more would fall in love if — if . . .

Reader, would you care to come with us for a few moments

to Petersburg, to one of the most important buildings in that city? Look! Before you is a spacious room, furnished, we do not say richly — that expression is too lowly — but seriously, representatively, imposingly. Are you conscious of a certain shiver of servility? Then know: you have entered a temple, a temple consecrated to the highest decorum, to abundantly loving virtue; in a word: to something not of this earth. What an occult, truly occult silence envelops you! The velvet portieres at the door, the velvet curtains at the windows, the fluffy, yielding carpet on the floor, all would seem to be predestined and adapted to the appeasement, to the amelioration of all coarse sounds and strong sensations. The sedulously suspended lamps inspire sedate feelings; a seemly scent suffuses the rather fusty air; even the samovar on the table hisses restrainedly and modestly. The mistress of the house, an important personage in the Petersburg world, talks almost inaudibly; she always speaks as if there were a difficult, all but dying patient in the room. In imitation of her the other ladies hardly even whisper; and her sister, who is pouring tea, moves her lips quite without making a sound, so that the young man sitting opposite her, who has happened to find himself in this temple of decorum, is bewildered to know what she wants of him, though she whispers to him for the sixth time: "*Voulez-vous une tasse de thé?*"

In the corners young, comely men are visible; a gentle aspiration shines in their gaze; imperturbably gentle, though surreptitious, is the expression on their faces; numerous marks of distinction gently glitter on their chests. The conversation also is of a gentle character: it is concerned with religious and patriotic matters, with F. N. Glinka's [1] "Mysterious Drop," the missions to the East, the monasteries and brotherhoods in Byelorussia. At rare intervals, softly treading over the soft carpet, liveried lackeys pass to and fro; their huge calves, enveloped in tight-fitting silk stockings, shiver noiselessly with every step; the respectful quiver of the sturdy muscles only deepens the general impression of splendid magnificence, splendid intentions, splendid veneration. . . . This is a temple! A temple!

"Have you seen Madame Ratmirova today?" one personage briefly asks.

[1] Russian soldier, author, and mystic poet (1786–1880). (Tr.)

"I met her today at Lise's," the mistress answers like an æolian harp. "I am sorry for her. . . . She has a malevolent mind — *elle n'a pas la foi.*"

"Yes, yes," the personage repeats, "it was Piotr Ivanich, I remember, who said of her, and said very truly, *qu'elle a — she has a malevolent mind.*"

"*Elle n'a pas la foi,*" the mistress's voice exhales like the smoke from incense. "*C'est une âme égarée.* She has a malevolent mind."

"She has a malevolent mind," the sister repeats with only her lips.

And that is why not all the young men are completely in love with Irena. . . . They are afraid of her — they are afraid of her "malevolent mind." Such is the stock phrase that has come into currency about her; in that phrase, as in all phrases, there is a grain of truth. And not only the young people are afraid of her; she is feared by their elders, and by the higher-placed persons, and even by the personages. No one else has such a gift for faithfully and subtly hitting off the ludicrous or the petty aspect of a character, no one else has such a power to stigmatize it so mercilessly in the unforgettable word. . . . And that word sears all the more painfully because it comes from fragrant, beautiful lips. . . . It is difficult to say what goes on in her soul; but among the crowd of her adorers rumor attaches the title of favorite to none.

Irena's husband is swiftly advancing along the road that the French call the path to glory. The stout general has surpassed him; the condescending general has been left behind. And in the same city in which Irena resides, our friend Sozont Potugin also resides; he rarely sees her, and she has no particular need to keep in touch with him. . . . The girl who was entrusted to his care died recently.

Fathers and Sons

1 8 6 1

I

WELL, Piotr, nothing to be seen yet?" asked a gentleman some forty years of age, bareheaded, and wearing a dusty coat and checkered pantaloons, as on May 20, 1859 he walked out on the low, small veranda of an inn on the X X X highroad; he addressed the question to his servant, a young and heavy-cheeked fellow with a very light down on his chin, and tiny, lackluster eyes.

The servant, who had a turquoise ring in his ear, pomaded hair of various hues, and respectful movements of the body — in a word, everything that distinguished a manservant of the later, more perfect generation — condescended to gaze along the road and replied: "Nothing to be seen, nothing at all."

"Nothing to be seen?" the master repeated.

"Nothing at all," the man replied a second time.

The gentleman sighed and sat down on the bench. We shall introduce the reader to him while he is sitting, gazing thoughtfully about, with his little legs tucked under him.

His name is Nikolai Piotrovich Kirsanov. Some ten miles from the inn he has a good estate of two hundred souls, or, as he puts it since he reached a land-rental agreement with his peasants and started a "farm," of thirty-five hundred acres of land. His father, a general on active service in 1812, semiliterate, a coarse but not really bad man, and a true Russian, had toiled and sweated all his life, first commanding a brigade, then a division, and had lived permanently in the provinces, where, owing to his rank, he played quite a considerable role. Like his elder brother, Pavel, of whom we shall be speaking later, Nikolai Piotrovich was born in the south of Russia, and until he was fourteen was educated at home, surrounded by inexpensive tutors, jaunty but servile adjutants, and other regimental and staff personalities. His mother, one of the

Kolyazin family, responded to the Christian name of Agathe while she was single, but was called Agafoklea Kuzminishna Kirsanova after she was married; she was the type of officer's wife known as "mother commander," wore extravagantly trimmed bonnets and rustling silk dresses, was always the first to go up to the cross in church, was a loud and garrulous talker, let the children kiss her hand each morning, blessed them at night — in a word, she lived a life of full content. As a general's son Nikolai Piotrovich — though he not only was undistinguished for his bravery, but even deserved to be called a little coward — was, like his brother, Pavel, to have entered military service; but he broke his leg on the very day the news of his commission arrived and, after lying two months in bed, was left "rather lame" for the rest of his life. His father gave him up in despair and allowed him to join the civil service. He carried him off to Petersburg as soon as he had reached the age of eighteen and entered him in the university. It so happened that just about then his brother joined a guards regiment as an officer. The two young men set up house together in one apartment, under the distant supervision of Ilia Kolyazin, an important official, their first cousin once removed on the mother's side. Their father returned to his division and his spouse and only occasionally sent his sons large sheets of gray paper folded in four, mottled with the secretary's flowing script. The last page of these fourfold sheets was adorned with the words "Piotr Kirsanov, Major General," industriously circumscribed with scrolls and flourishes. In 1835 Nikolai Piotrovich left the university with the degree of Bachelor, and in the same year General Kirsanov was placed on the retired list owing to an unsatisfactory military parade, and arrived with his wife to live in Petersburg. He intended to rent a house close to the Tauride Garden and had put his name down for membership in the English Club, but he died suddenly of a stroke. Agafoklea Kuzminishna soon followed him: she could not get accustomed to the lonely life of the capital; the misery of existence as a retired general's wife gnawed at her. Meantime, even while his parents were alive and to their no little chagrin, Nikolai Piotrovich succeeded in falling in love with the daughter of an official named Prepolovensky, the former owner of his apartment; she was a pleasant-looking and, as one says, a mentally developed girl: she read the serious articles in the "scientific" sections of the journals. He married her as soon as the period of mourning was past and, abandoning the post in the Ministry of Crown Lands that his father had obtained for him by pulling strings, he lived a blissful life with his Masha, first in a summer residence out of town near the Institute of Forestry, then in town, in a small and very comfortable apartment, with a clean staircase and a rather chilly reception room, and finally in the country, where he settled down completely and where his son, Arkady, was born soon after. The couple lived very well and quietly: they were hardly ever separated, they read together, played four-hand pieces on the piano, and sang duets; she planted flowers and supervised the poultry yard, he engaged in farming and occasionally went hunting, while Arkady grew and grew, also well and quietly. Ten years passed like a dream. In 1847 Kirsanov's wife died. He hardly withstood this blow, and went gray in a few weeks; he planned to go abroad, in order to get at least a little change — but then 1848 arrived. He was forced to return to the country and, after a rather prolonged period of inactivity, began to make changes in the running of the estate. In 1855 he took Arkady to the university; he lived three winters with him in Petersburg, going hardly anywhere and endeavoring to cultivate acquaintance with his son's youthful colleagues. He could not travel to Petersburg for Arkady's last winter, and so we see him in May 1859, now quite gray, rather stout, and a little bent in the back; he was waiting for his son, who, like himself earlier, had gained the degree of Bachelor.

Out of a sense of the proprieties, or possibly because he wanted to escape his master's eye, the servant went under the gateway and lit a pipe. Nikolai Piotrovich's head drooped, and he began to gaze at the rickety steps of the veranda; a large, speckled chicken decorously walked about it, firmly setting down its large yellow feet; a bedraggled kitten, delicately perched on the railing, watched the bird with animosity. The sun was burning hot. From the shady entrance to the inn came the smell of warm rye bread. Our Nikolai Piotrovich fell to dreaming: "My son . . . a Bachelor . . . dear Arkady . . . " the thoughts incessantly revolved in his head; he tried to think of something else, but those same thoughts returned again and again. He recalled his dead wife: "She didn't live to see it!" he whispered despondently. . . . A plump dove-gray pigeon flew down onto the road and hurriedly went to drink from a puddle by the well. Nikolai Piotrovich began to watch it, but now his ear caught the rattle of approaching wheels.

"I think they're coming," his man reported, diving out of the gateway.

Nikolai Piotrovich jumped up and gazed along the road. A tarantass drawn by a troika of hired horses appeared; in the tarantass could be seen the band of a student's peaked cap, the familiar features of a dear face.

"My dear Arkady! My dear Arkady!" Kirsanov shouted, and he ran, and he waved his arms. . . . A few moments later his lips were pressed to the young Bachelor's beardless, dusty, and sunburnt cheek.

II

"Let me brush myself down, Papa," Arkady said in a voice rather hoarse with the journey, but ringing with the tones of youth, as he gaily responded to his father's embraces. "I'll make you all dirty."

"That's all right, that's all right," Nikolai Piotrovich declared, smiling tenderly, and he brushed his hand once or twice over the collar of his son's topcoat and his own coat. "Now let me see you, let me see you," he added, stepping back. But he at once went with hurried steps toward the inn, calling: "This way, this way, and bring the horses quickly!"

Nikolai Piotrovich seemed to be far more moved than his son; he seemed even to be a little embarrassed, as though shy. Arkady halted him.

"Papa," he said, "let me introduce you to my good friend Bazarov, whom I have told you so much about in my letters. He has been so kind as to consent to stay with us."

Nikolai Piotrovich turned swiftly and, going up to a tall man in a long canvas coat with tassels, who had just climbed out of the tarantass, firmly squeezed his bare red hand, which the other man seemed reluctant to hold out to him.

"I'm sincerely glad," he began, "and grateful for your kind intention to visit us; I hope — may I know your Christian name and patronymic?"

"Yevgeny Vasiliev," Bazarov replied in an indolent but manly voice and, turning back the collar of his coat, revealed all his face to Nikolai Piotrovich's eyes. The face was long and lean, with a high forehead, a nose broad above and thin below, large, rather green eyes, and hanging side-whiskers of a sandy color; it was animated with a tranquil smile, and expressed self-confidence and intelligence.

"I hope, my dear Yevgeny Vasilich, that you will not be bored during your stay," Nikolai Piotrovich continued.

Bazarov's thin lips very slightly parted, but he made no answer and only raised his peaked cap. His ash-blond hair, long and thick, did not conceal the considerable protuberances of his ample cranium.

"Well, what do you think, Arkady?" Nikolai Piotrovich began again, turning to his son. "We'll have the horses harnessed up at once, shall we? Or would you like to rest?"

"We can rest at home, Papa; order them to be harnessed."

"At once, at once," his father took him up. "Hey, Piotr, d'you hear? See to things quickly, my lad!"

Piotr, who, being a perfect servant, did not come to kiss his young master's hand, but only bowed to him from a distance, again vanished through the gateway.

"I have the carriage here, but there is a troika of horses for your tarantass as well," Nikolai Piotrovich fussily said, while Arkady took a drink from an iron ewer brought by the mistress of the inn, and Bazarov lit a pipe and went up to the driver, who was unharnessing the horses. "But the calash has only two seats, and I don't know how your friend —"

"He'll ride in the tarantass," Arkady interrupted in an undertone. "Please don't stand on ceremony with him. He's a very fine fellow, and very unassuming in his ways, as you'll see."

Nikolai Piotrovich's coachman brought out the horses.

"Well, hurry up, thick-beard!" Bazarov said to the tarantass-driver.

"D'you hear that, Mitiukha?" remarked another driver who was standing close by with his hands thrust into the back slit of his sheepskin. "Did you hear what the gentleman called you? You're thick-bearded all right."

Mitiukha only dusted his cap and dragged the reins free of the sweating shaft-horse.

"Quicker, quicker, give him a hand, lads!" Nikolai Piotrovich exclaimed; "and you'll have something for vodka."

A few minutes later the horses were harnessed, the father and son took their seats in the calash, Piotr clambered on the box,

Bazarov jumped into the tarantass and rested his head against the leather cushion, and both the carriages rattled off.

III

"Well, and so you're a Bachelor at last and have come home," Nikolai Piotrovich said, touching Arkady now on the shoulder, now on the knee. "At last!"

"And how is Uncle? Quite well?" asked Arkady, who, despite the sincere, almost childish joy that possessed him, was anxious to turn the conversation as soon as possible from an emotional to a more matter-of-fact note.

"Yes, he's quite well. He wanted to come with me to meet you, but for some reason he changed his mind."

"And have you been waiting for me long?" Arkady asked.

"Why, about five hours."

"Good old Papa!"

Arkady energetically turned to his father and kissed him vigorously on the cheek. Nikolai Piotrovich laughed quietly.

"I have a fine horse ready for you!" he began; "you wait and see. And your room has been hung with wallpaper."

"And is there a room for Bazarov?"

"We can find one for him."

"Please, Papa, be nice to him. I can't tell you how much I value his friendship."

"You made his acquaintance quite recently, didn't you?"

"Yes."

"I thought I didn't see him last winter. What is he doing?"

"His chief subject is natural science. But he knows everything. Next winter he wants to study to be a doctor."

"Ah! So he'll be in the medical faculty!" Nikolai Piotrovich remarked, and then was silent for a moment or two. "Piotr," he added, pointing, "surely those are our peasants coming along?"

Piotr looked in the direction his master was pointing. Several peasants' carts drawn by unbitted horses were swiftly rolling along a narrow field track. Each cart carried a peasant, and many of them two, riding with their sheepskins flung wide open.

"That is so," Piotr observed.

"Where are they driving to? Into the town, surely?"

"They must be going to the town. To the pub," Piotr added contemptuously, and leaned a little toward the coachman, as though appealing to him. But the coachman did not even stir: he was a man of the old school and did not share Piotr's more modern views.

"I've had a lot of trouble with the peasants this year," Nikolai Piotrovich went on, turning to his son. "They're not paying their rent. But what can you do?"

"Are you satisfied with your hired laborers?"

"Yes." Nikolai Piotrovich let the word filter through his teeth. "But they're getting at them, that's the trouble; and there's no real effort being made even yet. They ruin the harness. But they haven't done the plowing at all badly. With thorough threshing there will be flour enough. But I suppose you're not interested in the farm at the moment?"

"We haven't any shade anywhere, that's the pity," Arkady remarked, without replying to the last question.

"I have had a large awning fitted over the balcony on the north side," Nikolai Piotrovich replied, "and now we shall be able even to dine in the open."

"It will be rather like a holiday house . . . but anyhow, these are all details. What air we have here! How gloriously it smells! Really, I think that nowhere in the world does the air smell as it does in these parts! And the sky —"

Arkady suddenly stopped, threw an oblique glance over his shoulder, and lapsed into silence.

"Of course," Nikolai Piotrovich remarked, "you were born here; everything about it ought to seem more than usually good to you."

"But, Papa, it doesn't matter where a man is born."

"None the less —"

"Really, it doesn't matter in the least."

Nikolai Piotrovich looked sidelong at his son, and the calash had covered nearly half a mile before the conversation was renewed.

"I don't remember whether I wrote and told you," Nikolai Piotrovich began, "your former nurse, Yegorovna, has died."

"Really? Poor old woman! But is Prokofich still here?"

"Yes, and he hasn't changed in the least. He still grumbles away just the same as ever. In fact, you won't find any great changes at Marino at all."

"Have you still got the same steward?"

"Except that I have changed the steward. I decided not to keep any freed servants or any of the former domestic serfs, or at least not to entrust them with any positions involving responsibility." (With his eyes Arkady indicated Piotr.) "*Il est libre, en effet,*" Nikolai Piotrovich remarked in an undertone, "but then, he is a valet. I now have a steward from the burgher class; he seems to be an efficient fellow. I have agreed to pay him two hundred and fifty rubles a year. But by the way," Nikolai Piotrovich added, rubbing his forehead and eyebrows with his hand, a gesture that was always a sign of his inward embarrassment, "I just told you that you won't find any changes in Marino. That is not quite correct. I consider it my duty to warn you, though — "

He hesitated for a moment, then went on in French:

"A strict moralist would find my frankness out of place, but to begin with, the matter can't be concealed, and secondly, as you know, I have always observed special principles in regard to relations between father and son. For that matter, you, of course, will be quite entitled to condemn me. At my age — In a word, that — that girl, of whom I expect you have already heard — "

"Fenichka?" Arkady asked easily.

Nikolai Piotrovich went red.

"Please don't mention her name aloud. Why, yes — she is living with me now. I have accommodated her in the house — where there were two small rooms. But in any case everything can be changed."

"But why should it, Papa?"

"Your friend will be staying with us . . . it will be awkward."

"Please don't be anxious on Bazarov's account. He's above all that."

"Well, you of course — " said Nikolai Piotrovich. "The small wing of the house is unsatisfactory, that's the trouble."

"But please, Papa," Arkady took him up, "you appear to be apologizing; you ought to be ashamed."

"Of course I ought to be ashamed!" Nikolai Piotrovich replied, going redder and redder.

"Now, that's enough, Papa, quite enough, please let it drop!" Arkady said, smiling amiably. "He's apologizing for something!" he thought, and his soul was filled with a feeling of condescending tenderness for his good and gentle father, a feeling mingled with a sense of secret superiority. "Please drop it," he repeated

172

yet again, involuntarily enjoying the consciousness of his own more advanced and free views.

Nikolai Piotrovich glanced at him from under the fingers of the hand with which he was still rubbing his forehead, and something plucked at his heart. But he at once rebuked himself.

"Well, here is the beginning of our land," he said after a long silence.

"And that is our wood ahead, isn't it?" Arkady asked.

"Yes, that is ours. Only I have sold it. It will be felled this year."

"Why did you sell it?"

"We needed the money; and besides, that land is to be handed over to the peasants."

"Who don't pay you their rent?"

"That is their business; but in any case they will pay some time or other."

"It's a pity about the wood," Arkady remarked, and began to look about him.

The district through which they were driving could not be called picturesque. Open field, unbrokenly open field stretched right away to the horizon, sometimes rising a little, then declining again; here and there small woods were visible, and gullies, with scanty and stunted scrub, wound in a manner reminiscent of the way they were represented on the ancient maps of Catherine's time. Here and there, too, were narrow streams with steep banks, and tiny ponds with crumbling dams, and little villages with low, tiny huts beneath gloomy, frequently tumbledown roofs, and crooked threshing-sheds with walls made of wattle and with yawning little gateways by abandoned threshing-floors, and churches, sometimes of brick with the stucco falling away, sometimes of wood with crosses awry and decayed burial-grounds. Arkady felt a little griping of the heart. As though of deliberate intent, all the peasants they fell in with were ragged, and were riding miserable little nags; wayside osier willows with hanging bark and broken branches stood like beggars in rags; emaciated, shaggy cows, looking as though gnawed to the bone, were greedily nibbling at the grass in the ditches. They seemed to have only just torn themselves away from menacing, death-dealing talons. And, evoked by the miserable aspect of these debilitated animals, a white phantom of joyless, endless winter with its blizzards, frosts, and snows arose in the midst of that spring day. "No," Arkady thought, "this is not a rich country, it does not suggest either affluence or industry; it cannot, it cannot be left like that, changes simply must be made . . . but how to effect them, how to set about it? . . ."

So Arkady meditated; but while he was meditating, spring came into its own. Everything around him was green shot with gold, everything broadly and gently undulated and shone beneath the gentle breath of the warming breeze — everything, the trees, the bushes, and the grass; everywhere the skylarks poured out endless, ringing streams of song; the pewits called as they hovered about the low-lying meadows or silently flitted from mound to mound; beautifully black, the rooks wandered amid the tender green of the still young and low spring crops; they were lost in the rye, which was already beginning to whiten; only rarely did their heads appear amid its smoky waves. Arkady gazed and gazed, and his meditations gradually faded, vanished. He flung off his greatcoat, and such a merry, such a youthful lad looked at his father that Nikolai Piotrovich embraced him once more.

"Not far now," the older man remarked. "As soon as we get to the top of that little hill the house will be in sight. We shall have a wonderful life together, Arkady; you'll help me on the farm, provided that doesn't bore you. Now we must come really close to each other, must know each other really well, mustn't we?"

"Of course," Arkady said; "but what a wonderful day it is today!"

"It is for your arrival, my dear boy. Yes, spring in all its glory. But, you know, I agree with Pushkin — you remember, in *Yevgeny Oniegin*?

> *To me how mournful is thy coming,*
> *Springtime, springtime, the time of love!*
> *How —*"

"Arkady!" Bazarov's voice came from the tarantass; "send me a match, I've nothing to light my pipe with."

Nikolai Piotrovich lapsed into silence, and Arkady, who had begun to listen to him not without a feeling of astonishment, yet not without sympathy, hurriedly took a silver matchbox from his pocket and sent Piotr with it to Bazarov.

"Would you like a cigar?" Bazarov shouted again.

"Send it along," Arkady replied.

Piotr returned to the calash and handed him the matchbox and a black cigar, which Arkady lit at once, spreading such a strong and acrid scent of well-seasoned tobacco that Nikolai Piotrovich, who had never smoked in all his life, involuntarily turned his nose away, though imperceptibly, in order not to upset his son.

Fifteen minutes later both carriages halted before the veranda of a new wooden house painted gray and covered with a red iron roof. This was Marino, also known as Novaya-Slobodka — the new settlement — or, as the peasants called it, One-man Hamlet.

IV

No swarm of domestics poured onto the veranda to meet their masters; only one girl, aged about twelve, appeared; she was followed out of the house by a lad who greatly resembled Piotr and was dressed in a gray livery jacket with white buttons adorned with armorial bearings, for he was Pavel Kirsanov's man. He silently opened the door of the carriage and unbuttoned the apron of the tarantass. Nikolai Piotrovich and his son, together with Bazarov, went through the dark and almost empty hall, where a young woman's face peered for a moment round one of its doors, and passed into the reception room, which was furnished in the latest style.

"So we're at home," Nikolai Piotrovich observed, removing his hat and shaking back his hair. "Now the chief thing is to have some supper and a rest."

"It certainly would not be a bad idea to have something to eat," Bazarov remarked, stretching himself, and he dropped on a divan.

"Yes, yes, let us have some supper, supper quickly." For no obvious reason Nikolai Piotrovich stamped his foot. "And here is Prokofich, just at the right moment."

Prokofich was a man of about sixty, white-haired, thin, and swarthy, in a brown frock coat with copper buttons, and with a rose-colored kerchief round his neck. He smirked, went to kiss Arkady's hand, and, after bowing to the guest, retired to the door and stood with hands folded behind his back.

"There he is, Prokofich," Nikolai Piotrovich began, "he's come back to us at last. . . . Well, what do you think of him?"

"He looks in the best of health," the old man declared, and he smirked again, but at once knitted his thick eyebrows. "Am I to lay the table?" he said meaningly.

"Yes, yes, please. But won't you go to your room first, Yevgeny Vasilich?"

"No, thank you, I don't need to. Only give orders for my small trunk to be taken to my room, and this garment can be put in there too," he added, taking off his light coat.

"Very good. Prokofich, take his coat." (Prokofich, who appeared to be amazed, took Bazarov's "garment" in both hands and, raising it high above his head, retreated on tiptoe.) "And how about you, Arkady, will you go to your room for a moment or two?"

"Yes, I must clean myself up," Arkady replied, and was about to go to the door; but at that moment a man of average height, dressed in a dark English suit, a fashionable low-cut cravat, and patent-leather shoes, entered the reception room. He was Arkady's uncle, Pavel Piotrovich Kirsanov. He appeared to be about forty-five years of age; his close-cut gray hair gleamed darkly like new silver; his face, choleric but unlined, unusually regular and pure, as though fashioned by a light and subtle chisel, revealed that at one time he had been remarkably handsome; his clear, black, rather elongated eyes were particularly fine. All the uncle's elegant and well-bred appearance retained a youthful harmony and that upward striving from the earth which a man almost entirely loses when he has passed the twenties.

Pavel Piotrovich took his beautiful hand with its long, rosy nails — a hand that seemed even more beautiful because of the snowy whiteness of his cuff, with its fastening of a single large opal — out of the pocket of his pantaloons and held it out to his nephew. Having accomplished this preliminary European handshake, he kissed him three times, Russian fashion; in other words, he touched his nephew's cheek three times with his perfumed mustaches, and pronounced:

"Welcome home."

Nikolai Piotrovich introduced him to Bazarov: Pavel Piotrovich bent his supple waist a little and smiled faintly, but did not give him his hand and even put it back in his pocket.

"I was beginning to think you would not arrive today," he said in a pleasant voice, affably swaying his body, twitching his shoulders, and displaying his splendid white teeth. "Did anything happen on the road?"

"Oh no," Arkady replied, "we were only delayed a little. But in consequence we are as hungry as wolves. Get Prokofich to hurry, Papa, and I'll be back in a moment."

"Wait, I'll come with you," Bazarov exclaimed, suddenly starting up from the divan. The two young men went out.

"Who is that?" Pavel Piotrovich asked.

"A friend of Arkady's, a very intelligent man, according to him."

"Is he going to stay with us?"

"Yes."

"That hairy man?"

"Why, yes."

Pavel Piotrovich drummed his nails on the table.

"I find that Arkady s'est dégourdi," he remarked. "I am glad he has returned."

They talked little at supper. Bazarov especially said almost nothing, but he ate a great deal. Nikolai Piotrovich told various incidents of his farming life, as he put it, discussed the forthcoming government measures, the committees, the deputations, the necessity of introducing machinery, and so on. Pavel Piotrovich slowly walked to and fro (he never ate supper), occasionally sipping from a glass filled with red wine, and still more rarely making some remark, or rather exclamation, in the nature of "Ah! Ehee! Hm!" Arkady told some of the latest Petersburg news, but he felt a little awkward — that awkwardness which a young man usually possesses when he has just ceased to be a child and has returned to a spot where everybody is used to seeing and regarding him as a child. He dragged out his talk unnecessarily, avoided the word "Papa," and even replaced it once by the word "Father," pronounced, truly, through his teeth; with excessive jauntiness he poured far more wine into his glass than he really desired, and drank it all. Prokofich did not take his eyes off him and only chewed his lips. After supper they all retired at once.

"But you have a rather eccentric uncle," Bazarov said to Arkady as he sat in a gown by his bed and sucked at a stocky pipe. "What elegance to find in the country, you know! Those nails of his, those nails! Why, you could send those nails to an exhibition!"

"Ah, but you don't know that he was a lion in his day," Arkady replied. "I'll tell you his story some time or other. He was really handsome, he turned the heads of all the women."

"You don't say! So it's all for old times' sake. Pity there's no one to captivate here. I stared and stared: at those amazing cuffs of his, looking just as though made of stone, and his chin so smoothly shaved. But you know it's ridiculous, isn't it, Arkady Nikolaich?"

"Maybe; but he really is a fine man."

"An archaic phenomenon! But your father's a great lad! He wastes his time reading poetry, and I don't suppose he's brilliant at farming, but he's a good sort."

"My father is a man with a golden heart."

"Have you noticed that he's shy?"

Arkady shook his head, as though he himself were never shy.

"It's an astonishing thing," Bazarov went on, "these old romantics. They develop their nervous system to the point of irritability, and so their equilibrium is disturbed. All the same, good night! I've an English washstand in my room, but the door won't fasten. Even so, that is something to be encouraged — English washstands; now that really is progress!"

Bazarov went out, and Arkady was overcome by a feeling of happiness. It is pleasant to fall asleep in your own house, on a familiar bed, under a blanket over which beloved hands have toiled, perhaps the hands of the nurse — those gracious, kindly, and unwearying hands. Arkady recalled his old nurse, Yegorovna, and sighed, and wished her "rest in peace." For himself he did not pray.

Both he and Bazarov soon dropped off, but other people in the house were a long time getting to sleep. His son's return had excited Nikolai Piotrovich. He got into bed, but did not put out the candles and, resting his head on his hand, thought long thoughts. His brother sat until well after midnight in his own room, in a broad leather armchair, before a hearth in which coal was faintly burning. Pavel Piotrovich did not undress, he only changed patent-leather shoes for red Chinese slippers without heels. He held the latest issue of *Galignani* in his hands, but he did not read; he stared fixedly at the hearth, where a flickering bluish flame died away and started up again. God knows where his thoughts wandered to, but they did not wander only in the past: the expression on his face was concentrated and morose, which is not the case when a man is occupied only with memories. But in a little back room the young woman named Fenichka sat on a large chest, in a blue dressing-jacket and with a white kerchief flung over her dark hair, sometimes listening, sometimes dozing, sometimes gazing at a half-open door, through which a child's cot could be seen and the regular breathing of a sleeping infant could be heard.

v

Next day Bazarov was awake and out of the house before anyone else. "Hm!" he thought as he looked about him, "not a very impressive spot!" When Nikolai Piotrovich had divided the land with his peasants, he had had to use nearly eleven acres of completely level and bare ground to make the new homestead. He built the house, the offices and farm buildings, made a garden, dug a pond and two wells; but the young trees did not do well, very little water gathered in the pond, and the well water proved to have a brackish taste. Only an arbor of lilac and acacias had flourished; the family sometimes drank tea and had dinner in it. In a few minutes Bazarov had traversed all the paths in the garden, had been in the cattle yard and the stable, had discovered a couple of yard boys, with whom he at once struck up an acquaintance, and went with them to a small marsh, about half a mile from the house, in search of frogs.

"What do you want frogs for, sir?" one of the boys asked him.

"Why, I'll tell you," answered Bazarov, who had the special gift of winning the trust of people of the lower orders, though he never encouraged them and treated them offhandedly. "I flatten out the frog and look to see what is happening inside it; and as you and I are also frogs, only we walk on two legs, I shall know what happens inside us too."

"But what do you want to know for?"

"In order not to make any mistake if you fall ill and I have to attend you."

"Are you a doctor, then?"

"Yes."

"Vaska, d'you hear, the gentleman says that you and I are frogs. That's queer!"

179

"I'm afraid of them—frogs, I mean," remarked Vaska, a barefooted boy about seven years of age with hair as white as flax, who was wearing a gray Cossack-style jacket with standing collar.

"What is there to be afraid of? They don't bite, do they?"

"Now, step into the water, philosophers!" Bazarov told them.

Meanwhile Nikolai Piotrovich also had risen and gone off to Arkady, whom he found fully dressed. The father and son went onto the terrace beneath the shade of the awning; a samovar was already boiling on a table by the railing, between great bouquets of lilac. A girl, the same who had been the first to meet the arrivals on the veranda the evening before, appeared and said in a piping voice:

"Fyodosia Nikolavna is not very well and cannot come; she told me to ask you whether you will pour out tea for yourselves or is she to send Dunia."

"I'll pour it out myself, myself," Nikolai Piotrovich hurriedly replied. "How do you drink tea, Arkady, with cream or with lemon?"

"With cream," Arkady replied, and after a momentary silence said interrogatively: "Papa dear?"

Nikolai Piotrovich looked at his son in some embarrassment.

"Well?" he said.

Arkady looked down.

"Forgive me, Papa, if my question seems out of place to you," he began, "but you yourself, by your frankness yesterday, call for frankness in me. You won't be angry?"

"Go on."

"You make me bold to ask you— Isn't it because—it isn't because I am here that Fen—that she won't come to pour out the tea, is it?"

Nikolai Piotrovich turned a little away from his son.

"It may be," he said at last, "she supposes—she is shy."

Arkady gave his father a swift look.

"There's no reason why she should be. To begin with, you know my way of thinking" (Arkady was delighted to say these words), "and secondly, I have no wish to be the least constraint on your life, on your habits. Besides, I am sure you could not make a bad choice; if you have allowed her to live under the same roof with you, then she is deserving of it; in any case, a son is not his father's judge, especially I, and especially a father like you, who have never imposed any restraints whatever on my freedom."

Arkady's voice trembled at first: he was conscious of all his magnanimity, but at the same time he realized that he was reading his father something in the nature of a homily; but a man is greatly affected by the sound of his own voice, and Arkady said the last wards firmly, and even with a certain flair.

"Thank you, Arkady," Nikolai Piotrovich said thickly, and his fingers again wandered over his eyebrows and forehead. "Your assumptions are quite correct. Of course, if this girl were not worthy — It is not a frivolous caprice. It is not easy for me to talk to you about it; but you understand that it was difficult for her to come here, with you present, especially on the first day after your arrival."

"In that case I shall go to her," Arkady exclaimed with a new access of magnanimous feeling, and he jumped up from the table. "I'll explain to her that she has no reason whatever to be shy with me."

Nikolai Piotrovich also rose.

"Arkady," he began, "do me the favor—how can you— There—I haven't warned you—"

But Arkady was already out of earshot and running from the terrace. Nikolai Piotrovich stared after him and dropped disconcertedly into his chair. His heart began to beat. As he sat there was he realizing that the relations between him and his son must in the future inevitably be strange, or was he conscious that Arkady could hardly have shown any greater respect for him if he had not touched on the matter at all, or was he reproaching himself for his weakness? It is difficult to say; all these feelings struggled within him, but in the form of sensations — and even they were far from clear; but the flush did not leave his face, and his heart beat.

He heard hurried steps, and Arkady returned to the terrace.

"We've made each other's acquaintance, Father," he exclaimed with an expression of gracious and kindly triumph on his face. "It is quite true Fyodosia Nikolavna isn't very well today and will come later. But why didn't you tell me I had a brother? I would have kissed him yesterday evening, just as I kissed him a moment ago."

Nikolai Piotrovich was about to blurt out some remark, was about to rise and open his arms. Arkady flung himself on his neck.

"What are you doing? Embracing again?" Pavel Piotrovich's voice sounded behind them.

Both father and son were equally glad of his appearance at that moment; there are certain situations that are very affecting, but which those who take part in them find rather trying.

"Why the surprise?" Nikolai Piotrovich said gaily. "At last I have lived to see Arkady home. I have not had time to take a good look at him since yesterday."

"I am not at all surprised," Pavel Piotrovich remarked. "Even I am not averse from embracing him."

Arkady went up to his uncle and again felt the light brush of his perfumed mustaches on his cheeks. Pavel Piotrovich sat down at the table. He was wearing an elegant morning suit of English cut, and his head was adorned with a little tarboosh. This tarboosh and the small, negligently tied cravat suggested the freedom of country life; but the tight-fitting collar of the shirt, which, to be sure, was not white, but colored, as it should be for the morning toilet, dug with its customary inflexibility into his clean-shaven chin.

"But where is your new friend?" he asked Arkady.

"He's gone out; he's in the habit of rising early and going off somewhere. The main thing is not to pay any attention to him; he doesn't like ceremony."

"Yes, that is evident." Pavel Piotrovich began unhurriedly to spread butter on his bread. "Is he going to stay with us for long?"

"As long as is convenient. He's come here on the way to his father."

"And where does his father live?"

"In our own province, fifty miles from here. He has a small estate there. He was formerly a regimental doctor."

"Ah, yes, yes, yes. I kept asking myself where I had heard the name of Bazarov before. Nikolai, I think I remember that there was a Dr. Bazarov in Father's division."

"I think there was."

"Exactly, exactly. So that doctor is his father? Hm!" Pavel Piotrovich wriggled his whiskers. "Well, and what exactly is Mr. Bazarov himself?" he asked with a drawl.

"What is Bazarov?" Arkady smiled. "If you like, uncle, I'll tell you just what he is."

"I shall be greatly obliged, nephew mine."

"He's a nihilist." [1]

"What?" Nikolai Piotrovich asked, but Pavel Piotrovich raised a knife with a piece of butter on its blade into the air and remained immobilized.

"He's a nihilist," Arkady repeated.

"A nihilist," Nikolai Piotrovich declared. "That is from the Latin *nihil*, or nothing, so far as I can judge; so the word means a man who — who recognizes nothing?"

"Rather say: who respects nothing," Pavel Piotrovich caught him up, and began again on the butter.

"Who approaches everything from a critical standpoint," Arkady remarked.

"But isn't that the same?" Pavel Piotrovich asked.

"No, it isn't. A nihilist is a man who does not bow to any authorities, who does not take any principle on trust, no matter with what respect that principle is surrounded."

"Well, and is that good?" Pavel Piotrovich interrupted him.

"It depends, uncle. It is good for some, and very bad for others."

"Really. Well, I can see that this is outside our province. We, the people of the older generation, we assume that without principles" (Pavel Piotrovich pronounced that last word evenly, in the French fashion, whereas Arkady, on the other hand, put the emphasis on the first syllable), "without principles taken, as you put it, on trust, it is impossible to move a single step forward, or to breathe. *Vous avez changé tout cela*, God grant you health and general's rank, but we shall only admire you, gentlemen — what did you call it?"

"Nihilists," Arkady distinctly declared.

"Yes. Formerly there were Hegelists, and now there are nihilists. We shall see how you will exist in a vacuum, in an airless expanse; but now, brother, please ring; it is time I had my cocoa."

Nikolai Piotrovich rang and called: "Duniasha!" But instead of Duniasha, Fenichka herself came onto the terrace. She was a young woman of twenty-three, with a clear white and soft skin, dark hair and eyes, crimson, childishly swollen lips, and delicate

[1] This word was coined by Turgenev. (Tr.)

little hands. She was wearing a neat cotton dress; a new azure triangular kerchief lay over her rounded shoulders. She brought a large cup of cocoa, and as she set it before Pavel Piotrovich she was completely abashed; the hot blood flooded in a crimson wave beneath the fine skin of her pleasant face. She lowered her eyes and halted by the table, resting lightly on the very tips of her toes. She seemed conscience-stricken at having come, and at the same time she seemed to feel that she had the right to come.

Pavel Piotrovich knitted his brows sternly, but Nikolai Piotrovich was confused.

"Good morning, Fenichka," he said between his teeth.

"Good morning," she replied in a voice not loud, but melodious, and, glancing sidelong at Arkady, who gave her a friendly smile, she quietly withdrew. She walked with a slight tendency to waddle, but it became her.

For a few moments there was silence on the race. Pavel Piotrovich began to sip his cocoa, but suddenly raise his head.

"And here is Mr. Nihilist coming to present himself to us," he said in an undertone.

He was right; Bazarov was coming through the garden, striding across the flower-beds. His canvas coat and pantaloons was soiled with mud; clinging marsh vegetation was wrapped round the crown of his old round hat; in his right hand he was carrying a small bag; in the bag something living was stirring. He came swiftly up to the terrace and, nodding his head, said:

"Good morning, gentlemen; pardon me for being late for tea; I'll be back in a minute; I must just put these prisoners in a safe place."

"What have you got, leeches?" Pavel Piotrovich asked.

"No, frogs."

'Do you eat them – or cultivate them?"

'For experiments," Bazarov said in an unconcerned tone, and went into the house.

"So he'll cut them up," Pavel Piotrovich remarked. "He doesn't believe in principles, but he believes in frogs."

Arkady gave his uncle a commiserative look. Nikolai Piotrovich surreptitiously shrugged his shoulders. Pavel Piotrovich himself felt that his witticism had fallen flat, and he began to talk about farming and the new steward, who the evening before had come to him to complain that one of the workmen was idling and had got out of hand. "That is the Æsop he is," he said in passing. "He always protested that he was a stupid man; he will live his day and will depart as stupid."

VI

Bazarov returned, sat down at the table, and hurriedly began to drink his tea. The two brothers gazed at him without speaking, but Arkady took stealthy glances first at his father, then at his uncle.

"Did you go for a long walk?" Nikolai Piotrovich asked at last.

"You have some marshland not far from here, by an ash grove. I started up five snipe; you can kill them, Arkady."

"You don't go hunting, then?"

"No."

"You yourself are studying physics, are you not?" Pavel Piotrovich asked in his turn.

"Yes, physics, and natural sciences generally."

"They say the Germans have had great successes recently in that field."

"Yes, the Germans can teach us a great deal in that respect," Bazarov answered carelessly.

Pavel Piotrovich had used the Russianized form of the word "Germans" instead of the original Slavonic word, with the intention of being ironic; but no one noticed it.

"Have you such a high opinion of the Germans?" Pavel Piotrovich asked with exquisite courtesy. He was beginning to feel a secret irritation. His aristocratic nature was revolted by Bazarov's completely free and easy manner. This doctor's son was not merely lacking in modesty; he even replied offhandedly and reluctantly, and there was something coarse, almost insolent, in the tone of his voice.

"Their scientists are an efficient lot."

"Yes, truly. But I suppose you haven't such a flattering opinion of Russian scientists?"

"I'm afraid you're right."

"That is very praiseworthy self-denial," Pavel Piotrovich remarked, straightening up and throwing his head back. "But how is it that Arkady Nikolaich has just told us you do not recognize any authorities? Don't you believe them?"

"Why should I trouble to recognize them? And what am I to believe? They tell me something to the point, I agree, and that's all there is to it."

"And do all Germans speak to the point?" Pavel Piotrovich said, and his face took on such a dispassionate, distant expression that he seemed to have departed beyond the clouds.

"Not all of them," Bazarov replied with a little yawn; evidently he had no desire to continue the verbal contest.

Pavel Piotrovich glanced at Arkady as though wanting to say to him: "Your friend is polite, you must admit."

"As for me," he said again, not without some effort, "I, sinful man that I am, do not feel any pity for the Germans. I will not say anything about the Russian Germans; we all know what they are like. But I have no liking even for the German Germans. Even in the old days they were all over the place; in those days they had — well, there was Schiller, and 'Gette,' wasn't it? My brother thinks very highly of them. . . . But now they are all chemists and materialists."

"A decent chemist is twenty times more useful than any poet," Bazarov interrupted.

"Really!" Pavel Piotrovich remarked, and slightly raised his eyebrows, as though dropping off to sleep. "So you do not recognize art, then?"

"The art of acquiring money, or no more hemorrhoids!" Bazarov exclaimed with a contemptuous sneer.

"Indeed! So that is your idea of a joke. And so you renounce everything? Granted. So you believe only in science?"

"I have already told you that I do not believe in anything; and what do you mean by science — science in general? There are sciences, just as there are crafts and professions; but there is no such thing as science in general."

"Very good! But with regard to other generally accepted conventions, do you hold to the same negative tendency?"

"What is this, a police inquiry?" Bazarov asked.

Pavel Piotrovich paled a little. Nikolai Piotrovich considered it advisable to intervene in the conversation.

"We'll discuss this subject with you in more detail some other time, my dear Yevgeny Vasilich; we shall ascertain your opinion, and we shall express our own. For my part I am very glad that you are studying natural science. I have heard that Liebig has made some remarkable discoveries concerning land fertilization. You may be able to help me in my agricultural work; you may be able to give me some useful advice."

"I am at your service, Nikolai Piotrovich; but how can we tackle Liebig? We have to learn the A B C first, only then can we turn to books; and so far we haven't even seen A for ourselves."

"Well, I see you are definitely a nihilist," Nikolai Piotrovich thought.

"Permit me none the less to turn to you if I require to," he added aloud. "But now, brother, I think it is time for us to go and have a talk with the steward."

Pavel Piotrovich rose from the table.

"Yes," he declared, not looking at anybody, "it is a misfortune to have lived five short years in the country, far from the great minds! You become such a perfect fool. You try not to forget what you were taught, but there — in a trice it transpires that all you have learned is nonsense, and you are told that sensible men no longer occupy themselves with such trifles, and that you are a backward nincompoop. But there is nothing to be done about it! Evidently the youngsters are wiser than we."

Pavel Piotrovich slowly turned on his heels and slowly left the terrace. Nikolai Piotrovich followed him.

"Tell me, is he always like that?" Bazarov unconcernedly asked Arkady as soon as the door closed behind the two brothers.

"Listen, Yevgeny, you treated him too harshly," Arkady remarked. "You've affronted him."

"Oh yes, I'll pamper them, these country aristocrats! Why, they're all self-esteem, with their habits of country lions and their foppery. He should continue his career in Petersburg, if that is what he is like. . . . But, in any case, I am not interested in him. Do you know I have found a quite rare specimen of the water beetle, *Dytiscus marginalis*? I'll show it to you."

"I promised to tell you his story," Arkady began.

"The story of the beetle?"

"Now, do stop it, Yevgeny. The story of my uncle. You'll see that he is not the man you imagine him to be. He is more deserving of pity than sneers."

"I don't dispute it; but how is it he has taken you in?"

"One must be fair, Yevgeny."

"What does that follow from?"

"But do listen. . . ."

And Arkady told him the story of his uncle. The reader will find it in the next chapter.

VII

Pavel Piotrovich Kirsanov was educated first at home, like his younger brother, Nikolai, and then in the *corps des pages*. Even as a child he was distinguished by his remarkably handsome appearance, and in addition he was self-confident, a little derisive, and amusingly splenetic — people could not help liking him. As soon as he became an officer he was to be seen everywhere. He was lionized, and he enjoyed himself, even played the fool, even put on airs, but that, too, became him. Women lost their wits over him, men called him a fop and secretly envied him. He lived, as we have said, in one apartment with his brother, of whom he was sincerely fond, though they were not in the least like each other. Nikolai Piotrovich limped a little, had small features, pleasant, but rather mournful small black eyes, and soft, thin hair; he was always ready to be lazy, but just as ready to read, and was afraid of society. Pavel Piotrovich never spent an evening at home; he was famous for his daring and dexterity (he had made gymnastics fashionable among the society youth) and read only five or six French books. At the age of twenty-eight he was already a captain; a brilliant career awaited him. Suddenly everything was changed.

About that time a certain woman, who is not forgotten even today, Princess R., made rare appearances in Petersburg society. She had a well-bred and decorous but rather stupid husband, and they had no children. She suddenly went abroad, suddenly returned to Russia, and altogether led a strange life. She was reputed to be a frivolous coquette, gave herself over enthusiastically to all kinds of pleasure, danced till she dropped, laughed and joked with young people, whom she received in a twilit reception hall before dinner, and at night wept and prayed, was never able to rest, and often wandered about the room until dawn, miserably wringing her hands, or sat, pale and cold, over a psalter. Day came, and she was again transformed into a society lady, she again paid visits, laughed, chattered, and literally threw herself in the way of anyone who could provide her with the least amusement. She was an amazing combination of physical characteristics: her tresses, of golden color, and as heavy as gold, fell below her knees, but no one would have called her a beauty; of all her features only her eyes were fine, and not even the eyes themselves — they were small and gray — but their look, swift and deep, was unconcerned to the point of audacity and thoughtful to the point of despondency — an enigmatic look. Something out of the ordinary shone in that look, even when her tongue was babbling the most empty of phrases. She dressed exquisitely. Pavel Piotrovich met her at a ball, danced a mazurka with her, during which she did not say one sensible word, and fell passionately in love with her. He was accustomed to triumphs, and once more he swiftly achieved his purpose; but the ease of the victory did not cool his ardor. On the contrary, he grew even more tormentedly, even more strongly attached to this woman, who, even when she yielded herself irrevocably, still seemed to retain something sacred and inaccessible, into which none could penetrate. What lurked in that soul, God knows! She seemed to be in the power of secret forces, unknown even to herself; they played with her as they wished; her little mind could not cope with their caprices. . . . All her conduct was a succession of incongruities: the only letters that could have aroused her husband's rightful suspicions were written to a man almost unknown to her; but her love was tinged with sorrow; she no longer laughed or jested with the man she had chosen, and listened to him and looked at him in bewilderment. Sometimes, very often quite suddenly, this bewilderment would pass into a frigid horror; her face acquired a dead and wild expression; she locked herself in her bedroom, and her maid, listening with one ear to the keyhole, could hear her bitter sobbing. Often, returning home after a rapturous meeting, Kirsanov felt within him that rending and bitter chagrin which rises in the heart after utter failure. "Yet what else do I want?" he asked himself, but his heart remained despondent. One day he gave her a ring with a sphinx carved on it.

"What is it," she asked, "a sphinx?"

"Yes," he answered, "and that sphinx is you."

"I?" she asked, and slowly raised her enigmatic gaze to him. "Do you know that that is very flattering?" she added with a faint smile; but her eyes still had that strange look.

It was hard for Pavel Piotrovich even when Princess R. loved him; but when she cooled in her feeling for him, and that happened quite quickly, he all but went out of his mind. He tormented himself and was jealous, would not give her any peace, and dragged after her everywhere; she grew tired of his importunate persecution, and she went abroad. Despite the requests of his friends, the exhortations of his higher officers, he went into retirement, and set off after the Princess; four years he spent in foreign countries, sometimes chasing after her, sometimes deliberately losing sight of her; he was ashamed of himself, he was furious at his own pusillanimity — but nothing was of avail. Her image, that incomprehensible, almost senseless, but enchanting image had been carved too deeply into his soul. At Baden he succeeded in renewing his former relations with her; it seemed that never before had she loved him so passionately. . . . But within a month it was all finished; the fire had flamed up for the last time, and it went out forever. Having a presentiment of the inevitable parting, he wanted at least to remain her friend, as if friendship with such a woman were possible. . . . She quietly left Baden, and thenceforth she persistently avoided him. He returned to Russia, tried to resume his old ways of life, but could not re-enter the old circles. With a poisoned soul he wandered from place to place; he still paid visits, he preserved all the habits of a man of society, he could boast of two or three new victories; but now he no longer expected anything remarkable either of himself or of others, and he did nothing. He grew old, went gray; to sit of an evening in the club, to be splenetically bored, to argue unconcernedly in bachelors' society, became a necessity to him, and that is a bad sign, as is well known. Of course he did not even think of marrying. Ten years passed in this way, drably, fruitlessly, and swiftly, terribly swiftly. Nowhere else does time speed past as in Russia; in prison, they say, it speeds even faster. One day, at dinner in the club, Pavel Piotrovich heard that Princess R. was dead. She had died in Paris, in a state verging on insanity. He rose from the table and walked a long time about the club rooms, halting, as though rooted to the ground, close to the card-players, but did not return home any earlier than usual. Some time later he received a packet addressed to him; it contained the ring he had given the Princess long before. She had drawn a cross over the sphinx and had given orders that he was to be told that the Cross was the solution.

This occurred at the beginning of 1848, just when Nikolai Piotrovich arrived in Petersburg after losing his wife. Pavel Piotrovich had hardly seen his brother since Nikolai's retirement to the country; Nikolai Piotrovich's wedding occurred during the very early days of Pavel Piotrovich's acquaintance with the Princess. On his return from abroad he had gone to his brother with the intention of staying with him for a couple of months, admiring his happiness; but he had remained only one week. The difference between the two brothers' lives was too great. In 1848 this difference had greatly diminished: Nikolai Piotrovich had lost his wife, Pavel Piotrovich had lost his memories; after the Princess's death he tried not to think of her. But Nikolai was left with the consciousness of a wisely spent life, his son was growing up before his eyes; Pavel, on the contrary, was a lonely bachelor and was entering on that vague, crepuscular time, the time of regrets that resemble hopes, of hopes that resemble regrets, when youth has passed, but old age has not yet arrived.

That time was more difficult for Pavel Piotrovich than for anyone else: having lost his past, he had lost all.

"I shall not invite you to Marino now," Nikolai Piotrovich said to him one day (he had called his estate Marino in honor of his wife); "you were bored there even when my wife was alive, and now I think you would be eaten up with yearning there."

"Then I was still stupid and flighty," Pavel Piotrovich replied, "but now I have sobered down, even if I have not grown any wiser. Now, on the contrary, if you will allow me, I am ready to settle down with you forever."

Instead of replying, Nikolai Piotrovich embraced him; but after this conversation eighteen months passed before Pavel Piotrovich decided to carry out his intention. On the other hand, once he had settled down in the country he did not go away again, not even during the three winters Nikolai Piotrovich spent in Petersburg with his son. He began to read, mostly English books; in fact, he ordered all his life in accordance with English tastes; he rarely met his neighbors and went visiting only during elections, and even then he was usually silent, only occasionally irritating and alarming landowners of old-fashioned ideas with his liberal ways, and not coming into any close contact with the representatives of the new generation. Both the one and the other group regarded him as arrogant; both groups respected him for his distinguished, aristocratic manners, for the rumors of his conquests; because he dressed excellently and always stayed in the best room of the best hotel; because he always dined well, and once had even dined with Wellington and Louis-Philippe; because he always carried a silver dressing-case and a portable bath around with him; because he was always scented with some unusual, amazingly "noble" perfume; because he was a splendid whist-player and always lost; finally, he was also respected for his irreproachable integrity. The ladies considered him an enchanting melancholist, but he did not mix with the ladies.

"And so you can see, Yevgeny," Arkady said as he ended his story, "how unjustly you judge my uncle! I do not even mention the fact that he has more than once rescued my father from difficulties, has given him all his money — you may not know that the estate was not divided between them — but he is always glad to help anyone and, I must say, always stands up for the peasants; though it is true that when talking to them he frowns and sniffs cologne."

"That's obviously nerves," Bazarov interrupted.

"Maybe, but he has a very good heart. And he's far from stupid. What very good advice he has given me — especially — especially in regard to relations with women!"

"Aha! He's scalded his lips with his own milk, so he blows on another's. We know that trick!"

"Well, in a word," Arkady went on, "he is deeply unhappy, believe me; to feel scorn for him would be wicked."

"But who feels any scorn for him?" Bazarov retorted. "All the same, I say that a man who staked all his life on the card of woman's love, and who, when that card failed him, grew sour and let himself sink to being incapable of anything at all, is not a man, but a male animal. You say he is unhappy; you should know best; but he hasn't lost all his stupidity. I am confident that he seriously imagines himself to be clever because he reads *Galignani* and once a month saves a peasant from a flogging."

"But remember his upbringing, the times in which he has lived," Arkady remarked.

"Upbringing?" Bazarov took him up. "Every man should bring himself up — well, as I have, for instance. . . . And as for the times, why should I be dependent on them? Let them rather be dependent on me. No, brother, all that is simply wanton and empty! And what are these mysterious relations between man and woman? We physiologists know what those relations are. You study the anatomy of the eye: what is the cause of that enigmatic look, as you put it? It's all romanticism, nonsense, rottenness, art. Let's rather go and look at that beetle."

And the two friends went off to Bazarov's room, which was already pervaded with the scent of medicaments, mingled with the smell of cheap tobacco.

VIII

Pavel Piotrovich did not stay long to listen to his brother's conversation with the steward, who was a tall and gaunt man with a wheedling, consumptive voice and knavish eyes, and who replied to all Nikolai Piotrovich's remarks with "Of course, that is well known," and endeavored to represent the peasants as drunkards and thieves. The husbandry only recently set on a new course was creaking like an ungreased wheel, cracking like home-made furniture of unseasoned timber. Nikolai Piotrovich did not despair, but he sighed rather frequently and was lost in thought: he felt that without money his affairs would make no progress, and his money had almost all gone. Arkady had told the truth: Pavel Piotrovich had helped his brother more than once; more than once, seeing him struggling and racking his head, wondering how to get out of his difficulties, Pavel Piotrovich had slowly gone across to the window and, thrusting his hands in his pockets, had muttered through his teeth: "*Mais je puis vous donner de l'argent*," and had given him money; but that day he himself had none, and he preferred to withdraw. The petty vexations of the farm made him feel miserable; moreover, it always seemed to him that Nikolai Piotrovich, despite all his fervor and industry, did not set about affairs in the right way, though he himself could not have pointed out just where his brother had gone wrong. "He is not sufficiently practical," he thought; "they fool him." Nikolai Piotrovich, on the other hand, had a high opinion of his brother's practical nature and always asked his advice. "I am soft and weak, I've spent my life in the lonely countryside," he used to say, "and you haven't lived so much among people for nothing, you know them well; you have an eagle eye." In reply

Pavel Piotrovich only turned away, but did not disillusion his brother.

Leaving Nikolai Piotrovich in his room, he went along the corridor separating the front from the back part of the house and, as he reached a low door, halted irresolutely, tugged at his whiskers, and knocked.

"Who's there? Come in," he heard Fenichka's voice.

"It is I," Pavel Piotrovich said, and opened the door.

Fenichka jumped up from the chair on which she was seated with her child and, handing the baby to a girl, who at once carried it out of the room, hurriedly adjusted her kerchief.

"Pardon me if I have disturbed you," Pavel Piotrovich began, without looking at her; "I simply wanted to ask you — I think they are sending to town today — to order them to buy some green tea for me."

"Very good," Fenichka replied; "how much do you wish them to buy?"

"Why, half a pound will be enough, I think. But I see you have made a change here," he added, looking about him with a swift glance, which also slipped over Fenichka's face. "Those curtains," he added, seeing that she did not understand what he meant.

"Yes, the curtains; Nikolai Piotrovich gave them to us; but they've been up a long time now."

"But then, I have not been here for a long time. It is very pleasant here now."

"Owing to Nikolai Piotrovich's kindness," Fenichka whispered.

"You are more comfortable here than in the other wing?" Pavel Piotrovich asked politely, but without smiling in the least.

"Of course."

"Whom have they put there in your place?"

"The laundresses are there now."

"Ah!"

He lapsed into silence. "Now he'll go," Fenichka thought. But he did not go, and she remained standing before him as though rooted to the ground, gently playing with her fingers.

"Why did you have your baby taken out?" Pavel Piotrovich said at last. "I am fond of children: let me see him."

Fenichka went quite red with embarrassment and pleasure. She was afraid of Pavel Piotrovich; he hardly ever spoke to her.

"Duniasha," she called, "bring in Mitya" (Fenichka spoke in the second person plural to everybody in the house, even the servants). "But wait a moment: we must dress him." She went to the door.

"But that doesn't matter," Pavel Piotrovich observed.

"I'll be back in a moment," Fenichka replied, and briskly left the room.

Now Pavel Piotrovich was left alone, and he looked about him with particular attention. The small, rather low room in which he was standing was very clean and cozy. It still smelt of the paint with which the floor had recently been painted, as well as of camomile and balm. Along the wall stood chairs with lyre-shaped backs; the late general had bought them in Poland, during a campaign. In one corner stood a little bed beneath a muslin canopy, beside an ironbound chest with a rounded lid. In the opposite corner a little lamp was burning before the large dark icon of Nicholas the Miracle-Worker; suspended from the halo by a red ribbon, a tiny marble egg hung on the saint's breast. Along the windowsills jars of last year's jam, carefully tied up, shed a green light; on their paper covers Fenichka herself had written "Gooseberry" in large letters; Nikolai Piotrovich was particularly fond of this kind of jam. A cage with a bobtailed siskin hung on a long cord from the ceiling; the bird chirruped and hopped about incessantly, and the cage rocked and quivered incessantly; hempseed fell with a quiet patter to the floor. On the wall between the windows, above a small cupboard, hung rather poor photographs of Nikolai Piotrovich in various positions, taken by a traveling artist; here, too, hung a photograph of Fenichka herself, a complete failure: an eyeless face smiled tensely in a dark little frame — it was impossible to distinguish anything else — and above Fenichka was General Yermolov in a Caucasian cloak, frowning sinisterly at distant Caucasian mountains from beneath a silk cowl for holding pins, which had fallen right over his brow.

Some five minutes passed; a rustling and whispering came from the other room. Pavel Piotrovich took a grease-stained book, an odd volume of Masalsky's *Sharpshooters*, from the cupboard and turned over several pages. . . . The door opened, and Fenichka entered with Mitya in her arms. She had dressed him in a little crimson shirt with a galloon at the neck, had combed his hair and wiped his face; he breathed deeply, struggled with all his body, and tugged with his little hands, as all healthy children do; but the elegant shirt obviously had an effect on him; all his chubby little figure expressed his satisfaction. Fenichka had tidied her own hair too and had arranged her kerchief better; but she could have remained as she was. And, in very deed, is there anything in the world more captivating than a young and beautiful mother with a healthy baby in her arms?

"What a chubby boy!" Pavel Piotrovich said in a condescending tone, and he tickled Mitya's double chin with the end of the long nail of his forefinger; the child fixed its eyes on the siskin and smiled.

"It's your uncle," Fenichka said, bending her head over the baby and gently shaking him, while Duniasha quietly set a lighted fumigating pastille on a kopek piece in the window.

"How many months is he now?" Pavel Piotrovich asked.

"Six months; it will soon be seven, on the 11th."

"Won't it be eight, Fyodosia Nikolavna?" Duniasha intervened a little shyly.

"No, seven; how could it be the eighth!" The child smiled again, fixed his eye on the chest, and suddenly clutched at his mother's nose and lips with all five fingers. "Naughty!" Fenichka said, without drawing her face away from his fingers.

"He is like my brother," Pavel Piotrovich observed.

"Who else should he be like?" Fenichka thought.

"Yes," he went on, as though talking to himself, "an undoubted likeness." He looked at Fenichka closely, almost sorrowfully.

"It's your uncle," she repeated, but now in a whisper.

"Ah! Pavel! So there you are!" They suddenly heard Nikolai Piotrovich's voice.

Pavel Piotrovich hurriedly turned round and knitted his brows; but his brother was looking at him so joyfully, so gratefully, that he could not but smile in reply.

"You have a splendid little fellow!" he pronounced, and looked at his watch, "but I dropped in here to see about some tea. . . ."

And, adopting an unconcerned expression, he at once left the room.

"Did he come here of his own accord?" Nikolai Piotrovich asked Fenichka.

"Yes; he knocked and came in."

"But Arkady hasn't been to see you again?"

"No. Don't you think I ought to transfer to the wing, Nikolai Piotrovich?"

"What for?"

"I think it might be better for the time being."

"N-no," Nikolai Piotrovich said hesitantly, and rubbed his forehead. "It should have been done earlier. . . . Good morning, tubby," he said with sudden vivacity, and, drawing close to the child, kissed him on the cheek; then he stooped a little and put his lips to Fenichka's hand, which showed as white as milk against Mitya's crimson shirt.

"Nikolai Piotrovich! What are you doing?" she stammered, and cast down her eyes; then she slowly raised them. Delightful was the expression of her eyes when she looked up from under her brows and smiled graciously and a little foolishly.

Nikolai Piotrovich had made Fenichka's acquaintance in the following manner. One day, some three years previously, he had had to spend the night at an inn in a distant county town. He was pleasantly struck by the cleanliness of the room he was given and the freshness of the bed linen; "surely a German woman must be the hostess here," he thought; but the hostess proved to be Russian, a woman about fifty years of age, neatly dressed, with an open, intelligent face and modest speech. He talked with her over the tea; he liked her very much. At that time Nikolai Piotrovich had only just entered into occupation of his new farm and, not wishing to keep serfs around him, was looking for hired servants; the innkeeper, for her part, complained of the few people who passed through the town, and of the difficult times. He proposed that she should come and work for him as housekeeper; she agreed. Her husband had died long before, leaving her with only one daughter, Fenichka. Some two weeks later Arina Savishna (as the new housekeeper was named) arrived with her daughter at Marino and settled in the wing. Nikolai Piotrovich's choice proved to be very satisfactory. Arina introduced order into the house. No one talked about Fenichka, who was then just past seventeen, and she was rarely to be seen: she lived very quietly, very modestly, and only on Sundays did Nikolai Piotrovich notice the delicate profile of her rather white face somewhere at one side in the parish church. Thus more than a year passed.

One morning Arina came to him in his room and, after bowing low, as usual, asked him whether he could help her daughter, as a spark from the fire had flown into her eye. Like all stay-at-homes, Nikolai Piotrovich tried his hand at doctoring and had even acquired a case of homeopathic remedies. He at once told Arina to bring in the sufferer. When Fenichka learned that the master had sent for her she was very frightened, but she came with her mother. Nikolai Piotrovich led her across to the window and took her head in both his hands. After closely examining her reddened and inflamed eye, he prescribed a lotion that he himself at once made up and, tearing his handkerchief to pieces, showed her how to bathe the eye. Fenichka listened to all he had to say and was about to go. "Kiss the master's hand, you little stupid," Arina told her. Nikolai Piotrovich did not give her his hand and, in his embarrassment, himself kissed her on her bowed head, on the parting. Fenichka's eye soon got better, but the impression she had made on Nikolai Piotrovich did not quickly pass. He was always calling to mind that pure, tender, timorously upturned face; he felt that soft hair beneath the palms of his hands, he saw those innocent, half-parted lips, behind which pearly little teeth gleamed humidly in the sunlight. He began to watch her more closely in the church, sought to fall into conversation with her. At first she avoided him, and one day, late in the afternoon, meeting him on a narrow path that walkers had made across a ryefield, she turned into the dense, tall rye, with its undergrowth of wormwood and cornflowers, so that he would not catch sight of her. He noticed her little head amid the golden entanglement of the rye, from which she was peering out like a little animal, and called to her graciously:

"Good afternoon, Fenichka! I don't bite."

"Good afternoon," she whispered, not emerging from her lair.

Little by little she began to grow accustomed to him, but she always remained timorous in his presence. Then suddenly her mother died of the cholera. Where was Fenichka to go? From her mother she had inherited a love of order, and sagacity and gravity; but she was so young, so entirely alone, Nikolai Piotro-

vich himself was so kind and modest. . . . There is nothing more
to be said.

"So my brother just came in to see you?" Nikolai Piotrovich
asked her. "He just knocked and came in?"

"Yes."

"Well, that is good. Let me give Mitya a swing."

And he began to throw the baby almost up to the ceiling, to the
great delight of the infant and the no little anxiety of the mother,
who, every time he flew up, stretched out her hands to his bare
feet.

But Pavel Piotrovich returned to his exquisite room, with its
walls hung with excellent paper of an extravagant color, with
weapons arranged against a variegated Persian wall carpet, with
walnut furniture, upholstered in dark green velveteen, with a
Renaissance bookcase of old black oak, with bronze statuettes on
the magnificent writing-desk, with a chimney hearth. . . . He
flung himself on a divan, put his hands behind his head, and remained motionless, staring almost with despair at the ceiling.
Whether because he wanted to conceal what was occurring in
his face even from the walls or for some other reason, he rose
and unfastened the heavy window curtains, then flung himself
back on the divan.

IX

On that same day Bazarov also made Fenichka's acquaintance. He
was walking about the garden with Arkady and explaining to him
why certain of the trees, especially the oak saplings, had not taken
root.

"What this place wants is more silver poplars and firs, and limes
if you like, to consolidate the black earth. Now, this arbor has
taken well," he added, "because acacias and lilacs are good children, they don't need attention. But there's somebody here."

Fenichka was sitting with Duniasha and Mitya in the arbor.
Bazarov came to a halt, but Arkady nodded to Fenichka as if she
were an old acquaintance.

"Who is that?" Bazarov asked him as soon as they had passed.
"She's very good-looking!"

"But whom are you talking about?"

"You know whom: only one of them was good-looking."

Arkady, not without some embarrassment, briefly explained who Fenichka was.

"Aha!" Bazarov exclaimed, "evidently your father has good taste. I like your father, really and truly I do! He's a dog! But I must make her acquaintance all the same," and he turned back to the arbor.

"Yevgeny!" Arkady shouted after him in alarm; "be careful, for God's sake!"

"Don't get agitated!" Bazarov said; "we're used to mingling with people, we've known town life."

As he approached Fenichka he removed his hat.

"Let me introduce myself," he began with a courteous bow. "I am a friend of Arkady Nikolaich's, and a quiet sort of man."

Fenichka half rose from the bench and looked at him without speaking.

"What a wonderful baby!" Bazarov continued. "Don't be alarmed, I've never yet given anyone the evil eye. Why has he got such crimson cheeks? Is he cutting his teeth?"

"Yes," Fenichka said, "he's already cut four teeth, but now the gums are swollen again."

"Let me look — don't be afraid, I'm a doctor."

Bazarov took the child in his arms, and, to the surprise of both Fenichka and Duniasha, Mitya made no resistance whatever and was not frightened.

"I see, I see. . . . It's all right, everything's going well; he'll have good teeth. If anything should go wrong, let me know. And you yourself are quite well?"

"Yes, God be thanked."

"God be thanked — that's best of all. And you?" Bazarov added, turning to Duniasha.

Duniasha, a girl who was very strict in the house and very forward when out of the master's sight, only snorted for answer.

"Well, that's fine. And here is your hero!"

Fenichka took the child back into her arms.

"How quiet he was with you!" she said half aloud.

"All children are quiet with me," Bazarov replied. "I know the trick."

"Children can feel who is fond of them," Duniasha observed.

"That's just it," Fenichka confirmed. "Mitya, for instance, won't let anyone else take him at all."

"But would he come to me?" asked Arkady, who, after standing a little way off for a time, had now come into the arbor.

He held out his arms to take Mitya, but the child threw his head back and began to bellow, which greatly embarrassed Fenichka.

"He'll come some other time, when he's used to me," Arkady said indulgently, and the two friends went off.

"What is her name, by the way?" Bazarov asked.

"Fenichka — Fyodosia, that is," Arkady replied.

"And her patronymic? I must know that too."

"Nikolavna."

"*Bene.* What I like about her is that she doesn't get too embarrassed. Maybe others would condemn that in her. But how absurd! Why should she be embarrassed? She's the mother, and so she is within her rights."

"She is within her rights," Arkady observed, "but my father, now — "

"And he is within his rights," Bazarov interrupted.

"Well, no, I don't think so."

"Evidently you don't like the idea of an extra little heir!"

"Aren't you ashamed to impute such ideas to me?" Arkady replied heatedly. "That isn't why I regard my father as in the wrong; I consider he ought to marry her."

"Hm!" Bazarov calmly commented. "Well, we are magnanimous! So you still attach importance to marriage; I hadn't expected that of you."

The friends walked on a few paces without speaking.

"I have had a look at your father's farm," Bazarov began again. "The cattle are poor, and the horses worn out. The buildings too are half drunk, and the workmen look like a lot of embittered drones; and the steward is either a fool or a rogue, I haven't yet completely decided which."

"You're severe today, Yevgeny Vasilich."

"And the good little peasants are cheating your father all the time. You know the saying: 'A Russian peasant would gobble up God.'"

"I am beginning to agree with my uncle," Arkady observed; "you have a downright poor opinion of the Russians."

"How terrible! The Russian is only good in the sense that he, too, has a very poor opinion of himself. The important thing is that twice two are four, and nothing else matters in the least."

"Including nature?" Arkady said, thoughtfully gazing at the checkered fields, beautifully and softly lit up by the setting sun.

"Even nature doesn't matter, in the sense in which you mean it at this moment. Nature isn't a temple, but a workshop, and man is the workman in that workshop."

At that very moment the languid sounds of a violoncello reached them from the house. Someone was playing Schubert's *Expectation* with feeling, though with an inexperienced hand, and the suavely flowing melody spread like honey through the air.

"What is that?" Bazarov asked in astonishment.

"It's Father."

"Your father plays the cello?"

"Yes."

"But how old is your father?"

"Forty-four."

Bazarov abruptly burst into laughter.

"What are you laughing at?"

"What do you think! A man of forty-four, a *pater familias*, in N . . . province, playing a cello!"

Bazarov went on laughing; but this time, despite all his respect for his teacher, Arkady did not even smile.

x

Some two weeks passed. Life in Marino flowed on in its normal course: Arkady played the sybarite, Bazarov worked. Everybody in the house had grown accustomed to him, to his perfunctory manners, his monosyllabic and fragmentary remarks. Fenichka especially grew so used to him that one night she asked for him to be awakened as Mitya had convulsions; and Bazarov went and, half joking as usual, half yawning, sat with her a couple of hours and treated the infant. On the other hand, Pavel Piotrovich came to hate Bazarov with all the strength of his soul: he regarded him as arrogant, insolent, cynical, plebeian; he suspected that Bazarov had no respect for him, that he all but had contempt for him — for him, Pavel Kirsanov! Nikolai Piotrovich was rather afraid of the young "nihilist" and doubted whether his influence over Arkady was beneficial; but he was always ready to listen to him and was glad to be present at his physical and chemical experiments. Bazarov had brought a microscope with him, and he pored over it for hours at a time. The servants also grew attached to him, though he was always deriding them: they felt that none the less he was one of them, and not a master. Duniasha was never slow to giggle with him and gave him sidelong, meaning glances as she ran past "like a little quail." Piotr, who was an extremely ambitious and stupid man who went with his forehead always tensely furrowed, and whose only virtue was that he looked honest, could spell out words, and frequently brushed his coat — even he smirked and came to life as soon as Bazarov paid any attention to him; while the yard boys ran after the "doctor" like little dogs. Only old Prokofich did not like him, wore a morose look as he handed him food at the table, called him a "knacker" and a "knave," and declared that with his side-whiskers he was a real swine in a bush. In his own way Prokofich was just as much an aristocrat as Pavel Piotrovich.

The first days of June arrived, the finest days of the year. The weather was set fair; there was a distant threat of cholera again, but by now the inhabitants of N . . . province had grown accustomed to its visits. Bazarov rose very early and went off for two or three miles not for a walk — he could not endure excursions without a purpose — but to collect grasses and insects. Sometimes he took Arkady with him. They usually fell into some argument on the way back, and as a rule Arkady lost, though he talked more than his companion.

One day they were gone rather a long time; Nikolai Piotrovich went out into the garden to meet them and, reaching the arbor, suddenly heard swift steps and the two young men's voices. They were passing on the farther side and could not see him.

"You don't know Father well enough," he heard Arkady say.

Nikolai Piotrovich froze where he stood.

"Your father's a very good fellow," Bazarov pronounced, "but he's on the retired list, his song is sung."

Nikolai Piotrovich pricked up his ears. . . . Arkady made no answer.

"The man on the retired list" remained standing for a minute or two, then slowly went back home.

"The day before yesterday I saw him reading Pushkin," Bazarov continued meanwhile. "Do explain to him that that will never do any good. After all, he's not a boy: it's time he threw aside that nonsense. Wanting to be a romantic, in these days! Give him something useful to read."

"What would you give him?" Arkady asked.

"Why, I think Büchner's *Stoff und Kraft* to begin with."

"I think so too," Arkady remarked approvingly. *Stoff und Kraft* is written in a popular style."

"So that's what you and I are," Nikolai said to his brother as he sat in his room after dinner that same day; "we've been put on the retired list, our song is sung. Well, what of it! Perhaps Bazarov is right. But I must admit I find one thing very upsetting: I was hoping that now at least I would come into close and friendly relations with Arkady, but it appears I have been left behind, he has gone on ahead, and we cannot understand each other."

"But why has he gone on ahead? And how is he so greatly different from us?" Pavel Piotrovich exclaimed impatiently. "All this has been put into his head by that *signor*, that nihilist. I hate that wretched doctor; in my view he is simply a charlatan; I am confident that with all his frogs he has not achieved much even in physics."

"No, brother, don't say that; Bazarov is intelligent and knowledgeable."

"And what repellent conceit!" Pavel Piotrovich again interrupted.

"Yes," Nikolai Piotrovich remarked, "he certainly is conceited. But evidently you cannot get on without it. And there is one thing I don't quite understand. I seem to do everything to keep up with the times: I've established my peasants on their own land, I've started a farm, so that I am even regarded as a Red all over the province; I read, I study, I do everything I can to keep abreast of contemporary requirements — but they say my song is sung. And now, brother, I am myself beginning to think that it really is sung."

"Why are you?"

"I'll tell you why. Today I was sitting reading Pushkin. I remember, I happened to light on *The Gypsies*. Suddenly Arkady comes up to me, and silently, with such a look of kindly commiseration on his face, he takes the book away from me as gently as if I were a child and puts another, a German book, in front of me. Then he smiled and walked away, taking Pushkin with him."

"You don't say! And what book did he give you?"

"This one."

And Nikolai took the notorious work by Büchner, its ninth edition, out of the back pocket of his frock coat.

Pavel Piotrovich turned it over in his hands.

"Hm!" he snorted. "Arkady Nikolaevich is taking your education in hand. Well, and have you tried to read it?"

"I have."

"And what was the result?"

"Either I'm stupid or this is all rubbish. I suppose I must be stupid."

"But you have not forgotten your German?" Pavel Piotrovich asked.

"I understand it well enough."

Pavel Piotrovich again turned the book over in his hands and looked at his brother with wrinkled brows. They were both silent.

"Why, that reminds me," Nikolai Piotrovich began, evidently wishing to change the conversation; "I've had a letter from Kolyazin."

"From Matvei Ilich?"

"Yes. He has arrived at X X X to hold an inquiry into the province. He's an important person now, and he writes that he would like to see us, as we're relations of his, and he invites me and you and Arkady to the town."

"Are you going?" Pavel Piotrovich asked.

"No; and you?"

"I shall not go either. Highly necessary to drag some thirty miles to eat jelly! Mathieu wants to exhibit himself to us in all his glory; but he can go to the devil! He'll get enough incense from the provincial authorities, he can manage without ours. A very important rank, a privy councilor! If I had continued in the service, stupidly toiling and slaving, I would have been an adjutant general by now. But now you and I are on the retired list."

"Yes, brother; evidently it's time we ordered our coffins and folded our hands across our chests," Nikolai Piotrovich remarked with a sigh.

"Well, I shall not surrender so soon," his brother muttered. "We shall yet have a tussle with that doctor, I foresee that."

The tussle occurred the very same day, during the evening tea. Pavel Piotrovich went into the reception hall all ready for battle, irritable and resolute. He waited only for a pretext to fling himself on the enemy, but for a long time that pretext did not offer itself. Bazarov always said little in the presence of the "old Kirsanovs," as he called both brothers, and that evening he felt out of sorts and silently drank cup after cup of tea. Pavel Piotrovich was consumed with impatience; but at last his desires were realized.

The talk had turned to discussion of one of the neighboring landowners. "He's a rotter, a petty aristocrat!" Bazarov, who had met him in Petersburg, unconcernedly remarked.

"Allow me to ask you," Pavel Piotrovich retorted, and his lips began to quiver. "In your conception do the words 'rotter' and 'aristocrat' have the same meaning?"

"I said: 'petty aristocrat,'" Bazarov observed, lazily taking a gulp of tea.

"You did; but I assume that you have the same opinion about aristocrats as you have about petty aristocrats. I consider it my duty to inform you that I do not share that opinion. I dare to say that everybody knows me as a man of liberal views and a lover of progress; but for that very reason I respect aristocrats, true aristocrats. Remember, my dear sir" (at these words Bazarov raised his eyes to Pavel Piotrovich), "remember, my dear sir," he repeated harshly, "the English aristocrats. They do not yield one iota of their rights, and so they respect the rights of others; they demand the fulfillment of obligations in regard to themselves, and so they themselves fulfill *their* obligations. It was the aristocracy that gave England freedom and maintains it."

"I've heard that song lots of times," Bazarov retorted; "but what are you trying to prove by it?"

"My dear sir, I am trying to prove by *this* —" (When he grew angry, Pavel Piotrovich deliberately used a distorted form of the Russian for "this," though he knew very well that grammar did not recognize such forms. This idiosyncrasy was a last survival of the tradition of Czar Alexander's times. On the rare occasions when the bigwigs of those days talked in their native language, some of them used the form *"efto,"* others *"echto,"* instead of *"eto,"* as though indicating: we, you know, are true Russians, and at the same time we are the magnates, who are permitted to ignore the school rules.) "By *this* I am trying to prove that without a sense of one's own worth, without respect for oneself — and in an aristocrat those feelings are developed — there is no stable basis for the social — *bien public* — the social edifice. Personality, my dear sir — that is the chief thing; the human personality should be strong as a rock, for on it everything is built. I know very well, for example, that you are pleased to consider my habits, my toilet, my very neatness, as absurd; but they all arise from a feeling of self-respect, from a feeling of duty, yes, yes, of duty. I live in the country, in a quiet spot, but I do not let myself down, I respect the man in me."

"Pardon me, Pavel Piotrovich," Bazarov rejoined; "you say you respect yourself and you sit with folded hands; what benefit to the *bien public* is that? You could be entirely without respect for yourself and do exactly the same."

Pavel Piotrovich turned pale.

"That is quite a different question. There is no reason whatever why I should explain to you now why I sit with folded hands, as you take the liberty of expressing it. I only wish to say that aristocratism is a principle, and in our times only immoral or empty people can live without principles. I said that to Arkady the day after his arrival, and I repeat it to you now. Is that not so, Nikolai?"

Nikolai Piotrovich nodded.

"Aristocratism, liberalism, progress, principles," Bazarov said. "Just think, how many foreign — and useless — words! They are quite unnecessary to a Russian."

"And what does he need, in your opinion? To listen to you, one would think we were outside humanity, outside all its laws. Pardon me, the logic of history requires — "

"Yes, but what do we want that logic for? We shall manage without it."

"How shall we?"

"Why, we just shall. You, I hope, have no need for logic in order to put a piece of bread into your mouth when you're hungry. What do we need those abstractions for?"

Pavel Piotrovich threw up his hands.

"After that I fail to understand you. You are insulting the Russian people. I do not understand how you can avoid recognizing principles, rules. What is the motive of your actions?"

"I have already told you, uncle, that we don't recognize any authorities," Arkady intervened.

"We act by the force of what we recognize as beneficial," Bazarov declared. "At the present time rejection is the most beneficial of all things, and so we reject."

"Everything?"

"Everything."

"How? Not only art, poetry — but also — it is a terrible thing to say — "

"Everything!" Bazarov repeated with complete imperturbability.

Pavel Piotrovich stared at him. He had not expected that, and Arkady even reddened with pleasure.

"None the less, allow me," Nikolai Piotrovich began. "You reject everything, or, to express it more exactly, you pull down everything. But then surely it is necessary to build up too?"

"That isn't our business. First we must clear the site."

"The present state of the people demands that," Arkady added sententiously. "We must meet those demands, we have no right to give ourselves over to the satisfaction of our personal egotism."

Evidently this last phrase did not please Bazarov: it had a waft of philosophy — in other words, of romanticism — for Bazarov called philosophy also romanticism. But he did not consider it necessary to contradict his young pupil.

"No, no!" Pavel Piotrovich exclaimed in a sudden outburst, "I am not prepared to believe that you, gentlemen, have a perfect knowledge of the Russian people, that you are the representatives of its requirements, its strivings! No, the Russian people is not such as you represent it. It sacredly respects the traditions, it is patriarchal, it cannot live without faith — "

"I shan't try to dispute that," Bazarov interrupted, "I am even ready to agree that *in this respect* you are right."

"But if I am right — "

"And all the same it proves nothing."

"It proves precisely nothing," Arkady repeated with the assurance of an experienced chess-player who has foreseen an apparently dangerous move by his opponent and so is not in the least perturbed.

"How does it prove nothing?" the bewildered Pavel Piotrovich muttered. "So you will go against the whole of the people?"

"And what if we do?" Bazarov exclaimed. "The people assume that when there is thunder it is the prophet Elijah driving across heaven in his chariot. Well, and are we to agree with them? And besides they are Russian, and am I not a Russian too?"

"No, you are no Russian after what you have just said. I cannot recognize you as Russian."

"My grandfather plowed the land," Bazarov replied with haughty pride. "Ask any of your own peasants whom they more readily recognize as their fellow countryman, you or me. You don't even know how to talk with them."

"But you talk with them, yet at the same time you are contemptuous of them."

"What of it, if they are deserving of contempt? You reject my attitude, but who told you that my attitude is something quite fortuitous, that it is not evoked by that same national spirit in the name of which you rant so much?"

"So you think! Great need we have of nihilists!"

"Whether there is need of them or not is not for you to decide. After all, even you regard yourself as not without use."

"Gentlemen, gentlemen, no personalities, please!" Nikolai Piotrovich exclaimed, and he half rose.

Pavel Piotrovich smiled and, laying his hand on his brother's shoulder, forced him to sit down again.

"Don't be alarmed," he said. "I shall not forget myself, precisely because of my feeling of worth, which Mr. — which the doctor ridicules so severely. Excuse me," he went on, turning again to Bazarov, "you, perhaps, think that your teaching is something new? That is quite a vain idea. The materialism that you preach has been in circulation more than once before and has always proved bankrupt — "

"Another foreign word!" Bazarov interrupted. He was beginning to be annoyed, and his face went a coarse, coppery color. "To begin with, we preach nothing; that is not our habit."

"Then what do you do?"

"This is what we do. Formerly, not so very long ago, we said that our officials take bribes, that we had neither roads, nor commerce, nor an impartial judiciary — "

"Why yes, yes, you are the accusers; that is what that is called, I think. With many of your accusations I agree, but — "

"But then we realized that to talk, everlastingly only talk about our ulcers is not worth the labor, that it leads only to platitudes

209

and doctrinairism; we saw that our sages also, the so-called advanced people and accusers, were good for nothing, that we were occupying our minds with rubbish, we were talking about art, about unconscious creation, about parliamentarism, about the bar, and the devil knows what else, when it was really a question of daily bread, when we were being smothered by the coarsest of superstitions, when all our corporations were going to smash simply because there was an insufficiency of honest people, when the very freedom the government was making so much fuss about would hardly be of any use to us, because our peasant is glad to rob himself just in order to get drunk in the pub."

"So," Pavel Piotrovich interrupted him, "so you were convinced of all this and decided that you yourselves would not do anything serious about it at any price."

"And we decided not to do anything about it at any price," Bazarov glumly repeated. He suddenly felt vexed with himself for expatiating so freely before this gentleman.

"But only revile everything?"

"And revile everything."

"And that is called nihilism?"

"And that is called nihilism," Bazarov again repeated, this time with especial insolence.

Pavel Piotrovich slightly narrowed his eyes.

"So that is the position!" he pronounced in a strangely calm tone. "Nihilism is to be our help in all misfortunes, and you, you are our saviors and heroes. Indeed! But why do you abuse others, even those very accusers? Are you not simply indulging in talk, like everybody else?"

"Whatever others may do, we do not commit that sin," Bazarov said through his teeth.

"So what, then? Are you doing something? Are you intending to act?"

Bazarov made no reply. Pavel Piotrovich began to tremble, but he mastered himself at once.

"Hm! To act, to break down—" he continued. "But how can you break down when you do not even know why you are doing it?"

"We break things down because we are a force," Arkady observed.

Pavel Piotrovich looked at his nephew and smiled wryly.

"Yes, and force does not render any account," Arkady pronounced, and drew himself up.

"Unhappy wretch!" Pavel Piotrovich roared; he was quite unable to restrain himself any longer; "if only you knew *what* you are supporting in Russia with your trivial sententiousness! Really, this would try the patience of an angel! Force! There is force in the savage Kalmuck and in the Mongol — but what use is it to us? To us civilization is precious, yes, yes, my dear sir; to us its fruits are precious. And tell me not that those fruits are insignificant; the wretchedest dauber, *un barbouilleur*, a dance pianist who gets five kopeks an evening, even they are of more use than you, because they are representatives of civilization, and not of the coarse Mongol force! You imagine yourselves to be advanced, but you ought to be sitting in a Kalmuck tent! Force! But do remember in the last resort, you forceful gentlemen, that there are only four and a half of you all together, while there are millions of these others, and they will not allow you to trample on their most sacred beliefs, they will crush you!"

"If they crush, then that's the road to go," Bazarov declared. "Only we shall see. There aren't so few of us as you assume."

"What? You seriously think that you can cope — can cope with the entire nation?"

"You know, all Moscow was set alight by a farthing candle," Bazarov replied.

"Yes, yes. First a pride almost satanic, then derision. That is what the youth are carried away by, that is what the inexperienced hearts of striplings surrender to. Look, there is one of them sitting beside you, and he is all but praying to you, enjoy the sight!" (Arkady turned away and frowned.) "And this infection has already been spread far and wide. I have been told that in Rome our artists never even set foot in the Vatican. They regard Raphael as all but a fool, because, they say, he represents authority; but they themselves are loathsomely impotent and barren, and they have no more imagination than will suffice for *A Girl at the Fountain*, say what you like! And even that girl is drawn atrociously. In your view they are splendid fellows, are they not?"

"In my view," Bazarov retorted, "Raphael also is not worth a brass farthing; and they are no better than he."

"Bravo! Bravo! Listen, Arkady — now, that is how the modern young people should talk! And what else could they do, think you, than follow you? Formerly young people had to study, they were not anxious to acquire the reputation of being ignoramuses, and so willy-nilly they worked. But now you only need say to them: 'Everything in the world is rubbish!' and the thing is done. The young people are delighted. And in very deed formerly they were simply blockheads, but now they have suddenly become nihilists."

"And now your boasted feeling of your own worth has betrayed you," Bazarov remarked phlegmatically, whereas Arkady flared up and his eyes glittered. "Our argument has gone too far — I think it would be better to bring it to an end. But I shall be ready to agree with you," he added as he rose, "when you present me with a single convention of our present-day existence, in family or social life, that does not call for complete and ruthless rejection."

"I shall provide you with millions of such conventions," Pavel Piotrovich exclaimed. "Millions! Why, take the peasants' community, for instance."

A frigid sneer twisted Bazarov's lips.

"Well, so far as the commune is concerned," he said, "you'd better talk with your brother about it. I think he has now learned by experience what the commune is: mutual responsibility, sobriety, and all that kind of thing."

"Then the family, the family, as it exists among our peasants!" Pavel Piotrovich cried.

"That question too, I think, it would be better for you not to analyze in detail. I expect you have heard of fathers sleeping with their daughters-in-law? Listen to me, Pavel Piotrovich, give yourself a couple of days — I don't think you'll find anything at once. Consider all our social strata, and think carefully over each of them, and meanwhile Arkady and I will — "

"Sneer at everything," Pavel Piotrovich caught him up.

"No, dissect frogs! Come along, Arkady; good-by, gentlemen."

The two friends went out. The brothers were left alone and at first only looked at each other.

"There!" Pavel Piotrovich began at last; "there you have our present-day youth! There they are — our heirs!"

"Heirs," Nikolai Piotrovich repeated with a despondent sigh. All through the argument he had sat like a cat on hot bricks, only taking stealthy, unhappy glances at Arkady. "Do you know what

I have just remembered, brother? One day I quarreled with our mother: she started to shout and wouldn't listen to me. . . . At last I told her that she couldn't understand me: we belonged to two different generations. She was terribly annoyed, but I thought: 'It can't be helped. It's a bitter pill, but it has to be swallowed.' And now our turn has come, and our heirs can say to us: 'You are not of our generation; swallow the pill.' "

"You are far too magnanimous and modest," Pavel Piotrovich objected. "I, on the contrary, am confident that you and I are far more right than these gentlemen, though perhaps we express ourselves in a rather old-fashioned way, *vielli*, and we do not have that impertinent self-confidence. . . . And how bombastic this present-day youth is! You ask one of them: what wine would you like, red or white? 'I have the habit of preferring red,' he answers in a bass voice and with such a serious face, as if all the universe were watching him at that moment. . . ."

"Do you want any more tea?" Fenichka asked, putting her head in at the door. She could not bring herself to enter the reception room so long as she could hear the sound of arguing.

"No, you can tell them to take the samovar away," Nikolai Piotrovich replied, and he rose to meet her. Pavel Piotrovich vehemently said: "*Bon soir*" to him and went off to his own room.

XI

Half an hour later Nikolai Piotrovich went into the garden, to his favorite arbor. He was obsessed with mournful thoughts. For the first time he clearly realized what a gulf separated him from his son; he had a presentiment that with every day the gulf would grow wider and wider. So in vain had he spent the winters in Petersburg, in vain had he sat for days on end over the latest publications, in vain had he listened to the young people's conversations, in vain had he rejoiced to get in some remark amid their heady speeches. "My brother says we are right," he thought, "and, putting aside all conceit, it does seem to me that they are farther from the truth than we are; but at the same time I feel that they have something we do not possess, some advantage over us. . . . Youth? No: not only youth. Doesn't it consist in the fact that they have fewer traces of gentility than we?"

Nikolai Piotrovich let his head sink, and he passed his hand over his face.

"But to reject poetry?" he thought again, "to have no feeling for art, for nature . . ."

And he looked about him as though seeking to understand how anyone could have no feeling for nature. Evening was coming on; the sun had hidden behind a small ash grove lying half a mile away from the garden: the shadow of the trees stretched endlessly across the silent fields. A peasant was trotting on a little white horse over a dark, narrow track at the very edge of the grove; in vain did he ride in the shadow: he was clearly visible in every detail, even to the patch on his shoulder. It was pleasant to see the little horse's legs twinkling so distinctly. The rays of sunlight penetrated into the grove from the other side and, making their way through the trees, flooded the trunks of the ashes with such a warm light that they came to resemble pine trunks, while their foliage turned almost blue, and above it rose a pale blue sky, faintly flushed with the sunset. The swallows were flying high; the wind had completely died away; belated bees were sluggishly and drowsily humming in the lilac flowers; gnats were swirling in a column above a single outjutting branch. "My God, how good it is!" thought Nikolai Piotrovich, and his favorite verses were about to come to his lips; he recalled Arkady, *Stoff und Kraft*, and was silent, but he continued to sit, continued to give himself over to the mournful and joyous play of single thoughts. He liked to indulge in dreams: his country life had developed this capacity in him. Was it so long since he had sat dreaming as he waited for his son at the inn? But since then there had already been a change, relations that then were still uncertain were already defined . . . and in what manner! He recalled again his dead wife, but not as he had known her over many years, not as the domesticated, efficient housewife, but as a young girl with a slender waist, an innocently curious gaze, and a tightly twisted pigtail coiled above her childishly thin neck. He recalled how he had seen her the first time. He was still a student then. He had met her on the staircase of the apartment in which he lived, and, accidentally jostling against her, had turned and tried to apologize, but had only muttered: "Pardon, monsieur," and she had bent her head, smiled, and suddenly taken fright and fled. But at the turn of the stairs she had glanced swiftly up at him, had put on a serious look, and had blushed. And then the first shy visits, the half-words, the half-smiles, and the misunderstandings, and the sorrow, and the raptures, and finally that panting joy. . . . Where had they all fled? She had become his wife, he had been happy as are few on this earth. . . . "But," he thought, "those first sweet moments — why couldn't we live on in them with an everlasting, undying life?"

He did not try to clarify his thought to himself, but he felt that he wanted to retain that blessed time with something stronger than memory; he wanted once more to feel that his Maria was near him, to be conscious of her warmth and breath, and he was even beginning to imagine that above him . . .

"Nikolai Piotrovich," Fenichka's voice sounded close at hand. "Where are you?"

He started. He did not feel pain, or shame. He did not concede even the possibility of comparison between his wife and Fenichka, but he regretted that she had thought of coming to look for him. Her voice at once reminded him of his gray hairs, his age, his present existence. . . .

The enchanted world that he had already entered, which had already emerged from the misty waves of the past, stirred — and vanished.

"I'm here," he replied; "I'm coming, you go on." "There they are, the traces of gentility," the thought flashed through his head. Fenichka glanced into the arbor without speaking and disappeared; but he noted with surprise that while he had been dreaming, the night had come on. Everything was darkening and was beginning to be still all around him, and past him slipped Fenichka's face, so white and small. He rose and was about to return to the house; but his heart, softened with tenderness, could not be still in his breast, and he began to walk slowly about the garden, now thoughtfully looking down at his feet, now raising his eyes to the sky, where the stars were already swarming and twinkling. He walked about a great deal, almost until he was tired, but the anxiety he felt, a kind of searching, indefinite, mournful anxiety, was still not alleviated. Oh, how Bazarov would have laughed at him, if he had discovered what went on within him during those moments! Even Arkady would have condemned him. He, this man of forty-four, an agriculturist and farmer, burst into tears, causeless tears; and that was a hundred times worse than the cello.

Nikolai Piotrovich continued to walk about and could not bring himself to go into the house, into that peaceful and cozy nest which gazed at him so invitingly with all its lighted windows. He had no strength to part with the darkness, the garden, the feeling of the fresh air on his face, and that sorrow, that anxiety. . . .

At a turn in the path he was met by Pavel Piotrovich.

"What is the matter with you?" his brother asked him. "You are as pale as a ghost; you are not well; why don't you go to bed?"

Nikolai Piotrovich briefly explained his spiritual condition to him and walked away. Pavel Piotrovich walked to the end of the garden, and he, too, was lost in thought, and he, too, raised his eyes to the sky. But in those handsome, dark eyes was reflected nothing but the light of the stars. He had not been born a romantic, and his exquisitely dry and sensual soul, misanthropic in the French manner, was incapable of dreaming.

"Do you know what?" Bazarov said to Arkady that same night. "A magnificent idea has occurred to me. Your father mentioned today that he had received an invitation from that eminent relative of yours. Your father won't go; so let's both slip away to X X X; the gentleman invites you as well. You see the weather that's settled here; so we'll have a ride and see the town. We'll spend five or six days there and then come away!"

"And will you be coming back here?"

"No, I must go and see my father. You know he lives twenty miles from X X X. I haven't seen him for a long time, nor my mother; the old people need a little comfort. They're very good to me, especially Father; he's very amusing and I am their only son."

"And will you be staying with them long?"

"I don't think so. I'm afraid I shall be bored."

"And will you call here on the way back?"

"I don't know, I'll see. Well, what d'you think? Shall we go?"

"If you like." Arkady lazily remarked.

Inwardly he was greatly delighted by his friend's suggestion, but he considered it his duty to conceal his feelings. Not for nothing was he a nihilist.

Next day he drove with Bazarov to X X X. The younger people at Marino regretted their departure; Duniasha even burst into tears . . . but the old men breathed more easily.

XII

The town of X X X, to which our friends drove, was in charge of one of the younger type of governor, both progressive and despot, as is the case everywhere in Russia. During the first year of his administration he managed to fall out not only with the provincial marshal of the nobility — a retired captain of the guards, a horse-breeder, and a convivial fellow — but with all his own officials. The ensuing conflict finally grew to such dimensions that the ministry at Petersburg found it necessary to commission a man of trust to inquire into the entire affair on the spot. The authorities' choice fell upon Matvei Ilich Kolyazin, the son of the Kolyazin who at one time had had the brothers Kirsanov under his patronage. He, too, was one of the "younger men"; in other words, he had recently passed his fortieth birthday; but he had already made his mark among statesmen and wore a star on each breast. One was a foreign decoration, to be sure, and not of the best at that. Like the governor whom he had come to judge, he regarded himself as a man of progress and, though already a bigwig, was unlike the majority of bigwigs. He had the very highest opinion of himself; his vainglory knew no limits; but he bore himself simply, looked approvingly, listened indulgently, and smiled so benevolently that at the beginning of an acquaintance he could even pass for a "very fine chap." On important occasions, however, he could make the sparks fly, as the saying is. "Energy is indispensable," he would say at such times, *"l'énergie est la première qualité d'un homme d'état";* none the less he was usually made a fool of, and any least experienced official could ride him. Matvei Ilich spoke with great respect of Guizot, and tried to give all and sundry the impression that he was not to be classified among the routine and backward bureaucrats, that he did not let a single important manifestation of social life pass unobserved. . . . He was good at all that kind of talk. He even followed, though truly with a negligent dignity, the development of contemporary literature — just as a grown man, meeting a procession of boys in the street, sometimes attaches himself to it. In reality Matvei Ilich was not greatly unlike those statesmen of Czar Alexander's times who, when preparing to spend an evening with Mme Svechina, who was living in Petersburg at the time, read a page from Condillac in the morning; only his manners were different, more modern. He was an accomplished courtier, a very sly fox, and nothing more; he had no understanding of affairs and no intelligence, but was capable of managing his own business; in that respect no one could put anything across him, and, after all, that is the main thing.

Matvei Ilich received Arkady with the benevolence proper to an enlightened dignitary, and we will say more, with jocosity. None the less he was astonished when he learned that the relatives he had invited had remained behind. "Your papa always was eccentric," he remarked, playing with the tassels of his superb velvet dressing-gown. And suddenly, turning to a young official in a very well-meant, tightly buttoned semi-uniform, he exclaimed with a preoccupied air: "Well?" The young man, who had been silent for so long that his lips had stuck together, half rose and gazed in bewilderment at his chief. But, having embarrassed his subordinate, Matvei Ilich paid no more attention to him. Our dignitaries generally are fond of embarrassing their subordinates; the methods they use in order to achieve this end are very varied. We may note in passing that the following method is much resorted to, "is quite a favorite," as the English say. A dignitary will suddenly cease to understand even the simplest of words and will go quite deaf. He asks, for instance: "What is today?"

They tell him very respectfully: "Today is Friday, Your Ex-ex-ex-cency."

"Well? What? What's that? What did you say?" the dignitary repeats tensely.

"Today is Friday, Your Ex-ex-ex-cency."

"How? what? What's Friday? Which Friday?"

"Friday, Your E-e-e-e-cency, a day of the week."

"No-ow! Are you trying to teach me?"

After all, Matvei Ilich was a dignitary, though he regarded himself as a liberal.

"I advise you, my friend, to call on the governor," he told Arkady. "You understand, I advise you to do so not because I hold to the ancient idea that it is necessary to go and pay your respects to the authorities, but simply because the governor is an honest man; and besides I expect you would like to make the acquaintance of local society. . . . For you're not a boor, I hope? And he is giving a great ball the day after tomorrow."

"Will you be at the ball?" Arkady asked.

"He is giving it in my honor," Matvei Ilich declared almost commiseratingly. "Do you dance?"

"Yes, but only badly."

"That's unfortunate. There are some pretty girls here, and besides, a young man should be ashamed not to dance. But again I say that not because I am dominated by ancient ideas; I don't think at all that the mind should be in the feet, but Byronism is absurd, *il a fait son temps*."

"But, uncle, it isn't at all because of Byronism that I — "

"I'll introduce you to the local ladies, I'll take you under my wing," Matvei Ilich interrupted him, and smiled conceitedly. "You'll like that, won't you?"

A servant entered and reported the arrival of the chairman of the criminal court, a honey-eyed old man with pursed lips, who was extremely fond of nature, especially on summer days, when, as he said: "every little bee takes a little consideration from every little flower." Arkady withdrew.

He found Bazarov in the inn where they had taken a room, and spent a long time persuading him to call on the governor. "It can't be helped!" said Bazarov at last; "in for a penny, in for a pound. We've come to have a look at the landowners, so let's look at them." The governor received the young men affably, but did not ask them to be seated and did not sit down himself. He was everlastingly fidgeting and hurrying; he had worn a tight-fitting semi-uniform and an extremely tight cravat since early morning, he had not had any proper food or drink, and he was continually issuing orders. In the province he was nicknamed Burdal, in allusion not to the well-known French preacher Bourdaloue, but to *burda*, the Russian word for bilge. He invited Kirsanov and Bazarov to attend the ball, and a couple of minutes later invited them again, now regarding them as two brothers and calling them both Kaisarov.

They were on their way home from the governor's when suddenly a little man in a Slavophil Hungarian hussar jacket jumped out of a passing droshky and, crying: "Yevgeny Vasilich," rushed to Bazarov.

"Ah, so it's you, Herr Sitnikov!" Bazarov remarked, continuing along the sidewalk. "What fate has brought you here?"

"Just imagine, quite an accident," the man replied. Turning to

the droshky, he waved his hand five times or so and shouted:
"Follow us, follow us! My father has business here," he went
on, jumping across the gutter, "and so he asked me. . . . I
learned of your arrival today and have already been to call on
you." (The two friends did, in fact, find a visiting-card waiting
for them on their return to their room; it had crumpled corners
and bore the name of Sitnikov, written in French on one side and
in Slavonic script on the other.) "I hope you are not coming
away from the governor's?"

"Then don't hope, we've come straight from there."

"Ah! In that case I'll go and call on him. . . . Yevgeny Vasilich, introduce me to your — to him."

"Sitnikov, Kirsanov," Bazarov snorted without halting.

"I am highly honored," Sitnikov began, falling in beside them,
smirking, and hurriedly pulling off his excessively elegant gloves.
"I've heard a great deal. . . . I am an old acquaintance of
Yevgeny Vasilich and, I can even say, his pupil. I am obliged to
him for my regeneration. . . ."

Arkady looked at Bazarov's pupil. A worried and stupid expression was imprinted on the small though pleasant features of
his very smooth face; the little eyes, which looked as though
they had been pushed in, had a fixed and anxious gaze, and he
smiled anxiously, with a fleeting, wooden smile.

"Will you believe," he went on, "that when Yevgeny Vasilich
said for the first time in my hearing that one should not recognize any authorities, I felt such exultation — as though I had come
to maturity. Now, I thought, at last I have found a man! By the
way, Yevgeny Vasilich, you simply must make the acquaintance
of a certain local lady who is quite capable of understanding you
and who will regard your visit as a real festival; I expect you have
heard of her?"

"What is her name?" Bazarov said reluctantly.

"Kukshina, Eudoxie, Yevdoksia Kukshina. She's a remarkable
character, *émancipée* in the true sense of the word, an advanced
woman. Do you know what? Let us all go along to her now. She
lives only a couple of steps away. We'll have breakfast there. I
don't suppose you have breakfasted yet?"

"Not yet."

"Well, that's excellent. She's gone a different road from her
husband, you know; she is dependent on no one."

"Is she good-looking?" Bazarov interrupted him.

"Nn-no, I can't say she is."

"Then what the devil are you asking us to go along to her for?"

"Now, you wag, you wag. . . . She'll bring out a bottle of champagne for us."

"Really! Now the practical man is evident. By the way, is your father still the local licensee?"

"Yes, he is," Sitnikov replied hurriedly, and squealed with laughter. "Well, are you coming?"

"I really don't know."

"You wanted to see the local people, so why not go with him?" Arkady observed in an undertone.

"But what about you, Mr. Kirsanov?" Sitnikov intervened. "You come too, we can't go without you."

"But how can all three of us drop in on her without warning?"

"That's all right. She's an eccentric sort."

"And there will be a bottle of champagne?" Bazarov demanded.

"Three!" Sitnikov exclaimed. "I'll guarantee that."

"What with?"

"My own head."

"Your father's purse would be better. But come on, then."

XIII

The small upper-class house in Moscow style in which Avdotia Nikitishna (or *Yevdoksia*) Kukshina lived was situated in one of the recently burned-down streets of the town of X X X (it is a well-known fact that our provincial towns are burned down every year). At the door, above a crookedly pinned visiting-card, was a bell handle, and in the porch the visitors were met by someone who might have been a servant, or perhaps a companion, in a cap — an obvious sign of the mistress's progressive trends. Sitnikov asked whether Avdotia Nikitishna was at home.

"Is that you, Victor?" a thin voice came from the next room. "Come in."

The woman in the cap at once vanished.

"I'm not alone," Sitnikov announced, spiritedly throwing off his hussar coat and revealing a coat like a sack or a Russian peasant coat. He gave Arkady and Bazarov a dashing look.

"It doesn't matter," the voice replied. "*Entrez!*"

The young men entered. The room in which they found them-

221

selves was more like a workroom than a reception room. Papers, letters, and stout issues of Russian periodicals, most of them with edges uncut, were lying about on dusty tables; the white butts of cigarettes were scattered everywhere. A lady, still young, fair-haired, rather disheveled, in a silk and not entirely tidy dress, with large bracelets on her short arms and a lace kerchief on her head, was reclining on a leather divan. She rose from the divan and, negligently drawing a short velvet coat lined with yellow-ing ermine fur round her shoulders, she drawled: "Good morn-ing, Victor," and squeezed Sitnikov's hand.

"Bazarov, Kirsanov," he introduced them impetuously, in imi-tation of Bazarov.

"You are welcome," she replied and, fixing Bazarov with her round eyes, between which was a little red snub nose, she added: "I know you," and squeezed his hand too.

Bazarov's face clouded. There was nothing really hideous in this emancipated woman's tiny and insignificant figure, but her facial expression had an unpleasant effect on the observer. In-voluntarily one wanted to ask her: "What is the matter — hun-gry? Or bored? Or shy? What are you all strung up for?" She, like Sitnikov, was everlastingly clawing at her soul. She talked and moved jauntily yet awkwardly; evidently she regarded her-self as a good-natured and simple creature, and yet, no matter what she did, one continually had the impression that that was precisely what she did not want to do; everything she did seemed to be "on purpose," as children say; in other words, it was not simple, not natural.

"Yes, yes, I know you, Bazarov," she repeated. (She had the habit, common to many provincial and Moscow ladies, of calling a man by his surname from the first day of their acquaintance.) "Would you like a cigar?"

"We don't mind a cigar," said Sitnikov, who was already sprawled in an armchair, with one leg cocked up, "but how about some breakfast? We're terribly hungry; and tell them to bring in a bottle of champagne."

"You sybarite," Yevdoksia declared, and smiled. (When she smiled, she laid bare her upper gum above her teeth.) "Isn't that so, Bazarov, isn't he a sybarite?"

"I am fond of the comforts of life," Sitnikov pronounced gravely. "That doesn't prevent my being a liberal."

"Oh, but it does, it does!" Yevdoksia exclaimed; none the less she ordered her lady help to see about both breakfast and champagne. "What is your view on that?" she added, turning to Bazarov. "I am sure you share my opinion."

"Well, no," Bazarov objected; "a piece of meat is better than a piece of bread, even from the chemical aspect."

"Do you study chemistry, then? That is my passion! I have even invented a kind of mastic myself."

"A mastic? You?"

"Yes, I. And do you know what it is for? To make dolls' heads, so that they don't break. You see, I'm practical, too. But it isn't ready yet. I must read Liebig first. By the way, have you read Kislyakov's article on female labor in the *Moscow News*? Do read it. You are interested in the woman question, aren't you? And in schools too? What does your friend do? What are his Christian name and patronymic?"

Mme Kukshina let her questions *drop* one after another with delicate negligence, without waiting for the answers; spoilt children talk to their nurses in the same way.

"My name is Arkady Nikolaich Kirsanov," Arkady said. "And I am not doing anything."

Yevdoksia burst into a roar of laughter.

"Now, that's charming! Why aren't you smoking? Victor, you know, I am angry with you."

"What for?"

"I hear you have begun to praise George Sand again. She's a backward woman and nothing more! How can you compare her with Emerson! She has no ideas whatever on education, or physiology, or anything. I am sure she has never even heard of embryology, and in our day what can you do without that?" (Yevdoksia even threw out her hands.) "Ah, what an amazing article Yelisievich has written on that question! Now, he's a gentleman of genius!" (Yevdoksia always used the word "gentleman" instead of "man.") "Bazarov, sit down by me on the divan. You may not know it, but I am terribly afraid of you."

"Why are you? Forgive my curiosity."

"You are a dangerous gentleman; you're such a critic! Ah, my God! it's absurd of me, I talk like some steppe landowner woman. For that matter, I really am a landowner. I run my own estate and, just imagine, I have a drunkard for head man — an amazing

223

type, exactly like Cooper's Pathfinder: there's something so forth-right in him! I have settled down finally here; it's an intolerable town, isn't it? But what can one do?"

"It's no worse than others," Bazarov observed unconcernedly.

"But they all have such petty interests, that's what makes it so horrible! I used to spend the winters in Moscow . . . but now my faithful consort, M'sieur Kukshin, lives there. And besides, Moscow today — I really don't know — it isn't what it was. I am thinking of traveling abroad; last year I was on the point of going."

"To Paris, of course?" Bazarov asked.

"To Paris and Heidelberg."

"Why Heidelberg?"

"Why, Bunsen is there, of course!"

To which Bazarov could find no reply.

"Pierre Sapozhnikov — do you know him?"

"No, I don't."

"But really, Pierre Sapozhnikov — he is always to be seen with Lydia Khostatova."

"I don't know her either."

"Well, he's undertaken to escort me. Thank God, I am free, I haven't any children — What did I say: '*Thank God*'! However, it's of no consequence."

Yevdoksia rolled a cigarette in her tobacco-stained fingers, ran her tongue along the edge, sucked at it, and lit it. Her lady help entered with a tray.

"Ah, here's breakfast! Would you like a bite of something? Victor, uncork a bottle; that's your department."

"Yes, that's mine, that's mine," Sitnikov mumbled, and again squealed with laughter.

"Are there any good-looking women here?" Bazarov asked as he drank his third glass.

"There are," Yevdoksia replied, "but they're all so empty-headed. For instance, *mon amie* Odintsova isn't at all bad-looking. Pity her reputation is rather — Not that that would matter, but she has no freedom of outlook, no breadth, nothing — of that sort. We have got to change the entire system of education. I've al-ready thought of that; our women are very stupidly brought up."

"You'll never do anything with them," Sitnikov retorted. "They're only deserving of contempt, and I do feel contempt for them, wholly and completely!" (The possibility of feeling contempt and expressing his contempt was the most pleasant feeling Sitnikov could have; he was especially fond of attacking women, not suspecting that within a few months he would be cringing before his own wife, simply because she was born Princess Durdoleosova.) "Not one of them would be able to understand our talk, not one of them is worthy of serious men like us talking about her!"

"But then there isn't any need for them to understand our talk," Bazarov observed.

"Whom are you talking about?" Yevdoksia intervened.

"Good-looking women."

"What? So you share Proudhon's opinion!"

Bazarov drew himself up haughtily. "I share no one's opinions; I have my own."

"Down with the authorities!" Sitnikov shouted, rejoicing at the opportunity to express himself strongly in the presence of a man to whom he toadied.

"But Macaulay himself — " Kukshina began.

"Down with Macaulay!" Sitnikov thundered. "Do you defend those petticoats?"

"Not the petticoats, but the rights of women, which I have sworn to defend to the last drop of my blood."

"Down — " But here Sitnikov stopped. "Well, I don't deny those rights," he declared.

"Ah, but I see you are a Slavophil."

"No, I am not a Slavophil, though of course — "

"Yes, yes, yes! You are a Slavophil. You are an adherent of the 'Rules of the Household.' [1] You should have a whip in your hand!"

"A whip is a good thing," Bazarov remarked; "only we have now reached the last drop — "

"Of what?" Yevdoksia interrupted.

"Of champagne, deeply respected Avdotia Nikitishna, of champagne, not of your blood."

"I cannot listen with equanimity when women are attacked," Yevdoksia continued. "It's terrible, terrible. Instead of attacking

[1] "Rules for Household Government," emphasizing the domination of the husband, which formerly circulated in manuscript among the common people of Russia. (Tr.)

them, you would do better to read Michelet's book *De l'amour*. That's a masterpiece! Gentlemen, we will now talk about love," Yevdoksia added, languidly letting her head fall back on the divan's crumpled cushion.

There was a sudden silence.

"But why talk about love?" Bazarov observed.

"You mentioned Odintsova just now. That is the name you said, I think? Who is this lady?"

"Charming, charming!" Sitnikov began to squeal. "I'll introduce you to her. She's intelligent, rich, and a widow. Unfortunately, she isn't sufficiently developed yet: she should make our Yevdoksia's closer acquaintance. I drink to your health, Eudoxie! Let's clink glasses! '*Et toc, et toc, et tin-tin-tin. Et toc, et toc, et tin-tin-tin!!*' "

"Victor, you're a madcap. . . ."

The breakfast went on for quite a long time. The first bottle of champagne was followed by a second, a third, and even a fourth. . . . Yevdoksia chattered away without stopping; Sitnikov echoed her. They talked a great deal about marriage, whether it was a prejudice or a crime, and how people were born, whether all identical or not, and what exactly individuality was. It ended at last with Yevdoksia, crimson with the wine she had drunk, and knocking her flat nails on the keys of an out-of-tune piano, beginning to sing in a hoarse voice first gypsy songs, then Seymour-Schiff's ballad "Drowsy Granada is dozing," while Sitnikov tied his head in a scarf and acted the dying lover when she came to the words:

> "And thy lips with mine
> Are fused in a burning kiss."

In the end Arkady could stand no more. "Gentlemen, this has grown rather like a madhouse," he observed aloud. Bazarov, who only rarely interjected a derisive remark — he was more occupied with the champagne — yawned noisily, rose, and, without taking leave of their hostess, went out with Arkady. Sitnikov jumped up to follow them.

"Well, now what do you say, what do you say?" he asked, dancing attendance on first one, then the other. "Didn't I tell you she was a remarkable personality? Now, that's the kind of woman we could do with more of! She is a highly moral phenomenon of her kind."

"And is that establishment of thy father also a moral phenomenon?" Bazarov remarked, pointing to a pub they were passing at that moment.

Sitnikov again squealed with laughter. He was deeply ashamed of his origin, and did not know whether to feel flattered or aggrieved by Bazarov's unexpected "thouing."

XIV

The governor's ball took place a few days later. Matvei Ilich was the genuine "hero of the celebrations." The provincial marshal announced to all and sundry that he was present entirely out of respect for Matvei Ilich, while the governor, even at the ball, even when standing still, continued to "issue orders." Matvei Ilich's benignity in his relations with others was only equaled by his majesty. He was gracious to all — to some with a nuance of fastidiousness, to others with a nuance of respect; he was expansive *en vrai chevalier français* in the ladies' company and incessantly laughed a large, resounding, and monotonous laugh, as is proper for a dignitary. Arkady he patted on the back and loudly called "little nephew"; Bazarov, who was attired in an old frock coat, he vouchsafed an abstracted but condescending glance out of the corner of his eye, and a vague but affable bellow in which the only intelligible sounds were "I . . . " and "mmm yes"; Sitnikov he gave one finger and a smile, but with his head turned away; even to Kukshina herself — who arrived at the ball without crinoline of any kind and wearing dirty gloves, but with a bird of paradise in her hair — even to Kukshina he said "*enchanté.*" There was a very large crowd and there was no lack of gentlemen partners; the civilians mostly thronged the walls, but the military danced zealously, especially one of them, who had lived for some six weeks in Paris, where he had learned various devil-may-care exclamations in the style of "*zut,*" "*Ah, fichtrrre,*" "*pst, pst, mon bibi,*" and suchlike. He pronounced them perfectly, with genuine Parisian chic, yet he said "*si j'aurais*" instead of "*si j'avais,*" and "*absolument*" in the sense of "certainly"; in a word, he expressed himself in that Great-Russian French dialect which the French laugh at so much when there is no need for them to assure us that we talk their language like angels, "*comme des anges.*"

Arkady was a poor dancer, as we know already, and Bazarov did not dance at all: they took up a position in one corner, where Sitnikov joined them. Putting a contemptuous smile on his face and letting fall venomous remarks, he looked about him insolently, and apparently felt genuine satisfaction. Suddenly his face changed and, turning to Arkady, he said, evidently in some embarrassment: "Odintsova has arrived."

Arkady looked round and saw a tall woman in a black gown standing at the entrance to the hall. She struck him by the dignity of her bearing. She carried her bare arms beautifully to set off her graceful figure; light sprigs of fuchsia fell beautifully from her gleaming hair to her sloping shoulders; her luminous eyes gazed calmly and intelligently — calmly was just the word, but not thoughtfully — from beneath a slightly beetling white brow, and her lips smiled a hardly perceptible smile. A gracious and gentle strength radiated from her features.

"Do you know her?" Arkady asked Sitnikov.

"Intimately. Would you like me to introduce you?"

"Please — after this quadrille."

Bazarov also turned his attention to Odintsova.

"Who is that person?" he said. "She is quite unlike any of the other women."

Sitnikov waited till the end of the quadrille, then led Arkady to Odintsova. But he could hardly have been intimately acquainted with her: he stammered as he spoke, and she gazed at him with some astonishment. None the less she smiled at Arkady when she heard his surname. She asked him if he wasn't the son of Nikolai Piotrovich.

"Yes, that is so."

"I have met your father twice, and I have heard a great deal about him," she continued. "I am very glad to make your acquaintance."

At that moment some adjutant flew up to her and asked her for a quadrille. She consented.

"Do you dance, then?" Arkady asked respectfully.

"Yes. But why should you think I don't? Or do I seem too old to you?"

"Oh, really, how could I — But in that case permit me to ask you for a mazurka."

She smiled indulgently.

"Very well," she said, and looked at Arkady not exactly patronizingly, but rather as married sisters look at very young brothers.

She was a little older than Arkady, for she had passed her twenty-ninth birthday; but in her presence he felt like a schoolboy, a young student, as though the difference in their ages was far greater. Matvei Ilich approached her with a majestic air and unctuous remarks. Arkady slipped aside, but he continued to watch her: he did not take his eyes off her even during the quadrille. She talked as unconstrainedly with her partner as with the dignitary; she rolled her head and eyes a little, and laughed quietly once or twice. Her nose was rather flashy, like almost all Russian noses, and her complexion was not perfectly clear; but even so, Arkady decided that he had never before met such a charming woman. The sound of her voice did not fade from his ears; even the folds of her gown seemed to be arranged round her differently, they fell more harmoniously and amply, and she moved with a very buoyant yet natural grace.

Arkady felt some bashfulness in his heart when, at the first sounds of the mazurka, he took his place beside his lady and prepared to enter into conversation, only to run his hand over his hair, finding not one word to say. But he was shy and agitated only for a few moments. Her composure was communicated to him: before fifteen minutes had passed he was talking easily about his father, his uncle, about life in Petersburg and in the country. She listened to him with polite sympathy, slightly opening and closing her fan; his chatter was interrupted when other male partners came to ask for her; Sitnikov, by the way, carried her off twice. She returned, sat down again, picked up her fan, and even her breast did not rise and fall more rapidly; but Arkady again began to chatter, completely absorbed in the happiness of finding himself close to her, of talking to her, of looking into her eyes, at her fine brow, at all her pleasant, serious, and intelligent face. She herself talked little, but knowledge of life was revealed in her words; from various of her remarks Arkady concluded that this young woman had already managed to feel and to think a very great deal. . . .

"Who was that you were standing with?" she asked him, "when Mr. Sitnikov led you to me?"

"Did you notice him, then?" Arkady asked in his turn. "Don't you think he has a very fine face? He is a friend of mine, named Bazarov."

He began to talk about "his friend."

He talked about him in such detail and with such enthusiasm that she turned toward him and looked at him attentively. Meanwhile the mazurka was nearing its end. Arkady felt regretful at having to part with his lady: he had so greatly enjoyed the hour or so he had spent with her! True, all that time he had felt continually that she was treating him indulgently, that somehow he ought to be grateful to her . . . but young hearts are not burdened by that feeling.

The music stopped.

"*Merci*," she said, rising. "You've promised to call on me; bring your friend with you. I shall be very curious to see a man who has the courage not to believe in anything."

The governor came up to her, announced that supper was ready, and with a preoccupied air gave her his hand. As she went out she turned to smile and nod to Arkady for a last time. He bowed low, gazed after her (how shapely he thought her waist, flooded with the gray shimmer of black silk!), and as he thought: "She has already forgotten my existence," he felt an exquisite humility in his soul. . . .

"Well?" Bazarov asked Arkady as soon as he returned to his friend in the corner, "satisfied? I've just been told by one gentleman that that lady is — oh, dear, dear! But that gentleman would appear to be a fool. Well, but what do you think, is she really — oh, dear, dear?"

"I don't quite understand that definition," Arkady replied.

"Really, now! What an innocent!"

"In that case I don't understand your gentleman. She is very nice, undoubtedly, but she behaves so coldly and severely that — "

"Still waters — you know!" Bazarov interrupted him. "You say she is cold. But that is just what gives the savor. You like ice cream, don't you?"

"Maybe," Arkady muttered, "I can't judge as to that. She wishes to make your acquaintance and asked me to take you along to see her."

"I can imagine how you described me! All the same, you did

well. Take me along. No matter who she may be, just a simple provincial lioness or an 'émancipé' like Kukshina, I haven't seen such shoulders as hers for a long time."

Arkady was rather jarred by Bazarov's cynicism, but, as often happens, he chided his friend with something a little different from the thing to which he objected.

"Why aren't you prepared to allow freedom of thought in women?" he said in an undertone.

"Because, dear brother, according to all my observations the only women who think freely are hideous."

There the conversation ended. The two young men left immediately after supper. Kukshina smiled after them with nervous malevolence, but not without some timidity; her self-esteem was deeply wounded by the circumstance that neither of them had paid any attention to her. She was the last to leave the ball, and at four in the morning she and Sitnikov danced a polka-mazurka in the Parisian manner. And with this instructive spectacle the governor's celebration came to its end.

xv

"We'll see what category of mammals this person belongs to," Bazarov said to Arkady next day as they went up the stairs of the hotel in which Mme Odintsova was staying. "My nose tells me that there is something not quite as it should be here."

"I am amazed at you!" Arkady exclaimed. "What? You, you, Bazarov, hold to that narrow-minded morality which — "

"Aren't you queer!" Bazarov interrupted him carelessly. "Don't you really know that in our dialect and for the likes of us 'not quite as it should be' means 'just as it should be'? It means that there's something in it to our advantage. Didn't you yourself say this morning that she had made a strange marriage? — though, in my view, to marry a wealthy old man is not in the least strange, but on the contrary is perfectly sensible. I don't believe the town rumors; but I like to think, as our cultured governor says, that they are justified."

Arkady did not answer; he knocked on the door. A young servant in livery led the two friends into a large room, furnished stupidly, like all the rooms in Russian hotels, but decorated with flowers. Soon Mme Odintsova herself appeared in a simple morning dress. By the light of the spring sunshine she seemed even younger. Arkady introduced her to Bazarov and with secret astonishment noted that he seemed to be embarrassed, whereas she remained perfectly composed, as she had been the previous evening. Bazarov himself felt that he was embarrassed, and he was chagrined. "Here's a fine thing; afraid of a woman!" he thought and, sprawling in his chair as negligently as Sitnikov, he began to talk with exaggerated jauntiness, while she did not remove her clear eyes from him.

Anna Sergeevna Odintsova was the daughter of Sergei Nikolaevich Loktiev, a notoriously handsome adventurer and gamester who, after keeping his head above water and causing a great sensation for fifteen years in Petersburg and Moscow, ended by being completely ruined and was forced to settle down in the country, where in any case he died soon after, leaving almost nothing to his daughters, Anna, aged twenty, and Katherine, aged twelve. Their mother, of Prince X's impoverished line, had died in Petersburg while her husband was still at the height of his career. After her father's death Anna's situation was very difficult. The brilliant upbringing she had received in Petersburg had not prepared her for the anxieties of estate management and domestic responsibilities or for quiet country existence. She knew absolutely no one in all the district, and she had no one with whom to take counsel. Her father had tried to avoid contact with the neighbors; he was contemptuous of them and they were contemptuous of him, each in their own fashion. She did not lose her head, however, and immediately sent for her mother's sister, Princess Avdotia Stepanovna X, a malicious and arrogant old woman who, on settling in her niece's house, at once took all the best rooms for herself, snorted and grumbled from morning till evening, and even when walking in the garden was accompanied by her sole serf, a glum-faced lackey in shabby pea-green livery with blue galloons and a tricorne. Anna patiently endured all her aunt's caprices, gradually set about her sister's education, and seemed to be reconciled to the thought of withering in her out-of-the-way house. . . . But fate had decided otherwise.

She chanced to be seen by a man named Odintsov, very rich, aged about forty-six, an eccentric, a hypochondriac, rather fat, heavy, and sour, yet neither stupid nor a bad man; he fell in love with her and offered her his hand. She consented to be his wife; he lived with her for six years and, on dying, left her all his fortune. For some twelve months after his death Anna Sergeevna did not leave her country home at all; then she went abroad with her sister, but stayed only in Germany; she grew miserable and returned to reside in her charming Nikolskoe, which was some twenty-five miles from the town of X X X. There she had a magnificent, excellently furnished house, and a beautiful garden with a conservatory — her husband had never denied himself anything. She visited the town very rarely, usually on business, and did not stay long. She was not liked in the province, there had been a terrible outcry over her marriage with Odintsov, all kinds of stories were told about her, people declared that she had helped her father in his swindling transactions, nor was it for nothing that she had traveled abroad, but out of the necessity to conceal certain unfortunate consequences. . . . "Do you realize what consequences?" the indignant narrators ended. "She has passed through fire and water," it was said of her; and a well-known wit of the province usually added: "and through copper tubes." [1] All these rumors reached her ears; but she took no notice of them; she had an independent and very resolute character.

She sat leaning against the back of her armchair, with one hand laid on the other, and listened to Bazarov. Contrary to his custom, he talked a great deal and obviously tried to interest his hostess, which greatly surprised Arkady. He could not make up his mind whether Bazarov had achieved his aim. It was difficult to judge from Anna Sergeevna's face what impression was made on her: it preserved one and the same expression, friendly but subtle; her fine eyes beamed with attention, but an imperturbable attention. Bazarov's affectation during the first few minutes of their visit had an unpleasant effect on her, like a bad smell or a harsh sound; but she at once realized that he felt embarrassed, which even flattered her. Only the trivial repelled her, and no one could have reproached Bazarov with trivialities. That day Arkady was astonished by one thing after another. He expected Bazarov to talk to her as though she were an intelligent woman, about his convictions and views; she herself had expressed the desire to hear a man "who has the courage not to believe in anything"; but instead he talked about medicine, about homeopathy, about

[1] "Through fire, water, and then copper tubes" — used of a slippery, artful person. (Tr.)

botany. It transpired that Mme Odintsova had not wasted her time in her seclusion: she had read several good books, and she expressed herself in correct Russian. She turned the talk to the subject of music, but, perceiving that Bazarov did not appreciate art, little by little she returned to botany, though Arkady was all ready to talk about the significance of folk melodies. She continued to treat him as a younger brother: apparently she appreciated his goodness and simplicity of youth — and that was all. For more than three hours the conversation went on, unhurriedly, yet varied and vital.

At last the two friends rose and began to take their leave. Anna Sergeevna looked at them graciously, extended her beautiful white hand to each of them in turn, and, after a moment's thought, said with an irresolute but pleasant smile:

"If you're not afraid of being bored, gentlemen, come and visit me at Nikolskoe."

"Why, of course, Anna Sergeevna," Arkady exclaimed. "I shall regard myself as particularly happy to."

"And you, M'sieur Bazarov?"

Bazarov only bowed — and Arkady was made to feel astonishment for a last time: he noticed that his friend blushed.

"Well?" he said to Bazarov when they reached the street, "are you still of the opinion that she is — oh, dear, dear?"

"Who can tell? You saw how she froze up!" Bazarov retorted. After a brief silence he added: "She's a duchess, an imperious person. She only needs a train to be carried behind her and a coronet on her head."

"Our duchesses don't talk Russian like that," Arkady remarked.

"She's been refashioned, my boy, she's tasted our bread."

"All the same she is enchanting," Arkady declared.

"Such a fine body!" Bazarov continued, "it ought to go at once to the anatomical theater."

"Stop it, for God's sake, Yevgeny! That talk is like nothing on earth."

"Now, don't be angry, you're too sensitive! I've said she's first-class. We'll have to go and visit her."

"When?"

"Well, say the day after tomorrow. What can we do here? Drink champagne with Kukshina? Listen to your relation, the liberal dignitary? . . . We'll slip off the day after tomorrow. As it happens, my father's little place isn't far from there. It's the Nikolskoe on the — road, isn't it?"

"Yes."

"*Optime*. There's no point in hanging about. Only fools dally — and wise men. I tell you it's a fine body!"

Two days later the two friends were driving along the road to Nikolskoe. The day was clear and not too hot, and the well-fed hired horses trotted along rapidly, gently waving their twisted and plaited tails. Arkady gazed at the road and smiled, himself not knowing why.

"Congratulate me!" Bazarov suddenly exclaimed; "today is the 22nd of June, the day of my angel. We shall see how he looks after me. They're expecting me home today," he added, lowering his voice. "Well, they can wait a little longer, it isn't so important as that!"

XVI

Anna Sergeevna's country house stood on a rolling, open rise, a little distance from a yellow brick church with a green roof, white columns, and, above the main entrance, an alfresco painting, representing *The Resurrection of Christ* in the Italian style. A swarthy, helmeted warrior, prone in the foreground, was particularly remarkable because of his swelling contours. Beyond the church a village extended in two long rows, with chimneys rising here and there above straw roofs. The gentry's house was built in the same style as the church, the style known to us as the Alexandrine; this house, too, was painted yellow, and it, too, had a green roof and white columns and a pediment with armorial bearings. The provincial architect had erected both edifices with the approval of the dead Odintsov, who could not endure any empty and, as he expressed it, arbitrary innovations. On both sides of the house were the dark trees of an old-world garden; an avenue of close-pruned firs led to the main entrance.

In the vestibule our friends were met by two well-built lackeys in livery; one of them immediately ran for the butler. The butler, a stout man in a black frock coat, appeared at once and led the guests up carpeted stairs into a separate room, which was already furnished with two beds and all the appurtenances of the toilet. It was evident that order reigned in the house, everything was clean, everything had a decorous odor, as in ministers' waiting-rooms.

"Anna Sergeevna requests you to present yourselves to her in half an hour," the butler reported, "and in the meantime have you any commands?"

"There will not be any commands whatever, my dear fellow," Bazarov replied, "except perhaps that you would be so kind as to bring us a glass of vodka."

"Very good," the butler replied, not without a touch of bewilderment, and he retired, his boots creaking.

"What a *grand genre*!" Bazarov observed, "that is what I think you call it? A duchess, and in every respect!"

"A fine duchess," Arkady retorted, "when at our first meeting she invites such distinguished aristocrats as you and me to call on her."

"Especially me, a future doctor, and a doctor's son, and a deacon's nephew. You know, of course, that I am a deacon's nephew? Like Speransky," [1] Bazarov added after a brief silence, with a twist of his lips. "But, all the same, she has indulged herself; oh, how this lady has indulged herself! Surely we ought to wear frock coats?"

Arkady only shrugged his shoulders, but he, too, felt a little embarrassment.

Half an hour later Bazarov and Arkady went down into the reception hall. It was a lofty, spacious room, furnished quite luxuriously, but without any particular taste. Heavy, expensive furniture stood in the usual starchy order along the walls, which were hung with brown wallpaper with a design in gold; Odintsov had ordered it from Moscow through his friend and agent, a wine merchant. Above the central divan hung a portrait of a flabby, fair-haired man — and it seemed to stare at the guests inimically. "That must be he *himself*," Bazarov whispered to Arkady and, wrinkling his nose, added: "Shall we clear out?" But at that moment their hostess entered. She was wearing a light *barège* gown; her hair, combed smoothly back behind her ears, conferred a maidenly expression on her pure, fresh features.

"Thank you for keeping your word," she began; "you will stay with me for a while, won't you? It really isn't bad here. I'll

[1] A Russian statesman of the early nineteenth century. (Tr.)

introduce you to my sister, she can play the piano well. To you, M'sieur Bazarov, that is a matter of indifference; but you, M'sieur Kirsanov, like music, I think; in addition to my sister my old aunt is living with me, and sometimes one of our neighbors drives over to play cards; and that is all the society we have. But now let us sit down."

She uttered all this little speech very meticulously, as though she had learned it by heart; then she turned to Arkady. It transpired that her mother had been acquainted with his mother and had even been a confidante of her love for Nikolai Piotrovich. Arkady began to talk enthusiastically about his dead mother, but meanwhile Bazarov examined some albums. "How humble I have become!" he thought.

A handsome borzoi with a blue collar ran into the room, its nails tapping on the floor, and it was followed by a girl of about eighteen, black-haired and swarthy, with a rather round but pleasant face and small dark eyes. She was carrying a basket full of flowers. "And this is my sister, Katya," Odintsova said, nodding toward the girl.

The girl made a little curtsy, seated herself by her sister, and began to pick over the flowers. The borzoi, which was called Fifi, approached each guest in turn, wagging its tail, and thrust its cold muzzle into their hands.

"Did you pick all those yourself?" Mme Odintsova asked.

"Yes," Katya replied.

"And is auntie coming for tea?"

"Yes."

When Katya spoke she smiled very pleasantly, bashfully and openly, and looked up with an amusingly severe expression. Everything about her was still youthfully verdant: her voice, and the down all over her face, and her rosy hands with whitish little rings in the palms, and the very slightly raised shoulders. . . . She blushed incessantly and breathed hurriedly.

Mme Odintsova turned to Bazarov.

"You're looking at those pictures only out of politeness, Yevgeny Vasilievich," she began. "You're not really interested in them. Come and join us, and let us have an argument about something."

Bazarov approached.

"What do you command us to argue about?" he asked.

"Whatever you like. I warn you that I am a terrible arguer."

"You?"

"Yes, I. That seems to surprise you. Why does it?"

"Because, so far as I can judge, you have a calm and cold disposition, and discussion calls for enthusiasm."

"How have you managed to get to know me so quickly? To begin with, I am impatient and insistent, you had better ask Katya about that; and secondly, I very easily grow enthusiastic."

Bazarov looked at her.

"Maybe; you should know best. Well, so you would like to argue; very good. I have just been looking at the views of the Saxon Switzerland in your album, but you have just remarked that they cannot interest me. You said that because you do not think I have any artistic inclinations, and certainly I have none; but I found those views interesting from the geological aspect, from the aspect of mountain formation, for instance."

"Excuse me, but as a geologist surely you would rather turn to a book, to some special work, than to a picture."

"A picture shows me at a glance what it takes dozens of pages of a book to expound."

She was silent for a moment.

"And you really haven't the least touch of artistic feeling?" she said, resting her elbows on the table and by this very movement bringing her face closer to Bazarov. "But how do you manage without it?"

"But what does one need it for, if you will permit me to ask?"

"Why, if only to be able to recognize and study people."

Bazarov smiled.

"In the first place, to do that, one relies on vital experience; and secondly, I have to inform you that the study of individual personalities is not worth the labor. All people are like one another, in both body and soul; each of us has a brain, a spleen, a heart, and lungs, all constructed alike; and the so-called moral qualities are one and the same in all: the tiny variations are of no significance. One needs only a single human specimen in order to judge of all the others. People are like trees in the forest; no botanist will stop to study every birch separately."

Katya, who was unhurriedly matching flower to flower, raised her eyes to Bazarov in astonishment and, meeting his swift and perfunctory look, flamed to her ears. Anna Sergeevna shook her head.

"Trees in a forest!" she repeated. "So in your view there is no difference between a stupid and an intelligent man, between good and evil."

"Yes, there is a difference like that between the sick and the healthy. The lungs of a consumptive are not in the same condition as yours and mine, though they are of identical construction. We know approximately what our physical maladies are caused by; but moral diseases are due to stupid upbringing, to all kinds of trash with which human heads are stuffed from childhood — to the monstrous state of society, in a word. Put society right, and there will not be any diseases."

Bazarov said all this with an air suggesting that meanwhile he was saying to himself: "Whether you believe me or not I don't care!" He ran his long fingers slowly over his side-whiskers, and his eyes darted from side to side.

"And do you consider," Anna Sergeevna said, "that when society is put right, there will no longer be any stupid or bad people?"

"At any rate, with a sound organization of society it will make no difference whatever whether a man is stupid or intelligent, bad or good."

"Yes, I understand; you mean they will all have one and the same spleen."

"Exactly so, madame."

She turned to Arkady.

"And what is your opinion, Arkady Nikolaevich?"

"I agree with Yevgeny," he replied.

Katya looked up at them from under knitted brows.

"You amaze me, gentlemen," Mme Odintsova declared; "but we will discuss the question with you again. Now I can hear auntie coming to tea; we must spare her ears."

Anna Sergeevna's aunt, Princess X, a rawboned little woman with features clenched like a fist and with staring, malignant eyes below a gray wig, entered and, hardly acknowledging the guests, dropped into a broad velvet armchair, in which only she was allowed to sit. Katya placed a stool beneath her feet; the old woman did not thank her, did not even glance at her, only fidgeted with her hands beneath the yellow shawl that covered almost all her puny body. The Princess liked yellow: even in her cap there were bright yellow ribbons.

"How did you rest, auntie?" Mme Odintsova asked, raising her voice.

"That dog here again," the old woman snorted in reply; noticing that Fifi had taken two irresolute steps in her direction, she cried: "Shoo! Shoo!"

Katya called Fifi and opened the door for her.

Fifi rushed out joyfully, hoping that she was to be taken for a walk. But, finding herself alone outside the door, she began to scrape and whine. The Princess frowned. Katya was about to go out.

"I think tea will be ready now," Mme Odintsova said. "Come, gentlemen; auntie, will you have some tea?"

The Princess rose from her chair without speaking and was the first to leave the room. Everybody followed her into the dining-room. At the table a page in livery noisily drew back an armchair, which also was sacred and was piled with cushions, into which the Princess dropped. Katya, who poured the tea, gave her the first cup, which was adorned with armorial bearings. The old woman put some honey into her cup (she considered it both sinful and extravagant to drink tea with sugar, though she herself never spent a kopek on anything) and suddenly asked in a hoarse voice:

"But what does Prince Ivan say in his letter?"

No one answered her. Bazarov and Arkady soon realized that nobody paid any attention to her, though everybody treated her with respect. "It's just the importance they attach to their princely line," Bazarov thought.

After tea Anna Sergeevna suggested a walk, but a fine rain began to fall, and the entire company, with the exception of the Princess, returned to the reception hall. Porfiry Platonich, the neighbor who was fond of playing cards, arrived. He was rather stout, rather gray-haired, with fingers rather stubby, as though they had been ground down, and a very polite and jocular man. Anna Sergeevna, who talked more and more to Bazarov, asked him whether he would like to try conclusions with them in an old-fashioned game of preference. Bazarov agreed, saying that he must prepare himself in advance for the country doctor's duties that awaited him.

"Beware!" Anna Sergeevna observed; "Porfiry Platonich and I will beat you hollow. And you, Katya," she added, "play something for Arkady Nikolaevich; he is fond of music, and we can listen too."

Katya reluctantly went over to the piano; and Arkady, though he did indeed like music, reluctantly went after her: he had the feeling that Anna Sergeevna was sending him away, and in his heart, as in that of any young man of his years, a vague and wearisome feeling, resembling the presentiment of love, began to work. Katya raised the lid of the piano and, without looking at Arkady, said in an undertone:

"And what shall I play for you?"

"Whatever you like," Arkady answered indifferently.

"What music do you like most?" Katya repeated, without changing her position.

"Classic," Arkady replied in the same tone.

"Do you like Mozart?"

"Yes, I like Mozart."

Katya selected Mozart's Sonata and Fantasia in C minor. She played very well, though somewhat meticulously and dryly. Fixing her eyes on the music and tightly pursing her lips, she sat motionless and upright, and only toward the end of the sonata did her face begin to burn and a tiny strand of unruly hair fell over her dark brow.

Arkady was particularly struck by the last part of the sonata, in which, amid the captivating merriment of a carefree refrain, there are sudden outbursts of such mournful, almost tragic sorrow. . . . But the thoughts aroused in him by Mozart's music had no reference to Katya. Looking at her, he only thought: "But, you know, this young lady doesn't play at all badly, and she herself isn't at all bad-looking."

When she had finished the sonata, Katya, without removing her hands from the keys, asked: "Have you had enough?" Arkady announced that he did not dare to burden her any more and began to talk to her about Mozart; he asked her whether she herself had chosen this sonata, or had someone recommended it to her? But Katya replied to him in monosyllables, she *concealed* herself, retired within herself. When this occurred with her it was long before she emerged again; at such times even her face took on an obstinate, almost stupid expression. She was not

241

exactly bashful, but distrustful, and she was rather afraid of the sister who had brought her up, a feeling that, of course, the sister did not suspect at all. Arkady ended by calling to Fifi, who had returned, and, to keep himself in countenance, began to stroke the dog on the head, smiling benevolently. Katya returned to her flowers.

But meanwhile Bazarov was fleeced. Anna Sergeevna played cards expertly, and Porfiry Platonich also could hold his own. Bazarov was left the loser, though not of any considerable sum, yet to an extent not exactly agreeable to him. Over the supper table Anna Sergeevna again turned the conversation to the subject of botany.

"We'll go for a walk the first thing in the morning," she told him. "I want you to tell me the Latin names of the wild flowers and their properties."

"What do you want to know the Latin names for?" Bazarov asked.

"Order is necessary in all things," she replied.

"What a marvelous woman Anna Sergeevna is!" Arkady exclaimed when he and his friend retired to their room.

"Yes," Bazarov replied, "she's a female with a brain. And she has seen the world, too."

"In what sense did you mean that, Yevgeny Vasilich?"

"In a good sense, in a good sense, my dear father, Arkady Nikolaich! I am confident that she also manages her estate excellently. But the miracle is not she, but her sister."

"What? That swarthy little creature?"

"Yes, that swarthy little creature. She is fresh, and untouched, and shy, and taciturn, and everything you could wish. Now there's somebody one could occupy oneself with. With her, what you plan, that you will accomplish; but the other, she's a sly vixen."

Arkady made no reply to Bazarov, and each of them went to sleep with his own thoughts.

Anna Sergeevna also thought about her guests that evening. She liked Bazarov because he was not of a flirtatious disposition, and for the very severity of his judgments. She saw in him something new, something she had never happened to meet before, and she was inquisitive.

Anna Sergeevna was quite a strange creature. Having no prejudices whatever, not even having any strong beliefs, she hesitated at nothing and never achieved anything. She was clearsighted in many respects, she was interested in many things, and nothing completely satisfied her; nor, in all probability, did she desire complete satisfaction. Her mind was inquisitive and indifferent at one and the same time; her doubts never faded into oblivion, and never grew into anxiety. If she had not been wealthy and independent she might have flung herself into battle, might have known passion. . . . But life was easy for her, though sometimes she was bored, and she continued to spend day after day never hurrying and only rarely getting excited. Rainbow tints sometimes glowed before her eyes, but she breathed easily when they faded, and she did not regret them. Her imagination traveled even beyond the limits regarded as permissible by the laws of ordinary morality; but even then her blood flowed as quietly as before in her enchantingly graceful and tranquil body. There were times when, stepping out of her perfumed bath, all warm and limber, she would dream of the insignificance of life, of its sorrow, of toil, and evil. . . . Her soul would be filled with a sudden audacity, would seethe with noble striving; but a draft would blow from a half-closed window, and Anna Sergeevna would huddle together, and complain, and be almost angry, and at such a moment the only necessity she felt was that that loathsome wind should not blow on her.

Like all women who have never succeeded in falling in love, she wanted something, not knowing exactly what. In reality she wanted nothing, though it seemed to her that she wanted everything. She could hardly endure her late husband (she had been calculating in her marriage, though probably she would not have consented to be his wife if she had not regarded him as a good man) and had developed a secret loathing for all men, whom she imagined only as slovenly, heavy and sluggish, impotently irksome creatures. Once, somewhere abroad, she had met a young, handsome Swede with a chivalrous expression and honest blue eyes beneath an open forehead; he made a strong impression on her, but that did not prevent her returning to Russia.

"A strange man, that doctor!" she thought as she lay in her sumptuous bed, on lacy pillows, beneath a light silk blanket. . . . From her father Anna Sergeevna had inherited some little of his love of luxury. She had been very fond of her sinful but good father, and he had worshipped her, had amiably joked with her as with an equal, and had confided in her completely, had taken counsel with her. She could hardly remember her mother.

"A strange man, that doctor!" she repeated to herself. She stretched herself, smiled, flung her arms behind her head, then skimmed through a couple of pages of a stupid French romance, let the book fall, and dropped off to sleep, all clean and cool, in clean and scented linen.

Next morning, immediately after breakfast, Anna Sergeevna set off to botanize with Bazarov and returned just before dinner; Arkady had not been anywhere and had spent about an hour with Katya. He did not feel bored with her, she herself offered to repeat yesterday's sonata to him, but when Anna Sergeevna returned at last, when he saw her — his heart momentarily stopped beating. . . . She was walking through the garden with a rather weary gait; her cheeks were crimsoned, and her eyes glittered more brightly than usual below her round straw hat. She was turning the slender stalk of some wild flower over and over in her hand, a light mantilla fell to her elbows, and the broad gray ribbons of her hat nestled against her breast. Bazarov was walking behind her, self-confidently and negligently, as always; but though the expression of his face was cheerful and even gracious, Arkady did not like it. Muttering through his teeth: "Good day," Bazarov went off to his room, while his companion abstractedly gave Arkady her hand and then she too walked past him.

" 'Good day,' " Arkady thought. "Is this the first time we have seen each other today, then?"

XVII

Time (as is well known) sometimes flies like a bird, sometimes crawls like a worm; but man feels especially happy when he does not even notice whether it is passing rapidly or quietly. That was exactly how Arkady and Bazarov spent fifteen days at Nikolskoe. This was due in part to the order that Mme Odintsova had introduced into her house and her life. She observed it strictly, and compelled others also to submit to it. Everything all through the day was done at a regular time. In the morning all the company gathered for tea punctually at eight o'clock; from tea to break-fast time everybody could do as he wished; the mistress herself was occupied with the steward (the estate was rented out to the peasants), with the butlers, with the head housekeeper. Before dinner the company again assembled for talk or for reading; the evening was devoted to a walk, to cards, to music; at half past ten Anna Sergeevna retired to her room, gave her orders for the following day, and went to bed. Bazarov did not like this measured, somewhat formal regularity of everyday life — "just as though you're running on rails," he declared; the liveried lackeys, the decorous butlers affronted his democratic feelings. He considered that, as matters had gone so far, the company should dine in the English fashion, in tail coats and white ties. One day he raised this question with Anna Sergeevna. Her atti-tude was such that anyone could express his views to her without circumlocutions. She listened to him to the end and observed: "From your viewpoint you are right — and perhaps in this respect I am a lady; but in the country it is impossible to live without order, you would be overcome with boredom," and she continued to go her own way. Bazarov snorted, but during their stay at Nikolskoe both he and Arkady found life so easy just because, among other things, everything in her house "ran as though on rails."

Meanwhile from the first day of their residence at Nikolskoe there was a change in the two young men. Bazarov, for whom Anna Sergeevna showed much predilection, though she rarely agreed with him, began to manifest an uneasiness he had never before displayed: he grew irritable quickly, spoke reluctantly, looked at the others angrily, and fidgeted in his seat as though something was worrying him. But Arkady, who now had decided that he himself was in love with Anna Sergeevna, began to give himself over to a quiet despondency. This despondency, however, did not prevent his growing intimate with Katya; it even helped him to enter into benevolent, friendly relations with her. "*She* does not appreciate me! So be it! . . . But here is a good creature who does not reject me," he thought, and his heart again tasted the joy of magnanimous feelings. Katya vaguely realized that in her company he was seeking consolation for something and did not deny either him or herself the innocent satisfaction of a half-bashful, half-trusting friendship. In Anna Sergeevna's presence they did not talk to each other: beneath her sister's keen gaze Katya always closed up; and, as is only proper for a man in love, when close to the object of his devotion, Arkady could not pay attention to anything else. But when alone with Katya, he was quite at ease. He felt that he had not the talents to interest Mme Odintsova; he grew shy and confused when left alone with her; and she did not know what to say to him: he was too young for her. On the other hand, with Katya Arkady was quite at home; he treated her with condescension and did not stop her telling him the impressions aroused in her by music, by the reading of novels, poems, and other such trifles, though he did not notice or did not realize that these trifles interested him also. For her part, Katya did not prevent his feeling sorrowful. Arkady felt at ease with Katya, Mme Odintsova with Bazarov; and so as a rule, after being together for a little while, the two couples went their own ways, especially when they were out for a walk. Katya *worshipped* nature, and Arkady was fond of it, though he would not have dared to confess the fact; but Mme Odintsova was rather indifferent to it, in which she was exactly like Bazarov. The almost constant separation of our two friends was not without its consequences: their relations began to change. Bazarov stopped talking to Arkady about Mme Odintsova and even stopped railing against her "aristocratic ways"; true, he continued to praise Katya as before and suggested only that her sentimental tendencies should be moderated; but his praises were hurried, his advice dry, and altogether he talked much less than formerly to Arkady; he seemed to avoid, seemed to be ashamed to meet him. . . .

Arkady noticed all these things, but he kept his observations to himself.

The real cause of all this "change" was the feeling Mme Odintsova inspired in Bazarov, a feeling that tormented and enraged him and that he would have denied immediately with contemptuous laughter and cynical abuse if anyone had even distantly hinted at the possibility of what was happening inside him. Bazarov was a great woman-chaser and devotee of feminine beauty, but love in the ideal sense, or, as he expressed it, the romantic sense, he called nonsense, an unforgivable stupidity; he regarded chivalrous feelings as something in the nature of a deformation or disease, and more than once expressed his surprise that Toggenburg [1] with all his minnesingers and troubadours had not been put away in a madhouse. "If you take a fancy to a woman," he used to say, "try to gain your end; but if you can't, well then, it's no matter, turn your back on her, the world is large enough." He had taken a fancy to Mme Odintsova, and the rumors spread about her, the freedom and independence of her thought, her undoubted predilection for him—everything appeared to be in his favor; but he soon realized that with her he would not "gain his end." To his own amazement, however, he found he had no power to turn his back on her. His blood began to burn as soon as he thought of her; he could easily have managed his blood, but something else had entered into it, which formerly he would never have tolerated, which he had always made fun of, and which stirred up all his pride. When talking to her he expressed his indifferent contempt for everything romantic even more than before; but when he was alone he angrily recognized the romanticism that was in himself. Then he went off into the forest and walked through it with great strides, breaking the branches that came in his way, and cursing half aloud both her and himself; or he climbed into the hayloft, into the coach-house, and, obstinately closing his eyes, forced himself to sleep, in which, of course, he was not always successful. Suddenly he imagined those undefiled arms some day twining around his neck, those proud lips responding to his kisses, those intelligent eyes tenderly—yes, tenderly—resting on his eyes, and his head whirled and he forgot himself for a moment, until indignation again flamed up within him. He caught himself thinking all kinds of "shameful" thoughts, as though he were being provoked by a demon. Sometimes it seemed to him that a change was occurring in her too, that something peculiar was revealed in the expression of her face, that, perhaps . . . But at this he usually stamped his foot or grated his teeth and shook his fist at himself.

Meanwhile Bazarov was not altogether wrong. He caught her imagination; he occupied it, she thought a great deal about him. In his absence she did not long for him, did not wait for him; but his arrival at once aroused her; she readily remained alone with him and readily talked with him, even when he made her

[1] Hero of Schiller's ballad of the same name. (Tr.)

247

angry or affronted her taste, her exquisite manners. She seemed to desire to try him, and to plumb herself.

One day as he was walking with her in the garden, he abruptly announced in a glum tone that he intended to travel on to see his father soon. She turned pale, as though something had stabbed at her heart, and had stabbed so violently that she was amazed, and for long after she meditated on what it could mean. Bazarov had informed her of his departure not with the intention of trying her, of seeing what would come of it; he never "created." That same morning he had had a meeting with his father's steward and his own former servant, Timofeich. This Timofeich, who was a shabby, brisk little old man with faded yellow hair, a red, weatherbeaten face, and little tears in his shrunken eyes, and was wearing a rather short coat of stout grayish-blue cloth belted with a leather strap and had tarry boots on his feet, arrived without warning to see Bazarov.

"Ah, old fellow, good morning!" Bazarov exclaimed.

"Good morning, Master Yevgeny Vasilich," the old man began, and he smiled joyfully, so that all his face was wrinkled.

"What have you come for? I suppose they've sent you to fetch me?"

"Why, of course not, master, how could they!" Timofeich stammered (he remembered the strict injunction his master had given him on his departure). "I was traveling to the town on the master's business, and I had heard you were here, so I dropped in on my way, just to take a look at you — otherwise how could I have dared to trouble you?"

"Now, don't lie!" Bazarov interrupted him. "Is this your way to the town?" Timofeich was disconcerted and did not reply. "Is my father well?"

"Yes, praise be."

"And my mother?"

"And Arina Vlasievna, praise be to God."

"I suppose they're expecting me?"

The old man cocked his little head on one side.

"Ah, Yevgeny Vasilich, how could they help waiting for you? Believe it or not, your parents' hearts are pining with looking for you."

"Well, good, good! Don't make a song of it. Tell them I shall be home soon."

"Very good," Timofeich answered with a sigh.

As he left the house, he clapped his peaked cap on his head with both hands, climbed into the wretched-looking light droshky he had left at the gate, and made off at a trot, but not in the direction of the town.

In the evening of the same day Mme Odintsova was sitting in her room with Bazarov, while Arkady was striding about the hall and listening to Katya's playing. The Princess had gone upstairs to her room; she never could endure guests, least of all these "new wild men," as she called them. In the best rooms she only sulked; but in her own room, in front of her maid, she sometimes exploded into such abuse that her cap danced on her head together with her wig. Mme Odintsova knew all about these outbursts.

"But how can you be intending to leave us?" she asked Bazarov. "What of your promise?"

He started.

"What promise?"

"Have you forgotten? You intended to give me a few lessons in chemistry."

"I can't help that! My father is waiting for me; I can't hang about any longer. And besides, you can read Pelouse and Frémy's *Notions générales de chimie;* it's a good book and clearly written. In it you'll find all you need."

"But remember you assured me that a book cannot take the place — I have forgotten how you expressed it, but you know what I am trying to say — do you remember?"

"I can't help that!" Bazarov repeated.

"Why go?" she said, lowering her voice.

He glanced at her. She had thrown her head against the back of the armchair and had folded her arms, bare to the elbows, over her breast. By the light of the single lamp, shielded with a shade of cut-out paper, she seemed more pale than usual. An ample white gown entirely enveloped her in its soft folds; the tips of her crossed feet were only just visible.

"But why remain?" Bazarov replied.

She turned her head a little.

"Why do you ask? Aren't you enjoying yourself here? Or do you think no one will miss you here?"

"I am convinced of that."

She was silent for a moment.

"You are wrong in thinking so. But, in any case, I don't believe you. You could not have said that seriously." He did not stir. "Yevgeny Vasilievich, why are you silent?"

"But what can I say to you? It is never worth regretting anybody, least of all me."

"Why do you say that?"

"I am a positive, uninteresting man. I don't know how to talk."

"You're fishing for compliments, Yevgeny Vasilievich."

"That is not one of my habits. Don't you really understand that the exquisite side of life, that side which you treasure so much, is inaccessible to me?"

She bit the corner of her handkerchief.

"Think what you like, but I shall be bored when you go."

"Arkady will remain," Bazarov remarked.

She shrugged her shoulders a little.

"I shall be bored," she repeated.

"You really will? In any case, you won't be bored for long."

"Why do you assume that?"

"Because you yourself told me that you are bored only when your order is violated. You have organized your life on such impeccably sound lines that there cannot be any room in it for boredom, or yearning — or any oppressive feeling whatever."

"And you find that I am impeccable — I mean, that I have organized my life so perfectly?"

"I should say! Why, for instance, in a few minutes ten o'clock will strike, and I know in advance that you will turn me out."

"No, I shall not turn you out, Yevgeny Vasilievich, you can remain. Open that window — I feel stifled, somehow."

Bazarov rose and pushed at the window. It at once flew open with a crash. He had not expected it to open so easily; moreover, his hand trembled. The dark, gentle night, with its almost black sky, its faintly rustling trees, and the fresh scent of the free, clean air, looked into the room.

"Lower that blind and sit down," she said. "I want to have a chat with you before your departure. Tell me something about yourself; you never talk about yourself."

"I endeavor to talk with you about useful subjects, Anna Sergeevna."

"You are very modest. . . . But I should like to know something about you, about your family, about your father, for whom you are abandoning us."

"Why is she using such words?" Bazarov pondered.

"All that is not in the least interesting," he said aloud, "especially to you. We are obscure people."

"But I, in your view, am an aristocrat?"

Bazarov raised his eyes to her.

"Yes," he said, with exaggerated harshness.

She smiled wryly.

"I see you know me very little, though you maintain that all people are alike and that it is not worth studying them. Some day I'll tell you the story of my life — but first you will tell me yours."

"I know you very little," Bazarov repeated. "Perhaps you're right; perhaps it is true that every man is an enigma. Take even you, for instance; you avoid society, you are oppressed by it — and you have invited two students to stay with you. Why do you, with your intelligence, with your beauty, live in the country?"

"What? What is that you said?" she interrupted vivaciously. "With my — beauty?"

Bazarov knitted his brows.

"It doesn't matter," he muttered; "I only wanted to say that I don't understand at all why you have settled down in the country."

"You don't understand that. But you have your own explanation for it, haven't you?"

"Yes. I suppose you remain permanently in one spot because you have spoilt yourself, because you are very fond of comfort, of convenience, and are very indifferent to everything else."

She smiled again.

"You completely refuse to believe that I am capable of having enthusiasms?"

He looked up at her from under his wrinkled brows.

"Out of curiosity, perhaps; but not in any other way."

"Indeed? Well, now I understand why you and I have come together; you see, you are just the same as I."

"We have come together —" Bazarov said thickly.

"Yes! — but I had forgotten that you want to go away."

He rose to his feet. The lamp burned dimly in the darkened,

perfumed, secluded room; occasionally the blind was blown back, and through it the stimulating freshness of night flooded, the mysterious whisper of night could be heard. She did not stir a single limb; but little by little a secret agitation took possession of her. . . . It was communicated to Bazarov. He suddenly realized that he was alone with a young, beautiful woman. . . .

"Where are you going?" she slowly queried

He made no answer and dropped into his chair.

"And so you consider me a calm, effeminate, spoilt creature," she continued in the same voice, not taking her eyes from the window. "But I know myself that I am very unhappy."

"You unhappy! Why? Surely you cannot attach any significance to worthless rumors?"

Her face clouded. She felt vexed that he had understood her in *that* way.

"I am not even amused by those rumors. Yevgeny Vasilich, and I am too proud to let them disturb me. I am unhappy because — because in me I have no desire, no wish, to live. You gaze at me distrustfully; you think: the one who is saying that is an 'aristocrat,' is all dressed in lace and is sitting in a chair of velvet. Nor do I conceal that I love all that you call comfort, yet at the same time I have little desire to live. Reconcile those contradictions as best you can. In any case, all this is romanticism in your eyes."

Bazarov shook his head.

"You are healthy, independent, wealthy; what else do you want? What is it you wish for?"

"What is it I wish for?" she repeated, and sighed. "I am very tired, I am old, I have the feeling that I have been living a very long time. Yes, I am old," she added, gently drawing the edges of her mantilla over her bare arms. Her eyes met Bazarov's eyes, and she reddened a little. "Behind me I have already so many memories: life in Petersburg, wealth, then poverty, then my father's death, marriage, then the journey abroad, everything in order. . . . Memories in plenty, but nothing to remember, and ahead, before me, is a long, long road, but no aim. . . . And I don't want to take the road."

"Are you so disillusioned?" Bazarov asked.

"No," she said deliberately, "but I am dissatisfied. I feel that if I could get strongly attached to something — "

"You would like to fall in love," he interrupted her, "but fall in love you cannot: there is your misfortune."

She turned to examining the sleeves of her mantilla.

"Am I really incapable of falling in love?" she said.

"I think so! Only I was wrong in calling that a misfortune. On the contrary, he to whom that happens is more deserving of commiseration."

"To whom what happens?"

"Falling in love."

"But how do you know that?"

"By hearsay," Bazarov answered angrily.

"You are being flirtatious," he thought, "you're bored and you're teasing me because you have nothing better to do, but I — " And in very deed his heart was beating violently.

"Moreover you are perhaps too exacting," he said, leaning all his body forward and playing with the fringes of his chair.

"Maybe. In my view, either all or nothing. A life for a life. You've taken mine, so give your own, without regret and without recall. Otherwise it is better not at all."

"Well," Bazarov remarked, "that is a just condition, and I am surprised that so far you — haven't found what you wished."

"But do you think it easy to give yourself wholly to anything at all?"

"It is not easy if you stop to consider and bide your time, and attach a price to yourself, if you value yourself, in other words; but it is very easy to give yourself without reflecting."

"How can one not value oneself? If I have no value whatever, who needs my devotion?"

"That is not my business; it is for someone else to decide what is my value. The main thing is to be able to give oneself."

She drew away from her chairback.

"You talk," she began, "as if you had experienced it all."

"Now you've said it, Anna Sergeevna; all this, you know, is outside my province."

"But would you be able to give yourself?"

"I don't know; I don't want to boast."

She made no comment, and Bazarov lapsed into silence. The sounds of the piano floated in from the reception hall.

"What is Katya playing so late for?" she remarked.

Bazarov rose.

"Yes, you're right, it is late, it's time you retired to rest."

"Wait, wait, what are you hurrying for? . . . I must say one word to you."

"What is it?"

"Wait a moment," she whispered. Her eyes rested on Bazarov; she seemed to be examining him closely.

He strode up and down, then suddenly drew near her, hurriedly said: "Good-by," squeezed her hand so hard that she all but cried out, and left the room. She raised to her lips her fingers, pressed together, blew on them, and suddenly, starting impetuously out of her chair, went with swift steps to the door, as though intending to call him back. . . . A maid entered the room with a carafe on a silver tray. Mme Odintsova halted, ordered her to go, sat down, and was again sunk in thought. Her braided hair unwound and fell like a dark snake over her neck.

The lamp burned for a long time after in Anna Sergeevna's room, and long she remained motionless, only occasionally running her fingers over her arms, which were gently nipped by the nocturnal cold.

But Bazarov, disheveled and morose, his boots wet with dew, retired to his bedroom some two hours later. He found Arkady at the writing-desk with a book in his hands, his jacket tightly buttoned,

"Haven't you gone to bed yet?" he said, as though annoyed.

"You sat a long time with Anna Sergeevna this evening," Arkady replied without answering his question.

"Yes, I sat with her all the time you and Katerina Sergeevna were playing the piano."

"I didn't play —" Arkady began, and said no more. He felt the tears starting to his eyes, and he had no desire to weep in front of his derisive friend.

XVIII

Next morning when Mme Odintsova came down for tea, Bazarov sat for some time bent over his cup, then suddenly glanced at her. She turned to him as though he had nudged her, and he had the impression that overnight her face had paled a little. She soon retired to her room and appeared again only for breakfast. The weather had turned rainy that morning, it was impossible to go for a walk. All the company assembled in the reception hall. Arkady picked up the latest number of a periodical and began to read aloud. The Princess, as was her habit, first looked her astonishment as though he were planning something unseemly, then angrily fixed her eyes on him; but he paid no attention to her.

"Yevgeny Vasilievich," Anna Sergeevna said, "come to my room, I want to ask you— You mentioned a certain textbook yesterday. . . ."

She rose and made her way to the door. The Princess looked about her with an expression indicating that she would like to say: "Look, look, how amazed I am!" and again fixed her eyes on Arkady; but he raised his voice and, exchanging glances with Katya, who was sitting beside him, continued his reading.

Mme Odintsova hurried to her room. Bazarov followed her briskly, not raising his eyes and only catching the fine rustle and swish of the silk dress gliding ahead of him. She dropped into the same chair in which she had sat the previous evening, and Bazarov took up his former position.

"Now what did you say that book was called?" she began after a brief silence.

"Pelouse and Frémy: *Notions générales* —" Bazarov replied. "However, I can also recommend Ganot: *Traité élémentaire de physique expérimentale*. In that work the drawings are more distinct, and altogether it —"

She stretched out her hand.

"Yevgeny Vasilievich, forgive me, but I did not ask you here to discuss primers. I wanted to continue our conversation of yesterday. You went so abruptly. . . . You won't be bored?"

"I am at your service, Anna Sergeevna. But just what was it you and I talked about yesterday?"

She threw him a sidelong glance.

"I think we were talking about happiness. I told you about myself. And, by the way, I have just mentioned the word 'happiness.' Tell me, why is it that even when we are enjoying something, music, for instance, a good evening, or a talk with congenial people, why does it all seem to be rather a hint at some immeasurable happiness existing somewhere than actual happiness, I mean such as we ourselves know? Why is that? But perhaps you never feel anything of the kind?"

"You know the saying: 'We pine for what is not,'" Bazarov replied. "And besides, you yourself said yesterday that you are discontented. But you are right, such thoughts never enter my head."

"Perhaps they seem absurd to you?"

"No, but they just don't come into my head."

"Do you mean that? You know, I should very much like to know what *you* think about."

"How? I don't understand."

"Listen, for some time I have been wanting to discuss something with you. There's no need for you to say — and you know it yourself — that you are no ordinary man; you are still young, you have all your life before you. What are you preparing yourself for? What future awaits you? I mean — what aim do you wish to achieve, where are you going, what is in your soul? In a word, who are you? What are you?"

"You astonish me, Anna Sergeevna. You know that I am studying natural sciences, but as for who I am — "

"Yes, who are you?"

"I have already informed you that I am a future provincial doctor."

Anna Sergeevna made a movement of impatience.

"Why do you say that? You yourself don't believe it. Arkady could answer me so, but not you."

"But what Arkady — "

"Stop! Is it possible that you would be content with such modest activity, and aren't you yourself always declaring that for you there is no such thing as medicine? You — with your ambition — a provincial doctor! You tell me that in order to evade me, because you do not trust me at all. But do you know, Yevgeny Vasilievich, that I could understand you: I myself have been poor and ambitious, like you; I, perhaps, have passed similar trials to yours."

"All that is very fine, Anna Sergeevna, but you must excuse me. I am not in the least in the habit of unburdening myself, and between you and me there is such a gulf — "

"What gulf? You will tell me again that I am an aristocrat? Enough, Yevgeny Vasilievich; I think I have told you — "

"Yes, and apart from that," Bazarov interrupted, "what pleasure is there in talking and thinking about the future, which to a large extent doesn't depend on us? If a chance occurs of doing something — excellent; but if it doesn't, at least you will be glad you haven't chattered unnecessarily beforehand."

"You call a friendly talk chatter? . . . Or, since I am a woman, perhaps you don't regard me as worthy of your trust? For you are contemptuous of us all, aren't you?"

"I feel no contempt for you, Anna Sergeevna, and you know that."

"No, I don't know anything — but let us assume that I understand your reluctance to talk of your future activity; but what is happening within you now — "

"Happening!" Bazarov repeated after her. "Anyone would think I was some state or society! In any case, it isn't at all interesting; and besides, can a man always proclaim aloud all that is 'happening' inside him?"

"But I don't see why you cannot speak out all that you have in your soul."

"Can *you?*"

"I can," Anna Sergeevna replied after a momentary hesitation.

Bazarov bowed his head.

"You are more fortunate than I."

She looked at him interrogatively.

"As you wish," she continued, "but, all the same, something tells me that we have not come together for nothing, that we shall be good friends. I am confident that your — how shall I put it? — your feeling of tension, of reserve, will vanish in the end."

"But have you noticed any reserve in me — and how else did you put it? — any tension?"

"Yes."

Bazarov rose and went over to the window.

"And you would like to know the cause of this reserve, you would like to know what is happening inside me?"

"Yes," she repeated, with a still incomprehensible feeling of fear.

"And you won't be angry?"

"No."

"No?" Bazarov was standing with his back to her. "Then I tell you that I love you idiotically, madly. . . . Now you know what you have forced from me."

She extended both hands in front of her, but Bazarov was resting his forehead against the glass of the window. He was panting; all his body was obviously quivering. But it was not the quiver of youthful timidity, not the pleasant dismay of a first declaration that possessed him: it was passion, strong and oppressive, that was struggling within him — a passion resembling malice and, perhaps, akin to it. . . . She suddenly felt afraid of and sorry for him.

"Yevgeny Vasilich," she said, and involuntarily a tender note sounded in her voice.

He turned swiftly, flung a consuming gaze at her — and, seizing her by both hands, violently drew her to himself. . . .

She did not free herself at once from his embrace; yet a moment later she was standing far off in a corner, staring at him. He started toward her.

"You haven't understood me," she whispered with urgent fear. It seemed that if he took another stride she would cry out. . . . He bit his lips and left the room.

Half an hour later a servant handed her a note from Bazarov; it consisted of one single sentence: "Am I to go away today, or can I remain till tomorrow?"

"Why go away? I didn't understand you — you haven't understood me," she replied. But her own thought was: "I didn't understand myself either."

She did not appear until dinnertime, and she walked to and fro in her room continually, her hands behind her, occasionally halting before the window, or before the mirror, and slowly rubbing her handkerchief round her neck, on which she still seemed to feel a burning patch. She asked herself what had made her force him to be frank, as he had put it, and why hadn't she suspected anything? . . . "I am to blame," she said aloud, "but I could not anticipate this." She was lost in thought, and flushed when she remembered Bazarov's almost bestial face as he rushed to her. . . .

"Or?" she suddenly said, and halted, and shook her curls. . . . She saw herself in the mirror; her head thrown back, and the mysterious smile in the half-closed, half-opened eyes and lips, seemed at that moment to be telling her something at which she herself was abashed.

"No," she decided at last, "God knows where that would lead to, one cannot play with that, tranquillity is after all the best thing in the world."

Her tranquillity was not disturbed; but she was distressed, and even burst into tears once, herself not knowing why, but certainly not from any outrage she had suffered. She did not feel outraged: rather she felt guilty. Under the influence of various vague feelings, the consciousness of departing life, the desire for novelty, she had forced herself to go as far as a certain line, had forced herself to look across it — and had seen beyond it not even an abyss, but emptiness . . . or infamy.

XIX

Despite all her self-possession, despite all her freedom from prejudices, even Mme Odintsova felt awkward when she went into the dining-room for dinner. The meal passed quite satisfactorily, however. Porfiry Platonich arrived, and he told a number of stories; he had just returned from the town. Among other things, he reported that the governor, "Burdal," had ordered his officials on special commissions to wear spurs, in case he needed to send them anywhere in haste on horseback. Arkady conversed with Katya in an undertone and diplomatically waited on the Princess. Bazarov was obstinately and morosely silent. Once or twice Mme Odintsova looked at him — directly, and not surreptitiously — at his face, stern and jaundiced, with downcast eyes and the impress of contemptuous resolution in every feature, and thought: "No . . . no . . . no. . . ." After dinner she and all the company went into the garden. Noticing that Bazarov wanted to have a word with her, she took several steps aside and halted. He came up to her, though even now he did not raise his eyes, and said thickly:

"I must apologize to you, Anna Sergeevna. You cannot but be angry with me."

"No, I am not angry with you, Yevgeny Vasilich," she replied, "but I am distressed."

"So much the worse. In any case, I am punished sufficiently. My position, as you will probably agree, is most stupid. You wrote to me: 'Why go away?' But I cannot and do not wish to remain. Tomorrow I shall no longer be here."

"Yevgeny Vasilich, why are you — "

"Why am I going away?"

"No, that isn't what I wanted to say."

"You can't bring back the past, Anna Sergeevna . . . and

sooner or later this was bound to happen. Consequently, I must go away. I know of only one condition on which I could remain; but that condition will never arise. For, after all, you — forgive my presumption — you do not love me and never will love me, will you?"

His eyes glittered for a moment beneath his dark brows.

She did not answer him. "I am afraid of this man," the thought flashed through her head.

"Good-by," he said, as though he had guessed her thought, and he went back to the house.

Anna Sergeevna walked slowly after him and, calling to Katya, took her by the arm. She kept her sister at her side all day. She did not play cards, and laughed more and more, which was quite out of keeping with her pale and discomposed look. Arkady was bewildered, and watched her, as young people do watch; in other words, he continually asked himself: what does all this mean? Bazarov shut himself away in his room; however, he came down for tea. Anna Sergeevna felt like saying some kindly word to him, but she did not know how to open conversation with him. . . .

An unexpected event rescued her from her difficulty: the butler announced that Sitnikov had arrived.

It is difficult to convey in words how this young progressive fluttered like a quail into the room. Having resolved, with the intrusiveness peculiar to him, to drive into the country to visit a woman whom he hardly knew, who had never invited him to do so, but with whom, according to the information he had gathered, such intelligent and intimate acquaintances of his were staying, he was now stricken with timidity to his very marrow, and instead of uttering the apologies and greetings he had planned, he muttered some idiotic remark to the effect that Yevdoksia Kukshina had sent him to inquire into Anna Sergeevna's health, and that Arkady Nikolaevich also always spoke to him in terms of the greatest praise. At this word he began to stammer and was so disconcerted that he sat on his own hat. As no one turned him out, however, and Anna Sergeevna even introduced him to her aunt and sister, he soon recovered, and his tongue began to wag in fine style. We often find that our lives are helped by some trivial event: it slackens the overtautened strings and sobers down self-confident or self-forgetful feelings by reminding them of its own close kinship with them. With Sitnikov's arrival everything seemed to grow more dull, more empty — and more simple; everybody even ate a more hearty supper and retired to sleep half an hour earlier than usual.

'I can repeat to you now," Arkady said in bed to Bazarov, who also was undressed, "what you once said to me: 'Why are you so sad? You must have paid some sacred debt?' " For some time past a hypocritically free and easy bantering had been going on between the two young men, a trick that always indicates secret dissatisfaction or unexpressed suspicions.

"I'm going home to Father tomorrow," Bazarov announced.

Arkady raised himself and rested on his elbow. He was both surprised and, for some reason, glad.

"Ah!" he uttered. "And is that why you are sad?"

Bazarov yawned. "You'll know a lot, you'll be an old man."

"But how about Anna Sergeevna?" Arkady went on.

"What about Anna Sergeevna?"

"I mean to say: will she really let you go?"

"I haven't hired myself out to her."

Arkady lay thinking, and Bazarov got into bed and turned his face to the wall.

Several minutes passed in silence.

"Yevgeny!" Arkady suddenly exclaimed.

"Well?"

"I'll leave too when you go tomorrow."

Bazarov made no reply.

"Only I'll go home," Arkady continued. "We'll travel together as far as the Little Russian hamlets, and there you'll get horses from Fyodot. I'd be delighted to make your people's acquaintance, but I'm afraid of making them, and you, feel awkward. But you will come back to us afterward, won't you?"

"I have left my things with you," Bazarov replied, without turning over.

"But why doesn't he ask why I am going? And just as suddenly as he!" Arkady thought. "And, in fact, why am I going, and why is he going?" he continued his meditations. He could find no satisfactory answer to his own questions, and his heart was filled with something corrosive. He felt that it would be difficult for him to part from this life, to which he had grown so accustomed; but it would be strange to remain here by himself. "Something has happened between them," he mentally decided, "but why should I hang around her after he has gone? I shall only completely upset her and shall lose my last chance." He began to recall Anna Sergeevna in his mind; but then, little by little, other features obscured the young widow's beautiful face.

"I'm sorry about Katya too," Arkady whispered into his pillow, on which tears were dropping. . . . He suddenly flung back his hair and said aloud:

"What the devil did that fool Sitnikov turn up for?"

Bazarov first stirred in his bed, then gave utterance to the following:

"You're still stupid, brother, I can see that. The Sitnikovs are necessary to us. I — you get this into your head — I need blockheads like him. After all, it's not for the gods to bake the pots."

"Aha!" Arkady thought, and only now was all the bottomless abyss of Bazarov's self-esteem momentarily revealed to him. "So you and I are gods? Or rather you're a god, but perhaps I'm the blockhead, is that it?"

"Yes," Bazarov repeated moodily, "you're still stupid."

Mme Odintsova did not show any particular surprise when next day Arkady told her that he was leaving with Bazarov; she seemed abstracted and tired. Katya gazed at him silently and seriously, the Princess even crossed herself beneath her shawl, in such a way that he could not but notice it, while Sitnikov was completely flabbergasted. He had only just come down to breakfast in new and elegant attire, this time not of Slavophil design; the previous evening he had astonished the man assigned to him by the quantity of linen he had brought, and now abruptly his comrades were deserting him! He fidgeted a little with his feet, cast about like a hunted hare on the edge of a forest — and suddenly, almost fearfully, almost with a shout, announced that he, too, intended to depart. Mme Odintsova made no attempt to dissuade him.

"I have a very comfortable carriage," the unhappy young man added, turning to Arkady; "I can take you, and Yevgeny Vasilich can have your tarantass, so that it will be even more convenient."

"But of course not, it is quite out of your way, and it is a long distance to my home."

"It's nothing, nothing; I've lots of time, and besides I've got business in that direction."

"In regard to licenses?" Arkady asked, rather too contemptuously.

But Sitnikov was in such a state of despair that, contrary to custom, he did not even smile.

"I assure you my carriage is extremely comfortable," he muttered, "and there will be room for everybody."

"Don't upset M'sieur Sitnikov with a refusal," Anna Sergeevna said.

Arkady glanced at her and bowed meaningly.

The guests departed after breakfast. As she said good-by to Bazarov, Mme Odintsova held out her hand to him and said:

"We shall see each other again, shan't we?"

"As you command," Bazarov replied.

"In that case, we shall see each other again."

Arkady was the first to go out on the veranda; he climbed into Sitnikov's carriage. He was respectfully helped into the carriage by a butler, but he would gladly have struck him or burst into tears. Bazarov seated himself in the tarantass. When they reached the Little Russian hamlets, Arkady waited while Fyodot, the innkeeper, harnessed up the horses, and then, going over to the tarantass, with his former smile he said to Bazarov:

"Yevgeny, take me with you; I should like to go to your place."

"Get in!" Bazarov said between his teeth.

Sitnikov, who, whistling blithely, was strolling by the wheels of his carriage, only gaped as he heard these words; but Arkady callously took his things out of the carriage, seated himself beside Bazarov, and, bowing respectfully to his former fellow traveler, shouted: "Whip them up!" The tarantass rolled off and soon disappeared from sight. . . . Sitnikov, now completely confused, stared at his coachman; but the man was playing his whip above the tail of the side-horse. He jumped into his carriage and, thundering at two passing peasants: "Put your caps on, you fools!" drove off to the town, where he arrived very late, and where, next day, during his visit to Kukshina, he said some bitter things about those two "repulsive stuck-ups and boors."

When he got into the tarantass beside Bazarov, Arkady gave his friend a strong squeeze of the hand and for a long time did not utter a word. Bazarov appeared to understand and appreciate both the handclasp and the silence. He had not slept all the previous night, and he had not smoked, or eaten much at all, for several days past. His emaciated profile was gloomy and harsh beneath the cap clapped on his head.

"Well, brother," he said at last, "give me a cigar. . . . And have a look, is my tongue yellow?"

"Yes," Arkady replied.

"As I thought . . . and the cigar doesn't taste pleasant. The machine's gone wrong."

"You certainly have changed during the last few days," Arkady observed.

"It's nothing! We'll get over it. The only thing that troubles me is that my mother is much too tender-hearted: if you haven't grown a paunch, and if you don't eat ten times a day, she worries herself to death. But Father's all right, he's been everywhere himself, and he has feasted and starved. No, I can't smoke," he added, and he flung the cigar into the dust of the road.

"It's fifteen miles to your estate, isn't it?" Arkady asked.

"Yes, fifteen. But ask that sage," he pointed to the peasant, one of Fyodot's workmen, sitting on the box.

But the peasant replied: "Who knows? We don't measure by miles here," and continued to swear at the shaft-horse in an undertone for "kicking up his muzzle" — in other words, for throwing up his head.

"Yes, yes," Bazarov began again, "there's a lesson for you, my young friend, a very instructive example. Damn it all, how idiotic everything is! Every man hangs by a thread, an abyss may open beneath him at any moment, yet he must needs go on thinking all kinds of unpleasant things for himself, spoiling his whole life."

"What are you hinting at?" Arkady asked.

"I am not hinting at anything, I am saying openly that you and I have behaved very stupidly. What is there to explain? But I've already observed at the clinic that anyone who fulminates against his pain invariably triumphs over it."

"I don't quite understand you," Arkady remarked, "I hardly think you had anything to complain about."

"As you don't quite understand me, I'll expound the following to you: 'It is better to be a stone in the road than to let a woman take possession of so much as the tip of your finger.' That is all — " Bazarov all but pronounced his favorite word, "romanticism," but he refrained, and said: " — rubbish. You won't believe me now, but I tell you: you and I found ourselves in women's company, and we liked it; but to cut yourself off from such company is just like having a cold shower on a hot day. A man has no time to occupy himself with such trifles; a man should be raging, says the excellent Spanish proverb. Now, take you," he added, turning to the peasant sitting on the box, "you, wise man, have you a wife?"

The man turned his flat and watery-eyed face to the two friends.

"A wife, d'you say? Yes. How could I do without a wife?"

"Do you beat her?"

"The wife, you mean? All kinds of things happen. We don't beat them without cause."

"That's splendid. Well, but does she beat you?"

The peasant tugged at the reins.

"A fine thing to say, master. You can always have your joke." He was obviously offended.

"D'you hear that, Arkady Nikolaevich? Yet you and I have been thrashed. That's what it means to be educated people."

Arkady smiled forcedly, but Bazarov turned away and did not open his mouth again for the rest of the journey.

The fifteen miles seemed a full thirty to Arkady. But now at last the small village where Bazarov's parents lived came into sight on the slope of a rolling hill. Beyond it, amid a young birch grove, appeared a small country house beneath a straw-thatched roof. At the first hut in the village two peasants were standing with their hats on, swearing at each other. "You're a great swine," said one to the other, "but you're worse than a little pig." "And your wife is a witch," the other retorted.

"By the unconstraint of their forms of address," Bazarov observed to Arkady, "and by the playfulness of their turns of speech, you can judge that my father's peasants are not greatly oppressed. And there he is himself coming out on the porch of his habitation. So he must have heard the carriage bell. It's he all right, I recognize his figure. Ah, but how gray he's gone, poor devil!"

XX

Bazarov hung out of the tarantass, while Arkady stretched his head round his comrade's back and saw a tall, gaunt man, with tousled hair and a fine aquiline nose, and dressed in an old military tunic wide open at the chest, standing in the little porch of the house. He stood with feet set wide apart, smoking a long pipe and screwing up his eyes against the sun.

The horses came to a halt.

"So you've turned up at last," Bazarov's father said to him, continuing to smoke, though the pipe was trembling between his fingers. "Well, climb out, climb out, and we'll greet each other properly."

He embraced his son. "Yevgeny, my dear little Yevgeny," a woman's quavering voice was heard. The door was flung wide open, and on the threshold appeared a round little, short little old woman, in a white mobcap and a short, varicolored jacket. She groaned, stumbled, and would certainly have fallen if Bazarov had not supported her. Her swollen little arms were at once wound round his neck, her head nestled against his chest, and there was a silence. Only her convulsive sobbing was to be heard.

Old Bazarov breathed deeply and screwed up his eyes even more.

"Well, that's enough, that's enough, Arina, my dear! Stop it!" he said, exchanging glances with Arkady, who was standing motionless by the tarantass, while the peasant on the box even turned away. "That's quite unnecessary, do please stop it!"

"Ah, Vasily Ivanich!" the old woman murmured, "at last, my dear, I see my little one, my little Yevgeny . . . " and, without unclasping her arms, she drew her wet, tearstained, crushed, and beaming face away from Bazarov, gazed at him with beatific and absurd eyes, then fell on his chest again.

"Well, yes, of course, that's all in the nature of things," Vasily Ivanovich said, "only we'd better go into the house. Here's a guest arrived with Yevgeny. You mustn't mind," he added, turning to Arkady, and slightly scraping one foot, "you understand, it's just a woman's weakness and a mother's heart, you know. . . ."

But his own lips and eyebrows were twitching, and his chin was quivering — though he obviously was trying to master himself and to appear all but unconcerned. Arkady bowed.

"Come on, Mother, Father's quite right," Bazarov said, and led the feeble old woman into the house. Seating her in a comfortable armchair, he once more hurriedly embraced his father and introduced Arkady to him.

"I am very glad to meet you," Vasily Ivanovich declared, "only you mustn't expect too much; everything of ours is simple, on a military footing. Arina Vlasievna, do calm down, be so good; what is all this weakness for? Our guest will have a poor opinion of you."

"My goodness!" the old woman said through her tears, "I haven't the honor of knowing your name and patronymic."

"Arkady Nikolaich," Vasily Ivanovich prompted her in an undertone, with an important air.

"You must pardon a stupid old woman." She blew her nose and, bending her head first to the right, then to the left, she diligently wiped one eye, then the other. "You must forgive me. You see, I was beginning to think I would die without seeing my d-d-d-ear boy."

"Well, you have lived to see him, madame," Vasily Ivanovich retorted. "Taniushka" — he turned to a barefoot girl aged about thirteen, in a bright red cotton dress, who was shyly peeping round the door — "bring your mistress a glass of water, on a tray, d'you hear? And you, gentlemen," he added with a kind of old-fashioned playfulness, "allow me to invite you into a retired veteran's private room."

"Let me put my arms round you just one little once more, Yevgeny my dear," Arina Vlasievna groaned. Bazarov bent over her. "But what a handsome fellow you've grown!"

"Well, handsome or not," Vasily Ivanovich observed, "he's a man, as they say, *ommfe*.[1] But now, Arina Vlasievna, I hope that, having satiated your maternal heart, you will see about satiating your dear guests, because, as you know, you mustn't feed nightingales on fairy stories."

The old woman got up from the chair.

"The table will be laid this very minute, Vasily Ivanich. I'll run into the kitchen myself and order the samovar to be got ready, we'll have everything, everything. Why, I haven't seen him for three years, I've given him neither food nor drink, and is that easy to bear?"

"Well then, hurry up about it, mistress, and don't bring shame on yourself; and I ask you, gentlemen, to follow me. And here's Timofeich come to pay his respects to you, Yevgeny. He is glad too, I think, the old spaniel. Well? You are glad, aren't you, you old spaniel? Please follow me."

[1] Russian transliteration of the French *homme fait*.

And Vasily Ivanovich bustled on in front, scraping and shuffling in his patched slippers.

The entire house consisted of six tiny rooms. One of them, the one to which he led our friends, was called the office. A stout-legged table, littered with papers black with ancient dust, as though they had been sprinkled with soot, occupied all the space between two windows; on the walls hung Turkish weapons, knouts, sabers, two maps, anatomical charts, a portrait of Hufeland,[1] a knot of hair in a black frame, and a diploma behind glass; a ragged leather divan with broken springs was placed between two enormous bookcases of Karelian birch; on the shelves was a disorderly crowd of books, boxes, stuffed birds, cans, and phials; in one corner stood a broken electrical machine.

"I warned you, my dear visitor," Vasily Ivanovich began, "that we live here, so to speak, in bivouac."

"Now stop it, what are you apologizing for?" Bazarov interrupted. "Kirsanov knows very well that you and I are not Crœsuses, and that you haven't a palace. Where shall we put him, that's the question."

"Why, of course, Yevgeny, I've got a very nice little room in the wing; he'll be very comfortable there."

"So you've a little wing now?"

"Why, of course; where the bathhouse is," Timofeich intervened.

"Really it's next to the bathhouse," Vasily Ivanovich hastened to add. "And it's summertime now. . . . I'll run along at once and see about it; and meanwhile you bring their things in, Timofeich. Of course, Yevgeny, I put my room at your disposition. *Suum cuique.*"

"Well, there you are! A very amusing old chap and one of the best," Bazarov added as soon as Vasily Ivanovich had gone out. "Just as much an eccentric as your father, only in a different way. And he talks an awful lot!"

"And your mother, too, seems to be a very fine woman," Arkady observed.

"Yes, she's quite a simple sort. You wait and see the dinner she gives us!"

---

[1] A prominent German physician (1762–1836). (Tr.)

"We weren't expecting you, master, and they haven't brought any beef," remarked Timofeich, who had just dragged in Bazarov's trunk.

"We'll manage without beef; what the eye doesn't see — Poverty is no crime, they say."

"How many souls does your father own?" Arkady suddenly asked.

"The property isn't his, but Mother's; I think there are fifteen souls."

"Twenty-two all together," Timofeich observed in a dissatisfied tone.

They heard the shuffling of slippers, and Vasily Ivanovich reappeared.

"In a few minutes your room will be ready to receive you," he exclaimed triumphantly, "Arkady — Nikolaich. That is your name, isn't it? An here is your servant," he added, pointing to a close-cropped lad in a blue out-at-elbow caftan and oversized boots who had entered with him. "His name's Fyodka. I repeat again, though my son forbids me, don't expect too much. However, Fyodka knows how to fill a pipe. You do smoke, of course?"

"I smoke cigars usually," Arkady replied.

"And very sensible on your part. I myself have a preference for cigars, but in these lonely parts it is extremely difficult to get them."

"Now, enough of playing the Lazarus," Bazarov again interrupted him. "You sit down here on the divan and let me have a look at you."

Vasily Ivanovich laughed and sat down. He had a strong facial resemblance to his son, only his forehead was lower and narrower, and his mouth rather wider, and he was always on the move, twitching his shoulders as though his coat were cutting into his armpits, blinking, coughing, and wriggling his fingers, whereas his son was distinguished by a negligent immobility.

"Play the Lazarus!" Vasily Ivanovich repeated. "Don't think, Yevgeny, that I want to win our guest's pity, so to speak, by appealing to the backwoods we live in. On the contrary, I am of the opinion that there is no such thing as backwoods for a thinking man. At least I endeavor, as far as possible, not to let any moss grow on me, as they say, not to lag behind the times."

Out of his pocket he pulled a new yellow foulard handkerchief, which he had managed to snatch up while running to Arkady's room, and waved it in the air as he went on:

"I say nothing of the fact that, for instance, not without sacrifices painful to myself, I have put the peasants on a rental basis and given them half of my own land. I regarded that is my duty, and in that case common sense itself commands, though other landowners do not even think of it. I am talking of science, of education."

"Yes; I see you have *The Friend of Health* for 1855," Bazarov remarked.

"An old comrade sends it to me," Vasily Ivanovich said hurriedly. "But we have some notion of phrenology, for instance," he added, talking, for that matter, more to Arkady and pointing to a small plaster-of-Paris head, divided into numbered parallelograms, standing on the bookcase. "Schönlein [1] has not remained unknown to us — nor Rademacher." [2]

"But do they still believe in Rademacher in X X X province?" Bazarov asked.

Vasily Ivanovich began to cough.

"In the province — Of course, gentlemen, you know better than we; and how can we hope to keep up with you? Why, you have come to take our places. Even in my day some humoralist named Hoffman, [3] or a Brown [4] with his vitalism seemed very absurd to us, but they too had made a noise in their time. You have found some new name to take Rademacher's place and to have your respect; but in twenty years they will be laughing at him too, probably."

"I tell you by way of consolation," Bazarov said, "that we now laugh at medicine altogether and do not respect anybody."

"How can you say that? Why, you want to be a doctor, don't you?"

"Yes. But the one doesn't hinder the other."

Vasily Ivanovich thrust his third finger into his pipe, where a little hot ash was still left.

"Well, maybe, maybe, I won't argue about it. After all, what

---

[1] German physician (1793–1864). (Tr.)
[2] German physician (1772–1849). (Tr.)
[3] German physician (1660–1742). (Tr.)
[4] Dr. John Brown (1735–88). (Tr.)

am I? A retired staff doctor, *volatou;* [1] and now I've dropped into agriculture. I served in your grandfather's brigade" — he turned again to Arkady. "Ye-es, ye-es, I've seen many things in my time. And the company I've kept, and the people I've been on respectful terms with! I, this same I whom you are pleased to see before you, I have felt the pulses of Count Witgenstein and Zhukovsky! [2] All the men in the Southern Army, after 1814, you understand" (here Vasily Ivanovich pursed his lips meaningly), "I knew them all through and through. But, after all, my work was not so important: a doctor should know his lancet, and that's enough! But your grandfather was a very estimable man, a real warrior."

"Confess that he was a fine tough old cudgel!" Bazarov remarked lazily.

"Ah, Yevgeny, the way you put things! Have a little pity! . . . Of course, General Kirsanov was not among those who —"

"Well, drop him!" Bazarov interrupted. "As we drove up I was delighted with your birch grove; it's grown splendidly."

Vasily Ivanovich brightened up.

"But wait till you see the garden I have now! I planted every tree myself. And there are fruits, and berries, and all kinds of medical herbs. You can be as clever as you like, you young people, but, all the same, old Paracelsus uttered the sacred truth: *in herbis, verbis et lapidibus* . . . after all, although, as you know, I have given up practicing, once or twice a week I have to shake up my old knowledge. They come for advice, and I can't throw them out on their necks. Sometimes poor people come for help. And there aren't any doctors in the district at all. Just imagine, one of our neighbors, a retired major — he gives treatment too. I inquire about him: has he studied medicine? They tell me: no, he hasn't studied, he does it more out of philanthropy. Ha ha, out of philanthropy! What? How? Ha ha ha!"

"Fyodka, fill my pipe!" Bazarov said harshly.

"But there is another doctor who came here to see a patient," Vasily Ivanovich went on in a kind of desperation, "and the patient was already *ad patres;* his man wouldn't let the doctor in and said he wasn't wanted any more. The doctor didn't expect that; he was disconcerted, and asked: 'Well, did the master hiccup

---

[1] *Voilà tout.*
[2] Russian poet (1783–1852). (Tr.)

before he died?' 'Yes, he hiccuped.' 'And did he hiccup a lot?' 'Quite a lot.' 'Oh well, that's good.' And off he went home. Ha ha ha!"

Only the old man laughed; Arkady set his lips in a smile. Bazarov simply pulled a long face. The talk continued in this fashion for about an hour; Arkady even had time to visit his room, which proved to be the bathhouse anteroom, but was very cozy and clean. At last Taniusha entered and reported that dinner was ready.

Vasily Ivanovich was the first to rise.

"Come along, gentlemen! Your magnanimous pardon if I have bored you. I expect my good mistress will satisfy you more than I can."

Though prepared in a hurry, the dinner was very good, and even plentiful; only the wine was not up to scratch, as they say; it was an almost black sherry, and had been bought by Timofeich from a merchant acquaintance in the town; it tasted perhaps of honey, perhaps of resin. And the flies, too, were a nuisance. In normal times a yard boy drove them off with a large green branch; but on this occasion Vasily Ivanovich sent him out, for fear of being condemned by the younger generation. Arina Vlasievna had found time to dress herself up; she had put on a high-standing cap with silk ribbons and a dove-blue shawl with arabesques. As soon as she saw her Yevgeny, she again burst into tears, but her husband did not have to admonish her: she herself quickly wiped away her tears, in order to avoid spotting the shawl. Only the young men ate; the master and mistress had had dinner long since. Obviously burdened with his unusual footwear, Fyodka waited on table, being helped by a hunchbacked woman with a masculine face, named Anfisushka, who performed the functions of housekeeper, poultry-keeper, and washerwoman. All dinnertime Vasily Ivanovich walked about the room and talked with a perfectly happy and even beatific air of the serious fears instilled in him by Napoleon III's policy and the confusion of the Italian problem. Arina Vlasievna did not pay any attention to Arkady and did not pick out the best bits for him; using her little fist to support her round face, on which the swollen, cherry-colored warts and moles on her cheeks and above her eyebrows conferred a very good-natured expression, she kept her eyes fixed on her son and sighed continually. She desperately wanted to find out how long he had come home for, but she was afraid to ask him. "Well, supposing he says two days," she thought, and her heart sank. After the roast Vasily Ivanovich disappeared for a moment and returned with an uncorked half-bottle of champagne.

"Look!" he exclaimed; "though we do live in the wilds, when we want to celebrate we know what to make merry with!" He poured champagne into three goblets and a wineglass, proposed the health "of our inestimable visitors," and tossed off his goblet in one gulp, military fashion, and made Arina Vlasievna drink her glassful down to the last drop. When the jams appeared, Arkady, who could not endure anything sweet, none the less considered it his duty to taste the four different kinds, only just made, especially as Bazarov refused outright and at once lit a cigar. Then tea, with cream and butter and cracknels, appeared on the scene; then Vasily Ivanovich led them all into the garden, in order to admire the beauty of the evening. As they passed a bench he whispered to Arkady: "I like to philosophize in this spot, gazing at the sunset; it befits a recluse. And there farther along I have planted several trees beloved of Horace."

"And what trees are they?" Bazarov, who overheard him, asked.

"Why — acacias, of course."

Bazarov began to yawn.

"I assume it is time for the travelers to retire to the embraces of Morpheus," Vasily Ivanovich observed.

"In other words, time for bed," Bazarov took him up. "A very sound observation. It certainly is time."

As he said good-night to his mother he kissed her on the forehead; but she embraced him and, behind his back, surreptitiously, blessed him three times. Vasily Ivanovich saw Arkady to his room and wished him "such an abundant repose as I enjoyed at your happy age." And, in fact, Arkady slept excellently in his bathhouse anteroom; it smelt of mint, and two crickets soporifically outchirruped each other behind the stove. Vasily Ivanovich went from Arkady to his office and, settling down on the divan at his son's feet, made ready to have a chat with him; but Bazarov at once sent him away, saying that he wanted to sleep. But he did not fall asleep until dawn came. Staring with wide-open eyes, he gazed malevolently into the darkness: the memories of childhood had no power over him, and besides he had not yet succeeded in escaping from his last bitter impressions. Arina Vlasievna first prayed to her heart's content; then had a long, long talk with Anfisushka. Standing as though rooted to the ground before her mistress and fixing her one eye on her, in a mysterious whisper the servant imparted all her observations and ideas concerning Yevgeny Vasilievich. The old mother's head absolutely swam with joy, with wine, with cigar smoke; her husband tried to talk to her, but gave it up.

Arina Vlasievna was a genuine Russian noblewoman of the old days; she should have been living two hundred years before, in the Old Moscow times. She was very pious and sensitive, believed in all kinds of signs and tokens, fortune-tellings, charms, and dreams; she believed in simpletons, in house goblins, in wood sprites, in unlucky encounters, in the evil eye, in popular remedies, in Maundy Thursday salt, in the imminent end of the world; she believed that if the candles do not go out during the service on Easter Eve the buckwheat will be a fine crop, and that mushrooms stop growing once a human eye has seen them; she believed that the devil loves to be where there is water, and that every Jew has a little bloody spot on his chest; she was afraid of mice, of grass-snakes, frogs, sparrows, leeches, thunder, cold water, drafts, horses, goats, red-headed people, and black cats and regarded crickets and dogs as unclean creatures; she ate neither veal nor pigeons, nor crabs, nor cheese, nor asparagus, nor Jerusalem artichokes, nor hare, nor watermelons, because a cut watermelon reminded her of the head of John the Baptist; and she could never speak of oysters without a shudder; she loved eating — and she fasted strictly; she slept ten hours a day — and never lay down at all if Vasily Ivanovich had a headache; she had never read a book, except *Alexis, or The Cabin in the Woods;* she wrote one or at the most two letters a year, but she was expert at domestic economy, in drying fruits and turning them into jam, though she never touched anything with her own hands and altogether shifted only reluctantly out of her seat. Arina Vlasievna was very kind and, in her own way, by no means stupid. She knew that in this world there were the gentlemen, who were there to give orders, and the ordinary people, who were there to obey — and so she was not revolted by the peasants' servility or by bows to the ground; but she was gracious and modest in her treatment of inferiors, never let a beggar pass without a gift, and never condemned anybody, though she did sometimes like a little slander. In her youth she had been very good-looking, she had played the clavichord and could make herself understood a little in French; but during many years of wandering with her husband, whom she had married against her parents' will, she had gone various ways and forgotten both music and French. She loved and was inexpressibly afraid of her son. She left the management of their property to Vasily Ivanovich and never put her nose into anything: she sighed, waved him off with her handkerchief, and in her terror raised her eyebrows higher and higher as soon as the old man began to talk to her about impending changes and about his plans. She was mistrustful, always expecting some great misfortune, and burst into tears as soon as she thought of anything sad. . . . Women like her are already dying out. God knows whether one should be glad of that!

XXI

On getting out of bed Arkady opened the window, and the first object that struck his eyes was Vasily Ivanovich. Attired in a Bokharan dressing-gown belted with a handkerchief, the old man was zealously exerting himself in the garden. He noticed his young guest and, resting on his spade, exclaimed:

"I wish you health! How were you pleased to rest?"

"Excellently!" Arkady replied.

"But, as you see, I am like Cincinnatus: I'm hoeing up some late turnips. In these days that have come now — thank God for it! — every man must provide his nourishment with his own hands; it's no use relying on others: you must labor for yourself. And it transpires that Jean-Jacques Rousseau was right. Half an hour ago, my dear sir, you would have seen me in quite a different position. Into one peasant woman, who was complaining of being loose — that is in their language, but we call it dysentery, I — how shall I put it? — I poured opium; and out of another I pulled a tooth. I proposed etherization to her, only she wouldn't agree. All this I do gratis, *anamater*.[1] For that matter, it's nothing to me: you see I 'm a plebeian, a *homo novus* — not one of the hereditary nobles, not like my faithful spouse. . . . But wouldn't you

[1] *En amateur.*

like to come out here into the shade, to breathe in the morning freshness before tea?"

Arkady went out to him.

"Pleased to meet you yet again!" Vasily Ivanovich said, putting his hand military fashion to the greasy skull-cap that covered his head. "I know you are accustomed to luxuries, to pleasure, but even the great of this world do not abhor to spend a brief period beneath the shelter of the cottage."

"But really," Arkady exclaimed, "how am I one of the great of this world? And I am not accustomed to luxuries."

"Allow me, allow me," Vasily Ivanovich objected with an amiable smirk. "Though I am relegated to the archives now, I have knocked about the world a bit, I know a bird by its flight. I am a psychologist too in my own way, and a physiognomist. If I hadn't had that — I dare to call it — talent, I would have gone under long since; I, a little man, would have been rubbed out. I tell you without seeking to pay compliments; the friendship that I observe between you and my son makes me sincerely glad. I have just seen him; as is his custom, of which you are probably aware, he jumped out of bed very early and ran off to see the district. Pardon my curiosity: have you known my Yevgeny long?"

"Since last winter."

"I see. And allow me also to ask — but perhaps we could sit down? Allow me to ask, as a father, with all frankness: what is your opinion of my Yevgeny?"

"Your son is one of the most remarkable people I have ever met," Arkady replied enthusiastically.

Vasily Ivanovich's eyes suddenly opened wide and his cheeks faintly burned. The spade fell from his hand.

"And so you think — " he began.

"I am sure," Arkady broke in, "that a great future awaits your son, that he will bring fame on your name. I was convinced of that at our very first meeting."

"How — how did it happen?" Vasily Ivanovich was hardly able to get the words out. An exultant smile parted his broad lips and did not leave them again.

"You want to know how we came to meet?"

"Yes — and in general — "

Arkady began to tell, and to speak about Bazarov with even

greater fervor, with greater enthusiasm than on that evening when he had had the mazurka with Mme Odintsova.

Vasily Ivanovich listened to him, listened, blew his nose, rolled his handkerchief in both hands, coughed, rumpled his hair — and finally could not restrain himself any longer: he leaned toward Arkady-and kissed him on the shoulder.

"You have made me perfectly happy," he said, without ceasing to smile; "I must tell you that I — worship my son; I won't say anything about my old woman: one knows what a mother feels. But I dare not express my feelings in his presence, because he doesn't like it. He is hostile to all effusive feelings; many people even condemn him for his hardness of disposition and see in it a sign of pride or lack of feeling; but people like him are not to be measured by the normal measures, don't you agree? For instance, others in his place would get all they could out of their parents, but he has never taken an unnecessary kopek, that is God's truth!"

"He's a disinterested, honest man," Arkady observed.

"Disinterested is just the word. But I, Arkady Nikolaich, not only worship him, I am proud of him, and all my ambition consists in hoping that in the course of time the following words will appear in his biography: 'The son of a simple army doctor, who, however, early realized his gifts and spared nothing to ensure his education — '" The old man's voice suddenly broke.

Arkady squeezed his hand.

"What do you think?" Vasily Ivanovich asked after a silence, "surely in a medical career he will not achieve the fame you prophesy for him?"

"Not, of course, in a medical career, though even in that sphere he will be one of our leading scientists."

"Then what in, Arkady Nikolaich?"

"That is difficult to say at this moment, but he will be celebrated."

"He will be celebrated!" the old man repeated, and buried himself in his thoughts.

"Arina Vlasievna ordered me to ask you to come to tea," Anfisushka said as she passed with an enormous dish of ripe raspberries.

Vasily Ivanovich started, and asked:

"And will there be iced cream with the raspberries?"

"There will."

"But make sure it really is cold! Don't stand on ceremony, Arkady Nikolaich, help yourself. Why doesn't Yevgeny come?"

"I'm here," Bazarov called from Arkady's room.

His father turned swiftly.

"Aha! You thought you would call on your friend; but you're too late, *amice*, and we've already had a long talk. Now we must go and have tea: your mother's summoned us. By the way, I want to have a talk with you."

"What about?"

"There's a peasant here who's suffering from icterus."

"Jaundice, you mean?"

"Yes, chronic and very obstinate icterus. I have prescribed centaury and hypericum, and made him eat carrots, and given him soda; but these are all *palliative* measures; it needs something more decisive. Though you laugh at medicine, I am sure you can give me valuable advice. But we'll have a talk about it later. Now let us go in to have some tea."

He nimbly jumped up from the bench and began to sing from *Robert*:

> "One law, one law, one law I set myself;
> In joy — in joy — in joyousness to live."

"Remarkable vitality!" Bazarov said as he turned from the window.

Noonday arrived. The sun scorched through a fine veil of serried, milk-white clouds. Everywhere there was silence; only the cocks called vigorously to one another in the village, arousing in all who heard them a strange sensation of drowsiness and boredom; and somewhere high in the summits of the trees the incessant squeak of a young hawk sounded in a lachrymose challenge. Arkady and Bazarov lay in the shadow of a small haystack, after spreading a couple of armfuls of dry and rustling, yet still green and scented grass to lie on.

"That aspen," Bazarov began, "reminds me of my childhood; it grows on the edge of a hole left from a brick shed, and in those days I was sure that that hole and aspen acted as a special talisman: I was never bored when I was near them. I did not understand then that the reason I was not bored was that I was a child. And now I am grown up, the talisman doesn't work."

"How long did you spend here all together?" Arkady asked.

"A couple of years without a break; then later we came here on visits. We lived a nomad life; we spent most of our time in towns."

"And has this house been standing long?"

"Very long. It was built by my grandfather, my mother's father."

"Who was he, your grandfather?"

"The devil knows. Some second-major. He served under Suvorov and was always telling the story of the crossing of the Alps. I expect he was lying."

"That explains why Suvorov's portrait is hanging in your reception room. But I like such little houses as yours, very old and very warm; and they have a peculiar scent of their own."

"It reminds me of shrine-lamp oil and melilot," Bazarov declared, yawning. "And the flies in these pleasant little houses — ! Pah!"

"Tell me," Arkady began after a brief silence, "you weren't treated harshly as a child?"

"You see the kind of parents I have: not at all strict."

"Are you fond of them, Yevgeny?"

"I am, Arkady!"

"They're very fond of you!"

Bazarov said nothing.

"Do you know what I am thinking?" he said at last, flinging his arms behind his head.

"I don't. What is it?"

"I am thinking my parents find life pretty good! At the age of sixty my father goes fussing around, talking about 'palliative' measures, curing people, playing the magnanimous gentleman to the peasants — in a word, he lives a merry life. And my mother is happy too: her day is so crammed with all kinds of occupations, with oh's and ah's, that she never has time to think of herself. But I — "

"And you?"

"But I am thinking: here am I lying under a haystack. . . . The narrow little spot I occupy is so tiny by comparison with all the rest of space where I am not and where nothing is concerned with me, and that part of time which I shall succeed in living is so insignificant in comparison with eternity, where I have never been and never will be — And yet in this atom, in this mathematical point, blood circulates, the brain functions, and even wants something. . . . What ignominy! What pettiness!"

"Allow me to observe that what you are saying applies to absolutely everybody — "

"You're right," Bazarov broke in. "I simply meant to say that they — my parents, I mean — are occupied and they don't worry about their own personal insignificance, it doesn't stink in their nostrils . . . but I — I feel only boredom and malice."

"Malice? But why malice?"

" 'Why?' Why do you ask? Have you forgotten, then?"

"I remember everything, but, all the same, I don't think you have any right to be annoyed. You're unhappy, I agree, but — "

"Ah, Arkady Nikolaevich, I see you conceive of love like all the modern young people: 'Cluck, cluck, cluck, little hen,' and as soon as the little hen begins to approach, God give you good legs! I'm not like that. But enough of this talk. What can't be helped is shameful to talk about." He turned on his side. "Aha! Look at that great little ant dragging that half-dead fly. Drag it along, brother, drag it along! Don't take any notice of its resistance, take advantage of the fact that you, as a living creature, do not have to yield to any feeling of compassion; you're not like us, who are self-humiliated."

"It's not for you to talk like that, Yevgeny! When did you humiliate yourself?"

Bazarov raised his head.

"That is the only thing I am proud of. I haven't humiliated myself, and so no dear little woman will ever humiliate me. Amen! Full stop! You won't hear another word from me on this subject."

The two friends lay for some time in silence.

"Yes," Bazarov began again. "A strange creature is man. As you look from outside and from a distance at the lonely life the 'fathers' live here, you wonder: what could be better? Eat, drink, and know that you are behaving in a very sound, very sensible fashion. But no: you're eaten up with yearning. You want to have contact with people, even if you curse them, so long as you can have contact with them."

"One needs so to arrange one's life that every moment in it is of significance," Arkady declared thoughtfully.

"Easy to say! Though at times the significant is false, it is always sweet; but then again one can be reconciled to the insignificant too. . . . But petty annoyances, petty annoyances — now, they're a real misfortune."

"Petty annoyances don't exist for a man, provided he isn't prepared to recognize them."

"Hm — what you have said is an *inverted platitude*."

"What? What do you mean by that?"

"Why, just this: to say, for instance, that education is beneficial is a platitude; but to say that education is detrimental, that is an inverted platitude. It seems to be more subtle, but essentially it is the same thing."

"Yes, but where is the truth, on which side?"

"Where? I answer you, like an echo: where?"

"You're in a melancholy mood today, Yevgeny."

"Really? The sun must have cooked me, and one shouldn't eat so many raspberries."

"In that case it wouldn't be a bad idea to have a nap," Arkady observed.

"By all means; only don't look at me: any man's face looks stupid when he's asleep."

"But aren't you quite unconcerned what people think of you?"

"I don't know what to say to that. A real man ought not to be concerned about it at all; a real man is the one who isn't thought about, but who has to be listened to or hated."

"Strange! I don't hate anybody," Arkady observed after reflection.

"But I hate so many people. You're a gentle soul, and spineless, how could you hate! . . . You're timid, you have little hope in yourself — "

"But have you any hope in yourself?" Arkady interrupted. "Have you any high opinion of yourself?"

Bazarov was silent.

"When I meet any man who stands up to my conception of things," he declared deliberately, "then I shall change my opinion of myself. Oh, to hate! You, for instance, said today as we were passing our head man Philip's hut — it's so beautifully kept and whitewashed — 'Now,' you said, 'Russia will achieve perfection when the very poorest peasant has a house like that, and every one of us should help to achieve that state.' But I hated that poorest peasant, that Philip or Sidor, for whom I have got to wear myself out and who won't even say thank-you to me for it . . . and, in any case, what do I want his thanks for? Well, he'll be living in a whitewashed hut, but docks will be growing out of me; and then 'what?'"

"No more of this, Yevgeny — listening to you talking today, one cannot but agree with those who reproach us with having no principles."

"You talk like your uncle. There aren't any such things as principles, you haven't even yet realized that! But there are sensations. Everything depends on them."

"How does it?"

"Why, like this. For instance, I, I hold to a negative trend, by virtue of my sensations. I find it pleasant to reject, my brain is arranged that way — and that's all there is to it! Why am I fond of chemistry? Why are you fond of apples? Also because of your sensations. It is all the same thing. Man will never penetrate deeper than that. Not everybody would tell you this, and even I shan't tell you a second time."

"Yes, but is honesty also a sensation?"

"I should say!"

"Yevgeny!" Arkady began in a miserable voice.

"Well? What? Don't you like it?" Bazarov broke in. "No, brother! Having decided to mow everything down, then mow yourself down too! . . . All the same, we have philosophized enough. 'Nature is singing the silence of sleep,' said Pushkin."

"He never said anything of the sort," Arkady declared.

"Then if he didn't say it, he ought to have in his capacity as poet. Which reminds me: he must have served in the army."

"Pushkin never was in the army!"

"Pardon me, but on every page of his you will find: 'To battle, to battle, for the honor of Russia!'"

"What are you making up all these stories for? Why, it's simply slander."

"Slander! Very serious, that! What a word to think of in order to frighten me! No matter how much you slander a man, he really deserves twenty times worse."

"Let's have a nap!" Arkady said in an annoyed tone.

"With the greatest of pleasure," Bazarov replied.

But neither of them could sleep. An almost inimical feeling had taken possession of the two young men's hearts. Five minutes later they opened their eyes and silently exchanged glances.

"Look," Arkady said suddenly, "a dry maple leaf has broken off and is falling to the ground; its movements are exactly like those of a butterfly in flight. Isn't it strange? The most mournful and dead thing resembles the most merry and living."

"Oh, my friend, Arkady Nikolaich!" Bazarov exclaimed; "one thing I ask you: don't talk beautifully."

"I talk as I can. And besides, that is despotism on your part. A thought came into my head, so why shouldn't I express it?"

"Yes; but why shouldn't I, too, express my thoughts? I consider that to talk beautifully is indecent."

"But what is decent? To abuse everything?"

"Ah, I see you are firmly resolved to follow in your uncle's steps. How that idiot would rejoice if he heard you!"

"What did you call Pavel Piotrovich?"

"I called him what he ought to be called: an idiot!"

"But that is intolerable!" Arkady exclaimed.

"Aha! The family feeling speaks," Bazarov said imperturbably. "I have noticed before how obstinately it persists in people. A man is prepared to renounce everything, to give up all kinds of prejudices; but to admit that his brother, who steals other people's clothes, for instance, is a thief — that is too much for him. And besides, when you come down to it, *my* brother, *mine*, yet not a genius — is that possible?"

"It was a simple feeling of justice that spoke within me and not a family feeling at all," Arkady retorted fierily. "But as you don't understand that feeling, as you haven't got that *sensation*, you cannot judge of it either."

"In other words, Arkady Kirsanov is too exalted for my understanding; I bow and am silent."

"Please do stop, Yevgeny; we shall end by quarreling in earnest."

"Ah, Arkady! Do me the favor, let us have at least one really good quarrel — to the death, to annihilation."

"But then if we do, surely we'll end by — "

"By coming to blows?" Bazarov interrupted. "Well, what of it? Here in the hay, in such idyllic surroundings, far from the world and human gaze — that doesn't matter. But you will never master me. I shall seize you at once by the throat — "

Bazarov opened his long, cruel fingers. Arkady turned and jokingly prepared to resist. But his friend's face suddenly appeared so sinister, such a far from joking threat did he think he saw in the crooked smile of those lips, in those burning eyes, that he felt involuntary misgiving. . . .

"Ah, so that's where you've got to!" Vasily Ivanovich's voice sounded at that moment, and the old army doctor, wrapped in a home-made linen jacket and wearing a straw hat, also home-made, on his head, appeared above the young men. "I've been looking and looking for you. . . . But you've chosen an excellent spot and are devoting yourselves to a fine occupation. Lying on the 'earth,' and gazing up at 'heaven.' Do you know, there is a special significance in that!"

"I gaze up at heaven only when I want to sneeze," Bazarov snorted and, turning to Arkady, said in an undertone: "Pity he interfered."

"Now, no more of that," Arkady whispered, and surreptitiously squeezed his friend's hand. But no friendship will long survive such clashes.

"I look at you, my young friends," Vasily Ivanovich was saying meanwhile, shaking his head and resting his crossed hands on a cunningly twisted stick of his own fashioning, with the figure of a Turk for a knob, "I look, and I cannot but enjoy the sight. How much strength there is in you, youth in its finest blooming, abilities, talents! Absolutely — Castor and Pollux!"

"Now listen — he's gone right off into mythology!" Bazarov declared. "You can see at once that he was strong at Latin in his time. Why, I remember, you won a silver medal for composition, didn't you?"

"Dioscuri, Dioscuri!" Vasily Ivanovich repeated.

"But that's quite enough, Father, don't get sentimental."

"Just once in a lifetime one may" the old man murmured. "However, I didn't come to look for you, gentlemen, in order to pay you compliments, but in order, firstly, to report that we shall be having dinner soon; and secondly, I wanted to warn you, Yevgeny — you're a sensible man, you know what people are like, and you know what women are like, and so you will excuse — your mother wanted to have a church service to celebrate your homecoming. Don't imagine I am summoning you to be present at that service; it's already finished; but Father Alexei — "

"The parson?"

"Why, yes, the priest; he's going to — dine with us. I didn't expect that and didn't even advise — but somehow it happened — he didn't understand me. . . . And then — and Arina Vlasievna — But in any case he's a very good and sensible man."

"Why, he won't eat my share of dinner, will he?" Bazarov asked.

Vasily Ivanovich laughed. "Really, the things you say!"

"And I don't demand any more than that. I am ready to sit down at table with any man."

Vasily Ivanovich adjusted his hat.

"I was sure in advance," he said, "that you are above all prejudice. And, for that matter, I, an old man, in my sixty-second year, I, too, haven't any." (Vasily Ivanovich did not dare to confess that he himself had desired the service. He was just as devout as his wife.) "And Father Alexei was very anxious to make your acquaintance. You'll like him, you see. He isn't averse from a game of cards, and even — but this is between ourselves — smokes a pipe."

"All right, then; after dinner we'll sit down to a round of whist, and I'll strip him."

"He-he-he, we'll see! 'The old woman spoke for both.' "

"Why, you aren't still troubled by the old passion, are you?" Bazarov said with peculiar emphasis.

Vasily Ivanovich's bronze cheeks vaguely reddened.

"You ought to be ashamed, Yevgeny. What has been, has been. Well, yes, I am prepared to admit before *them* that I had the passion in my youth, truly; yes, and I paid for it too. But isn't it hot? May I sit down with you? I shan't be in the way, shall I?"

"Not in the least," Arkady replied.

With much groaning Vasily Ivanovich sat down on the hay. "Your present couch reminds me, gentlemen," he began, "of my military, bivouac life, of dressing-stations, also arranged somewhere beside a haystack, and thank God even for that." He sighed. "Much, very much, have I experienced in my time. For instance, if you like, I'll tell you a curious incident of the plague in Bessarabia."

"For which you were given the Vladimir cross?" Bazarov intervened. "We know, we know. . . . By the way, why aren't you wearing it?"

"Didn't I tell you I hadn't any prejudices?" Vasily Ivanovich muttered (he had ordered the crimson ribbon to be removed from his coat only the previous evening), and he began to tell them about the incident during the plague. "But look, he's fallen asleep," he suddenly whispered to Arkady, pointing to his son and winking good-naturedly. "Yevgeny, get up!" he added aloud. "Let's go to dinner."

Father Alexei, a man of full and imposing figure, with thick, carefully combed hair, and wearing an embroidered belt around a lilac silk cassock, proved to be a very astute and resourceful man. He himself hastened to shake Arkady's and Bazarov's hands, as though realizing in advance that they had no need of his blessing, and altogether he was perfectly self-possessed. He did not degrade himself, nor did he provoke others; he neatly joked at seminary Latin, and spoke in defense of his bishop; he drank two glasses of wine and refused a third; he accepted a cigar from Arkady, but did not smoke it at once, saying that he would take it home. He had one not altogether pleasant habit: from time to time he slowly and cautiously raised his hand in order to catch a fly on his face and sometimes crushed it in doing so. He sat down at the card-table with a moderate demonstration of satisfaction, and ended by stripping Bazarov of two rubles fifty kopeks in notes; in Arina Vlasievna's house there was no thought of anyone settling in silver.

She sat as before beside her son (she did not play cards), resting her cheek on her little fist as before, and got up only to order some more refreshments to be brought. She was afraid to fondle Bazarov, and he did not encourage her, did not provoke her to caresses; and besides, Vasily Ivanovich had advised her not to "disturb" him very much. "The young people are not fond of it," he told her (there is no need to say how excellent the dinner was that day; Timofeich in his own person had galloped off at break of dawn for some special Circassian beef; the head man had ridden in the opposite direction for turbots, ruffes, and crayfish; for mushrooms alone the peasant women had received forty-two copper kopeks). But Arina Vlasievna's eyes, inseparably fixed on Bazarov, expressed not only devotion and tenderness; they also revealed sorrow, mingled with curiosity and fear; they contained a kind of humble reproach.

Bazarov, however, was not in the mood to analyze exactly what his mother's eyes expressed; he rarely turned to her, and then only with a brief question. Once he asked her for her hand "for luck"; she quietly laid her soft little hand on his rough, broad palm.

"Well," she asked after waiting a little, "hasn't it helped?"

"It's still worse," he replied with a careless smile.

"They're taking great risks," Father Alexei declared almost with commiseration, and he stroked his handsome beard.

"The Napoleonic principle, Father, the Napoleonic," Vasily Ivanovich retorted, and led an ace.

"And that brought him to St. Helena," observed Father Alexei, and he covered the ace with a trump.

"Would you like some currant juice, Yevgeny, my dear?" Arina Vlasievna asked.

Bazarov only shrugged his shoulders.

"It's no good!" he said to Arkady next day, "I'm leaving here tomorrow. I'm bored; I want to work, but I can't here. I'll go back to your village; I've left all my specimens there. At least I can shut myself away in your house. But here my father tells me: 'my office is at your service — no one will interfere with you,' but he himself won't leave me for a second. And besides, I feel conscience-stricken at shutting myself away from him. And my mother too. I hear her sighing on the other side of the wall, but if I go out to her, there's nothing I can say to her."

"She'll be very upset," Arkady said, "and he too."

"I'll come back to them."

"When?"

"Why, on my way to Petersburg."

"I'm especially sorry for your mother."

"What's that? Has she been treating you to berries?"

Arkady lowered his eyes.

"You don't know your mother, Yevgeny. She is not only a splendid woman, she is very intelligent, really and truly. This morning she talked to me for half an hour, and so much to the point, so interestingly."

"I expect she talked about me the whole time."

"You weren't the only one we talked about."

"Maybe; you can see better, you're outside it. If a woman can maintain a conversation for half an hour, that is a good sign at any rate. But I shall go all the same."

"It won't be easy for you to tell them this news. They're always wondering what we shall be doing in two weeks' time."

"Not easy! The devil provoked me into annoying Father today! The other day he ordered one of his peasant tenants to be whipped — and it was very sensible of him; yes, yes, don't look at me in such horror — it was very sensible, for the man is a terrible thief and drunkard; only Father hadn't expected that it would come to my ears, as they say. He was quite crestfallen, and now in addition I've got to upset him. . . . It can't be helped! The wound will heal."

Bazarov had said: "It can't be helped!" but the whole day passed before he could bring himself to inform Vasily Ivanovich of his intentions. Finally, as he was saying good-night to him in the office, he remarked with a prolonged yawn:

"Ah yes. I almost forgot to tell you. Order our horses to be sent to Fyodot tomorrow for a relay."

Vasily Ivanovich was amazed.

"But surely Mr. Kirsanov isn't going away?"

"Yes, he is; and I'm going with him."

Vasily Ivanovich spun round where he stood.

"You're going?"

"Yes . . . I've got to. Please give orders about the horses."

"Good . . ." the old man began to stammer, "for a relay — good — only — only — Why are you going?"

"I must drive over to his place for a short while. I'll come back here afterward."

"Yes! For a short while. . . . Good." Vasily Ivanovich pulled out his handkerchief and, blowing his nose, bowed down almost to the floor. "All right then — that — will be done. I did think you would be staying with us — longer. Three days. That, that, after three years, is rather short, rather short, Yevgeny!"

"But I tell you I shall soon be coming back. I must go."

"Must — oh well! You must do your duty above all. . . . Send the horses, then? Good. Of course, Arina and I hadn't expected this. She's asked a neighbor to let her have some flowers, she was intending to decorate your room." (He did not even mention that each morning at daybreak, standing with unstockinged feet in his slippers, he held a conference with Timofeich; with trembling hands taking out one torn banknote after another, he commissioned him to make various purchases, especially insisting on stocks of food and red wine, which, so far as he was able to observe, the young men greatly liked.) "The main thing is liberty; that is my rule — no one must be constrained — no — "

He stopped short and made toward the door.

"We'll see each other soon, really, Father."

But Vasily Ivanovich did not turn round, he only waved his hand and went out. On going to his bedroom he found his wife in bed and began to whisper his prayers, in order not to disturb her. But she did wake up.

"Is that you, Vasily Ivanovich?" she asked.

"Yes, it's me."

"Have you been with Yevgeny? Do you know, I'm worried: I wonder whether he sleeps well on the divan. I ordered Anfisushka to put your camp mattress and new pillows under him; I'd have given him our feather bed, but I know he doesn't like to sleep on anything soft."

"Don't you worry, mother, that's all right. He's comfortable. Lord, forgive us sinners," he continued his prayer in an undertone. Vasily Ivanovich spared his old wife; he did not feel like telling her that night the sorrow that awaited her.

Bazarov and Arkady drove off next day. From early morning everybody in the house was in the dumps; a utensil fell from Anfisushka's hands; even Fyodka was astonished, and ended by taking off his boots. Vasily Ivanovich fussed about more than ever; he was obviously screwing up his courage, he talked loudly and stamped with his feet, but his cheeks were sunken, and his gaze continually slipped past his son. Arina Vasilievna wept quietly; she would have been completely broken up and would have had no control over herself if her husband had not argued with her for a full two hours in the early morning. And when, after repeated promises to return in any case within a month, Bazarov tore himself at last out of the embraces restraining him and seated himself in the tarantass, when the horses started off and the carriage bell began to jingle and the wheels to turn, and now there was nothing to gaze after, and the dust had settled again, and Timofeich, all huddled and staggering as he went, wandered back into his little room; when the two old folk were left alone in their home, which suddenly seemed to cringe and grow decrepit, then Vasily Ivanovich, who at the porch only a few moments before had been bravely waving his handkerchief, dropped into a chair and let his head fall on his breast.

"He's deserted, deserted us," he began to stammer; "he's thrown us over; he was bored with us. I'm as lonely as a finger now, as lonely as a finger," he repeated several times, and each time he thrust his hand out in front of him with the index finger separate from the others.

Then Arina Vlasievna went over to him, rested her gray head against his gray head, and said: "It can't be helped, Vasily! Our son is a piece cut off the loaf. He's like an eagle: he wanted to come, so he flew here; he wanted to go, so he's flown away; but you and I are like mushrooms in a hollow stump, we sit side by side and never stir from our place. Only I shall always be the same to you forever, just as you will to me."

Vasily took his hands from his face and put his arms round his wife, his comrade; so tightly he had never embraced her in his youth; she comforted him in his sorrow.

XXII

Our friends drove to Fyodot's in silence, only rarely exchanging insignificant remarks. Bazarov was not altogether satisfied with himself. Arkady was not satisfied with him. Moreover, in his heart he felt that causeless sorrow which is familiar only to very young people. The coachman changed horses and, climbing onto the box, asked: "To the right or the left?"

Arkady started. The road to the right led to the town, and thence to his home; the road to the left led to Mme Odintsova's house.

He glanced at Bazarov.

"Yevgeny," he asked, "to the left?"

Bazarov turned away.

"What stupidity are you thinking of now?" he muttered.

"I know it's stupid," Arkady answered, "but where's the harm of it? It isn't as though it was the first time."

Bazarov pulled his peaked cap over his brow.

"As you like," he said at last.

"Take the left!" Arkady shouted.

The tarantass rolled off in the direction of Nikolskoe. But, having decided on a stupidity, the friends were still more obstinately silent than before, and even seemed to be angry.

By the very manner in which the butler met them on the veranda the two friends could guess that they had acted imprudently in yielding to the fantastic idea that had suddenly occurred to them. They were obviously not expected. They were left sitting for quite a long time and with quite idiotic physiognomies in the reception hall. Mme Odintsova came out to them at last. She greeted them with her usual amiability, but was astonished at their speedy return and, so far as one could judge from the deliberation of her movements and speech, was not overjoyed by it. They hastened to announce that they had only dropped in as they were passing and in four hours would be driving on, to the town. She confined herself to a faint exclamation, asked Arkady to greet his father in her name, and sent for her aunt. When the Princess appeared, she looked very sleepy, which made her scowling, aged face seem even more malevolent. Katya was not well, she did not leave her room. Arkady suddenly felt that he at least wanted just as much to see Katya as Anna Sergeevna. The four hours passed in meaningless desultory talk; Anna Sergeevna both listened and talked without smiling. Only at the very moment of parting did her former friendliness seem to stir in her soul.

"I've a touch of hypochondria now," she said, "but don't take any notice of it and come back again — I say that to you both — a little later."

Both Bazarov and Arkady replied with a silent bow, got into their carriage, and without making any further calls drove home to Marino, where they arrived safely the following evening. All the way neither of them even mentioned the name of Odintsova. Bazarov in particular hardly opened his mouth and gazed steadily to one side, away from the road, with a harsh concentration.

At Marino everybody was highly delighted to see them. His son's protracted absence had begun to alarm Nikolai Piotrovich; he cried out, kicked his feet about, and bounced on the divan when Fenichka ran in to him with shining eyes and announced the "young gentlemen's" arrival; even Pavel Piotrovich felt a little pleasant agitation and smiled condescendingly as he shook the returned wanderers' hands. Then there was talk and cross-questioning; Arkady talked more than Bazarov, especially after supper, which continued long past midnight. Nikolai Piotrovich ordered several bottles of porter only just arrived from Moscow to be brought in, and he himself made merry to such an extent that his cheeks went a raspberry color, and he laughed and laughed with rather a childish, rather a nervous laugh. The general excitement spread even to the servants. Duniasha ran to and fro like a lunatic and banged the doors constantly; and even at three in the morning Piotr was still trying to play a Cossack waltz on his guitar. The strings sounded mournfully and pleasantly in the still air; but with the exception of a brief preliminary *fioritura* nothing resulted from the cultured valet's efforts; nature had denied him musical talent as well as all others.

But meanwhile life was not proceeding altogether satisfactorily at Marino, and poor Nikolai Piotrovich was in a bad way. His worries over the farm were growing with every day — worries that were disconsolate, pointless. His troubles with the hired laborers were becoming intolerable. Some were demanding to be paid off or were asking for a raise, others went off after getting an advance; the horses were ailing; the harness vanished as though burned in a fire; work was done carelessly; the threshing-machine ordered from Moscow proved to be useless because of its weight; another broke down the first time it was used; half the cattle shed was burned down because a blind old woman, one of the servants, went in windy weather with a firebrand to fumigate her cow. True, the old woman declared that all the mischief arose because the master had taken it into his head to make some cheese and dairy produce never known before. The steward suddenly grew lazy and even began to get fat, as any Russian gets fat who has fallen into "money for jam." Catching sight of Nikolai Piotrovich from a distance, in order to demonstrate his zeal he would fling a piece of stick at a little pig that happened to run past, or threaten some half-naked lad, but, in any case, he spent most of his time asleep. The peasants placed on a tenant basis did not bring the rent at the dates fixed, and stole the timber. Almost every night the watchmen caught peasant horses grazing on the farm meadows, and sometimes brought them in by force. Nikolai Piotrovich would impose a monetary fine for the damage done to the meadow, but usually the affair ended with the horses being returned to their owners after being kept for a day or two on the master's fodder. To complete the mischief, the peasants began to quarrel among themselves; brothers demanded that their land should be shared out among them, their wives could not live together in one house; a fight would suddenly flare up, and everybody suddenly started to his feet as though by command, everybody ran to gather in front of the office porch, went crawling to the master, often with bleeding snouts, or drunk, and demanded trial and punishment; there was uproar, howling, women's sniveling squeals mingled with men's curses. Then it became necessary to separate the warring parties, to shout oneself hoarse, knowing in advance that in any case it was impossible to come to a just decision. There were not sufficient hands for the harvest; so, with the most innocent of faces, a neighboring freeholder arranged to supply reapers at two rubles per four acres and cheated in the most unconscionable manner; the Kirsanovs' own women charged incredible prices for their labor, and meanwhile the grain was falling out of the ear, and then they couldn't manage to get the mowing finished, and then the council for widows and orphans began to threaten and demand an immediate payment of interest up to date. . . .

"I haven't the strength to keep up with it!" Nikolai Piotrovich exclaimed in despair more than once. "I mustn't join in the fight myself, and my principles won't allow me to send for the district policeman, yet without the threat of punishment one cannot do anything!"

"*Du calme, du calme,*" Pavel Piotrovich remarked at this, though he himself muttered, frowned, and tugged at his whiskers.

Bazarov kept away from all these "worries," and in any case it was not for him, a guest, to intervene in other people's affairs. The day after his arrival at Marino he set to work on his frogs, on his infusoria, and chemical constituents, and was occupied with them all the time. Arkady, on the other hand, considered it his duty, if not to help his father, at least to appear as if he were ready to help him. He listened to him patiently and once offered some advice, not expecting it to be followed, but in order to show his sympathy. He felt no antipathy to farm management; he even thought with satisfaction of undertaking agricultural activity; but at this time other ideas were swarming in his head. To his own amazement, he was thinking continually of Nikolskoe; yet formerly he would only have shrugged his shoulders if anyone had told him that he would be bored under the same roof as Bazarov. And under which roof? Under his parental roof! Yet he was in fact bored, and he felt drawn to get away. He thought of walking till he was tired, but that did not help. While talking to his father one day, he learned that Nikolai Piotrovich possessed several quite interesting letters that Mme Odintsova's mother had written to his wife, and Arkady gave him no rest until he had got hold of these letters, for which his father had to rummage through twenty different boxes and chests. When he gained possession of these half-crumbling papers, Arkady seemed to be more at rest, as though he saw before him the end toward which he should proceed. " 'I say that to both of you,' she said," he muttered to himself again and again. "I'll drive over, I'll drive over, damn it all!" But he recalled the last visit, the chilly reception, and his previous awkwardness, and he was troubled by a sense of misgiving. Yet the "chance it" of youth, the secret desire to try his fortune, to test his strength alone, without anyone's patronage, conquered at last. Only ten days after his return to Marino he again dashed off to the town on the pretext of desiring to study the organization of Sunday schools, and thence to Nikolskoe.

Continually urging on his driver, he sped there like a young officer into battle: he felt both afraid and gay, and impatience choked him. "The main thing is that one mustn't think," he assured himself. His hired driver proved to be a spirited sort; he came to a halt before every tavern, saying: "Just one?" or "Surely just one?" But on the other hand, having had "just one," he did not spare the horses. Now at last the high roof of the well-known house appeared. "What am I doing?" the thought suddenly flashed through Arkady's head. "Well, but you can't turn back!" The troika dashed along merrily; the driver whooped and whistled. Now the little bridge was thundering beneath the hoofs and wheels, now the avenue of clipped firs was approaching.

A rose-colored gown was glimpsed amid the dark green, a young face peered out from beneath the light fringe of a parasol. . . . He recognized Katya, and she recognized him. Arkady ordered the driver to pull up his galloping horses, jumped out of the carriage, and went to her.

"So it's you!" she said, and slowly all her face went crimson. "Let us go to my sister, she's here in the garden; she will be glad to see you."

Katya led Arkady into the garden. It seemed to him that the meeting with her was a particularly fortunate omen; he rejoiced to see her as though she were a sister. Everything had happened so excellently: no butler, and no announcing his arrival. At a turn in the path he saw Anna Sergeevna. She was standing with her back toward him. Hearing steps, she slowly turned round.

Arkady was at a loss for words, but her very first remark at once reassured him. "Good morning, runaway," she said in her even, gracious voice, and came to meet him, smiling and screwing up her eyes against the sun and the wind. "Where did you find him, Katya?"

"I have brought you, Anna Sergeevna," he began, "something that you don't in the least expect. . . ."

"You have brought yourself; that is the best of all."

XXIII

After seeing Arkady off with sarcastic commiseration and making it quite clear that he was not under any illusion as to the real object of his friend's journey, Bazarov withdrew completely into himself; he was possessed with a fever for work. He no longer quarreled with Pavel Piotrovich, especially as in his presence the older man adopted an excessively aristocratic demeanor and expressed his opinion more in sounds than in words. On one occasion Pavel Piotrovich did, indeed, enter into competition with the *nihilist* in regard to the question, then fashionable, of the rights of the Ostsee gentry.[1] But he suddenly stopped, after muttering with frigid courtesy: "However, you and I cannot understand each other; I, at any rate, do not have the honor of understanding you."

"I should say not!" Bazarov exclaimed. "Man is capable of understanding everything — how the ether throbs, and what goes on in the sun — but he is quite incapable of understanding how another man can blow his nose in a different manner from the way he blows his own."

"Well, is that a clever remark?" Pavel Piotrovich said interrogatively, and walked away.

He sometimes asked permission to be present at Bazarov's experiments, however, and once even set his face, scented and

---

[1] The "Baltic barons," of German origin and culture, had retained extensive privileges, which later were whittled down. (Tr.)

washed with excellent detergents, against the miscroscope in order to see how a transparent infusorian swallowed up a green
speck and fussily digested it with what appeared to be very nimble little fists situated in its throat. Nikolai Piotrovich visited Bazarov much more frequently than did his brother; he would have
gone every day to "learn," as he expressed it, if the anxieties of
the farm had not dragged him away. He was no constraint on the
young naturalist experimenter; he sat in a corner of the room and
watched attentively, occasionally allowing himself a cautious
question. During dinner and supper he tried to turn the conversation to physics, geology, or chemistry, as all other subjects, even
economic, not to mention political ones, might lead, if not to
clashes, at least to mutual dissatisfaction. Nikolai Piotrovich
guessed that his brother's hatred of Bazarov had not diminished
in the least. One insignificant incident, among many others, confirmed his assumption. Cholera began to make its appearance here
and there in the neighborhood, and even "removed" two people
from Marino itself. One night Pavel Piotrovich had quite a severe
attack. He suffered agonies all night, but did not resort to Bazarov's skill. And when next day Bazarov asked: "But why didn't
you send for me?" he replied, still very pale, but already carefully brushed and combed and shaved: "Why, I remember you
yourself said that you don't believe in medicine!" So the days
passed. Bazarov worked persistently and morosely. . . . But
meanwhile in Nikolai Piotrovich's house there was one being with
whom he did talk readily, even though not to unburden his soul.
That person was Fenichka.

He usually met her early in the morning, in the garden or the
yard; he did not call on her in her room, and she approached his
door only once, in order to ask him whether she should bathe
Mitya or not. She not only trusted him, not only was not afraid
of him, but was even more free and at ease in his presence than
with Nikolai Piotrovich. It is difficult to say why this was so;
perhaps because she unconsciously felt that Bazarov lacked all
the qualities of a nobleman, lacked all the superiority that both
attracts and repels. In her eyes he was both an excellent doctor
and a plain sort of man. When attending to her child she was unconstrained by his presence, and one day, when her head suddenly
swam and began to ache, she took a spoonful of medicine that he
administered. If Nikolai Piotrovich was present she behaved more

distantly, doing so not out of cunning, but from a feeling of propriety. She was more afraid of Pavel Piotrovich than ever before; he had been watching her for some time past, and would turn up unexpectedly, as though sprung out of the ground behind her back, in his English suit, with a fixed, keen gaze and his hands in his pockets. "He makes you go cold all over," Fenichka complained to Duniasha, and in reply the girl sighed and thought of another "unfeeling" man. Bazarov, quite unwittingly, had become the *ruthless tyrant* of her soul.

Fenichka liked Bazarov, but he liked her too. Even his face changed when he talked with her; it acquired a clear, almost kind expression, and with his usual negligence was mingled a jocular kind of attention. Fenichka grew more good-looking with every day. There is a time in young women's lives when they suddenly begin to blossom and unfold like summer roses; such a time had come in Fenichka's life. Everything conduced to this, even the prevailing July heat. Dressed in a light, white dress, she herself seemed whiter and lighter; she did not get sunburned, and the heat, from which she could not escape, slightly flushed her cheeks and ears and, pouring a gentle sluggishness into all her body, was reflected in the drowsy languor of her pretty little eyes. She was almost unable to work; her hands always slipped down to rest on her knees. She did hardly any walking and continually groaned and complained with amusing impotence.

"You should bathe more frequently," Nikolai Piotrovich said to her. He had arranged a large bathing spot, enclosed with canvas, in a pond that was not yet completely dried up.

"Oh, Nikolai Piotrovich, while I am getting to the pond I shall die, and as I come back I shall die. There isn't any shade at all in the garden."

"You're quite right, there isn't any shade," Nikolai Piotrovich replied, and he rubbed his eyebrows.

One day, about seven in the morning, as Bazarov was returning from a walk he found Fenichka in the long since faded, but still dense and green lilac arbor. She was sitting on the bench with a white kerchief flung over her head, as usual; beside her lay quite a heap of red and white roses still wet with dew. He greeted her.

"Ah! Yevgeny Vasilich!" she said, and she raised the edge of her kerchief a little to look at him, baring her arm to the elbow as she did so.

"What are you doing here?" Bazarov said, sitting down beside her. "Making posies?"

"Yes; for the breakfast table. Nikolai Piotrovich likes it."

"But it's a long time yet to breakfast. What a mass of flowers!"

"I've picked them now because later it will get hot, and it will be impossible to come out of the house. Now is the only time you can breathe. I've gone quite weak with this heat. I'm beginning to fear I shall fall ill."

"What an idea! Let me feel your pulse." Bazarov took her hand, felt for the regularly beating artery, and did not even bother to count the beats. "You'll live to be a hundred," he said, dropping her hand.

"Ah! God forbid!" she exclaimed.

"Why? Don't you want to live long, then?"

"But a hundred years! We had a granny eighty-five years old, and what a martyr she was! She was black in the face, deaf, and hunchbacked and was always coughing; she was only a burden to herself. And what sort of life d'you call that!"

"So it is better to be young?"

"Why, of course it is, isn't it?"

"But how is it better? Tell me!"

"How is it better? Why, now I am young I can do everything —I can go, and come, and carry, and I never have to ask anybody for anything. . . . What could be better?"

"And yet for me it is all the same whether I am young or old."

"How can you say that? It's all the same? What you're saying isn't possible."

"But you judge for yourself, Fyodosia Nikolavna, what good is my youth to me? I live alone, like a recluse. . . ."

"That depends entirely on you."

"Not entirely on me! If someone would only have pity on me!" Fenichka gave Bazarov a sidelong look, but did not say anything.

"What is the book you have there?" she asked after waiting a moment or two.

"This? It is a scientific book, a difficult one."

"But are you always studying? And aren't you bored? As it is, I think you know everything."

"Evidently I don't know everything. You try reading a little of it."

"Why, I shan't understand a word. Is it a Russian book?" Fenichka asked, taking the solidly bound volume in both hands. "How thick it is!"

"Yes, it's Russian."

"All the same, I shan't understand a word."

"But I didn't give it to you for you to understand. I just wanted to watch you as you read. When you read, the end of your little nose wrinkles very charmingly."

Fenichka, who had begun to read in an undertone from the article "On Creosote" at which she had happened to open the book, laughed and dropped it — it slipped from the bench to the ground.

"I like to see you laugh, too," Bazarov remarked.

"Now, do stop!"

"I like to hear you talk. It's just like a little stream rippling."

Fenichka turned her head away.

"You are a one!" she said, fingering the flowers. "And why should you listen to me? You have had conversations with such intelligent ladies."

"Ah, Fyodosia Nikolavna! Believe me, all the intelligent ladies in the world are not worth your little elbow."

"Now! There's a thing to say!" Fenichka whispered, and she covered her arms.

Bazarov picked the book up from the ground.

"This is a medical book. Why did you throw it down?"

"Medical?" Fenichka repeated, and turned to him. "But do you know what? Ever since you gave me those drops, do you remember, Mitya sleeps so well! I can't imagine how to thank you; really, you are so good."

"But doctors have to be paid properly," Bazarov remarked with a smile. "Doctors are mercenary people, as you know."

Fenichka raised her eyes to Bazarov; they seemed even darker because of the whitish reflection that fell on the upper part of her face. She did not know whether he was joking or not.

"If you wish, we'll be very glad. . . . We shall have to ask Nikolai Piotrovich — "

"But you don't think I want money?" Bazarov interrupted her. "No, I don't want money from you."

"Then what?" Fenichka said.

"What?" Bazarov echoed. "Guess."

"I'm not a thought-reader!"

"Then I'll tell you; I want — one of those roses."

Fenichka laughed again and even made a gesture of surprise, so amusing did Bazarov's wish seem to her. She laughed, and at the same time she felt flattered. He gazed at her fixedly.

"Certainly, certainly," she said at last and, bending over the bench, began to sort out the roses. "Which would you like, red or white?"

"Red, and not too large."

She straightened up.

"Here you are," she said, but she at once drew back her outstretched hand and, biting her lips, looked toward the entrance to the arbor, then listened intently.

"What's the matter?" Bazarov asked. "Nikolai Piotrovich?"

"No. He has gone off to the fields . . . and besides, I'm not afraid of him — but Pavel Piotrovich, now — I thought — "

"What?"

"I thought that he was walking past. No, there's no one. Take it." Fenichka gave Bazarov the rose.

"Why are you afraid of Pavel Piotrovich?"

"He's always frightening me. It isn't so much what he says, but he looks so meaningly. And you don't like him either, do you? You remember, you were always arguing with him at one time. I don't even know what you argue about, but I see that you get him so tied up, and so — "

Fenichka showed with her hands how, in her opinion, Bazarov tied up Pavel Piotrovich.

Bazarov smiled.

"But if he were to get the better of me," he asked, "would you take my part?"

"How can I take your part? But, in any case, no one could get the better of you."

"Do you think so? But I know a hand that if it wished could twist me round its little finger."

"Whose hand is that?"

"But don't you really know? Just smell what a beautiful scent this rose you gave me has."

Fenichka stretched forward her little neck and put her face

close to the flower. The kerchief slipped from her head to her shoulders, to reveal a soft mass of black, gleaming, rather disheveled hair.

"Wait a moment, I want to smell it with you," Bazarov said. He bent over and kissed her vigorously on her parted lips.

She quivered, and pressed her hands against his chest; but she pressed feebly, and he was able to renew and prolong his kiss.

A dry cough came from behind the lilac. Fenichka immediately shifted away to the other end of the bench. Pavel Piotrovich appeared, bowed stiffly, said with malevolent gloominess: "So you're here," and went away. Fenichka at once gathered up all the roses and left the arbor. "Shame on you, Yevgeny Vasilich!" she whispered as she went. A tone of unfeigned reproach sounded in that whisper.

Bazarov recalled another recent scene, and he felt conscience-stricken and contemptuously chagrined. But he at once shook his head, ironically congratulated himself on his formal entry into the company of Céladons,[1] and went to his room.

Pavel Piotrovich left the garden and slowly made his way to the wood. He remained there quite a long time, and when he returned for breakfast Nikolai Piotrovich anxiously asked him whether he was well, so darkened was his face.

"You know I sometimes suffer from an excess of bile," his brother calmly answered.

XXIV

Two hours later he knocked on Bazarov's door.

"I must apologize for interrupting you in your scientific occupations," he began, seating himself in a chair by the window and resting both hands on a handsome stick with an ivory knob (he usually went about without a stick), "but I am compelled to ask you to afford me five minutes of your time — no more."

"All my time is at your service," replied Bazarov, over whose face a strange look passed as Pavel Piotrovich entered.

"Five minutes will be sufficient for me. I have come to put before you a certain problem."

"A problem? What is it?"

"Be so good, then, as to listen. At the beginning of your stay

[1] Céladon: a stock name for a courtly lover, from the name of the hero of the French romance *Astrée* by Honoré d'Urfé (1568–1625).

in my brother's house, before I denied myself the pleasure of conversing with you, I had the opportunity to hear your views on many subjects; but, so far as I remember, neither between us, nor even in my presence, was there ever any talk of duels, of duels generally. Permit me to inquire what your opinion is on that subject."

Bazarov, who had risen to meet him, sat down on the edge of the table and folded his arms.

"Well, my opinion is," he said, "that from the theoretical aspect a duel is ridiculous; from the practical aspect, however, it is another matter."

"In other words, you mean to say, if I have understood you aright, that no matter what may be your theoretical view of a duel, in practice you would not allow yourself to be insulted without demanding satisfaction."

"You have guessed my thoughts perfectly."

"Very good. I am very pleased to hear you say that. Your words save me from uncertainty."

"From indecision, you mean to say."

"That is just the same; I express myself in order to be understood; I — am not a seminary rat. Your words save me a certain mournful necessity. I have decided to fight a duel with you."

Bazarov's eyes started out of his head.

"With me?"

"Undoubtedly with you."

"But what about? Please inform me."

"I could give you a reason," Pavel Piotrovich began. "But I prefer to be silent in that respect. To my taste, you are superfluous here; I cannot endure you, I despise you, and if that is not enough for you — "

His eyes began to flash. Bazarov's eyes also flamed.

"Very good!" he drawled; "no further explanations are necessary. You have had the fantastic idea of testing your chivalrous soul on me. I could refuse you that satisfaction, but since things have gone so far — "

"I am deeply obliged to you," Pavel Piotrovich answered, "and I can hope now that you will accept my challenge, without compelling me to resort to methods of violence."

"In other words, speaking without allegories, to that stick?" Bazarov observed unconcernedly. "That is perfectly correct.

There is no necessity whatever for you to insult me. Nor is it altogether safe. You can remain a gentleman. I accept your challenge also like a gentleman."

"Excellent," Pavel Piotrovich said, and he stood the stick in one corner. "In a moment we'll have a few words to say concerning the conditions of our duel; but first I would wish to know whether you consider it necessary to resort to the formality of a small quarrel, which might serve as the pretext for my challenge."

"No, better without formalities."

"That is what I think. I also consider it irrelevant to enter into the real causes of our conflict. We cannot endure each other. What more does one require?"

"What more does one require?" Bazarov repeated ironically.

"As for the actual conditions of the duel, as we shall not have seconds — for where are we to get them?"

"Precisely, where are we to get them?"

"I have the honor to propose the following: we shall fight tomorrow morning, I suggest, at six o'clock, behind the grove, with pistols; at ten paces from the line."

"At ten paces? That is just; that is the distance at which we hate each other."

"We can make it eight," Pavel Piotrovich observed.

"We can; why not?"

"Each to fire twice; and against possible eventualities each is to have in his pocket a letter in which he blames himself for his end."

"Now, with that I do not entirely agree," Bazarov said. "It is just a little like a French romance, just a little improbable."

"Maybe. However, you must agree that it is unpleasant to be placed under suspicion of murder."

"I agree. But there is a means of avoiding that mournful charge. We shall have no seconds, but there can be a witness."

"Who, namely, if I may ask."

"Why, Piotr."

"Which Piotr?"

"Your brother's valet. He is abreast of present-day ideas, and he will perform his role with all the *comme il faut* requisite in such circumstances."

"I have the feeling that you are jesting, my dear sir."

"Not in the least. When you have considered my proposal, you will be convinced that it is marked by its common sense and simplicity. You cannot hide a needle in a sack, and I undertake to prepare Piotr for his role and to bring him to the battlefield."

"You are still jesting," Pavel Piotrovich declared, rising from his chair. "But after the amiable readiness to meet me that you have displayed, I have no grounds for objection. Well, so everything is arranged. By the way, you haven't any pistols, have you?"

"Why should I have pistols, Pavel Piotrovich? I am not a warrior."

"In that case I offer you mine. You can be assured that it is five years since I last fired them."

"That is very comforting news."

Pavel Piotrovich picked up his stick.

"After which, dear sir, it only remains for me to express my gratitude to you and to let you return to your occupations. I have the honor to take my leave."

"Till our next pleasant meeting, my dear sir," Bazarov said, showing out his guest.

Pavel Piotrovich had left the room, but Bazarov remained standing before the door. Suddenly he exclaimed: "Pah, the devil! How noble, and how idiotic! What a comedy we played! Trained dogs dance on their hind legs like that. But it was impossible to refuse him; why, if I had he would have struck me, and then — " Bazarov turned pale at the very thought; all his pride rose on its hind legs. "Then I would have had to strangle him like a kitten." He returned to his microscope; but his heart was profoundly disturbed, and the calm necessary to scientific observation had vanished. "He saw us this morning," he thought; "but did he really take this step for the sake of his brother? And over what a serious matter — a kiss! There's something else behind all this. Why, I suppose he isn't in love with her himself? Of course he is! That's as clear as daylight. What a tangle! Who'd have thought it! . . . It's bad!" he decided at last, "it's bad, whichever way you look at it. To begin with, I shall have to face a bullet, and in any case I shall have to go away; and then there's Arkady, and that ladybird, Nikolai Piotrovich. It's bad, bad."

Somehow the day passed unusually quietly and languidly. It was as though Fenichka did not exist: she remained in her little room like a mouse in its hole. Nikolai Piotrovich had a preoccupied air. It had been reported to him that rust had appeared in his wheat, a crop on which he particularly relied. Pavel Piotrovich oppressed everybody, even Prokofich, with his icy courtesy. Bazarov started to write a letter to his father, but tore it up and flung it under the table. "If I die," he thought, "they will hear about it; but I shan't die. I shall hang about this world a long time yet." He ordered Piotr to come to him on important business next morning as soon as day broke; Piotr got it into his head that Bazarov wanted to take him with him to Petersburg. Bazarov went to bed late, and all night he was tormented by disjointed dreams. . . . Mme Odintsova hovered around him, and she was his mother too; she was followed about by a kitten with black whiskers, and the kitten was Fenichka; but Pavel Piotrovich appeared to him in the guise of a great forest, which he had to fight none the less. Piotr awakened him at four o'clock; he at once dressed and went out with him.

The morning was glorious, fresh; little speckled clouds hung like fleeces in the pallidly clear azure; a fine dew was sprinkled over the leaves and the grass, and glistened with silver on the spider-webs; the moist, dark earth still seemed to retain the ruddy traces of the dawn; from all the sky poured the songs of sky-larks. Bazarov reached the grove, sat down in the shade at the edge, and only then revealed to Piotr what service he expected from him. The educated valet was terrified to death; but Bazarov calmed him with the assurance that he would have nothing to do but stand some distance off and watch, and that he would not have to undertake any responsibility at all. "But meanwhile," he added, "think of the important role you will have to play!" Piotr flung out his hands, cast down his eyes, and, looking quite green, leaned against a birch.

The road from Marino wound round the little wood; on it lay a light dust, as yet untouched by wheel or foot. Bazarov involuntarily gazed along that road and tore up and chewed grass, but continually told himself: "How idiotic!" The morning chill made him shiver once or twice. . . . Piotr looked at him despondently, but Bazarov only smiled; he was not afraid.

The sound of horses' hoofs along the road came to their ears. . . . A peasant appeared round the trees. He was driving two hobbled horses before him, and as he passed Bazarov he looked at him with a strange look, not removing his hat, an omission that evidently troubled Piotr as a bad omen. "Now, that man also has risen early," Bazarov thought, "but at least he is going about his business; but we . . . "

"I think they're coming," Piotr suddenly whispered.

Bazarov raised his head and saw Pavel Piotrovich. Dressed in a light check jacket and snow-white pantaloons, he was walking swiftly along the road; under his arm was a box wrapped in green baize.

"Pardon me, I am afraid I have kept you waiting," he said, bowing first to Bazarov, then to Piotr, for whom he now felt some respect as a kind of second. "I did not wish to disturb my valet."

"It's quite all right," Bazarov replied. "We have only just arrived."

"Ah! So much the better!" Pavel Piotrovich looked about him. "There is no one in sight, no one will interfere. . . . Can we begin?"

"We can."

"I assume you do not require any further explanations?"

"I do not."

"Would you like to load them?" Pavel Piotrovich asked as he took the pistols from the case.

"No; you load them, and I will measure the paces. I have longer legs," Bazarov added with a smile. "One, two, three . . . "

"Yevgeny Vasilich," Piotr stammered with difficulty (he was shivering as if in a fever), "say what you like, I am going — "

"Four — five. Go then, friend, go away; you can even stand behind a tree and stop your ears, so long as you don't shut your eyes; but if anyone falls, run and pick him up. Six — seven — eight — " Bazarov halted. "Enough?" he asked, turning to Pavel Piotrovich, "or shall I add two more paces?"

"As you wish," Pavel Piotrovich said, inserting a second bullet.

"Well then, we'll add two more paces." Bazarov made a line on the ground with the toe of his boot. "And there's the line. But, by the way, how many paces is each of us to walk away from the line? That's an important question too. We didn't discuss it yesterday."

"I think, ten paces," Pavel Piotrovich replied, handing Bazarov both pistols. "Will you be so good as to choose?"

"I will be so good. But you must agree, Pavel Piotrovich, that our duel is extraordinary to the point of absurdity. Just look at our second's physiognomy."

"So you still feel like jesting," said Pavel Piotrovich. "I do not deny the strangeness of our duel, but I consider it my duty to warn you that I am intending to fight seriously. *A bon entendeur, salut!*"

"Oh, I haven't any doubt that we have decided to exterminate each other; but why not laugh and why not combine *utile dulci*? There, now: you talk to me in French, and I to you in Latin."

"I shall fire to hit," Pavel Piotrovich repeated, and took up his position. Bazarov for his part counted out ten paces from the line and halted.

"Are you ready?" Pavel Piotrovich asked.

"Absolutely."

"We can advance."

Bazarov slowly moved forward, and Pavel Piotrovich advanced toward him, with his left hand in his pocket and gradually raising the pistol barrel. . . . "He's aiming straight at my nose," Bazarov thought, "and how industriously he is screwing up one eye, the brigand! All the same, this is an unpleasant sensation. I shall fix my eyes on his watch-chain. . . ." Something whizzed sharply past Bazarov's ear, and at the same moment a shot rang out. "I heard it, so nothing has happened," the thought had time to flash through his head. He advanced once more and, without taking aim, pressed the trigger.

Pavel Piotrovich quivered a little and pressed his hand to his thigh. A thin stream of blood began to flow down his white pantaloons.

Bazarov threw his pistol away and went up to his opponent.

"Are you wounded?" he asked.

"You were entitled to bring me to the line," Pavel Piotrovich said, "and this is nothing. According to our conditions each has one more shot."

"Well, you'll excuse me, but that must be some other time," Bazarov replied, and put his arm round Pavel Piotrovich, who was turning pale. "Now I am no longer a duelist but a doctor, and my first task is to look at your wound. Piotr! Come here, Piotr! Where have you hidden yourself?"

"It's only a trifle — I don't need anyone's help," Pavel Piotrovich said deliberately, "and — we — must — again — " He was about to tug at his mustache, but his hand grew weak, his eyes rolled, and he lost consciousness.

"There's a fine thing! He's fainted! What on earth!" Bazarov involuntarily exclaimed as he lowered him to the grass. "Let's see what has happened." He took out his handkerchief, wiped away the blood, and groped around the wound. . . . "The bone is whole," he muttered between his teeth; "the bullet passed through at no great depth, only the muscle, the *vastus externus*, is torn. He'll be dancing again in three weeks! So it's a faint! Oh, I do like these nervous people! Why, look how thin his skin is!"

"Is he dead?" Piotr's quavering voice whispered behind his back.

Bazarov looked round.

"Go and get water quickly, friend, and he'll yet outlive both you and me."

But apparently this perfect servant did not understand his words, and he did not stir from the spot. Pavel Piotrovich slowly opened his eyes. "He's dying!" Piotr whispered, and began to cross himself.

"You're right — what a stupid physiognomy!" the wounded gentleman said with a forced smile.

"Go and get some water at once, damn you!" Bazarov shouted.

"There's no need. It was only a momentary *vertige*. . . . Help me to sit up . . . that's right . . . I only need to hold something against this scratch, and I shall walk home, or they can send a droshky for me. If you agree, the duel will not be renewed. You have acted magnanimously — today, only today, please note."

"There's no point in recalling the past," Bazarov retorted, "and as for the future, it is not worth racking one's brains over that either, because I intend to slip away at once. Let me bandage your leg now; your wound is not dangerous, but it will be best to stop the blood. But first we must bring this mortal back to life."

Bazarov shook Piotr by the shoulder and sent him off for a droshky.

"Listen now, don't frighten my brother," Pavel Piotrovich said to him; 'you're not to think of reporting this business to him."

Piotr dashed off; while he was gone for the droshky the two opponents sat on the ground and were silent. Pavel Piotrovich tried to avoid looking at Bazarov; even now he was not prepared to be reconciled to him; he was ashamed of his own arrogance, his failure, he was ashamed of all the things he had devised, though he felt also that it could not have ended in any more satisfactory manner. "At any rate he won't be hanging about here," he reassured himself, "and thanks for that." The prolonged silence grew heavy and awkward. They both felt uncomfortable. Each of them realized that the other understood him. To friends such a realization is pleasant, but it is highly unpleasant to people who are not friends, especially when they can neither have an explanation nor part company.

"I haven't bandaged your leg too tightly, have I?" Bazarov asked at last.

"No, it is quite all right, it is excellent," Pavel Piotrovich replied. After a momentary pause he added: "There is no way of deceiving my brother; we shall have to tell him we quarreled over politics."

"Very good," said Bazarov. "You can say that I cursed all Anglophils."

"That is an excellent idea. What do you think, what is that man thinking about us now?" Pavel Piotrovich went on, pointing to the same peasant who had driven the hobbled horses past Bazarov a few minutes before the duel, and who, as he returned along the road, "fussed" and removed his hat at the sight of the "gentlemen."

"Who is to know what he thinks?" Bazarov replied; "most probably he isn't thinking at all. The Russian peasant is the same mysterious stranger of whom Mrs. Radcliffe once said so much. Who can understand him? He doesn't even understand himself."

"So that is what you think!" Pavel Piotrovich began, but abruptly exclaimed: "Look what your stupid fool Piotr has done! Why, there is my brother galloping toward us."

Bazarov turned, and saw Nikolai Piotrovich's pale face as he came along in the droshky. He jumped out before it stopped, and rushed to his brother.

"What does this mean?" he said in an agitated tone. "Yevgeny Vasilich, pardon me, but what is all this?"

"It is nothing," Pavel Piotrovich replied, "there was no need to alarm you. I have had a little quarrel with Mr. Bazarov, and I have paid a little for it."

"But what was it all about, for God's sake?"

"It is difficult to explain. Mr. Bazarov spoke disrespectfully of Sir Robert Peel. I hasten to add that I alone am to blame for everything, and Mr. Bazarov conducted himself admirably. I challenged him."

"But you're bleeding, look at you!"

"But did you think I had water in my veins? This bloodletting will even be beneficial. Is that not so, doctor? Help me to get into the droshky, and do not let it depress you. I shall be well again tomorrow. That is right; excellent! You can start, coachman."

Nikolai Piotrovich walked behind the droshky; Bazarov was about to fall back. . . .

"I must ask you to attend to my brother," Nikolai Piotrovich said to him, "until another doctor can arrive from the town."

Bazarov nodded without speaking.

An hour later Pavel Piotrovich was lying in bed with an artistically bandaged leg. All the house was plunged into consternation; Fenichka was taken unwell. Nikolai Piotrovich surreptitiously wrung his hands, but Pavel Piotrovich laughed and joked, especially with Bazarov; he put on a thin batiste shirt, an elegant morning jacket, and a fez, dĭd not allow the window blinds to be lowered, and divertingly grumbled about the necessity to abstain from food.

By nightfall, however, he was running a fever; his head began to ache. The doctor from the town arrived. (Nikolai Piotrovich paid no heed to his brother, and Bazarov himself wanted the doctor to be sent for; he had sat all day in his room, jaundiced and ill-tempered, and went only on the very shortest of visits to see the patient; once or twice he happened to fall in with Fenichka, but she turned and fled from him in terror.) The new doctor advised cooling drinks, but confirmed Bazarov's assurance that no danger whatever was to be anticipated. Nikolai Piotrovich told him that his brother had wounded himself through not taking precautions, to which the doctor replied: "Hm!" but on being given twenty-five silver rubles in cash he said: "You don't say so! That does happen quite often, I know."

No one in the house went to bed or undressed. From time to time Nikolai Piotrovich tiptoed in to his brother and tiptoed out again; Pavel Piotrovich was dozing; he groaned a little, said to him in French: "*Couchez-vous*," and asked for a drink. On one of these occasions Nikolai Piotrovich made Fenichka take him a glass of lemonade; Pavel Piotrovich gazed at her fixedly and drank every drop of the liquid. Toward morning the fever increased a little, and the patient was slightly delirious. At first he uttered incoherent remarks; then he suddenly opened his eyes and, seeing his brother anxiously bending over him, he said:

"But don't you agree, Nikolai, Fenichka has something in common with Nelly?"

"With which Nelly, Pavel?"

"How can you ask that? With Princess R. Especially in the upper part of her face. *C'est de la même famille.*"

Nikolai Piotrovich made no answer, but inwardly he was astonished at the vitality of such long-past feelings in his brother. "Coming up after all this time!" he thought.

"Ah, how I love that empty creature!" Pavel Piotrovich groaned, throwing his arms behind his head with a yearning movement. "I cannot endure that some insolent nincompoop should dare to touch . . ." he stammered a few moments later.

Nikolai Piotrovich only sighed; he had no suspicion of the person to whom these words really referred.

Bazarov called on him the next morning, at eight o'clock. He had already packed and had set free all his frogs, insects, and birds.

"You have come to say good-by?" Nikolai Piotrovich said, rising to meet him.

"Exactly."

"I understand, and I entirely approve. Of course, my poor brother is to blame, and for that he is punished. He has told me he placed you in a position in which it was impossible for you to do otherwise. I believe it was impossible for you to avoid that duel, which — which to some extent is explained only by the constant antagonism of your mutual views." (Nikolai Piotrovich was getting his words mixed.) "My brother is a man of the old school, fiery and obstinate. . . . Thank God that it has ended as it has. I have taken all necessary measures to avoid publicity. . . ."

"I shall leave you my address, in case any trouble arises," Bazarov remarked perfunctorily.

"I hope that trouble will not arise, Yevgeny Vasilich. . . . I am very sorry that your stay in my house has had such — such an end. It is all the more upsetting for me because Arkady — "

"I expect I shall see him," replied Bazarov, who was always provoked to impatience by any kind of "explanation" and "declaration." "In the contrary case, I ask you to greet him for me and to accept the expression of my regrets."

"And I ask . . ." Nikolai Piotrovich replied with a bow; but Bazarov went out without waiting to hear the end of his phrase.

Learning that Bazarov was leaving, Pavel Piotrovich expressed the wish to see him and shake his hand. But Bazarov remained as cold as ice; he realized that Pavel Piotrovich wanted to display his magnanimity. He did not have a chance to say good-by to Fenichka: he only exchanged glances with her from the window. He thought her face seemed mournful. "I suppose she'll be ruined," he said to himself. "Well, she'll get away, somehow." On the other hand, Piotr was so upset that he wept on Bazarov's shoulder, until he froze the valet with the question: "Aren't your eyes on a wet spot?" And Duniasha had to flee to the grove in order to conceal her agitation. The cause of all this unhappiness climbed into his cart and lit a cigar. And when, at a turn in the road, some two miles away, he had a last view of the Kirsanov estate, stretching in a single line, with its masters' new house, he only spat and, muttering: "Damned petty gentry!" wrapped himself more closely in his greatcoat.

Pavel Piotrovich soon began to mend; but he had to lie in bed for about a week. He endured his "captivity," as he expressed it, quite patiently, but he took a lot of trouble over his toilet and continually ordered the servants to sprinkle his room with eau de Cologne. Nikolai Piotrovich read magazines to him; Fenichka waited on him as before, brought him bouillon, lemonade, soft-boiled eggs, and tea; but a secret horror took hold of her every time she entered his room. Pavel Piotrovich's unexpected behavior had alarmed all the people in the house, but her above all the others; only Prokofich was not perturbed; he explained that in his time too the gentlemen had made holes in one another, "but only noble people among themselves; they'd have ordered such upstarts to be flogged in the stable for their insolence."

Conscience hardly troubled Fenichka at all; but the thought of the real cause of the quarrel tormented her at times; and Pavel Piotrovich, too, looked at her so strangely . . . so that even when she turned her back on him she felt his eyes on her. She went thin with the incessant inward anxiety and, as so often happens, grew even more attractive.

One day — it was in the morning — Pavel Piotrovich felt very well and shifted from his bed to the divan, and Nikolai Piotrovich, after inquiring after his health, went off to the threshing-floor. Fenichka brought a cup of tea and, setting it on a little table, was about to retire. Pavel Piotrovich called her back.

"Where are you off to in such a hurry, Fyodosia Nikolavna?" he began. "Have you something you must do, then?"

"No-o — ye-es. I've got to go and pour out the tea."

"Duniasha can do that without you; sit a little while with a sick man. And, by the way, I have something I want to talk about to you."

Fenichka silently sat down on the edge of an armchair.

"Listen," Pavel Piotrovich said, and he tugged at his whiskers. "I have long been wanting to ask you: you seem to be afraid of me?"

"I-I?"

"Yes, you. You never look at me, as though you hadn't a clear conscience."

Fenichka reddened, but she glanced at Pavel Piotrovich. Somehow he seemed strange, and her heart began gently to palpitate.

"But your conscience is clear, is it not?" he asked her.

"Why shouldn't it be clear?" she whispered.

"Is there not good reason? However, whom can you have wronged? Me? That is incredible. Other people here in the house? That also is not to be believed. Unless it be my brother? But then, you love him?"

"I love him."

"With all your soul, with all your heart?"

"I love Nikolai Piotrovich with all my heart."

"Is that true? Look at me, Fenichka" (it was the first time he had addressed her by this diminutive of her Christian name). ". . . You know, lying is a great sin!"

"I am not lying, Pavel Piotrovich. If I did not love Nikolai Piotrovich I wouldn't want to live."

"And you will never desert him for anyone else?"

"Whom else can I desert him for?"

"Are there so few! Why, there is that gentleman who has just left us."

Fenichka rose to her feet.

"Good Lord, Pavel Piotrovich, what are you torturing me for? What have I done to you? How can you say such things? . . ."

"Fenichka," Pavel Piotrovich said in a mournful tone, "you see, I saw —"

"And what did you see?"

"Why, there — in the arbor."

Fenichka reddened to her ears and the roots of her hair.

"But how am I to blame for that?" she uttered with difficulty. Pavel Piotrovich half raised himself.

"You are not to blame? No? Not in the least?"

"I love only Nikolai Piotrovich in all the world, and I shall love him forever!" Fenichka said with sudden strength, though sobs rose in her throat. "But as for what you have seen, I shall say even at the Day of Judgment that I was not in the least to blame for it, and never have been, and it would be better for me to die here and now if I am to be suspected of such a thing, that to my protector, Nikolai Piotrovich, I — "

But now her voice betrayed her, and at the same time she felt Pavel Piotrovich seize and squeeze her hand. . . . She stared at him, and was petrified. He had gone even paler; his eyes were glittering and, most surprising of all, a single heavy tear rolled down his cheek.

"Fenichka!" he said in a peculiar whisper, "love, love my brother! He is such a good, kind man! Never betray him for anyone in the world, never listen to anyone's speeches! Think, what can there be worse than to love and not be loved! Never desert my poor Nikolai!"

Fenichka's tears dried, and her fear passed, so great was her astonishment. But what happened to her when Pavel Piotrovich, Pavel Piotrovich himself, pressed her hand to his lips, and so remained with his lips pressed to her hand, not kissing it, and only sometimes sighing convulsively. . . .

"Lord," she thought, "he isn't having a fit, is he?"

But at that moment all his past ruined life was quivering within him.

The staircase creaked under hurried steps. . . . He pushed her away and flung his head back on the pillow. The door opened — and Nikolai Piotrovich appeared, cheerful, fresh, ruddy. Mitya, as fresh and ruddy as his father, was dancing in only his little shirt at Nikolai's chest, clinging with bare little feet to the large buttons of his country coat.

Fenichka rushed to him and, twining her arms round him and their son, dropped her head on his shoulder. Nikolai Piotrovich was amazed: never before had the bashful and modest Fenichka caressed him in the presence of a third person.

"What is the matter?" he said, looking at his brother, and he handed Mitya to her. "You don't feel any worse?" he asked, going over to Pavel Piotrovich.

His brother buried his face in his batiste handkerchief.

"No — it is — it is nothing. . . . On the contrary, I feel very much better."

"You were in too much of a hurry to get onto the divan. Where are you going?" Nikolai Piotrovich added, turning to Fenichka; but she had already slammed the door behind her. "I thought I would bring you my hero to show to you; he was anxious to see his uncle. Why did she carry him off? All the same, what is the matter with you? Has anything happened between you here?"

"Brother!" Pavel Piotrovich solemnly pronounced.

Nikolai Piotrovich shivered. He suddenly had a feeling of dread, though he did not understand why.

"Brother," Pavel Piotrovich repeated, "give me your word that you will fulfill my one request."

"What request? Speak!"

"It is very important; as I understand it, on it depends all the happiness of your life. All this time I have pondered a great deal on what I want to say to you now. . . . Brother, fulfill your obligation, the obligation of an honest and a noble man, put an end to this scandal and evil example, which you, the finest of men, are setting!"

"What are you trying to say, Pavel?"

"Marry Fenichka. . . . She loves you; she — is the mother of your son."

Nikolai Piotrovich fell back a step and flung out his hands.

"Do you say that, Pavel? You, whom I have always regarded as an inflexible opponent of such marriages! You say that! But don't you really know that it is only out of respect for you that I have not done what you so rightly call my duty?"

"In that case your respect for me was wasted," Pavel Piotrovich retorted with a dreary smile. "I am beginning to think that Bazarov was right when he reproached me with aristocratism. No, dear brother, we have done enough posing and caring what the world thinks: we are old and humble now; it is time we laid aside all vanity. We shall simply, as you say, begin to do our duty; and, you see, we shall be given happiness into the bargain."

Nikolai Piotrovich rushed to embrace his brother.

"You have finally opened my eyes!" he exclaimed. "I knew I was right in always declaring that you are the kindest and wisest man in the world; but now I see that you are as sensible as you are magnanimous."

"Quieter, quieter," Pavel Piotrovich interrupted him. "Don't irritate the leg of your sensible brother, who when just under fifty fought a duel like any ensign. And so the question is decided: Fenichka will be my — *belle-sœur*."

"My dear Pavel! But what will Arkady say?"

"Arkady? He will be delighted, I should think. Marriage is not one of his principles, but on the other hand his feeling of equality will be flattered. And really why should there be castes in the *dix-neuvième siècle*?"

"Ah, Pavel, Pavel! Let me kiss you once more. Don't be afraid, I'll do it gently."

The brothers embraced.

"What do you think, should you not inform her of your intention at once?" Pavel Piotrovich asked.

"What is the hurry?" Nikolai Piotrovich objected. "Have you two had a conversation, then?"

"We two had a conversation? *Quelle idée!*"

"Well, that's all right. You get well first, and this matter will not be lost sight of, we must think it over well, take into consideration — "

"But you have decided, have you not?"

"Of course I have decided, and I thank you with all my heart. I shall leave you now; you must rest; any agitation is harmful to you. . . . But we'll talk about it again. You have some sleep, my dear brother, and God grant you your health again."

"What is he so thankful to me about?" Pavel Piotrovich thought when he was left alone. "As though it did not depend on him! But I, as soon as he is married, I shall go off somewhere, to Dresden or Florence, and shall live there until I die."

Pavel Piotrovich moistened his brow with eau de Cologne and closed his eyes. Lit up by the brilliant daylight, his handsome, emaciated head lay on the white pillow like the head of a corpse. . . . And, indeed, he was a corpse.

XXV

At Nikolskoe, in the garden, in the shadow of a tall ash, Katya and Arkady were sitting on a grassy bank; Fifi had made herself comfortable beside them, giving her long body that elegant contour which among hunters is called "hare's lair." Both Arkady and Katya were silent; he held a half-open book in his hands, while she was picking out the crumbs of white bread left in a basket and throwing them to a little family of sparrows that, with their peculiar cowardly impudence, were hopping and twittering right by her feet. A gentle breeze, whispering in the leaves of the ash, quietly shifted pale golden patches of light backward and forward, over the dark path and over Fifi's yellow back; a level shadow enveloped Arkady and Katya; only occasionally did a brilliant streak catch fire in her hair. They were both silent; but in the very way they were silent, in the way they were sitting side by side, a trustful friendship was revealed; each of them seemed not to be thinking of his or her companion, yet secretly was rejoicing in their proximity. Their faces, too, had changed since we last saw them: Arkady seemed to be more tranquil, Katya more animated and bolder.

"Don't you think," Arkady began, "that in Russian the ash is very well named? There is no other tree that rises so lightly and serenely into the air." [1]

Katya raised her eyes and said: "Yes"; but Arkady thought: "Now *she* won't reproach me with expressing myself *beautifully*."

"I am not fond of Heine," Katya began, indicating with her eyes the book Arkady held in his hands, "either when he laughs or when he weeps; I am fond of him when he is thoughtful and sad."

"But I like him when he laughs," Arkady remarked.

"That is because you still have traces of your former satirical tendencies." ("Former tendencies!" thought Arkady; "if Bazarov

---

[1] A play on words: *yasen*, ash; *yasno*, brightly, serenely. (Tr.)

were to hear that!") "You wait a little longer, and we shall change you completely."

"Who will change me? You?"

"Who will? Why, my sister; Porfiry Platonovich, whom you have already stopped quarreling with; my aunt, whom you escorted to church three days ago."

"But I couldn't refuse her! And as for Anna Sergeevna, you remember that she herself agreed with Yevgeny on many things."

"My sister was under his influence then, just as you were."

"Just as I was! Have you noticed, then, that I have now freed myself of his influence?"

Katya was silent.

"I know," Arkady continued, "that you never liked him."

"I cannot judge him."

"Do you know what, Katerina Sergeevna? Whenever I hear that reply I do not believe it. . . . There isn't a man alive on whom we cannot pass judgment! That is simply an excuse."

"Well, then I will say that he — it isn't that I don't like him, but I feel that he is alien to me, and I to him. . . . And you, too, are alien to him."

"Why am I?"

"How can I tell you? . . . He's a wild animal, and you and I are domesticated."

"Am I domesticated too?"

Katya nodded.

Arkady scratched himself behind his ear.

"Listen, Katerina Sergeevna: really, that's rather insulting."

"Why, would you like to be wild?"

"Not wild, but strong, and energetic."

"That is something you cannot hope for. . . . Your friend, on the other hand, doesn't want it, but it is in him."

"Hm! So you think he had great influence on Anna Sergeevna?"

"Yes. But no one can dominate her for long," Katya added in an undertone.

"Why do you think that?"

"She is very proud — that's not what I wanted to say — she greatly treasures her independence."

"But who doesn't?" Arkady asked. But the thought flashed through his head: "What is she getting at?" "What am I getting at?" flashed through Katya's head too. One and the same thoughts are incessantly occurring to young people who meet often and with cordial feelings for each other.

Arkady smiled and, shifting a little closer to Katya, said in a whisper:

"Confess that you are a little afraid of her."

"Of whom?"

"Of *her!*" Arkady repeated meaningiy.

"And are you?" Katya asked in her turn.

"I too; note that I said: 'I *too!*'"

Katya shook a threatening finger at him.

"That surprises me," she began; "never was my sister so well disposed toward you as she is now; much more than on your first visit."

"You don't say!"

"But haven't you noticed it? Aren't you pleased?"

Arkady sat thinking.

"How have I managed to win Anna Sergeevna's favor? Surely not by bringing her your mother's letters?"

"That was one thing, and there are other reasons too, which I shan't tell you."

"Why not?"

"I shan't tell you."

"Oh! I know you are very obstinate."

"Yes, I am obstinate."

"And observant."

Katya gave Arkady a sidelong look.

"Perhaps that annoys you? What are you thinking of?"

"I am wondering where you could have got that power of observation which you really do possess. You are so shy, so distrustful; you avoid everybody. . . ."

"I have lived a great deal alone; you can't help beginning to think about things then. But do I really avoid everybody?"

Arkady looked at her gratefully.

"All this is very fine," he went on, "but people in your position, I mean to say with your fortune, rarely possess that gift; it is as difficult for the truth to reach them as it is to reach a czar."

"But then, you see, I am not rich."

Arkady was astonished and did not immediately understand what she meant. "And of course she's right, the estate belongs entirely to her sister," the thought struck him. This thought was not unpleasant.

"How well you said that!" he observed.

"What do you mean?"

"You said it well; quite simply, without any sense of shame and without affectation. And I must say I think that anyone who knows and who says that he is poor must possess some special feeling, something rather like pride."

"Because of my sister's kindness I have never felt anything like that; I mentioned my fortune only because the question happened to come up."

"Truly; but confess that you, too, have a tiny bit of that pride I have just referred to."

"For example?"

"For example, I am sure you — forgive my question — you wouldn't marry a wealthy man?"

"If I loved him very much — no, I think even then I wouldn't."

"Ah! So you see!" Arkady exclaimed. After waiting a moment he added: "But why wouldn't you marry him?"

"Because of what even the song sings about the poor girl who married a rich man."

"Perhaps you want to domineer or — "

"Oh no! What for? On the contrary, I am ready to be submissive, except that inequality is oppressive. But to respect oneself and be submissive, that I understand; that is happiness; but a subjugated existence — no, I'd rather be as I am."

" 'I'd rather be as I am,' " Arkady echoed her. "Yes," he continued, "it is not for nothing that you are of the same blood as Anna Sergeevna; you are just as independent as she, only you are more secretive. I am sure that not for anything would you be the first to express your feelings, no matter how strong and sacred they were. . . ."

"But how could it be otherwise?" Katya asked.

"You are just as intelligent; you have just as much character as she has, if not more — "

"Please don't compare me with my sister," she hurriedly interrupted; "that is too much to my disadvantage. You seem to have forgotten that my sister is both beautiful and clever, and — you especially, Arkady Nikolaich, should not say such things, and with such a serious expression too."

"What do you mean by: 'you especially,' and why do you conclude that I am joking?"

"Of course you're joking."

"Do you think so? But supposing I am convinced of what I am saying? Supposing I consider that even now I haven't expressed myself strongly enough?"

"I don't understand you."

"You really don't? Now I see that I have overestimated your powers of observation after all."

"How?"

Arkady made no answer and turned away. Katya found a few more crumbs in the basket and began to throw them to the sparrows; but she swung her hand too violently, and they flew off without getting a peck.

"Katerina Sergeevna!" Arkady suddenly began, "I expect it is all one to you; but I tell you that I wouldn't exchange you either for your sister or for anybody else in all the world."

He rose and walked swiftly away, as though he had taken fright at the words that had burst from his lips.

But Katya dropped both hands and the basket on her knees and, turning her head, gazed long after Arkady. Little by little a crimson hue began to tinge her cheeks; but her lips did not smile, and her dark eyes expressed bewilderment and some other, at that moment still nameless feeling.

"Are you alone?" Anna Sergeevna's voice sounded beside her. "I thought you came into the garden with Arkady."

Unhurriedly Katya turned her eyes to her sister (elegantly, even exquisitely dressed, Anna Sergeevna stood on the path and tickled Fifi's ears with the tip of her open parasol) and unhurriedly she said:

"I am alone."

"I see that," her sister replied with a laugh; "so he must have gone to his room."

"Yes."

"Were you reading together?"

"Yes."

Anna Sergeevna took Katya by the chin and raised her face.

"You haven't quarreled, I hope?"

"No," Katya said, and gently removed her sister's hand.

"How solemnly you answer! I thought I would find him here

and was intending to ask him to come for a walk with me. He is always asking me to come. Some shoes have arrived for you from the town; go and try them on. I noticed yesterday that your others are quite worn out. You don't pay anything like enough attention to them, and yet you have such enchanting little feet! You have fine hands too — only they're rather large; so you must conquer with your feet. But you're not a flirt, I know."

Anna Sergeevna continued along the path, her beautiful dress rustling a little; Katya rose from the bank and, taking Heine with her, also went off — only, not to try on her shoes.

"Enchanting little feet," she thought as she slowly and easily walked up the stone steps of the terrace, which were burning hot in the sun. "Enchanting little feet, you say. . . . Well, and he will be down at those feet."

But immediately she felt ashamed, and she ran nimbly upstairs.

Arkady was walking along the corridor to his room when the steward overtook him and reported that Mr. Bazarov was sitting in his room.

"Yevgeny!" Arkady muttered almost in alarm. "Has he been here long?"

"He arrived this very minute and said that I wasn't to inform Anna Sergeevna about him, but ordered me to take him straight to you."

"I hope nothing has happened at home," Arkady thought. Hurriedly running up the stairs, he flung open the door. Bazarov's appearance at once reassured him, though a more experienced eye would probably have discovered signs of internal emotion in the unexpected guest's still energetic, but hollow-cheeked figure. With a dusty greatcoat over his shoulders, his cap on his head, he was sitting on the windowsill; he did not rise even when Arkady flung himself on his neck with noisy exclamations.

"Now this is unexpected! What fate has brought you here?" Arkady asked, fussing about the room like a man who imagines and wishes to show that he is delighted. "Everything is all right at home, they're all well, aren't they?"

"Everything is all right, but they are not all well," Bazarov said. "But don't make so much commotion, order them to bring me some kvass, and sit down and listen to what I have to tell you in a few but, I hope, quite strong words."

Arkady calmed down, and Bazarov told him about his duel with

Pavel Piotrovich. Arkady was greatly astonished and even saddened, but he did not deem it necessary to say so; he only asked whether his uncle's wound really was not dangerous and, receiving the reply that it was extremely interesting, only not in a medical sense, he smiled forcedly. But his heart felt horrified and somehow ashamed. Bazarov seemed to understand his feelings.

"Yes, brother," he said, "that is what happens through living with feudalists. You yourself become a feudalist and take part in knightly jousts. Well, and so I am on my way back to my 'fathers,'" he concluded, "and on the way I turned aside here — to tell you all this, I would say, if I did not regard a useless lie as stupid. No, I turned aside here — the devil knows why. You see, sometimes it is good for a man to take himself by the forelock and pull himself up like a turnip out of a bed; that is what I have accomplished during the last few days. . . . But I felt I wanted to take one more glance at all I have parted from, at the bed in which I was planted."

"I hope those words don't apply to me," Arkady said agitatedly; "I hope that you are not thinking of parting from *me*."

Bazarov gazed at him fixedly, almost piercingly.

"Does that upset you so very much? It seems to me that *you* have already parted from me. You are so fresh-looking and clean-looking — your affair with Anna Sergeevna must be going well."

"What affair have I with Anna Sergeevna?"

"Why, didn't you come on here from the town because of her, you fledgling? And by the way, how are the Sunday schools getting on in the town? Aren't you in love with her? Or have you begun to be mock-modest?"

"Yevgeny, you know I have always been frank with you; I can assure you, I can swear by God to you that you are mistaken."

"Hm! A new phrase!" Bazarov remarked in an undertone. "But you have nothing to get worked up about, it is a matter of complete indifference to me. A romantic would say: 'I feel that our roads are beginning to separate,' but I simply say that we have begun to pall on each other. . . ."

"Yevgeny —"

"My dear fellow, that is no misfortune; isn't there much else yet to pall on us in the world? But now I am thinking, shouldn't we say good-by? Ever since I was here I have been feeling filthy, just as though I had read too much of Gogol's letter to the Kaluga governor's wife. I may mention that I did not order the horses to be unharnessed."

"But, really, that is impossible."

"Why is it?"

"I don't speak of myself; it will be most discourteous to Anna Sergeevna, who certainly will wish to see you."

"Well, there you are mistaken."

"But, on the contrary, I am sure I am right," Arkady retorted. "And what are you dissembling for? Now the question has arisen, haven't you yourself come here because of her?"

"That, maybe, is true, but, all the same, you are mistaken."

But Arkady was right. Anna Sergeevna did want to see Bazarov, and through the butler she invited him to come to her. Bazarov changed his clothes before he went: it transpired that he had packed his new suit so that it was right to hand.

She received him not in the room where he had so unexpectedly declared his love to her, but in the reception hall. She amiably extended the tips of her fingers to him, but her face expressed an involuntary strain.

"Anna Sergeevna," Bazarov hurried to say, "above all else I must reassure you. Before you stands a mortal who has long since come to his senses, and who hopes that others have forgotten his stupidities. I am going away for a long time, and you will agree that though I am not a soft creature, it would be unpleasant for me to go with the thought that you think of me with loathing."

Anna Sergeevna sighed deeply, like a man who has just reached the summit of a lofty hill, and her face brightened with a smile. She again held out her hand to Bazarov and responded to the pressure of his hand.

"Who remembers the past, let him go hence," she said, "the more so as, to tell the truth, I, too, was to blame then, if not with my coquetry, then with something else. In a word: we will be friends as before. It was a dream, wasn't it? But who remembers dreams?"

"Who remembers them? And besides, love — is an affectation."

"Is it really? I am very glad to hear it."

So Anna Sergeevna said, and so Bazarov said; they both thought they were speaking the truth. Was the truth, all the truth, expressed in their words? They themselves did not know, and the author knows even less. But the conversation proceeded as though they absolutely believed each other.

Anna Sergeevna, among other things, asked Bazarov what he had done at the Kirsanov's house. He all but told her of his duel with Pavel Piotrovich, but refrained at the thought that she might think he was trying to win her interest, and replied that he had worked all the time.

"But I," said Anna Sergeevna, "first had an attack of hypochondria, God knows why, and I even planned to go abroad, just imagine! . . . Then that passed, your friend, Arkady Nikolaich, arrived, and I again fell into my groove, my true role."

"And what is that role, if I may ask?"

"The role of aunt, of preceptress, of mother, whatever you like to call it. By the way, do you know, I didn't understand your close friendship with Arkady Piotrovich very well before; I found him rather uninteresting. But now I have come to know him better, and I am convinced that he is intelligent. . . . But the main thing is that he is young, young — not like you and me, Yevgeny Vasilich."

"Is he still just as bashful in your presence?" Bazarov asked.

"But surely — " Anna Sergeevna began; but after a moment's thought she added: "Now he has grown more confiding, and he talks to me. Formerly he avoided me. For that matter, I for my part have not sought out his company. He and Katya are great friends."

Bazarov felt annoyed. "A woman cannot help being artful," he thought.

"You say he avoided you," he said with a cold smile. "But probably it was no secret to you that he was in love with you?"

"What? He too?" the words burst from her.

"He too," Bazarov repeated with a humble bow. "Do you mean to say you didn't know that, and that I've told you news?"

Anna Sergeevna cast down her eyes.

"You are mistaken, Yevgeny Vasilich."

"I don't think so. But perhaps I should not have mentioned it." ("But in future don't you be artful," he added to himself.)

"Why shouldn't you mention it? But I think that here also you are attaching too much importance to a momentary impression. I am beginning to think that you are inclined to exaggerate."

"We'd better not talk about it, Anna Sergeevna."

"Why not?" she retorted, but she herself changed the conversation to a different subject. Even now she felt awkward with Bazarov, though she had told him, and assured herself, that everything was forgotten. When exchanging even the simplest of remarks with him, even when joking with him, she felt a slight pang of fear. So people on board a steamship on the sea talk and laugh unconcernedly about one thing and another, as if they were on dry ground; but let the least hitch occur, let the least sign of something unusual be manifest, and at once a peculiar expression of alarm appears on all faces, testifying to the constant recognition of a constant danger.

Anna Sergeevna's talk with Bazarov did not continue much longer. She began to go into a reverie, to answer abstractedly, and finally suggested that they should go into the hall, where they found the Princess and Katya. "But where is Arkady Nikolaich?" the mistress asked. Learning that he had not been seen for more than an hour, she sent for him. He was not speedily found: he had made his way to the most remote part of the garden and, resting his chin on his folded arms, was sitting buried in thought. They were deep and serious, were those thoughts, but not sorrowful. He knew that Anna Sergeevna was sitting closeted with Bazarov, but he felt no jealousy as he had in the past; on the contrary, his face slowly lit up; seemingly he was amazed and delighted, and had decided on something.

XXVI

Mme Odintsova's late husband had not liked innovations, but he had allowed "some play of refined taste," and so had had an edifice in the style of a Greek portico of Russian brick erected in the garden, between the conservatory and the pond. In the rear, dead wall of this portico, or colonnade, six niches were made to hold statues that Odintsov had intended to order from abroad. These statues were to have represented *Isolation, Silence, Meditation, Melancholy, Bashfulness,* and *Sensibility.* One of them, the goddess *Silence,* with finger to her lips, had been brought to Nikolskoe and set up; but on the very same day the yard boys knocked her nose off, and although a neighboring plasterer undertook to give her a new nose "twice as good as the old," Odintsov had ordered her to be taken down and she was relegated to a corner of the threshing-shed, where she stood for many long years, arousing the superstitious horror of the peasant women. The front of the portico had long since been overgrown with dense bushes; only the capitals of the columns were to be seen above the pillars. It was cool inside the portico, even at noon. Since the time she had seen a grass-snake in it, Anna Sergeevna was not fond of visiting the spot; but Katya often went and sat on the large stone bench set up below one of the niches. Enveloped in coolness and shade, she read, worked, or gave herself over to that sensation of complete silence which is probably known to everybody, the charm of which consists in the barely conscious, mute observation of the broad stream of life incessantly rolling both around us and within us.

The day after Bazarov's arrival Katya was sitting on her favorite bench, and beside her Arkady was sitting once more. He had entreated her to go with him to the portico.

There was about an hour left to lunchtime; the dewy morn had already been succeeded by the burning day. Arkady's face retained its expression of the previous afternoon; Katya had a preoccupied air. Immediately after tea her sister had summoned her to her room and, after a preliminary caress, which always frightened Katya a little, had advised her to be more prudent in her behavior with Arkady, and especially to avoid conversations alone with him, as apparently they had been remarked upon by their aunt, and by all the house. In addition, the previous evening Anna Sergeevna had been out of spirits; and Katya herself had felt some embarrassment, as though she recognized her own culpability. When she yielded to Arkady's request she told herself that it was for the last time.

"Katerina Sergeevna," he began with a bashful jauntiness, "ever since I have had the happiness of living in the same house as you, I have talked much with you, and yet there is something that for me is a very important — question, which I have never yet referred to. You remarked yesterday that I had been changed here," he added, both catching and avoiding Katya's gaze, fixed on him interrogatively. "In fact, I have changed in many respects, and you know that better than anyone else — you, to whom essentially I am obliged for this change."

"I? Me?" Katya said.

"I am no longer the presumptuous lad that I was when I first arrived here," Arkady went on; "it is not for nothing that I have passed my twenty-third birthday; I still wish to be useful, I wish to devote all my powers to the truth; but I no longer seek my ideals where I sought them formerly; they present themselves to me as — much nearer. Hitherto I have not understood myself, I have set myself tasks that are beyond my strength. . . . Recently my eyes have been opened, thanks to a certain feeling. . . . I am expressing myself not quite clearly, but I hope that you will understand me. . . ."

Katya made no answer, but she ceased to look at him.

"I think," he began again, now in a more agitated tone, while above him amid the leaves of a birch a chaffinch lightheartedly sang its little song, "I think that it is the duty of any honest man to be completely frank with those — with those people who — in a word, with those who are near to him, and so I — I have the intention — "

But here Arkady's eloquence betrayed him; he stumbled, hesitated, and was forced into silence for a moment. Katya did not raise her eyes at all. It seemed as though she did not even understand what all this was leading to and was waiting for something.

"I foresee that I shall surprise you," Arkady began again, collecting his strength, "the more so as this feeling is connected to a certain extent — to a certain extent, note that — with you. Yesterday, I remember, you reproached me with lacking in seriousness," he went on, with the air of a man who has walked into a marsh and feels that with every step he is sinking more and more, yet still hastens forward, in the hope of wading out of it the sooner. "That reproach is often directed to — falls upon — young people, even after they have ceased to deserve it; and if I had more self-confidence — " ("Oh, help me, do help me!" he thought in despair, but still Katya did not turn her head) "if I could hope — "

"If I could be sure of what you are saying," Anna Sergeevna's clear voice sounded at that moment.

Arkady at once lapsed into silence, and Katya turned pale. Past the bushes covering the portico ran a path. Anna Sergeevna, accompanied by Bazarov, was walking along that path. Katya and Arkady could not see them, but they heard every word, the rustle of her dress, their very breathing. They took a few steps farther and then, as though of intent, halted right in front of the portico.

"Don't you see," Anna Sergeevna continued, "you and I blundered; neither of us is any longer in our first youth, especially I; we have seen life, we have grown tired; both of us — why should we stand on ceremony? — are intelligent; at first we interested each other, our curiosity was aroused — but then — "

"But then I played myself out," Bazarov caught her up.

"You know that was not the cause of our disagreement. But no matter how it was, we had no need of each other, that is the main thing; in us there was too much — how can I express it? — homogeneity. We didn't realize that at first. On the contrary, Arkady — "

"Do you have any need of him?" Bazarov asked.

"Enough, Yevgeny Vasilich! You say he is not indifferent to me, and I myself have always had the impression that he liked me. I know I am old enough to be his aunt, but I do not wish to conceal from you that I have begun to think of him more often. In that young and fresh feeling there is a charm — "

"The word 'fascination' is the one more commonly used in such cases," Bazarov interrupted her; a seething rancor could be distinguished in his calm but muffled voice. "Arkady was rather secretive with me yesterday and talked neither about you nor about your sister. . . . That is a serious symptom."

"He is just like a brother with Katya," Anna Sergeevna said, "and I like that quality in him, though perhaps I ought not to allow such intimacy between them."

"Is that the — sister speaking in you?" Bazarov drawled.

"Of course. . . . But what are we standing here for? Let us walk on. What a strange conversation we are having, aren't we? And could I have ever imagined that I should talk like this to you? You know I am afraid of you — and at the same time I confide in you, because essentially you are very good."

"To begin with, I am not at all good; and secondly, I have lost all meaning for you, and you tell me I am good. . . . That is exactly like laying a wreath of flowers at a dead man's head!"

"Yevgeny Vasilich, we have no power — " Anna Sergeevna began; but a wind blew up, set the leaves rustling, and carried her words away.

"But you are free," Bazarov said after a moment.

It was impossible to distinguish any more; the footsteps passed into the distance . . . everything grew silent.

Arkady turned to Katya. She was sitting in the same position, only her head hung still lower.

"Katerina Sergeevna," he said in a quivering voice and clenching his hands, "I love you forever and irrevocably, and I love nobody but you. I wanted to tell you that, to learn what you think and to ask your hand, because I, too, am not rich, and I feel that I am ready for any sacrifice. . . . You don't answer? You don't believe me? You think I am speaking frivolously? But remember these last few days! Haven't you surely long since realized that everything else — understand me aright — everything, everything else, has long since vanished without trace? Look at me, say one word to me. . . . I love — I love you . . . do believe me!"

Katya glanced at Arkady with a serious and luminous glance and, after a long reverie, hardly smiling, she said: "Yes."

Arkady jumped up from the bench.

"Yes! You said 'Yes,' Katerina Sergeevna! What does that mean? Does it mean that you realize I love you, that you believe me? . . . Or — or — I do not dare to finish — "

"Yes," Katya repeated, and this time he understood her. He seized her large, beautiful hands and, panting with rapture, pressed her to his heart. He could hardly stand on his feet and only uttered: "Katya, Katya . . . " but she innocently fell to weeping, and laughing at her tears. Anyone who has never seen such tears in the eyes of a beloved one cannot fathom to what extent, all overcome with gratitude and shame, a human being can be happy on earth.

Next day, early in the morning, Anna Sergeevna asked for Bazarov to come to her room, and with a forced laugh she handed him a folded sheet of writing-paper. It was a letter from Arkady: in it he asked for her sister's hand.

Bazarov read the letter swiftly, forcing himself to conceal the feeling of malicious pleasure that momentarily flamed up in his breast.

"There now," he said, "and you, I believe, no longer ago than yesterday were thinking that he loved Katerina Sergeevna with a brotherly love. But what do you intend to do now?"

"What do you advise me to do?" she asked, still laughing.

"Why, I think," Bazarov replied, also with a laugh, though he did not feel in the least cheerful and had no desire whatever to laugh, any more than she had, "I think you must give the young people your blessing. The match is good in every respect; Kirsanov's fortune is not too bad, he is his father's only son, and his father's a fine sort, he won't thwart it."

Mme Odintsova walked about the room. Her face went red and pale in turn.

"Do you think so?" she said. "All right, I don't see any obstacles. . . . I am glad for Katya—and for Arkady Nikolaich. Of course, I shall await his father's reply. I'll send Arkady himself to him. Well, and so it transpires I was right yesterday when I told you that we were both old people. . . . How is it I didn't have any idea of this? It amazes me!"

She again began to laugh, but at once turned away.

"The youth these days have grown very artful," Bazarov remarked, and he laughed too. After a momentary silence he spoke again. "Good-by. I wish for your sake that the affair may end in the happiest of ways; but I shall rejoice at a distance."

She turned swiftly back to him.

"Are you going away, then? Why shouldn't you remain *now*? Remain—it is cheerful talking to you—just as though one were walking on the edge of a precipice. First one feels nervous, and then courage comes from somewhere or other. Remain."

"Thank you for your invitation, Anna Sergeevna, and for your flattering opinion of my conversational powers. But I consider that I have already circled too long in a sphere alien to me. Flying fish can survive in the air for a certain time, but they soon have to slap back into the water; allow me also to flop back into my element."

She gazed at Bazarov. A bitter sneer twisted his pale face. "This man loved me!" she thought. She felt sorry for him, and she sympathetically held out her hand to him.

But he, too, understood her.

"No!" he said, and he fell back a pace. "I am a poor man, but I have never yet accepted alms. Good-by, and fare well."

"I am convinced that this is not the last time we shall meet," Anna Sergeevna declared with an involuntary gesture.

"All kinds of things happen in this world!" Bazarov replied; he bowed and went out.

"And so you've thought to build yourself a nest?" he said to Arkady that same day as he squatted down, packing his trunk. "Well, it's a good idea. Only you were sly unnecessarily. I expected you to take quite a different direction. Or perhaps it rather surprised you yourself?"

"I certainly wasn't expecting it when I left you," Arkady replied, "but are you yourself being sly now in saying it's 'a good idea,' as though I didn't know your views on marriage?"

"Ah, my dear friend," Bazarov declared, "how you express yourself! Do you know what I am doing? There's some room left in my trunk, and I am putting hay into it; and that happens in our life's trunk too: we'll fill it up with anything rather than have an empty place in it. Please don't be annoyed; I expect you remember what opinion I have always held of Katerina Sergeevna. Another young lady only gets the reputation of being intelligent because she sighs intelligently; but yours stands up for herself, and stands so firmly that she will take you, too, in hand — why, yes, and that's how it should be." He slammed down the lid and rose from the floor. "But now in parting I will repeat to you — because there is no point in deluding ourselves — we are parting forever, and you are conscious of that yourself . . . you have acted sensibly; you were not created for our bitter, caustic, solitary life. You haven't either audacity or malevolence, but you have youthful daring and a youthful fervor; that is no good for our affairs. The likes of you, a nobleman, cannot get any farther than a noble humility or a noble indignation, and they are both trivial. You, for instance, don't fight — and yet you imagine yourselves as brave young lads — but we want to fight. And then what? Our dust will make your eyes smart, our filth will soil you, and besides, you haven't grown up to our level, you cannot help admiring yourself, you find it pleasant to swear at yourself; but we find it boring — give us others; we need to smash others! You're a fine fellow; but all the same you're a rather soft liberal nobleman's son — e volatou,[1] as my parent puts it."

"Are you saying good-by to me forever, Yevgeny," Arkady said mournfully, "and you haven't anything else to say to me than this?"

Bazarov scratched the nape of his neck.

"I have, Arkady, I have something else; only I shan't say it, be-

[1] Et voilà tout.

cause it is romanticism — and that means using too much syrup. But you get married quickly; and you arrange your nest and have as many children as possible. They'll be clever, if only because they will be born in their time, not like you and me. Aha! I see the horses are ready. Time I was off! I have said good-by to everybody. . . . Well, what now? Shall we embrace?"

Arkady flung himself on the neck of his former preceptor and friend, and the tears started from his eyes.

"Such is youth!" Bazarov said calmly. "But I rely on Katerina Sergeevna. You see how quickly she will comfort you!"

"Good-by, brother!" he said to Arkady when he had climbed into the cart. Pointing to a pair of daws perching side by side on the stable roof, he added: "There you are! Learn from them!"

"What does that mean?" Arkady asked.

"What? Are you so weak in natural history, then, or have you forgotten that the jackdaw is a very respectable family bird? An example for you! . . . Good-by, signor!"

With a rattle of wheels the cart rolled away.

Bazarov had spoken the truth. In conversation with Katya that evening Arkady completely forgot his preceptor. He was already beginning to be subordinated to her, and Katya felt that and was not surprised. He was to drive to Marino the following day, to see his father. Anna Sergeevna did not wish to constrain the young people and only out of propriety did not leave them too long alone. She magnanimously made sure that they were not troubled with the company of the Princess, who had been reduced to a lachrymose fury by the news of the forthcoming marriage. At first Anna Sergeevna was afraid lest the spectacle of their happiness should prove too depressing to her, but quite the contrary occurred; far from depressing her, this spectacle interested and in the end moved her. Anna Sergeevna was both delighted and saddened at the realization. "Evidently Bazarov is right," she thought; "curiosity, only curiosity, and love of peace, and egotism. . . ."

"Children," she said aloud, "tell me, is love an affectation?"

But neither Katya nor Arkady even understood her. They shunned her company; the involuntarily overheard conversation could not be forgotten. Anna Sergeevna soon set them at rest, however. And that was not difficult for her: she was herself set at rest.

XXVII

The old Bazarovs were all the more delighted at their son's abrupt arrival because it was entirely unexpected. Arina Vlasievna was so overcome and went running about the house in such a fashion that Vasily Ivanovich likened her to a little partridge; the short tail of her rather short jacket did, indeed, give her a birdlike quality. But he himself only mooed and chewed the amber mouth-piece of his pipe and, clutching his neck with his hands, twisted his head, as though testing to see whether it was screwed on properly, then suddenly opened his mouth wide and laughed without making a sound.

"I have come to stay with you for a whole six weeks, old man," Bazarov said to him. "I want to work, so please don't get in my way."

"You'll forget what I look like, that is how much I shall get in your way!" Vasily Ivanovich replied.

He kept his promise. Accommodating his son in his office as before, he all but hid away from him, and saw that his wife did not make any unnecessary demonstrations of affection. "You know, mother," he said to her, "Yevgeny got rather fed up with us on his first visit; this time we must be wiser." Arina Vlasievna agreed with her husband, but she gained little by doing so, for she saw her son only at the table and was completely afraid to talk to him. "Dear Yevgeny," she would say, and before he could look round she was fingering the strings of her reticule and stammering: "It's nothing, nothing, I just — " and then she would go off to Vasily Ivanovich and, supporting her cheek on one hand, say to him: "My dear, how am I to find out what our dear Yevgeny would like for dinner today, cabbage soup or borsch?" "But why didn't you ask him yourself?" "Because he gets fed up with me!" For that matter, Bazarov himself soon ceased to put up resistance: the fever of work fled from him and was replaced by a yearning boredom and dull anxiety. In all his movements a strange weariness was revealed; even his step, once firm and impetuously bold, was changed. He ceased to go off for lonely walks and began to seek company; he drank tea in the reception room, wandered about the garden with Vasily Ivanovich and smoked with him "in silence"; and one day he asked after Father Alexei. At first Vasily Ivanovich was delighted with this transformation, but his joy did not last long.

"Yevgeny distresses me," he quietly complained to his wife; "it isn't that he is dissatisfied or angry, that wouldn't be anything to worry about; he is embittered, he's sad — that is the terrible thing. He's always silent; if only he'd scold you and me; he's getting thin, and the color of his face isn't at all satisfactory."

"Lord, Lord," the old woman whispered, "I'd put a holy charm round his neck, but he wouldn't allow me."

Several times Vasily Ivanovich attempted very cautiously to question his son about his work, his health, about Arkady. . . . But Bazarov replied reluctantly and perfunctorily and one day, noticing during a conversation that his father was gradually leading up to something, said to him in a vexed tone: "What are you hovering about me for, just as though you were on tiptoe? That is worse than your previous manner."

"Now, now, now, I'm not doing anything," poor Vasily Ivanovich hurriedly replied.

His political allusions provoked just as little response. One day he talked about the imminent emancipation of the peasants, about progress, hoping to arouse his son's sympathy; but Bazarov unconcernedly remarked: "Yesterday as I walked past the fence I heard the local peasant lads singing, and not one of the old folk songs, but bawling the ballad: 'The time so true is coming now, my heart is conscious of love.' . . . And there's your progress!"

Sometimes Bazarov went off to the village and, quizzical as usual, fell into conversation with one of the peasants. "Well," he would say to him, "tell me all about your views on life, brother; for you know they say all the strength and the future of Russia are in you, with you a new epoch in history will begin; you will give us a real language, and laws."

The peasant either made no answer at all, or said something such as: "But we can — also, because you see — look, for instance, how our share of the land is situated."

"You tell me about your mir system, your communal organization," Bazarov interrupted him. "And is it the same mir that stands on three fishes?" [1]

[1] A play on words: "Mir" = both the Russian peasants' village community and the world. (Tr.)

"Ah, sir, it's the earth that stands on three fishes," the peasant explained reassuringly, with a patriarchally good-natured melodiousness of voice. "But it is well known that the masters are against our mir — our community, that is; because you are our fathers. And the more sternly the master demands, the sweeter it is for the peasant."

After listening to one such speech Bazarov shrugged his shoulders contemptuously and turned on his heel, while the peasant wandered home.

"What did he talk to you about?" the man was asked by another peasant of middle age and a morose visage, who, standing at the door of his hut, had been distantly present at the conversation. "About the arrears, I suppose?"

"Why about the arrears, brother of mine?" the first peasant replied, and there was no longer any trace of patriarchal melodiousness in his voice, but, on the contrary, a brusque austerity. "Why, he babbled away; he just wanted to let his tongue wag. We all know he's one of the masters; can he understand anything?"

"Yes, how can he?" the other peasant answered, and, shaking their hats and pulling down their belts, they turned to consideration of their affairs and their needs. Alas! Bazarov, contemptuously shrugging his shoulders, the Bazarov who knew how to talk to the peasants (as he had boasted in his dispute with Pavel Piotrovich), this same self-confident Bazarov did not even suspect that in their eyes he was in fact something of a jackanapes.

In the end, however, he found an occupation. One day in his presence Vasily Ivanovich bandaged a peasant's injured leg, but the old man's hands shook and he could not manage the bandages; his son helped him, and after that he began to take part in his father's practice, while continuing to make fun of the remedies he himself recommended and of his father, who at once put them into practice. But Bazarov's sneers did not trouble Vasily Ivanovich in the least; they even gave him some comfort. Holding his greasy dressing-gown together over his belly with two fingers, and smoking his pipe, he listened with pleasure; and the more malicious his son's observations, the more amiably did the gratified father chuckle, displaying every one of his blackened teeth. He even repeated Bazarov's occasional stupid or senseless remarks and, for instance, for several days on end he inappropriately and incessantly exclaimed: "Well, that's a ninth affair!" simply because his son had used that phrase on learning that his father attended morning service. "Thank goodness he's free of his hypochondria!" he whispered to his wife; "the way he rapped back at me today, it was marvelous!" Furthermore, the thought that he had such an assistant filled him with pride. "Yes, yes," he said to some peasant woman in a peasant overcoat and a horned headdress as he handed her a glass of Huillard water or a box of ointment, "you, my dear, should thank God every minute of the day that I have my son staying with me; we're treating you by the most scientific and up-to-date method now, do you understand that? The Emperor of the French, Napoleon, even he hasn't got a better doctor." But the woman, who had come to complain that she had the stitch (for that matter, she herself could not have explained what she meant by these words) only bowed and slipped her hand into her bosom, where she was carrying four eggs wrapped in the end of a towel.

On one occasion Bazarov even extracted a tooth from a peddler selling piece-goods, and although the tooth was quite ordinary, Vasily Ivanovich preserved it as a rarity and showed it to Father Alexei, repeating again and again:

"Look at those roots! What strength Yevgeny has! The peddler rose right into the air. . . . I think he could send an oak flying out of the ground!"

"Very praiseworthy!" Father Alexei said at last, not knowing how to answer and how to get rid of the ecstatic old man.

One day a peasant from a neighboring village brought to Vasily Ivanovich his brother, who was sick with typhoid. The unfortunate wretch was dying as he lay face-downward on a bunch of straw in a cart; his body was covered with dark patches; he had long since lost consciousness. Vasily Ivanovich expressed his regret that no one had thought of resorting to the aid of medicine before and announced that there was no hope. In fact, the peasant did not get his brother back home alive: the man died in the cart.

Three days later Bazarov entered his father's room and asked whether he had any silver nitrate.

"I have; what do you want it for?"

"I need it—to cauterize a small cut."

"Whom for?"

"Myself."

"Yourself? What's all this about? What kind of small cut? Where is it?"

"Here, on my finger. I've been to the village that typhoid case came from, you remember? For some reason they decided to open him up, and I haven't had any practice in that for a long time."

"Well?"

"Well, so I asked the county doctor to let me do it; well, and I cut myself."

Vasily Ivanovich suddenly turned white and, saying not a word, ran to his office, returning at once with a small piece of silver nitrate in his hand. Bazarov was about to take it from him and go out.

"For the very God's sake," Vasily Ivanovich said, "let me do it myself."

Bazarov smiled wryly.

"You're always keen on practicing!"

"Please don't jest. Show me your finger. It isn't a big cut, truly. Does that hurt?"

"Squeeze harder, don't be afraid."

Vasily Ivanovich stopped.

"What do you think, Yevgeny, wouldn't it be better to cauterize it with a hot iron?"

"That should have been done before, but now even silver nitrate isn't much use to tell the truth. If I have infected myself, it's too late now."

"How — too late —" Vasily Ivanovich could hardly get the words out.

"I should say! Four hours and more have passed since I did it."

Vasily Ivanovich cauterized the cut a little more.

"But do you mean to say the county doctor didn't have any silver nitrate?"

"No, he hadn't!"

"How was that, for God's sake! A doctor, and he hasn't such an indispensable article?"

"You should see his lancets!" Bazarov said, and went out.

All the rest of that day and all the following day Vasily Ivanovich resorted to every possible pretext to enter his son's room;

and although he did not even mention the cut, but tried to talk of indifferent matters, he looked so insistently into his son's eyes and watched him so anxiously that Bazarov lost his patience and threatened to go away. Vasily Ivanovich promised not to disturb him, especially as Arina Vlasievna, from whom he had of course concealed the whole affair, began to worry him by asking why he didn't sleep and what had happened to him. For two whole days he kept up his spirits, though he was far from satisfied with the look of his son, whom he watched surreptitiously. . . . But at dinner on the third day he could restrain himself no longer. Bazarov sat with head hanging and did not touch a single dish.

"Why aren't you eating, Yevgeny?" he asked, looking as cheerful as possible. "I think the food is nicely cooked."

"I don't want it, and so I don't eat it."

"Haven't you any appetite? How is your head?" he added in a diffident tone. "Is it aching?"

"Yes. Why shouldn't it ache?"

Arina Vlasievna straightened up and began to listen.

"Please don't be angry, Yevgeny," Vasily Ivanovich went on, "but won't you let me feel your pulse?"

Bazarov half rose.

"I can tell you without feeling it that I have a temperature."

"And have you had any rigor?"

"Yes, I have. I'll go and lie down; and you make me some lime tea. I must have caught a chill."

"I thought I heard you, you were coughing during the night," Arina Vlasievna remarked.

"I've caught a chill," Bazarov repeated, and went out.

Arina Vlasievna set to work to make some tea of lime flowers, but Vasily Ivanovich went into the next room and silently clutched at his hair.

Bazarov did not get up again that day, and he passed all the night in a heavy, semi-oblivious doze. At about one in the morning, opening his eyes with an effort, by the light of a little lamp he saw his father's pale face bent over him and ordered him to go out; the old man obeyed, but at once returned on tiptoe and, half hidden behind the doors of the bookcase, kept a steadfast watch on his son. Arina Vlasievna also did not go to bed and, opening the door of the room a very little, from time to time crept in to listen to "how her dear boy was breathing" and to look at Vasily Ivanovich. She could see only his motionless, bowed back, but even that gave her some relief.

In the morning Bazarov attempted to get up; his head swam, the blood started from his nose; he lay down again. His father silently waited on him; his mother went in to him and asked him how he felt. He replied: "Better," and turned to the wall. Vasily Ivanovich waved his wife away with both arms; she bit her lip to avoid bursting into tears, and went out. Everything in the house seemed suddenly to darken; all faces grew longer, a dreadful silence settled; a garrulous cock was carried from the yard down to the village and for long could not understand why he had been treated so.

Bazarov continued to lie with his face turned to the wall. Vasily Ivanovich tried to talk to him about various things, but talking wearied him, and the old man sat silent in his armchair, only cracking his fingers occasionally. He went into the garden for a few moments, stood there like a statue, as though struck by unexpressed astonishment (a look of astonishment never left his face at all during these days), and returned to his son, trying to avoid his wife's questionings. At last she seized him by the arm and convulsively, almost threateningly, said: "But what is the matter with him?" At this he stammered and forced himself to answer with a smile, but, to his own horror, instead of a smile, from somewhere inside him a laugh burst forth. He had sent for the doctor as soon as dawn came. He considered it necessary to warn his son of this step, so that he would not be angry.

Bazarov suddenly turned over on the divan, stared at his father fixedly and dully, and asked for a drink.

Vasily Ivanovich gave him some water and took the opportunity to feel his forehead. It was burning.

"Old fellow," Bazarov began in a hoarse and slow voice, "I'm in a bad way. I'm infected, and in a few days you will be burying me."

Vasily Ivanovich staggered back as though someone had struck him on the legs.

"Yevgeny!" he stammered, "what are you saying! . . . God forbid! You've caught a chill — "

"Enough of that!" Bazarov unhurriedly interrupted him. "It's not permissible for a doctor to talk like that. I have all the symptoms of infection, you know that yourself."

"But where are the symptoms — of infection, Yevgeny? . . . Don't say that!"

"But what is this?" Bazarov said, and, raising the sleeve of his shirt, he showed his father the sinister, crimson spots that had come up under his skin.

Vasily Ivanovich shivered and went cold with fear.

"Let us assume," he said at last, "let us assume — even — even if there is something in the nature of — infection — "

"Pyemia," his son prompted him.

"Why, yes — in the nature of — an epidemic — "

"*Pyemia*," Bazarov repeated harshly and distinctly. "Or have you forgotten your primers already?"

"Well, yes, yes, as you wish. . . . All the same, we shall cure you."

"Well, you hope! But that's not the point. I did not expect to die so soon; that is a chance that, to tell the truth, is very unpleasant. Now you and Mother must both rely on the fact that you are deeply religious; here's an opportunity for you to put it to the test." He drank a little more water. "But I want to ask you one thing — while my head is under my control. Tomorrow or the day after, my brain, as you know, will apply to be retired. Even now I am not quite sure whether I am making myself clear. While I was lying here I had the impression that red dogs were running round and round me, but you were pointing at me as if I were a grouse. I feel just as though I were drunk. Do you understand me all right?"

"Why, Yevgeny, you are talking quite naturally."

"So much the better; you told me you have sent for the doctor. . . . You comforted yourself with that — now comfort me: send a messenger urgently — "

"To Arkady Nikolaich?" the old man interrupted.

"Who is Arkady Nikolaich?" Bazarov said, as though uncertain. "Ah, yes! that fledgling! No, don't trouble him: he's fallen among the daws now. Don't look astonished, I'm not delirious yet. But you send a messenger urgently to — Anna Sergeevna Odintsova; there's a landowner of that name. . . . Do you know of her?" (Vasily Ivanovich nodded.) "He's to say that Yevgeny Bazarov sends his greetings and informs her that he is dying. Will you do that?"

"I will do it. . . . Only is it possible that you should die, you,

Yevgeny? . . . Judge for yourself! Where will there be any justice after that?"

"That I don't know; but you just send the messenger urgently."

"I'll send him this minute, and I'll write a letter myself."

"No, why bother? Say that I sent my greetings, that is all that is necessary. But now I'll go back to my dogs. Strange! I want to fix my thoughts on death, but nothing comes of it. I see a kind of patch . . . and nothing else."

He again turned heavily to the wall; but Vasily Ivanovich left his room and, making his way to his wife's bedroom, crumpled to his knees before the icons.

"Pray, Arina, pray!" he groaned; "our son is dying."

The doctor, the same county doctor who did not have any silver nitrate with him, arrived and, after examining the patient, advised resort to waiting methods, and at once remarked on the possibility of Bazarov's getting well.

"But have you ever happened to see anyone in my condition who did *not* depart to Elysium?" Bazarov asked. Suddenly seizing the leg of a heavy table that stood by the divan, he shook it and shifted it from its place.

"There's strength for you, strength," he said; "it's still here, but I've got to die! . . . An old man has at least had time to get unused to life, but I — But you try to deny death. It denies me, and that's all! Who's that crying?" he added after a pause. "Mother? Poor Mother! Whom will you feed now with your amazing borsch? But you, Vasily Ivanovich, you, too, seem to be down in the dumps? Well, if Christianity is of no help, be a philosopher, a stoic, won't you? After all, you did boast that you were a philosopher, didn't you?"

"What sort of philosopher am I!" Vasily Ivanovich began to bawl, and the tears rolled down his cheeks.

Bazarov grew worse with every hour; the fever took a rapid course, as it usually does with surgical infection. He had not yet lost consciousness and understood what was said to him; he still struggled. "I don't want to be delirious," he whispered, clenching his fists, "that's just idiotic!" And he added at once: "Well, if you take ten from eight, what is left?" Vasily Ivanovich went about like a lunatic, suggested first one remedy, then another, and in the end did nothing but cover his son's legs. "Wrap in cold sheets . . . an emetic . . . mustard plasters to the belly . . . bloodletting," he said tensely. The doctor, whom he implored to remain, assented to everything he proposed, gave the sick man lemonade, and asked for a pipe and something "strengthening and warming" — in other words, vodka — for himself. Arina Vlasievna sat on a low bench by the door and only went from time to time to pray; a few days previously a hand mirror had slipped out of her hand and had been shattered, and she always regarded that as a bad sign; even Anfisushka did not know what to say to her. Timofeich had been sent to tell Mme Odintsova.

The night was far from good for Bazarov. . . . The high fever tormented him. Toward morning he felt easier. He asked Arina Vlasievna to comb his hair, kissed her hand, and drank a couple of sips of tea. Vasily Ivanovich cheered up a little.

"God be thanked!" he declared; "the crisis has arrived . . . the crisis has come."

"Pah, just think of that!" Bazarov remarked. "All that that word means! He's found it, said it: 'crisis,' and he's comforted. It's astonishing how much man believes in words. Tell him, for instance, that he's a fool and don't thrash him, and he's miserable; call him a wise man and don't give him a farthing, and he feels satisfied."

This little speech, which was reminiscent of Bazarov's former sallies, deeply affected Vasily Ivanovich.

"Bravo! Excellently said, excellently!" he exclaimed, pretending to clap his hands.

Bazarov smiled mournfully.

"Well, what do you think," he said, "has the crisis arrived or passed?"

"You're better, that's what I see, that's what makes me glad," Vasily Ivanovich replied.

"Well, that's excellent; there's never any harm in being glad. But have you sent to her, you know who?"

"Yes, of course."

The change for the better did not last long. The attacks of fever were renewed. Vasily Ivanovich sat beside Bazarov. The old man seemed to be racked by some peculiar torment. He made several times as if to say something — and could not.

"Yevgeny!" he said at last; "my son, my dear, my darling son!"

This unusual call had an effect on Bazarov. He turned his head a little and, evidently striving to fight his way through from beneath the burden of the oblivion weighing upon him, he said: "What is it, my father?"

"Yevgeny," Vasily Ivanovich continued, and he dropped on his knees beside his son, though Bazarov did not open his eyes and could not see him. "Yevgeny, you're better now; if God pleases, you will get well; but take this opportunity, comfort me and your mother, fulfill the duty of a Christian! I have something to say to you, it is terrible; but still more terrible — you see, it's forever, Yevgeny — you just think, how — "

The old man's voice broke, but a strange look passed over his son's face, though he continued to lie with closed eyes.

"I do not refuse, if that may comfort you," he said at last; "but it seems to me that there is no need for haste. You yourself say that I am better."

"You're better, Yevgeny, you're better; but who knows? After all, it's in God's will, and when you have done your duty — "

"No, I'll wait," Bazarov interrupted. "I agree with you that the crisis has arrived. But if you and I are mistaken, well, after all, they administer the rites to unconscious people."

"But please, Yevgeny — "

"I'll wait. But now I want to sleep. Don't disturb me."

And he laid his head in its previous place.

The old man rose, sat down in the armchair, and, resting his chin on his hand, began to bite his fingers. . . .

The rattle of a springed carriage, the rattle that is so peculiarly audible in the quietness of the countryside, suddenly struck his ear. Nearer, still nearer rolled the light wheels; now he could hear the horses snorting. . . . Vasily Ivanovich jumped up and rushed to the little window. A two-seated chaise, harnessed to a four-in-hand, drove into the yard of his house. Not stopping to think what it might mean, in an outburst of thoughtless joy he ran out on the steps. . . . A liveried lackey opened the door of the chaise; a lady wearing a black veil, and in a black mantilla, emerged from it. . . .

"I am Odintsova," she said. "Is Yevgeny Vasilich still alive? Are you his father? I have brought a doctor with me."

"Benefactress!" Vasily Ivanovich exclaimed, and, seizing her hand, pressed it convulsively to his lips, while the doctor Anna Sergeevna had brought with her, a little man in spectacles, German to judge by his face, slid unhurriedly out of the chaise. "He's still alive, my Yevgeny's still alive, and now he will be saved! Wife! Wife! . . . An angel has come to us from heaven. . . ."

"Lord, what is all this!" the old woman stammered as she ran out from the reception room. Having no idea whatever of what was happening, in the anteroom she fell at Anna Sergeevna's feet and began to kiss her dress like a madwoman.

"What are you doing! What are you doing!" Anna Sergeevna cried, but Arina Vlasievna did not listen to her, and Vasily Ivanovich only repeated: "An angel! An angel!"

"*Wo ist der Kranke?*" the doctor said at last, not without a touch of annoyance.

Vasily Ivanovich recovered his wits.

"Here, here, please follow me, *wertester Herr Kollege*," he added as his memory of the past came back to him.

"Eh!" the German pronounced, and bared his teeth in a sour smile.

Vasily Ivanovich led him into his son's room.

"A doctor come from Anna Sergeevna Odintsova," he said bending right down to the sick man's ear. "And she's here too."

Bazarov suddenly opened his eyes.

"What did you say?"

"I said Anna Sergeevna Odintsova is here and has brought a doctor to see you."

Bazarov ran his eyes round the room.

"She's here? . . . I want to see her."

"You shall see her, Yevgeny; but first we must have a talk with the doctor. I shall tell him all the history of the case, as Sidor Sidorich has gone" (Sidor Sidorich was the county doctor) "and we'll hold a little consultation."

Bazarov glanced at the German.

"Well, get the talk over quickly; only not in Latin, for I know the meaning of *jam moritur*."

"*Der Herr scheint des Deutschen mächtig zu sein?*" the new foster-child of Æsculapius began, turning to Vasily Ivanovich.

"*Ich — gabe —* We'd better talk Russian," the old man said.

"Ah, ah! so diss iss de diss iss — Please . . ."

And the consultation began.

Half an hour later Anna Sergeevna, accompanied by Vasily Ivanovich, entered the room. The doctor had managed to whisper to her that there was not the least hope of the patient getting better.

She glanced at Bazarov — and halted at the door, so struck was she by his inflamed, yet deathly face with its dull eyes fixed on her. She was simply terrified with a cold and exhausting terror; the thought that this was not the feeling she would have experienced if she had really loved him flashed through her head.

"Thank you," he said with difficulty, "I hadn't expected this. This is kind on your part. So we have seen each other again, as you promised."

"Anna Sergeevna has been so good," Vasily Ivanovich began.

"Father, leave us. Anna Sergeevna, will you allow — ? I think, now — "

With his head he indicated his outstretched, helpless body.

Vasily Ivanovich went out.

"Well, thank you," Bazarov repeated. "This is regal of you. They say czars also visit the dying."

"Yevgeny Vasilich, I hope — "

"Oh, Anna Sergeevna, let us speak the truth. I'm done for. I've fallen under the wheel. And it transpires that there was no point in thinking about the future. It's an old story, is death, but to every man it comes anew. So far I have not been a coward . . . and then unconsciousness will come, and *fuit!*" (He feebly waved his hand.) "Well, and what have I to say to you — that I loved you? That was entirely without meaning even before, and now far more. Love is a form, but my personal form is already disintegrating. Rather let me say — how wonderful you are! And now you stand there, so beautiful — "

Anna Sergeevna involuntarily shuddered.

"It's all right, don't be alarmed — sit there. . . . Don't come near me: my illness is infectious."

Anna Sergeevna swiftly crossed the room and sat down in the chair beside the bed in which Bazarov was lying.

"Great-hearted!" he whispered. "Oh, how close, and how

346

young, fresh, pure . . . in this loathsome room! . . . Well, good-by! Live long, that is the best of all, and enjoy it, while there is time. Look, what a hideous spectacle: a half-crushed worm, and still puffing itself up! And yet it also thought: 'I'll achieve a great deal in my life, I shan't die, why should I? I have a task; why, I'm a giant!' But now the giant's whole task is to die decorously, though it is nothing to do with anyone. . . . All the same, I shan't wag my tail."

Bazarov was silent and with his hand began to grope for his glass. Anna Sergeevna gave him some drink, not taking off her gloves, and breathing apprehensively.

"You will forget me," he began again, "the dead is no comrade for the living. My father will tell you what a man Russia is losing. . . . That's all nonsense, but don't disillusion the old fellow. What comfort they get out of a child — you know. And make a fuss over Mother. After all, you won't find such people as they in your great world, even if you look for them with a candle in daylight. . . . Russia needs me. . . . No, evidently she doesn't. And who is needed? She needs the cobbler, she needs the tailor, needs the butcher — he sells meat — the butcher — wait, I'm getting mixed up. . . . There is a forest here — "

He laid his hand on his brow.

Anna Sergeevna bent over him.

"Yevgeny Vasilich, I am here."

He at once took her hand and half raised himself.

"Good-by," he said with sudden strength, and his eyes gleamed with a last gleam. "Good-by. . . . Listen — after all, I didn't kiss you that time. . . . Blow on the fading lamp, and let it go out. . . ."

Anna Sergeevna set her lips to his forehead.

"And that suffices!" he said, and fell back on the pillow. "Now — darkness . . ."

Anna Sergeevna quietly went out.

"Well?" Vasily Ivanovich asked her in a whisper.

"He's fallen asleep," she answered almost inaudibly.

Bazarov was not fated to awaken again. Toward evening he became completely unconscious, and he died the next day. Father Alexei performed the rites of religion over him. When the extreme unction was administered, when the consecrated chrism touched his breast, one of his eyes opened, and apparently, at the sight of the priest in his vestments, the smoking censer, the candle in front of the icon, something akin to a shudder of horror was momentarily reflected on his deathly face. But when at last he breathed his final breath and a general wailing arose in the house, Vasily Ivanovich was possessed by a sudden frenzy. "I said I would start to complain," he shouted hoarsely, with flaming, distorted face, shaking a fist in the air, as though threatening someone; "and I shall complain, I shall complain." But Arina Vlasievna, all in tears, hung on his neck, and they fell to the ground together. "And so they lay side by side," Anfisushka afterward related in the servants' room, "and hung their heads, just like lambs at noontide."

But the noontide sultriness passes, and evening and night come on, and then the return to the quiet refuge, where there is sweet sleep for the tormented and weary. . . .

XXVIII

Six months had passed. It was a white winter, with the cruel stillness of cloudless frosts, packed, scrunching snow, a rosy hoarfrost on the trees, a pallidly emerald sky, caps of smoke above the chimneys, billows of steam from momentarily opened doors, the faces of people fresh as though nipped, and the fussy trot of shivering little horses. The January day was now drawing to its end; the evening chill clenched the motionless air still more strongly, and the blood-red sunset swiftly faded. Lights were lit in the windows of the house at Marino; Prokofich, in a black frock coat and white gloves, with unusual solemnity was laying the table for seven places. A week before, in the small parish church, two weddings had been celebrated quietly and privately: Arkady to Katya, and Nikolai Piotrovich to Fenichka; and on this very day Nikolai Piotrovich was giving a farewell dinner for his brother, who was going on business to Moscow. Anna Sergeevna had departed for that city immediately after the wedding; she had been munificent to the young couple.

They all came to the table at three o'clock exactly. Mitya also was accommodated; he now had a nurse in a brocade headdress. Pavel Piotrovich sat between Katya and Fenichka: the husbands were placed beside their wives. Our acquaintances had changed of recent months; they had all seemed to improve in their appearance and had matured; only Pavel Piotrovich was thinner, which, however, conferred still more refinement and the air of the *grand seigneur* on his expressive features. . . . Fenichka, too, had changed. In a new silk gown, a broad velvet fillet for her hair, and a golden chain round her neck, she sat deferentially motionless, deferential to herself, to everybody around her, and smiled as though she were wanting to say: "You must excuse me, I'm not to blame." And not she alone — all the others smiled, and they, too, seemed to be apologizing; they all felt a little awkward, a little sad, and fundamentally very happy. Each waited on the others with amusing anticipation, as though they had all agreed to play out some good-natured comedy. Katya was the calmest of all: she looked about her trustfully, and one could see that Nikolai Piotrovich had already come to love her obliviously. Before the dinner ended he rose and, taking his glass in his hand, turned to Pavel Piotrovich.

"You are abandoning us — you are abandoning us, dear brother," he began; "of course, not for long; but all the same I cannot but express to you that I — that we — how much I — how much we — There is all the trouble, that we do not know how to make speeches. Arkady, you say it."

"No, Papa, I haven't prepared myself."

"But I have prepared myself very well! Simply, brother, allow me to embrace you, to wish you all the best, and a very speedy return to us!"

Pavel Piotrovich kissed them all, not excluding Mitya, of course; in Fenichka's case he also kissed her hand, which she did not yet know how to hold out properly, and, drinking a second glass, said with a deep sigh: "Be happy, my friends! Farewell!" [1]

This English epilogue passed unnoticed; but they were all moved.

"In memory of Bazarov," Katya whispered into her husband's ear, and clinked glasses with him. In answer Arkady squeezed her hand, but could not bring himself to propose this toast aloud.

And that, it would seem, is the end? But perhaps some of our readers would like to know what each of the persons we have

[1] "Farewell" is in English in the Russian text.

introduced is doing now, just now. We are prepared to satisfy them.

Anna Sergeevna recently married, not for love, but out of conviction, one of the coming Russian public figures, a very intelligent man, a lawyer, with strong practical sense, resolute will, and a remarkable gift of speech, a man still young, good, and as cold as ice. They are living in great harmony with each other, and will live, perhaps, to see happiness — perhaps to love. Princess X has died, to be forgotten from the very day of her death. The Kirsanovs, father and son, have settled down at Marino. Their affairs are beginning to mend. Arkady has become a zealous master, and the "farm" is already beginning to bring in a considerable income. Nikolai Piotrovich has been elected an arbitrator between the landowners and peasants and is laboring with all his powers; he is continually driving about his district; he makes long speeches (he holds to the opinion that the peasants have to be "explained to"; in other words, by the frequent repetition of one and the same words he reduces them to weariness); none the less, to tell the truth, he does not completely satisfy either the educated noblemen, who talk sometimes with chic, sometimes with melancholy, of "*man*cipation" (saying the "an" through their noses), or the uneducated noblemen, who unceremoniously curse "this muncipation." Both the one and the other group think he is too easy-going. Katerina Sergeevna has a son, called Kolia, while Mitya is already running about in great style and prattles away garrulously. After her husband and Mitya, Fenichka — Fyodosia Nikolavna, that is — worships no one more than Arkady's wife, and when Katya sits down at the piano she is quite happy to stay with her all day. Here we may well mention Piotr. He has gone quite wooden with stupidity and importance, he pronounces all his "ye's" as "yu's," but he too has married and received a goodly dowry with his bride. She was a town gardener's daughter, who had refused two good grooms simply because they didn't have a watch; but Piotr not only had a watch, he had patent-leather boots.

In Dresden, on the Brühl Terrace, between two and four o'clock, at the most fashionable hour for walks, you may meet a man of about fifty, now quite gray and seemingly suffering from the gout, but still handsome, exquisitely attired, and with that peculiar impress which is conferred only by long mingling with the higher levels of society. He is Pavel Piotrovich. From Moscow he traveled abroad for the benefit of his health and remained to reside in Dresden, where he is well acquainted with the English and with passing Russians. With the English he behaves simply, almost modestly, but not without dignity; they find him rather boring, but respect in him the "perfect gentleman." With the Russians he is freer, he gives vent to his spleen, jeers at himself and at them; but it all proves to be very pleasant in his case, and offhand and becoming. He holds to Slavophil views: it is well known that in high society that is regarded as *très distingué*. He never reads anything in Russian, but on his writing-table there is a silver ashtray in the shape of a peasant's bast shoe. Our tourists run after him a great deal. While *in temporary opposition*, Matvei Ilich Kolyazin majestically called on him when passing through Dresden on his way to the Bohemian waters; and the natives, whom, however, he rarely meets, all but worship him. No one can so easily and quickly obtain a ticket for the court *Kapelle*, the theater, and so on as *der Herr Baron von Kirsanow*. He still does as much good as he can; he still makes quite a stir, even today; it is not for nothing that he was once a lion; but he finds life oppressive — more oppressive than he himself suspects. It is worth taking a glance at him in the Russian church, as, leaning against the side wall, bitterly pursing his lips, he is lost in thought and for a long time makes no movement at all, then abruptly starts and almost imperceptibly crosses himself. . . .

Kukshina also has gone abroad. She is in Heidelberg now and is no longer studying natural sciences, but architecture, in which, according to her, she has discovered new laws. As before, she hobnobs with students, especially with the young Russian physicists and chemists with whom Heidelberg is filled, and who, at first astonishing the native German professors with their sober view of things, now astonishes those same professors with their absolute inactivity and utter laziness.

In Petersburg Sitnikov rubs shoulders with two or three such chemists, who are not able to distinguish oxygen from hydrogen, but who are filled with nihilism and self-esteem; and he is on nodding terms with the great Yelisevich. Sitnikov also is preparing to be great and, if we may accept his assurance, is continuing Bazarov's "work." They say someone recently thrashed him, but he did not let the debt go unpaid; in a certain obscure little article, printed in a certain obscure little journal, he hinted that the man who had thrashed him was a coward. He calls this irony. His father domineers over him as before, and his wife regards him as a little fool — and a man of letters.

There is a small village cemetery in one of the remote little districts of Russia. Like almost all our cemeteries, it has a mournful appearance: the ditches surrounding it have long since been overgrown; the gray wooden crosses have faded and rotted beneath their once painted roofs; the tombstones have all shifted, as though someone were pushing at them from below; two or three meager little trees barely provide a miserable shade; sheep wander unhindered over the graves. . . . But among those graves is one that no man touches, that no creature tramples on; only the birds settle on it and sing in the dawn. An iron fencing surrounds it; two young spruces are set one at each end; in this grave Yevgeny Bazarov is buried. It is often visited by two now decrepit old people, a husband and wife from the near-by village. Supporting each other, they go with leaden steps; they approach the fencing, drop and remain on their knees, and weep long and bitterly, and gaze long and fixedly at the speechless stone beneath which their son lies; they exchange a brief word, they brush the dust from the stone, and tend the branches of the spruce trees, and pray again, and cannot tear themselves away from this spot where they seem to be nearer to their son, to memories of him. . . . Surely their prayers, their tears, are not fruitless? Surely love, their sacred, devoted love, is not lacking in omnipotence? Ah no! No matter what passionate, sinful, turbulent heart is concealed in the grave, the flowers growing on it look at us serenely with their innocent eyes; not of eternal peace alone, of that great peace of "indifferent" nature do they speak to us; they speak also of eternal reconciliation and life everlasting.

First Love

1860

THE GUESTS had long since departed. The clock struck half past twelve. Only the host, Sergei Nikolaich, and Vladimir Piotrovich were left in the room.

The host rang and ordered the servant to clear the supper table.

"Well, so it's agreed," he said, making himself more comfortable in his armchair and lighting a cigar. "Each of us undertakes to tell the story of his first love. You begin, Sergei Nikolaich."

Sergei Nikolaich, a portly man with a fair, puffy face, first looked at his host, then fixed his eyes on the ceiling. "I never had a first love," he said at last. "I started with my second."

"But how could you have done that?"

"Quite simply. I was eighteen when I first began to chase after a certain very attractive young lady; but I courted her exactly as if it were nothing new for me at all, exactly as — I paid court to others, later. To tell the truth, the first time I fell in love — and the last — was at the age of six, with my nurse; but that was very long ago, I have quite forgotten the details of our relations, and even if I could remember them, who would be interested?"

"Well, what am I to say?" the host began. "There isn't much of interest to tell about my first love either. I never fell in love with anyone until I met Anna Ivanovna, my present wife; and everything went like clockwork then: our fathers arranged our betrothal, we very quickly fell in love with each other, and we got married without delay. So my story can be told in very few words. I confess, gentlemen, that when I raised this question of first love I was relying on you, — I won't say old bachelors, and yet you're not exactly young. Surely you'll amend matters for us with some story, Vladimir Piotrovich?"

"It so happens that my first love was not exactly ordinary," Vladimir Piotrovich replied after some hesitation. He was about forty years old, and had black hair streaked with gray.

"Ah!" The host and Sergei Nikolaich exclaimed in one voice. "So much the better. . . . Tell us the story."

"With pleasure. . . . But no, I won't tell you the story; I am no good at telling stories, I make them either dry and short, or long-winded and untrue to life. But if you'll allow me I'll write down all I can remember and read it to you."

At first his two friends would not agree, but he insisted on having his way. Two weeks later they met again, and he kept his promise.

This is what he had written.

I

At that time I was sixteen; it happened in the summer of 1833.

I was living with my parents in Moscow. They had rented a house for the summer close to the Kaluga Gate, opposite the Nieskuchny Gardens. I was preparing to enter the university, but I worked very little and at my leisure.

No one put any restraints on my freedom. I did what I liked, especially after I had parted from my last tutor, a Frenchman who could never get used to the idea that he had fallen "like a bomb" (*comme une bombe*) into Russia, and who spent days on end lying in bed with a fierce expression on his face. My father treated me with negligent kindness; my mother paid hardly any attention to me, though I was her only child: she was preoccupied with other cares. My father, a man still young and very handsome, had married her for money; she was ten years older than he. She had a miserable life; she was always getting upset, always jealous, always angry—but never in my father's presence. She was terribly afraid of him, and he treated her sternly, coldly, distantly. I have never known any other man so artificially calm, self-assured, and autocratic.

I shall never forget the first few weeks I spent in that house by the Kaluga Gate. The weather was perfect; we moved out of town on May 9, St. Nicholas's Day. I went walking in our garden, or about the Nieskuchny Gardens, or out beyond the city gate, taking a book with me—Kaidanov's *Course*, for instance—but rarely opening it. I spent much of my time reciting poems, for I knew very many by heart. My blood was coursing through my veins, and I was melancholy, so delightfully and absurdly; I was always expecting something, always afraid of something, and I was astonished at everything, and always at the ready. My imagination played and danced continually around the same ideas, like swifts round a belfry at dawn. I was lost in thought, I sorrowed and even wept. But through the tears and through the sorrow inspired by some melodious poem, or by the beauty of the evening, a joyous feeling of youthful and effervescent life sprang up like grass in spring.

I had a saddle-horse. I saddled her myself and rode alone to some distant spot, the farther the better; I shook out the reins in a gallop and imagined myself a knight at a tourney (how merrily the wind blew in my ears!). Or, turning my face to the sky, I took its radiant light and azure into my soul.

I remember that in those days my mind hardly ever visualized the image of a woman, the apparition of woman's love, in any definite shape; but in all my thoughts, in all my feelings, lurked a half-recognized, bashful presentiment of something new, something inexpressibly sweet — something feminine.

This presentiment, this expectation, suffused all my being: I drew it in with my breath, it flowed through my veins in every drop of my blood . . . it was fated to have speedy realization.

Our house consisted of a large timber dwelling with a columned portico and two low wings; in the left-hand wing was a tiny manufactory of cheap wallpapers; I sometimes went there to watch a dozen thin and shock-headed, hollow-cheeked boys in greasy gowns, who jumped from time to time on the wooden levers that worked the square blocks of the press and so, with the weight of their puny bodies, stamped the patterns on the wallpaper. The small wing on the right was empty, but was to be rented. One day, three weeks or so after May 9, the shutters of this wing were thrown open, and women's faces appeared at the windows: a family had come to live there. I remember that same day at dinner my mother asked our butler who our new neighbors were, and, when he mentioned the name of Princess Zasiokina, remarked not without a touch of respect: "Ah, a princess!" then added: "She cannot be very well off."

"They arrived in three droshkies," the butler observed as he respectfully presented the dish. "They haven't a carriage of their own, and the furniture they brought is hardly worth mentioning."

"Maybe," my mother replied, "but all the same a princess is better."

My father gave her a frigid look; she said no more.

Certainly the Princess Zasiokina could not have been wealthy: the small wing she had rented was so tumbledown and tiny that anyone at all well off would never have agreed to live in it. However, I paid no attention to any of this conversation. The Princess's title made little impression on me: I had recently been reading Schiller's *Robbers*.

2

I had the habit of wandering about our garden every evening with a gun and taking pot shots at the rooks. I had long felt hatred for those prudent, rapacious, and cunning birds. On the day I have already spoken of I went off into the garden as usual and, after walking fruitlessly along all the avenues (the rooks recognized me and only cawed brokenly in the distance), I happened to approach the low fence separating our domain from the narrow strip of garden extending beyond and attached to the right-hand wing. I walked along with my head sunk on my breast. Suddenly I heard voices. I looked over the fence and was petrified: I saw a strange sight.

A few paces away, in a glade between bushes of green raspberry, was a tall, graceful girl in a striped, rose-colored dress and with a white kerchief on her head; four young men were pressing round her, and she was smacking each of them in turn on the forehead with those small gray flowers — I don't know their names, but they are well known to children: the flowers form small bags and burst with a pop when you strike them against anything hard. The young men thrust out their foreheads so readily, and there was something so charming, so imperative, so gracious, amusing, and pleasant in the girl's movements, that I all but cried out with amazement and delight, and I think I would have given everything else on earth for those enchanting fingers to strike me on the forehead too. My gun slipped to the grass, I forgot everything; my eyes were fixed on that graceful waist and neck and the beautiful hands, and the rather untidy, fair hair beneath the white kerchief, and that one half-closed, intelligent eye (I was watching her from the side) and those eyelashes and the tender cheek below them. . . .

"Young man! Now, young man!" I suddenly heard a voice right beside me. "Is it permissible to stare like that at strange young ladies?"

First Love

I trembled all over, I was put to confusion. Beside me, but beyond the fence, a man with close-cut black hair was standing and gazing at me with an ironical expression. The girl turned toward me at that same moment. I saw her large gray eyes in her vivid, animated face, and all that face suddenly began to quiver, to smile; her white teeth gleamed, her eyebrows were raised amusingly. I crimsoned, snatched up my gun from the ground, and, pursued by a ringing but not ill-natured laugh, ran to my room, flung myself on my bed, and covered my face with my hands. My heart was dancing within me; I felt deeply abashed and gay; I felt an agitation I had never known before.

After a rest I combed my hair, made myself tidy, and went downstairs to tea. The image of the young girl went before me; my heart ceased to dance, but it felt a pleasant twinge.

"What is the matter with you?" my father suddenly asked me. "Have you killed a rook?"

I felt like telling him everything, but I refrained and only smiled to myself. When I went to bed, for some unknown reason I spun round three or four times on one leg, greased my hair, got into bed, and slept like a log all night. In the early morning I woke for a moment, raised my head, looked around me rapturously, and fell off to sleep again.

3

"How can I make their acquaintance?" was my first thought the moment I awoke in the morning. I went out into the garden before tea, but did not go close to the fence and did not see anyone. After we had had tea I walked up and down the road in front of the house several times and took glances at the windows from this distance. . . . I thought I saw her face behind a curtain, and in my alarm I hurriedly retreated. "All the same, we must make their acquaintance," I thought as I wandered aimlessly over the sandy waste that extends beyond the Nieskuchny Gardens. "But how? That's the problem." I recalled the tiniest details of the previous day's meeting; for some reason I remembered very clearly how she had laughed at me. But while I was working myself up and making all kinds of plans, fate was already taking care of me.

While I was out, my mother received a letter from her new neighbor; it was on gray paper and sealed with a brown seal such as is used only for postal notices and to seal the corks of cheap wine-bottles. This letter, which was written in illiterate terms and slovenly handwriting, asked my mother to extend her protection to the Princess: according to her, my mother was intimately acquainted with certain important people who had the fate of the Princess and her children in their hands, as she was involved in very serious judicial cases. "I adress myself to you," she wrote, "as one noble lady to another, and moreover it is a plesure for me to have this oportunity." In conclusion she asked my mother's permission for her to call. I found my mother in an unpleasant frame of mind: my father was not at home, and she had no one with whom to discuss the letter. It was impossible not to reply to a "noble lady," and a Princess at that, but how to reply my mother could not imagine. She thought it would not be correct to write a note in French, but she herself was not very good at Russian orthography, she knew that; and she was anxious not to compromise herself. She was delighted at my arrival and at once ordered me to go to the Princess and tell her in person that my mother was always ready to do Her Excellency any service that lay in her power, and to ask her to call at one o'clock. The unexpectedly rapid fulfillment of my secret desires both delighted and frightened me. But I did not reveal the confusion into which I was plunged, and first went to my room to put on a new coat and cravat, for when at home I still went about in a jacket and turn-down collar, though I was deeply mortified at having to wear them.

4

All my body trembling uncontrollably, I entered the close and unpleasant lobby of the Zasiokins' wing and was met by an old, gray-headed servant with a dark, copper-colored face, moody little pig's eyes, and such deep furrows on the forehead and temples as I had never seen in all my life. He was carrying a picked herring backbone on a tray; shutting the door leading to the other room with his foot, he asked abruptly: "What do you want?"

"Is the Princess Zasiokina at home?" I asked.

"Vonifaty?" a jarring feminine voice shouted from the other side of the door.

The servant silently turned his back on me, revealing that the back of his livery was badly worn and had a single rusty button stamped with an armorial bearing, and went off, after setting the tray on the floor.

"Have you been to the policeman?" the same voice asked. The servant muttered something. "What? Someone come? Our neighbor's son? Well, ask him in."

The servant returned to me. "Please go into the recption room," he said as he picked up the tray from the floor. I tidied myself and went in.

I found myself in a small and not very neatly arranged room with poor furniture that looked as though it had been set out in a hurry. A woman aged about fifty, straight-haired and plain-looking, in an old green dress and with a varicolored triangular worsted neckerchief round her neck, was sitting by the window, in an armchair with a broken arm. Her small black eyes were fixed on me.

I went up to her and bowed.

"Have I the honor of speaking to Princess Zasiokina?"

"I am Princess Zasiokina. And are you Mr. V.'s son?"

"That is so. I have called with a message from my mother."

"Please sit down. Vonifaty! Where are my keys? Have you seen them?"

I told the Princess my mother's answer to her note. As she listened she tapped her fat red fingers on the windowsill, and when I had finished she fixed her eyes on me once more.

"Very good; I shall call without fail," she said. "But how young you still are! How old are you, if I may ask?"

"Sixteen," I replied with an involuntary stammer.

The Princess took some greasy, scribbled papers out of her pocket, raised them right to her nose, and began to sort them over.

"A fine age!" she said suddenly, turning and fidgeting in her chair. "But please don't stand on ceremony. I have simple ways."

"Too simple," I thought, with involuntary squeamishness running my eyes over all her unsightly figure.

At that moment another door of the reception room was swiftly flung open and the girl I had seen in the garden the previous evening entered. She raised her hand, and a derisive smile flitted over her face.

"And this is my daughter," the Princess said, pointing to the girl with her elbow. "Zenia, my dear, this is the son of our neighbor, Mr. V. What is your name, if I may ask?" She turned to me.

"Vladimir," I replied, rising, and stuttering in my agitation.

"And your patronymic?"

"Piotrovich."

"Indeed. I knew a chief of police once whose name was Vladimir Piotrovich too. Vonifaty! Don't look for the keys. I have them in my pocket."

The young girl was still gazing at me with the same smile, her eyes half-closed and her head cocked a little on one side.

"I've already seen M'sieur Voldemar," she began. (The silvery sound of her voice ran over me like a pleasant chilliness.) "You will allow me to call you that, won't you?"

"Please!" I stammered.

"Where did you see him?" her mother asked.

The young Princess did not reply. "Are you busy now?" she said, not taking her eyes off me.

"Not at all."

"Would you like to help me ball some wool? Come with me to my room."

She nodded to me and went out. I followed her.

In the room we entered the furniture was rather better and was arranged with greater taste. At that moment, however, I was not in a state to notice anything: I walked as though in a dream, and in all my being I felt an idiotically tense felicity.

The Princess sat down, picked up a skein of crimson wool, and, pointing me to a chair opposite her, carefully opened the skein and put it over my hands. All this she did without saying a word, with an amusing deliberation of movement and with the same bright and crafty smile on her slightly parted lips. She began to wind the wool onto a card folded double, and suddenly transfixed me with such a clear and swift glance that I involuntarily cast down my eyes. When her eyes, which usually were half-closed, were opened to their full extent, her face changed completely: it was as though light had flooded over it.

"What did you think of me yesterday, M'sieur Voldemar?" she asked, after a moment. "I expect you condemned me?"

"I — Princess — I didn't think anything — how could I?" I answered in some embarrassment.

"Listen!" she retorted. "You don't know me yet; I am exceedingly strange; I always like to be told the truth. I heard that you're sixteen, and I am twenty-one; you see I am much older than you, and so you should always tell me the truth — and do as I tell you," she added. "Look at me; why don't you look at me?"

I was still more embarrassed; none the less, I raised my eyes to her. She smiled, only not with her previous, but with a different, approving smile. "Look at me," she said, caressingly lowering her voice. "I don't dislike being looked at. I like your face; I have a feeling we shall be friends. And do you like me?" She added craftily.

"Princess — " I began.

"To begin with, call me Zinaida Alexandrovna; and secondly, what is this habit children" (she corrected herself) — "young people have of not saying frankly what they feel? That's all right for grown-ups. Now, you do like me, don't you?"

Though I found it very pleasant to have her talking to me so frankly, none the less I was a little annoyed. I wanted to show her that she was not dealing with a boy, and so, adopting as nonchalant and serious an air as possible, I said: "Of course I like you very much, Zinaida Alexandrovna; I have no intention of concealing that."

She shook her head deliberately. "Have you a tutor?" she suddenly asked.

"No. I haven't had a tutor for a long time."

I was lying; it was not a month since I had parted with my Frenchman.

"Oh; why, so I see; you're quite big, really."

She gently tapped my fingers. "Hold your hands straight." And she set to work diligently to wind the wool.

I took advantage of the circumstance that she did not raise her eyes and began to scrutinize her, at first surreptitiously, then more and more openly. Her face seemed even more charming than it had looked the previous evening, so fine, intelligent, and pleasant was everything about it. She was sitting with her back to the window, which was hung with a white blind; the sunlight, filtering through this blind, flooded her fluffy, golden hair, her innocent neck, her drooping shoulders and tender, untroubled breast with soft light. I looked at her, and how dear and close she grew to me! I felt that I had known her a very long time, that I had never known anything and had never even lived until

I met her. . . . She was wearing a dark, rather shabby dress and an apron; I think I would willingly have caressed every fold in that dress and that apron. The toes of her shoes peered out from under her dress: I would have bowed myself down to those shoes in adoration. "And so I am sitting in front of her," I thought; "I have made her acquaintance. . . . What happiness — really, what happiness!" I all but sprang off the chair in my rapture, but I only kicked my feet a little, like an infant enjoying some treat.

I felt as good as a fish in water, and I would have remained in that room forever; I would never have left that spot.

Her eyelids slowly rose, and again her shining eyes beamed before me, and again she smiled.

"How you are staring at me!" she said slowly, and threatened me with one finger.

I crimsoned. . . . "She understands everything, she sees everything," the thought flashed through my head. "And how can she help understanding and seeing everything?"

Suddenly there was a tapping sound in the next room, and a saber clattered.

"Zenia!" the Princess called from that room. "Belovzorov has brought you a kitten."

"A kitten!" Zinaida exclaimed, and, rising impetuously from the chair, she flung the ball of wool onto my knees and ran out.

I also rose and, laying the skein and ball of wool on the window-sill, went into the reception room and halted in astonishment: in the middle of the room a tabby kitten was lying with her paws spread out, and Zinaida was on her knees before it, carefully raising its tiny head. Close to the Princess was a flaxen and curly-haired young hussar with crimson face and goggling eyes; he covered almost all the wall space between the two windows.

"How funny it is!" Zinaida declared. "And its eyes are not gray, but green; and what big ears it has! Thank you, Victor Yegorich! You are very kind!"

The hussar, whom I recognized as one of the young men I had seen the previous evening, smiled and bowed, clattering his spurs and jingling the chain of his saber.

"You were so kind yesterday as to say that you wanted a tabby kitten with large ears — and here it is! Your word is law!" He bowed again.

First Love

The kitten squealed faintly and began to sniff the floor.

"Oh, it's hungry!" Zinaida exclaimed. "Vonifaty! Sonia! Bring some milk."

A maid in an old yellow dress, with a faded kerchief round her neck, brought in a saucer of milk and set it before the kitten. The kitten trembled, screwed up its eyes, and began to lap.

"What a rosy little tongue it has!" Zinaida observed, bending her head down almost to the floor and gazing at the animal from one side, with her eyes right by its nose.

The kitten drank till it had had enough and then began to purr, finically lifting its paws. Zinaida got up and, turning to the maid, said in an indifferent tone: "Take it out!"

"In exchange for the kitten, your little hand!" the hussar said, grinning and drawing up all his powerful body, which was tightly constricted in his new uniform.

"Both hands!" Zinaida retorted, and held out her hands to him. While he was kissing them she looked at me across her shoulder.

I stood rooted to the spot and did not know whether I ought to smile, to say something, or keep silent. Suddenly through the wide-open door leading to the lobby I caught sight of our servant Fyodor. He made signs to me. I mechanically went out to him.

"What do you want?" I asked.

"Your mother has sent for you," he said in a whisper. "She is angry because you haven't come back with a reply."

"But have I been here so long, then?"

"An hour and more."

"An hour and more!" I involuntarily repeated. Going back to the reception room, I began to take my leave and scrape my feet.

"Where are you going?" the young Princess asked me, looking round the hussar's body.

"I must go home. So I am to say" — I turned to her mother — "that you will call on my mother at one o'clock."

"Yes, you tell her that, my boy."

She hurriedly picked up a snuffbox and took a pinch so noisily that I shuddered. "Yes, tell her that," she repeated, blinking tearfully and wheezing.

I bowed once more, turned, and left the room with the feeling of awkwardness in the back that a very young man always feels when he knows people are staring after him.

"But don't forget to come and see us, M'sieur Voldemar," Zinaida called, and she again burst into a laugh.

"What is she always laughing for?" I thought as I returned home with Fyodor, who said not one word to me, but followed me with a disapproving air. My mother scolded me and wondered what I could have been doing so long in that Princess's place. I did not tell her and went off to my room. I suddenly felt very sad. . . . I tried not to cry. . . . I was jealous of that hussar!

5

The Princess kept her promise and called on my mother, who did not take any liking to her. I was not present at their meeting, but at table my mother told my father that she thought Princess Zasiokina *une femme très vulgaire*, that she had grown very tired of the Princess's requests that she should intercede with Princess Sergei on her behalf, that she was always involved in lawsuits and affairs, *des vilaines affaires d'argent*, and that she must be a terrible intriguer. My mother added, however, that she had invited the Princess and her daughter to dine with us next day (when I heard the words "and her daughter," I bent my head over my plate), because, after all, she was our neighbor, and a Princess. To which my father said he remembered now what sort of lady she was: in his youth he had known the late Prince Zasiokin, who had been very well brought up, but had been an empty and quarrelsome fellow. In society he had been known as *"le Parisien,"* because he had lived many years in Paris; at one time he had been very wealthy, but he had gambled away all his fortune. And for some unknown reason, possibly for money — though in any case he could have made a better choice, my father added with a frigid smile — he married the daughter of some lawyer's clerk and then began to indulge in speculation and ruined himself completely.

"So long as she doesn't ask us to lend her money," my mother observed.

"That is extremely possible," my father said calmly. "Does she speak French?"

"Very badly."

"Hm! But that doesn't matter. I think you said you had invited her daughter too; someone has assured me that she is a very pleasant and well-educated girl."

"Ah! In that case she doesn't take after her mother."

"Nor her father!" my father retorted. "He was educated too, but stupid!"

Mother sighed and was lost in thought. My father said no more. During this conversation I felt very awkward.

After dinner I went into the garden, but without my gun. I had pledged myself not to go near the Zasiokin garden, but an irresistible force drew me that way — and not for nothing. When still some distance from the fence, I saw Zinaida. This time she was alone. She was holding a small book in one hand and was walking slowly along the path. She did not notice me.

I all but let her pass, but suddenly I stopped short and coughed.

She turned, but did not stop; with one hand she threw back the broad blue ribbon of her round straw hat, then she looked at me, quietly smiled, and fixed her eyes on her book again.

I took off my cap and hesitated for a moment, then turned away with a heavy heart. *"Que suis-je pour elle?"* I thought (God knows why) in French.

I heard familiar steps behind me. I looked round: my father was coming toward me with his swift and easy stride.

"Is that the young Princess?" he asked me.

"Yes."

"Do you know her, then?"

"I saw her this morning when I called on her mother."

My father halted and, turning sharply on his heels, walked back. As he drew level with Zinaida he bowed to her politely. She bowed in reply, not without a look of astonishment, and let her book fall. I saw her following him with her eyes. My father always dressed exquisitely, in his own original and simple manner; but never had his figure seemed more finely proportioned, never had he worn his gray hat more beautifully on his still quite thick, curly hair.

I thought of going to Zinaida, but she did not even glance at me. She picked up her book and walked away.

6

I spent all that evening and the following morning in a despondent torpor. I remember I tried to work, and picked up Kaidanov, but the scrawling lines and pages of that famous primer flickered before me in vain. Ten times in succession I read the sentence: "Julius Cæsar was distinguished by his martial courage"; I understood not one word and threw the book down. Before dinner I again greased my hair and put on my coat and cravat.

"What are you wearing them for?" my mother asked. "You're not a student yet, and goodness knows whether you'll pass the entrance examination. And it isn't so long since you had the jacket made for you. You mustn't stop wearing it altogether."

"We're having guests," I whispered almost in despair.

"What rubbish! What sort of guests do you call them?"

I had to submit. I exchanged my coat for the jacket, but I did not take off the cravat. The Princess and her daughter arrived half an hour or so before dinner; the older woman was wearing the green dress I had already seen, had thrown a yellow shawl round her shoulders, and had put on an old-fashioned bonnet with flame-colored ribbons. She at once began to talk about her promissory notes, complained of her poverty, and was "importunate," but did not stand on ceremony in the least: she took snuff just as nosily, and shifted and fidgeted on her chair just as freely. Apparently it did not even occur to her that she was a Princess. On the other hand, Zinaida behaved very correctly, almost haughtily, like a real princess. Her face wore a look of cold immobility and importance, and I did not recognize her, did not recognize her looks or her smiles, though in this new guise also she seemed beautiful to me. She was wearing a light *barège* dress with pale blue figurework; her hair fell in long curls at the side of her cheeks, in the English fashion; this coiffure suited the cold expression of her face. My father sat next to her at dinnertime and entertained her with his own distinctive, elegant, and imperturbable courtesy. Occasionally he glanced at her, and occasionally she glanced at him, but so queerly, almost inimically. They carried on conversation in French; I remember I was astonished by the purity of her pronunciation. At table the older Princess was just as unconstrained as before; she ate a great deal and praised the cooking. My mother was obviously depressed by her and replied with a mournful disdain; from time to time my father knitted his brows a little. My mother did not take to Zinaida either. "She's so haughty," she said next day. "And what has she got to be haughty about, *avec sa mine de grisette?*"

"Evidently you've never seen grisettes," my father remarked.

"And thank goodness for that!"

"Of course, thank goodness — only, how can you pass judgment on them?"

Zinaida did not pay any attention to me whatever. Soon after dinner the Princess took her leave.

"I shall hope to have your protection, Maria Nikolaevna and Piotr Vasilievich," she said in a drawling voice to my father and mother. "What can I do? There were days — but they have passed. And here am I, an Excellency," she added with an unpleasant laugh; "but what's the good of honor if you haven't any food for dinner?" My father bowed to her respectfully and accompanied her to the door of the lobby. I stood beside him in my tailless jacket and stared at the floor, as though condemned to death. Zinaida's treatment of me had completely overcome me. But imagine my surprise when, as she walked past me, with the old gracious expression in her eyes she hurriedly whispered: "Come along at eight o'clock, do you hear, without fail. . . ." I was astonished, but she was already departing, throwing a white scarf over her head as she went.

7

At eight o'clock exactly, wearing my coat and with my hair combed up at the front, I entered the lobby of the small wing that the Princesses occupied. The old servant stared at me glumly and rose reluctantly from the bench. Merry voices could be heard coming from the reception room. I opened the door and started back in amazement. The young Princess was standing on a chair in the middle of the room, holding out a man's hat in front of her; five men were crowded round the chair. They were trying to put their hands into the hat, but she raised it and shook it vigorously. When she saw me she cried: "Wait, wait! We have a fresh guest; he must be given a ticket too." Lightly jumping down from the chair, she took me by the lapel of my coat. "Come on," she said, "what are you waiting for? Messieurs, let me introduce you. This is M'sieur Voldemar, our neighbor's son. And these," she added, turning to me and pointing to the guests one after another, "are Count Malevsky, Dr. Lushin, the poet Maidanov, retired Captain Nirmatsky, and Belovzorov, the hussar you have seen before. Please be friends, and good friends."

I was so embarrassed that I did not even bow to anyone. Dr. Lushin I recognized as the same swarthy gentleman who had so ruthlessly put me to shame in the garden. I did not know the others at all.

"Count!" Zinaida continued, "write a ticket for M'sieur Voldemar."

"That is unfair," the Count objected in a slightly Polish accent. He was a very handsome and fashionably dressed man with black hair, expressive hazel eyes, a thin white nose, and a scanty mustache above a very small mouth. "He hasn't played forfeits with us."

"It's unfair," Belovzorov and the gentleman described as a retired captain both repeated. The captain was a man about forty years of age, hideously pockmarked, with hair as frizzy as a Negro's, rather stocky, bowlegged, and wearing a military jacket without epaulets, flung round his shoulders.

"Write a ticket, I tell you," the Princess repeated. "What do you call this, mutiny? M'sieur Voldemar is with us for the first time, and today the law does not apply to him. Stop grumbling and write a ticket; that is my wish."

The Count shrugged his shoulders but, humbly bowing his head, took the pen in his white, beringed hand, tore off a piece of paper, and began to write on it.

"At any rate, do let us explain to Mr. Voldemar what it is all about," Lushin said in a scoffing tone, "for he looks completely bewildered. You see, young man, we're playing forfeits. The Princess has had to pay a forfeit, and the one who draws the lucky ticket will have the right to kiss her hand. Did you understand what I said?"

I only glanced at him and continued standing as before. But the Princess jumped onto the chair again and shook the hat. All the men drew round her, and I with the others.

"Maidanov," she said to the tall young man with emaciated face, small, shortsighted eyes, and extraordinarily long black hair; "you, as a poet, should be magnanimous and surrender your ticket to M'sieur Voldemar, so that he has two chances instead of one."

But Maidanov shook his head and whirled his hair. I was the last to thrust my hand into the hat. I drew out a ticket and unfolded it. Lord, what did I feel like when I read the words: "A kiss!"

"A kiss!" I involuntarily exclaimed.

"Bravo! He's won!" Zinaida cried. "I am glad!" She got down

from the chair and looked into my eyes so lucidly and sweetly that my heart beat violently. "But are you glad?" she asked me.

"I?" I stammered.

"Sell me your ticket," Belovzorov suddenly said ineptly right in my ear. "I'll give you a hundred rubles for it."

I gave him such an indignant look that Zinaida clapped her hands, while Lushin exclaimed: "Good lad!"

"But," Lushin went on, "I, as the master of ceremonies, am bound to see that all the rules are observed. M'sieur Voldemar, go down on one knee. That is our custom."

Zinaida stood in front of me with her head bent a little to one side, as though to examine me the better, and dignifiedly stretched out her hand. My eyes went misty; I tried to go down on one knee, but fell down on both my knees; and so clumsily did I press my lips against her fingers that I scratched the tip of my nose with her nail.

"Enough!" Lushin cried, and he helped me to rise.

We went on playing at forfeits. Zinaida seated me beside her. The forfeits she thought of! In one case she had to represent a "statue," and she chose the ugly poet Maidanov as her pedestal; she ordered him to lie face-downward, and even to tuck his head into his chest. The merriment did not cease for one moment. I was a privately and soberly educated lad, brought up in a genteel, sedate home, and all this noise and racket, this unceremonious, almost violent gaiety, these unprecedented relations with strangers, went to my head. I was just as intoxicated as if I had drunk too much wine. I began to laugh and talk even louder than the others, so that even the old Princess, who was closeted in the next room with some lawyer's clerk summoned into conference with her, came out to stare at me. But I felt so happy that, as we say, I did not care a fig and took no notice of anyone's sneers and wry looks. Zinaida continued to show preference for me and did not let me leave her side. In one forfeit I had to sit beside her, our heads covered with the one silk kerchief: I was supposed to tell her my greatest secret. I still remember how close together our heads were in that stifling, translucent, scented veil, how in that twilight her eyes shone very mildly and very close to me, and her parted lips breathed on me hotly, and I saw her teeth, and her hair tickled and scorched me. I was silent; she smiled mysteriously and roguishly and whispered at last: "Well, and now what?" But I only went red and laughed and turned away, and could hardly get my breath. We grew tired of forfeits, so we began to play a game in which we all had to stand in a circle holding a string, while she was in the middle. And my goodness! What rapture I felt when I forgot what I was doing and she gave me a strong, sharp smack on my extended fingers! And how I tried after that to pretend that I was forgetting again! But she only teased me and would not smack my fingers, though I left them extended.

What else did we do in the course of that evening! We played the piano and we sang and we danced and we acted a gypsy encampment. Nirmatsky was dressed as a bear and given salt water to drink. Count Malevsky showed us card tricks and ended by shuffling the cards and dealing himself a hand that held all the trumps, at which Lushin "ventured to congratulate him." Maidanov recited parts of his poem "The Murderer" (this was at the height of the romantic period in our literature), which he proposed to publish in a black jacket with the title in blood red. We stole the hat off the knees of the lawyer's clerk and made him do the Cossack dance as ransom; we dressed old Vonifaty in a bonnet, while Zinaida put on a man's hat. I could not tell you all we did. Only Belovzorov withdrew more and more into one corner, morose and angry. At times his eyes were suffused with blood, he flushed and looked as though at any moment he would charge down on us and scatter us in all directions, like splinters. But the Princess looked at him and threatened him with her finger, and once more he skulked in his corner.

At last we were worn out. Zinaida's mother was now ready for anything, as she herself expressed it, and no amount of shouting disturbed her; but even she felt tired and wanted to rest. Supper was served at midnight, and consisted of a piece of old, dry cheese and some cold patties of chopped ham, which I thought more tasty than any meat pie; there was only one bottle of wine, and that bottle was queer: dark, with a swollen neck, and the wine inside it was a rose color; however, no one drank any of it. When I left I was weary and happy to the point of exhaustion; at parting Zinaida squeezed my hand firmly and again smiled enigmatically.

The night breathed heavily and humidly into my flaming face; a storm appeared to be gathering; black clouds were growing and crawling over the sky, visibly changing their smoky outlines. A breeze trembled restlessly in the dark trees, and somewhere beyond the horizon thunder seemed to be grumbling to itself angrily and hollowly.

I made my way to my room through the back entrance. My servant was sleeping on the floor, and I had to step across him. He awoke, saw me, and reported that my mother had been annoyed with me again and had wanted to send for me to come home, but my father had restrained her. (I never went to bed without saying good-night to my mother and asking her blessing.) But there was nothing to be done about it now!

I told my man that I would undress and get myself to bed and put out the candle. . . . But I did not undress and I did not lie down.

I sat down on a chair, and sat there for a long time as though enchanted. What I felt was so new and so sweet: I sat looking about me and not stirring, breathing slowly, and only silently laughing at my memories from time to time, then going cold at the thought that I was in love, that this was it, this was love. Zinaida's face silently floated before me in the darkness — it floated up, and did not float past — her lips still enigmatically smiling, her eyes looking at me a little sidelong, interrogatively, thoughtfully, and tenderly, as they had at our parting. At last I rose, tiptoed over to my bed, and cautiously laid my head on the pillow without undressing, as though afraid that by some abrupt movement I would disturb the feeling with which I was overflowing. . . .

I lay down, but I did not even close my eyes. I quickly noticed that pallid gleams of light were continually flickering across the room toward me. I half raised myself and glanced at the window. Its transom showed up distinctly against the mysteriously and mournfully glimmering panes. A thunderstorm, I thought; and I was right, it was a thunderstorm. But it was a very long way off, and no thunder was to be heard; only dull, long, sheet lightning lit up the sky incessantly; it did not flash so much as flutter and quiver like the wings of a dying bird. I got up, went across to the window, and remained standing there till dawn came. . . . The lightning did not cease for a moment; it was what the common people call a "sparrows' night." I gazed at the silent sandy plain, at the dark mass of the Nieskuchny Gardens, at the yellowish façades of distant buildings, which seemed to be quivering with every feeble flash. I gazed and could not tear myself away; that mute lightning, those temperate flashes, seemed to be in accord with the mute and secret emotions that were flaming up inside me. The dawn began to break; the sunrise drew on in crimson patches. As the sun approached, the lightning grew paler and less frequent; it flickered more and more intermittently, and finally ceased, overborne by the sobering and indubitable light of the oncoming day . . .

Within me, too, my own lightnings faded. I felt a great weariness and stillness. . . . But Zinaida's image continued to hover triumphantly over my soul. Only, that very image seemed to grow composed: like a swan flying up from the reeds of a marsh, it separated from the other, unpleasant shapes surrounding it and, as I dropped off to sleep, I fell once more at its feet in a valedictory and trustful adoration.

O gentle feelings, tender sounds, the benignity and assuagement of the deeply moved soul, the melting joy of love's first emotions — where are you now, where are you now?

8

When I went down to tea next morning, my mother scolded me, but not so much as I had expected, and made me tell her how I had spent the previous evening. I replied in few words, omitting many of the details and trying to make it all appear as innocent as possible.

"All the same, they are not people *comme il faut*," Mother remarked, "and there is no reason why you should go chasing after them, instead of preparing for your examination and keeping yourself occupied."

As I knew that my mother's anxiety about my occupations was confined to these few words, I did not think it necessary to protest. But after tea my father took me by the arm and, leading me into the garden, made me tell him all I had seen at the Zasiokins' the previous evening.

My father had a strange influence over me, and our relations, too, were strange. He took hardly any interest in my education and upbringing, but he never upset me, he respected my freedom, and, if I may put it so, he was even polite to me . . . only he never let me draw close to him. I loved him, I admired him, he seemed to me the perfect pattern of a man, and, upon my word, how passionately I would have become attached to him if I had not continually felt that he was thrusting me off! On the other hand, if he wished, with just one word, one gesture, he could suddenly win my unbounded confidence in him. My soul would lay itself bare, I would talk to him as if he were an understanding friend, or an indulgent tutor . . . and then, just as abruptly, he would abandon me, and he again thrust me off, kindly and gently, but none the less he thrust me off.

Sometimes a spirit of gaiety came over him, and then he was ready to sport and romp with me like a boy (he was fond of all vigorous physical movement). Once — only once — he caressed me so tenderly that I all but burst into tears. But his gaiety and his tenderness vanished without trace, and the intimacy that had sprung up between us afforded me no hope whatever for the future — I might have dreamed it. There were times when I would study his intelligent, handsome, lucid face . . . my heart would begin to quiver, and all my being would be vehemently drawn toward him. . . . He seemed to feel what was going on inside me, he would pat me casually on the cheek, and either would go off or would occupy himself with something, or would go quite set and cold, as he alone could, and at once I would shrink and go cold too. His rare outbursts of feeling for me were never to be evoked by my mute but intelligible entreaties; they always came unexpectedly. In later days, when I pondered on my father's character, I came to the conclusion that he had no time for me, or for family life; he was fond of something else, and thoroughly enjoyed that something else. "You yourself take all you can, but never put yourself in someone else's hand; belong to yourself: that is the whole art of life," he once said to me. On another occasion I, as a young democrat, ventured to reflect on freedom in his presence (that day he was "good," as I used to say, and at such times I could talk with him about anything). "Freedom," he repeated. "But do you know what it is that can give man freedom?"

"No, what?"

"Will; his own will; and it gives him power too, which is better than freedom. Know how to desire, and then you will be free, and you will command."

First and foremost my father wanted to live . . . and he did live. Perhaps he had a presentiment that he would not be able to enjoy the "art" of life for long: he died at the age of forty-two.

I told my father all about my visit to the Zasiokins. He listened to me half-attentively, half-abstractedly, sitting on a bench and drawing in the sand with the butt of his whip. Very occasionally he smiled, and looked at me brightly and amusingly, and encouraged me to go on by asking brief questions and making interjections. At first I could not bring myself even to mention Zinaida's name, but I could not restrain myself, and I began to refer to her. My father went on smiling. Then he was lost in thought; he yawned and rose to his feet.

I remembered that on leaving the house he had ordered his horse to be saddled. He was an excellent horseman and could control the very wildest of horses.

"Shall I ride with you, Papa?" I asked him.

"No," he replied, and his face adopted its usual indifferent and kindly expression. "Go for a ride by yourself if you like; and tell the coachman I'm not going."

He turned his back on me and walked away swiftly. I followed him with my eyes; he vanished through the gate. I saw his hat moving along above the fence; he turned in at the Zasiokins' gate.

He remained there over an hour, but then went off at once to town and did not return home till the evening.

After dinner I myself went to call on the Zasiokins! I found only the old Princess in the reception room. When she saw me she scratched her head under her cap with the end of a knitting-needle and suddenly asked me if I would write out a soliciting letter for her.

"With pleasure," I replied, and sat down on the edge of a chair.

"Only write in a large letters," she said as she handed me a dirty sheet of paper. "But could you do it today, my dear?"

"I'll write it out this very day."

The door leading to the next room was opened very slightly and Zinaida's face appeared in the opening; it was pale, thoughtful, and the hair was thrown back negligently. She stared at me with great, cold eyes and quietly closed the door again.

"Zenia, Zenia!" her mother called. But Zinaida did not answer. I took away the Princess's letter and sat over it all the evening.

My "passion" began from that day. I remember I felt rather as a man must feel who has just entered the Czar's service: I had ceased to be a boy; I was in love. I have said that my passion began from that day; I could add that my torments also dated from that day. In Zinaida's absence I languished; my mind was a blank, everything dropped out of my hands, and for days on end I thought tensely only about her. . . . I languished. . . . But I felt no better in her presence. I was jealous, I realized my insignificance, I stupidly sulked and stupidly fawned; and even so an irresistible power drew me to her, and every time I crossed the threshold of her room I felt an involuntary throb of happiness. She guessed at once that I was in love with her, nor did I think to conceal the fact; she made fun of my passion, played with me, petted and tormented me. It is sweet to be the sole source, the autocratic and irresponsible cause, of another being's greatest joys and deepest sorrows — and in Zinaida's hands I was as the softest wax. For that matter, I was not the only one in love with her: all the men who visited her home went crazy over her, and she kept them all in leading strings, at her feet. She found amusement in arousing their hopes, or their fears, in twisting them round her finger at her whim (she called this knocking people against one another), and they did not even think of resisting and readily submitted to her. In all her being, so vital and beautiful, was a peculiarly enchanting blend of cunning and unconcern, artificiality and simplicity, stillness and high spirits; everything she did, or said, her every movement, was invested with a light, subtle charm, a playful strength. Her face, too, was incessantly changing, and it played too; almost in the same instant it would express derision, thoughtfulness, and passion. The most varied of feelings, light and swift, sped momentarily over her eyes and lips, like the shadows of clouds on a sunny, windy day.

She had need of every one of her devotees. Belovzorov, whom she sometimes called "my animal" and sometimes simply "mine," would readily have thrown himself into the fire for her; though he could put no hope in his mental capacity or any other qualities, he was continually proposing to her, hinting that others only talked. Maidanov answered to the poetic elements in her soul: though he was rather cold, like almost all authors, he tensely assured her, and possibly himself too, that he worshipped her, he lauded her in innumerable poems and read them to her with an unnatural yet sincere rapture. She felt sympathy for him, and at the same time she rather made fun of him; she did not really believe him and, after listening to his effusions, made him read Pushkin, in order to clear the air, as she said. Dr. Lushin, mocking and cynical of speech, knew her better than did any of the others, and loved her more than any of the others, though he ran her down behind her back and to her face. She respected him, but she did not release him and sometimes took a particular, malignant pleasure in making him feel that he, too, was in her hands. "I am a coquette, I am heartless, I have an actress's nature," she said to him once in my presence. "Well, all right! Give me your hand; I'll stick a pin in it; you will feel shame in front of this young man, it will hurt you; but all the same, Mr. Self-righteous, you've got to laugh!" Lushin flushed, turned away and bit his lips, but finished by putting out his hand. She pricked him, and he did begin to laugh . . . and she laughed too as she pushed the pin in quite deep and looked into his eyes, which vainly tried to avoid her gaze.

Least of all could I understand the relations between Zinaida and Count Malevsky. He was good-looking, adroit, and intelligent, but even I, a sixteen-year-old lad, found something dubious, something false in him, and I was amazed that Zinaida did not notice it. But perhaps she did notice this falsity and was not repelled by it. Her unsatisfactory upbringing, her strange acquaintances and habits, her mother's constant presence, the poverty and disorder of the home — everything, beginning with the very liberty that this young woman enjoyed, and her consciousness of superiority to everybody around her, developed a half-contemptuous negligence and lack of squeamishness in her. There were times when it did not matter what happened — Vonifaty might come to report that there was no sugar in the house, some petty calumny would come out, or the guests would quarrel with one another — she only shook her curls, said: "It's all nothing," and was not worried in the least.

On the other hand, there were times when all my blood boiled as I saw Malevsky go up to her, his body swaying craftily, like a fox, and then elegantly lean on the back of her chair and whisper into her ear with a self-satisfied and ingratiating little smile, while she folded her arms on her breast, looked at him attentively, and she too smiled and gently swayed her head.

"What pleasure do you get out of seeing Monsieur Malevsky?" I asked her one day.

"But he has such handsome little mustaches!" she replied. "In any case, it's nothing to do with you."

"You mustn't think I'm in love with him," she said to me on another occasion. "No, I'm not. I cannot love a man like him, a man I have to look down at. I need someone who will break me. . . . But I shall never meet such a man, thank God! I shall never be caught by anyone; no, never!"

"So you will never fall in love?"

"But how about you? Don't I love you, then?" she said, and struck me on my nose with the end of her glove.

Yes, Zinaida was always making fun of me. For three weeks I saw her every day, and there was little that she did not do with me! She rarely called on us, and I did not regret this; in our house she was transformed into a young lady, into a young princess, and I shunned her. I was afraid of betraying myself in front of my mother, who was very unfriendly to Zinaida and watched us inimically. I was not so afraid of Father; he did not appear to notice me, and he talked only little with Zinaida, though when he did he talked with particular intelligence and meaning in his words. I stopped working, reading, I even stopped wandering about the district and riding. Like a beetle tied by one leg, I continually hovered about the home of my beloved; I think I would have remained there forever . . . but that was impossible: my mother grumbled at me, and sometimes Zinaida herself drove me away. Then I locked myself in my room or went off to the very end of the garden, climbed onto the ruins of a lofty stone conservatory, and, dangling my feet from the wall overlooking the road, sat there for hours and gazed and gazed, seeing nothing. Around me white butterflies lazily fluttered over the dusty nettles, a saucy sparrow settled not far away on a broken red brick and irritatingly chirruped, incessantly twisting and turning all its body and spreading wide its tail; the rooks, still distrustful of me, occasionally cawed as they sat high up on the bare crown of a birch tree, the sun and the wind played gently among the tree's supple branches, from time to time the sounds of the bells of the Donskoi Monastery floated calmly and despondently to my ears; but I sat, gazed, listened, and was entirely filled with a nameless feeling that included all feelings: sadness, and joy, and presentiment of the future, and desire, and fear of life. But at that time I understood nothing of all this, and I could not have given a name to any of the feelings that possessed me, or else I would have given all of it just one name, the name of Zinaida.

But Zinaida went on playing with me, like a cat with a mouse. At one moment she would flirt with me, and I grew excited and melted like wax; the next instant she drove me away, and I did not dare to go near her, did not dare to glance at her.

I remember she was very cold to me for several days in succession; I grew quite diffident, and when I timidly went to call on them I tried to keep near the old Princess, even though just then she was scolding and shouting a great deal: she was in a bad way with her promissory notes, and she had already had to see the police twice.

One day I was passing the well-known fence in the garden when I happened to see Zinaida: she was sitting very still on the grass, resting her head on both hands. I tried quietly to retreat, but she suddenly raised her head and beckoned to me imperatively. I was petrified: at first I did not understand her gesture. She repeated it. I at once jumped over the fence and ran up to her joyfully; but she halted me with a look and pointed to the path two steps away from her. In my confusion, not knowing what to do, I went down on my knees at the edge of the path. She was so pale, and such a bitter sorrow, such profound weariness, was expressed in all her features that my heart sank and I muttered involuntarily: "What is the matter?"

She stretched out her hand, pulled up some weed, bit it, and threw it away, as far as she could throw it.

"Do you love me very much?" she said at last. "Do you?"

I made no answer; and besides, why should I answer?

"Yes," she said, looking at me as before. "That is true. Just the same eyes," she added, then was lost in thought and covered her face with her hands. "Everything has grown repulsive to me," she whispered. "I would go off to the end of the world; I cannot bear this, I cannot cope with it. . . . And what awaits me in the future? . . . Ah, it is hard for me. . . . My God, how hard!"

"Why is it?" I asked timidly.

She did not answer and only shrugged her shoulders. I re-

378

mained on my knees, looking at her with deep despondency. Every word she uttered was a stab in my heart. I think that at that moment I would willingly have given my life if only she had ceased to grieve. I looked at her and, still not understanding why she was so depressed, I vividly pictured her coming suddenly, in an outburst of uncontrollable sorrow, into the garden and falling to the ground as though mown down. It was bright and green all around us; the wind was rustling among the leaves of the trees and occasionally swaying the long cane of a raspberry above Zinaida's head. Somewhere doves were cooing, and the bees were humming as they flew low over the scanty grass. Above us the sky was a gracious azure — but I felt so sad. . . .

"Say some poetry to me," she said in an undertone, and leaned on her elbows. "I like you to say poems. You sing them, but that's nothing, that's the way of youth. Say 'On the Hills of Georgia' [1] to me. Only sit down first."

I sat down and recited "On the Hills of Georgia."

" 'That my heart simply cannot help loving' " — Zinaida repeated the line. "That is where poetry is so good: it tells of something that is not, something that not only is better than the reality, but is even more like the truth. . . . 'That my heart simply cannot cease loving.' It would like to, but it cannot." She was silent again and suddenly started and rose. "Let's go. Maidanov is with Mamma; he brought me his poem, but I left him. And now he is upset too — but it cannot be helped. You will find out some day — only don't be angry with me!"

She hurriedly squeezed my hand and ran off in front. We returned to the house. Maidanov began to read us his "Murderer," which had just been printed; but I did not listen to it. He shouted out his four-foot iambics in a singsong voice; the rhythms alternated and jingled like sleighbells, empty and loud; but I gazed continually at Zinaida and continually tried to fathom the meaning of her last words.

> *"Or is it that a secret rival*
> *Suddenly has conquered thee?"*

Maidanov exclaimed in a nasal tone, and my eyes met Zinaida's eyes. She let them drop and faintly blushed. I saw her blush, and I went cold with alarm. I had already felt jealous, but only at

[1] An eight-line, one-stanza poem by Pushkin. (Tr.)

that moment did the thought that she was in love flash through my head. "My God! She's fallen in love!"

10

Now I was really tormented. I racked my brains, I thought, and thought again, and watched her persistently, though as far as possible secretly. A change had occurred in her, that was evident. Now she went off for walks by herself, and long walks too. Sometimes she did not come out of her room when there were visitors, but sat there for hours. This had not formerly been her habit. I suddenly became — or thought I became — extremely observant. "Isn't it he? Or perhaps it is he?" I asked myself, anxiously considering one devotee after another. Secretly I thought Count Malevsky more dangerous than the others, though for Zinaida's sake I felt ashamed of admitting this possibility.

My powers of observation did not extend beyond my own nose, and my secrecy probably did not deceive anybody; at least, Dr. Lushin soon saw through me. By the way, he, too, had changed of late: he had grown thinner, and though he laughed just as much, his laugh was more hollow, evil, and curt; his previous light irony and exaggerated cynicism were replaced by an involuntary nervous irritability.

"What are you always dragging along here for, young man?" he asked me one day when he was alone with me in the Zasiokins' reception room. (The young Princess had not yet returned from a walk, and her mother could be heard on the mezzanine floor loudly scolding her maid.) "You ought to be studying and working while you are young; but you — what are you doing?"

"You don't know whether I work or not at home," I retorted, not without a touch of hauteur, but also in some embarrassment.

"What work is there to be done here? That's not what is worrying you. But I won't argue with you — at your age this is to be expected. Only your choice is far from commendable. Don't you see the kind of house this is?"

"I don't understand you," I remarked.

"You don't understand? So much the worse for you. I consider it my duty to warn you. People like me, old bachelors, may call here with safety, what can happen to us? We have been well steeled, nothing whatever can make any holes in us. But you've still got a delicate skin; and the air here is injurious to you, believe me. You may catch the infection."

"What do you mean?"

"What I say. Tell me, are you really well, even now? Are you in any normal state? Is what you are feeling of any value to you, any good to you?"

"Well, and what am I feeling?" I said, though in my heart of hearts I had to admit that he was right.

"Ah, young man, young man!" he went on in a tone of voice that suggested there was something very insulting to me in those two words. "What are you trying to be clever for? After all, thank God you still reveal in your face what is going on in your soul. But there, why talk? I myself would not come here if — " (he clenched his teeth) — "if I were not just as big a fool as you are. Only this is the thing that amazes me: how is it that you, with your intelligence, don't perceive what is happening all around you?"

"But what is happening, then?" I retorted, and I went tense with expectation.

The doctor looked at me with derisive commiseration.

"And I'm a fine one too," he said, apparently to himself. "Much need I have to say all this to him! In a word," he added, raising his voice, "I repeat: this atmosphere is not good for you. You like being here; but then, why shouldn't you? It is pleasant to smell the scents of a conservatory, only you cannot go and live in it. Now take my advice and go back to Kaidanov."

The Princess entered and began to complain to him of the toothache. A little later Zinaida returned.

"Now do scold her, doctor," her mother said. "All day she is drinking nothing but ice water, and is it really good for her, with her weak chest?"

"Why do you do that?" Lushin asked Zinaida.

"What harm is there in it?"

"What harm is there in it? You may catch a chill and die."

"Really? Surely not? And in any case, what of it? If that is the way I am to go."

"You don't say!" the doctor snorted. Zinaida's mother went out.

"You don't say!" Zinaida repeated. "Is life so cheerful, after

381

all? Look around you. . . . Well, are you satisfied? Or do you think that I don't realize it all, don't feel it all? I enjoy drinking ice water, and can you seriously assure me that such a life is so worth while that it is not to be risked for a moment of enjoyment? . . . I won't speak of happiness."

"That's just it," Lushin remarked. "Caprice and independence: those two words sum up all your being, they express the whole of your character."

She laughed a nervous laugh.

"You've missed the post, doctor. You are not very good at observation, you're left behind. Put your spectacles on. I am not interested in caprices now; making a fool of you, making a fool of myself — how very cheerful! And as for independence — M'sieur Voldemar," she suddenly cried, stamping her little foot, "don't pull that melancholy face. I cannot stand it when people show me commiseration." She swiftly left the room.

"This atmosphere is bad for you, young man; very bad," Lushin said to me once more.

II

That evening all the usual guests were gathered in the Zasiokins' reception room; I was among them.

The conversation turned to Maidanov's poem. Zinaida praised it, and quite sincerely. "But do you know what?" she said to him. "If I were a poet I would choose other subjects. Perhaps it is all nonsense, but sometimes strange thoughts come into my head, especially when I am lying awake, before dawn, when the sky begins to turn rosy and gray. For instance, I would — You won't laugh at me?"

"No! No!" we all exclaimed with one accord.

"I would picture a whole company of young girls in a large boat on a quiet river at night," she went on, folding her hands over her chest and gazing to one side. "The moon is shining, and they are all in white and wearing garlands of white flowers, and they're singing something, a kind of hymn, you know."

"I understand, I understand; go on," Maidanov said in a meaningful and dreamy tone.

"Suddenly there is noise, and laughter, torches, tambourines on the bank. . . . It is a crowd of bacchantes running with singing and clamor. And here you have to describe the scene, Mr. Poet.

. . . Only I would like the torches to be crimson and smoking a great deal, and the bacchantes' eyes must be glittering beneath their garlands, and the garlands should be of a dark color. And don't forget the tigerskins and the goblets . . . and gold, lots of gold."

"But where is the gold to be?" Maidanov asked, throwing back his straight hair and dilating his nostrils.

"Where? On their shoulders, on their arms, on their legs, everywhere. They say that in ancient times the women wore gold bangles round their ankles. The bacchantes call to the girls in the boat to join them. The girls have stopped singing their hymn — they cannot go on with it — but they do not stir. The river carries them to the bank. And now, suddenly, one of them quietly rises. . . . This must be described very well: how she quietly stands up in the moonlight, and how her friends are afraid. . . . She has stepped over the edge of the boat, the bacchantes surround her, they dash off into the night, into the darkness. . . . Here you must describe the smoke as floating in great billows, and everything is confused. Only their shrieks are to be heard, and her garland is left lying on the bank."

She was silent. ("Oh, she has fallen in love indeed!" I thought again.)

"And is that all?" Maidanov asked.

"Yes," she replied.

"That cannot be the subject for a whole poem," he said seriously. "But I shall make use of your idea in a lyric."

"In the romantic genre?" Malevsky asked.

"Of course, in the romantic genre, the Byronic."

"But in my view Hugo is better than Byron," the young Count said with a negligent air. "He is more interesting."

"Hugo is a first-class writer," Maidanov retorted, "and my friend Tonkosheev, in his Spanish novel El Trovador —"

"Ah, that is the book with the question marks round the wrong way, isn't it?" Zinaida interrupted him.

"Yes, that's the way the Spaniards write it. I was about to say that Tonkosheev —"

"Now you'll start arguing about classicism and romanticism again," Zinaida once more interrupted him. "I'd rather have a game —"

"Of forfeits?" Lushin broke in.

"No, forfeits are boring; we'll play comparisons." (This was a game she herself had invented; some object was named, and each player tried to compare it with something else, and the prize went to the one who made the best comparison.) She went across to the window. The sun had only just set; long, crimson clouds were floating high in the heavens.

"What are those clouds like?" she asked, and went on without waiting for us to answer: "I think they are like those purple sails on Cleopatra's golden vessel when she sailed to meet Antony. Do you remember, Maidanov? You told me all about it recently."

Like Polonius in *Hamlet*, we all decided that the clouds did remind us of those very sails, and that not one of us could ever think of a better comparison.

"But how old was Antony then?" she asked.

"I'm sure he was a young man," Malevsky remarked.

"Yes, he was young" Maidanov confirmed in a tone of conviction.

"Pardon me!" Lushin exclaimed; "he was over forty."

"Over forty," Zinaida repeated, giving him a swift glance.

I went home soon after. "She's in love," my lips involuntarily whispered. "But with whom?"

12

The days passed. Zinaida grew more and more strange, more and more incomprehensible. One day I went to see her and found her sitting on a rush chair with her head pressed against the sharp edge of the table. She straightened up. . . . All her face was wet with tears.

"Ah! So it's you!" she said with a harsh, sneering smile. "Come here."

I went to her; she laid her hand on my head, suddenly seized my hair, and began to twist it.

"That hurts," I said at last.

"Ah! So it hurts, does it? But doesn't it hurt me? Doesn't it?" she repeated.

"Oh!" she cried out suddenly as she saw that she had torn out a thin strand of hair. "What have I done? Poor M'sieur Voldemar!"

She carefully straightened out the strand of hair, wound it round her finger, and twisted it into a little ring.

"I shall put your hair in a medallion, and I shall wear it," she said, while her eyes glittered with tears. "Perhaps that will comfort you a little. . . . But now good-by."

I returned home, to find an unpleasant situation awaiting me. My mother was having a scene with my father. She was reproaching him with something or other, but he, as usual, was coldly and courteously silent, and not long after, he drove off. I could not catch what my mother was saying, nor was I particularly interested. I remember only that afterward she sent for me to go to her room and talked in a very dissatisfied tone about my visits to the Princess, who, in her words, was *une femme capable de tout*. I kissed her hand (I always did that when I wanted to cut short the conversation) and went to my room. Zinaida's tears had baffled me completely. I simply did not know what to make of it all, and I, too, was ready to cry: after all, I was a child, despite my sixteen years. Now I no longer thought of Malevsky, though Bolovzorov grew more and more threatening every day and looked at the shifty Count like a wolf at a sheep. Indeed, I did not think of anything or anybody. I was lost in conjecture, and was always going off to lonely spots. I grew especially fond of the conservatory. I would climb up to the top of the high wall, would sit down, and go on sitting there, such an unhappy, lonely, and sorrowful lad that I began to feel sorry for myself. And how comforting did I find those mournful feelings, how I reveled in them!

Well, one day, as I was sitting on the wall, gazing into the distance and listening to the church bells, suddenly something passed over me . . . like a little breeze; not a shiver, but literally a waft, literally a sensation that someone was in the vicinity. . . . I looked down. Below me Zinaida was hurriedly walking along the road; she was in a gray dress and had a rose-colored parasol over her shoulder. She saw me, halted, and, throwing back the brim of her straw hat, raised her velvety eyes to me.

"What are you doing up there, so high?" she asked me with a strange smile. "Listen! You're always declaring that you love me; jump down here to me, if you really do love me."

She hardly had time to say the words before I flew down just as though someone had pushed me in the back. The wall was about fourteen feet high. I reached the ground on my feet, but the drop was so great that I could not keep my balance: I fell and lost consciousness for a moment. When I came to, without opening my eyes I felt that Zinaida was kneeling beside me. "My dear boy," she said as she bent over me, and an anxious tenderness sounded in her voice; "what made you do that, what made you do as I told you? . . . You see, I love you. . . . Get up."

Her breast rose and fell beside me, her hands touched my head, and suddenly — ah, what happened to me then! — her soft, fresh lips began to cover all my face with kisses . . . they touched my lips. . . . But then she must have guessed by the expression of my face that I had come round, though I had not opened my eyes, for, swiftly rising, she said: "Now get up, you madcap, you stupid! What are you lying in the dust for?" I got up. "Hand me my parasol," she said; "I dropped it somewhere. And don't stare at me like that. . . . What a stupid thing to do! You haven't hurt yourself, have you? I expect you've stung yourself in the nettles. Don't stare at me, I tell you. Oh, he doesn't understand a thing, he doesn't say a word," she added, as though to herself. "Go home, M'sieur Voldemar, and brush yourself off, and don't dare to follow me or I'll be angry, and then never again — "

She did not finish the sentence and briskly walked away, while I sat up in the road. My legs would not support me. The nettles had stung my hands, my back ached, and my head was swimming, but the feeling of bliss that I experienced at that moment has never visited me again. It was like a pleasant pain in all my limbs, and it was resolved at last in rapturous jumps and exclamations of joy. Truly, I was still a child.

13

I was so gay and proud all that day, I retained the feeling of Zinaida's kisses so vividly on my face, I remembered her every word with such shuddering rapture, I cherished my unexpected happiness so deeply that I began to feel frightened, I did not even wish to see her, the cause of these new sensations. I felt that now I could demand nothing more of fate, that now I ought to "sigh deeply for the last time, and die." On the other hand, when I went to call on the Zasiokins next day, I felt great embarrassment, which I vainly tried to conceal beneath a modest jauntiness, proper to a man who wishes to indicate that he can keep a secret. Zinaida received me very simply, without any sign of agitation; she only threatened me with her finger and asked whether I had any bruises. All my modest jauntiness and mysterious secrecy vanished in a moment, and with it my embarrassment. Of course, I had not expected anything in particular, but Zinaida's calm was like a douche of cold water. I realized that in her eyes I was a child, and I felt very miserable. She walked backward and forward, smiling swiftly whenever she glanced at me; but her thoughts were far away, I saw that clearly. . . . "Shall I be the first to refer to yesterday?" I thought. "Shall I ask where she was off to in such a hurry, so that I can find out definitely? . . ." But I only dismissed the idea and sat down in a corner.

Belovzorov came in; I was glad to see him.

"I haven't found you a riding-horse, not a quiet one, yet," he began in a harsh tone. "Freitag says he has one, but I'm not sure about it. I'm afraid."

"What are you afraid of?" Zinaida inquired. "May I ask?"

"What am I afraid of? Why, you cannot ride yet. God preserve us from anything happening! And what is this mad idea that has suddenly come into your head?"

"Well, that's my business, M'sieur my animal. In that case I shall ask Piotr Vasilich." (My father's name was Piotr Vasilich, and I was surprised to hear her mention his name so lightly and easily, as though she was quite sure of his readiness to serve her.)

"So that's it?" Belovzorov retorted. "So it's with him that you want to go riding?"

"Either with him or with someone else, it makes no difference to you. In any case it won't be with you."

"Won't be with me?" Belovzorov repeated. "As you wish. What of it? I'll get you a horse."

"Only, listen, I don't want any old nag. I warn you that I want to gallop."

"Gallop by all means. But whom are you going to ride with? Malevsky, by any chance?"

"And why not, warrior knight? Now calm down," she added, "and don't flash your eyes. I'll take you with me too. You know what I think about Malevsky now — pooh!" She shook her head.

"You say that just to console me," he snorted.

Zinaida half closed her eyes. "Does it console you, then? Oh, oh, oh, you warrior!" she said at last, as though she could not think of anything else to call him. "And what about you, M'sieur Voldemar? Would you go riding with us?"

"I'm not fond of riding — with lots of other people," I muttered without raising my eyes.

"So you prefer it to be tête-à-tête? Well, the free has his choice, the saved has — paradise," she said, sighing. "Go and see what you can do, Belovzorov. I need a horse for tomorrow."

"All very well, but where are we to get the money?" her mother intervened.

Zinaïda knitted her brows.

"I shan't ask you for it. Belovzorov will give me credit."

"He will, he certainly will," the Princess replied, and suddenly shouted at the top of her voice: "Dunia!"

"*Maman*, I have given you a bell to ring," Zinaïda observed.

"Dunia!" the old woman called again.

Belovzorov took his leave; I went with him. Zinaïda did not detain me.

14

Next morning I rose early, cut myself a stick, and went for a walk out beyond the city turnpike. I thought I would walk off my misery. The day was beautiful, bright, and not too hot; a cheerful, fresh breeze was roving over the earth, and it blew and played gently, stirring everything and disturbing nothing. I wandered a long time over the hills, through the forest; I did not feel happy — I had left home with the intention of giving myself over to dejection; but my youth, the fine weather, the fresh air, the pleasure of the swift walk, the delight of lying alone on the thick grass, all had their way: the memory of those unforgettable words, of those kisses, again forced itself upon my soul. It was pleasant to think that at all events Zinaïda would have to admit my resolution, my heroism. . . . "She may find others better than I," I thought, "and let her! On the other hand, others only say they'll do a thing, but I do it. And what else couldn't I do for her!" My imagination began to run riot. I imagined how I would save her from the hands of enemies, how, all streaming with blood, I would wrest her from a dungeon, how I would die at her feet. I remembered a picture that hung in our reception room; it depicted Maleque Adèle carrying off Mathilde [1] . . . and at that very moment my attention was distracted by the

[1] The hero and heroine of *Mathilde*, by the French woman novelist Marie Cottin (1770–1807).

sight of a great spotted woodpecker, which fussily climbed the slender trunk of a birch and peered anxiously out from behind it, first to the right, then to the left, like a musician from behind the neck of his double-bass.

Then I began to sing: "Not white are the snows," and went on to a ballad well known at that time, "I wait for thee, whenas the playful zephyr"; then I began to declaim Yermak's apostrophe to the stars, from Khomyakov's tragedy of the same name; I would have tried my hand at writing something in a sentimental style, I even thought of the line that was to end the poem: "O Zinaida, Zinaida!" But nothing came of it. Meanwhile the dinner hour was approaching. I dropped down into a valley; a narrow, sandy path wound along it in the direction of the city. I followed this path. . . . The hollow drumming of horse-hoofs sounded behind me. I looked round, involuntarily halted, and removed my cap: my father and Zinaida were riding toward me, side by side. My father was saying something to her, leaning all his body across and resting his hand on her horse's neck. He was smiling. Zinaida was listening to him without speaking, her eyes strictly cast down and her lips compressed. At first I saw no one else, but some moments later Belovzorov appeared round a bend in the valley; he was in his hussar uniform, with a pelisse, and was riding a foaming black horse. The good horse shook its head, snorted, and fretted; the rider was continually reining it in and spurring it on. I stepped aside. My father gathered up his reins and drew away from Zinaida; she slowly raised her eyes to him, and they both set off at a gallop. . . . Belovzorov tore after them, his saber clattering. "He's as crimson as a lobster," I thought. "And she — why is she so pale? They've been riding all the morning, and yet she's pale."

I hastened my steps and arrived home just before dinnertime. My father, who had washed and changed his clothes, was already sitting by my mother's chair and reading a *feuilleton* from the *Journal des débats* to her in his even, musical voice. But my mother was only half listening; when she saw me, she asked me where I had been all day, and added that she did not like people going off God knows where and God knows with whom. I felt like replying: "I have been for a walk by myself"; but I looked at my father, and for some reason I kept silent.

During the next five or six days I hardly saw Zinaida at all; she pleaded that she was unwell, which, however, did not prevent the usual visitors from reporting for duty, as they themselves put it — all except Maidanov, who grew depressed and bored as soon as he had no chance to rhapsodize. Belovzorov sat moodily in a corner, red of face, his coat tightly buttoned up. An unpleasant smiled roved continually over Count Malevsky's thin features. The Count certainly had fallen out of favor with Zinaida and now waited diligently on the old Princess, even driving with her in a hired carriage to see the Governor General. This journey proved a failure, however, and even led to some unpleasantness for Malevsky; they reminded him of some incident or other in which he had been involved with road engineers, and he had to plead in his justification that at that time he was lacking in experience. Lushin called a couple of times every day, but did not remain long. I was a little afraid of him after our last talk, but at the same time I was genuinely drawn toward him. One day he went for a walk with me in the Nieskuchny Gardens; he was very good-natured and amiable, told me the names and properties of various herbs and flowers, and suddenly went off at a tangent and exclaimed, striking himself on the forehead: "But I, fool that I am, thought she was a flirt! Evidently it is pleasant to sacrifice oneself for others!"

"What are you trying to convey?" I asked him.

"I'm not trying to convey anything to *you*," he retorted vehemently.

Zinaida avoided me: my arrival always made an unpleasant impression on her, as I could not help noticing. She involuntarily turned away from me — involuntarily, that was what made it so bitter, what upset me most of all. But there was nothing I could do about it, and I tried to keep out of her sight and watched over her only from a distance, which was not always possible. As before, something incomprehensible was happening to her: her features changed, she changed altogether. One warm, still evening I was particularly struck by the change that had occurred in her. I was sitting on a low bench under a spreading elder bush; I was fond of this spot, for from it I could see the window of Zinaida's room. I was sitting there, and above my head amid the darkened foliage a little bird was fidgeting; a gray kitten, arching its back, cautiously stole into the garden, and the first May bugs were buzzing noisily in the air, which was still translucent, though the day was fading. I sat and gazed at the window and waited to see whether it would open. Yes, it did open, and Zinaida appeared at it. She was wearing a white dress, and she herself, her face, her shoulders, her arms, were all as white as a sheet. She stood a long time without stirring and gazed a long time fixedly from under her wrinkled brows. I had not realized that she could look like that. Then she clenched her fists, strongly, very strongly, shook her curls, and, nodding with an air of decision, slammed the window shut again.

Three days later I met her in the garden. I tried to slip away, but she herself stopped me.

"Give me your hand," she said with all her former kindness. "You and I haven't had a talk for a long time."

I glanced at her. Her eyes were beaming mildly, and her face was smiling, as though through a mist.

"Are you still unwell?" I asked her.

"No, it's all past now," she replied as she picked a small red rose. "I'm a little tired, but that will pass too."

"And will you be again as you were before?" I asked.

She raised the rose to her face, and I had the impression that the brilliant color of the petals was reflected in her cheeks. "Have I changed, then?" she asked.

"Yes, you have changed," I replied in a low voice.

"I have been cold to you, I know," she began. "But you shouldn't have taken any notice of it. . . . I could not be otherwise. But why talk about it?"

"You don't want me to love you, that's what it is," I exclaimed moodily in an involuntary outburst.

"You're wrong; do go on loving me, but not as before."

"How, then?"

"We shall be friends, that's how." She held out the rose for me to smell. "Listen; after all, I am much older than you. I could quite well be your aunt, really I could; or if not your aunt, then your elder sister. But you —"

"You regard me as a child," I interrupted her.

"Why, yes. you are a child, but a dear, good, intelligent child whom I love very much. Do you know what? From today I appoint you my page; and you must not forget that pages should never leave their mistresses' side. Here is the token of your new dignity," she added, putting the rose in my buttonhole. "A token of my favor."

"I have had other favors from you in the past," I muttered.

"Ah!" she said, and looked sidelong at me. "What a memory he has! Well, what if I did? I'm just as ready now."

And, bending toward me, she printed a pure, tranquil kiss on my forehead.

I only gazed at her; but she turned away and went toward the house, saying: "Follow me, my page." I followed her, continually in a muse. "Is this gentle and sober-minded girl the same Zinaida whom once I knew?" I thought. "Surely not?" Even her walk seemed more staid, and all her figure more majestic and harmonious.

But my goodness! With what new strength did my love flame up within me!

16

After dinner guests again gathered in the Zasiokins' reception room, and Zinaida came out to join them. All the company was present that had assembled on that first unforgettable evening. Even Nirmatsky dragged himself along. This time Maidanov was the first to arrive; he brought some new verse. We played forfeits again, but now they were lacking in the previous ingenuity, and there was not the former foolery and hubbub; the gypsy element had vanished. Zinaida set a new mood for our gathering. I sat beside her, as was my right as a page. Among other things she suggested that the one who drew a forfeit should tell a dream he had had. But this was not a success. The dreams proved either uninteresting (Belovzorov had dreamed that he fed his horse on carp, and that his mount had a wooden head) or unnatural, invented. . . . Maidanov treated us to a whole novel: it included graveyard vaults, and angels with lyres, and flowers that talked . . . and sounds coming from afar. Zinaida would not let him finish. "Now we have begun to make up stories," she said, "let each of us tell some story, only it must be really made up." It fell to Belovzorov to begin.

The young hussar was disconcerted. "I can't think of anything," he exclaimed.

First Love

"What nonsense!" Zinaida rebuked him. "Imagine, for instance, that you are married, and tell us how you would spend the time with your wife. Would you keep her locked in?"

"I would keep her locked in."

"And would you sit with her yourself?"

"Of course I would."

"Excellent. But supposing she got bored with all this and was false to you?"

"I would kill her."

"But supposing she ran away?"

"I would go after her, and I would kill her just the same."

"Yes, but supposing I were your wife, what would you do then?"

He was silent for a moment, then replied: "I would kill myself."

Zinaida laughed. "I see your song isn't a long one."

She herself drew the second forfeit. She gazed up at the ceiling and was lost in thought. "Now listen to what I have made up," she said at last, "Imagine a magnificent palace, a summer night, and a marvelous ball. The ball is being given by the young Queen. Everywhere there is gold, marble, crystal, silk, lights, amber, flowers, incense, all the whims of luxury."

"You're fond of luxury, aren't you?" Lushin interrupted.

"Luxury is beautiful," she retorted. "I am fond of all beautiful things."

"More than fine things?" he asked.

"That is too subtle, and I don't understand it. Don't interrupt me. And so, it is a magnificent ball. There are a large number of guests, they are all young, fine, and brave, they are all madly in love with the Queen."

"But aren't there any women among the guests?" Malevsky asked.

"No — but wait, yes, there are."

"And they're all ugly?"

"They're all charming, but all the men are in love with the Queen. She is tall and graceful . . . she has a small gold diadem on her black hair."

I gazed at Zinaida, and at that moment she seemed so much taller than the rest of us, and such lucid intelligence and such authority beamed from her white forehead, from her knitted brows, that I thought: "You yourself are this Queen."

"They all crowd round her," she continued, "they all make her highly flattering speeches."

"But is she fond of flattery?" Lushin asked.

"How unbearable you are! You're always interrupting. . . . Who doesn't like flattery?"

"Just one last question," Malevsky interposed. "Has the Queen a husband?"

"I hadn't thought about that. No, why should she have a husband?"

"Of course," Malevsky caught her up; "why should she have a husband?"

"*Silence!*" Maidanov, who spoke French badly, exclaimed in French.

"*Merci,*" Zinaida said to him. "And so the Queen listens to these speeches, she listens to the music, but her eyes are not on any of her guests. Six windows are open from top to bottom, from ceiling to floor, and beyond them is the dark sky with great stars, and the dark garden with great trees. The Queen is gazing into the garden. There, by the trees, is a fountain; in the dusk it shows up white, and long, very long, like an apparition. Through the talk and the music the Queen hears the quiet splashing of the water; she gazes and thinks: 'All you gentlemen are of noble birth, you are all intelligent, and wealthy, you crowd round me, you treasure my every word, every one of you is ready to die at my feet, I rule over you. . . . But there, by the fountain, by that splashing water, the one I love, the one who rules over me, is standing and waiting for me. He is wearing neither sumptuous attire nor precious gems; no one knows him, but he is waiting for me and is sure that I shall come. And I shall go to him, and there is no power that could halt me when I desire to go to him and remain with him, and to be lost with him there in the darkness of the garden, beneath the rustling of the trees, beneath the splashing of the fountain.'"

She was silent.

"Is this — all made up?" Malevsky asked craftily.

Zinaida did not even look at him.

"But, gentlemen, what would we do," Lushin suddenly asked, "if we were among those guests and knew about that fortunate one by the fountain?"

"Wait, wait!" Zinaida interrupted him. "I myself will tell you what each of you would do. You, Belovzorov, would challenge him to a duel; you, Maidanov, would write an epigram on him. But no, you don't know how to write epigrams; you would write long iambic verse about him, in the manner of Barbier,[1] and you would publish your poem in the *Telegraph*. You, Nirmatsky, would borrow from him. . . . No, you would lend him money at interest. You, Doctor — " She paused. "As for you, I don't know what you would do."

"In my capacity as court physician," he said, "I would advise the Queen not to give balls if she hadn't time for her guests."

"Perhaps you'd be right. But you, Count — "

"And I?" Malevsky asked, with his unpleasant smile.

"You would offer him a poisoned sweet."

Malevsky's face twisted a little in a grimace and looked Jewish for a moment, but he immediately burst into a roar of laughter.

"And as for you, Voldemar — " Zinaida continued. "But no more of this; let us play some other game."

"M'sieur Voldemar, in his capacity as the Queen's page, would hold her train as she ran into the garden," Malevsky observed venomously.

I flared up; but Zinaida swiftly laid her hand on my shoulder, rose a little in her seat, and declared in a voice that shook a little: "I have never given Your Excellency any right to be insolent, and so I must ask you to withdraw." She pointed to the door.

"Forgive me, Princess!" Malevsky muttered, turning pale.

"The Princess is right!" Belovzorov exclaimed, and he, too, rose.

"By God, I never expected you to take it like that," Malevsky added. "I don't think there was anything of that nature in what I said. . . . It never occurred to me to insult you even in thought. . . . Do pardon me."

Zinaida gave him a cold look and coldly laughed. "If you wish you can remain," she declared with a negligent gesture. "I and M'sieur Voldemar were angry over nothing. You find it pleasant to wound! May you enjoy it!"

"Forgive me!" Malvesky repeated yet again; and I, remembering Zinaida's gesture, thought again that even a real queen could not have pointed an audacious man to the door with greater dignity.

[1] Henri Auguste Barbier (1805–82) French poet known chiefly by his satirical poems *Iambic Verses*.

The game of forfeits did not continue for long after this little incident; everybody felt rather awkward, not so much because of what had happened as because of another, not altogether defined, yet oppressive feeling. No one referred to it, but each of us was conscious of it, both in himself and in his neighbor. Maidanov read his poems to us, and Malevsky praised them with exaggerated enthusiasm. "Isn't he anxious to show how kind he is!" Lushin whispered to me. We soon broke up. Suddenly Zinaida went into a reverie; the Princess sent in to say that she had a headache; Nirmatsky began to complain of his rheumatism.

I was a long time getting to sleep; I had been impressed by Zinaida's story. "Was she hinting at something, perhaps?" I asked myself. "And at whom, at what was she hinting? And if there really is something to hint at, how is one to decide? . . . No, no, it cannot be that," I whispered, turning over from one hot cheek to the other. But I remembered Zinaida's face as she told her story. I remembered the exclamation that had burst from Lushin in the Nieskuchny Gardens, the sudden changes in her behavior toward me, and I was lost in conjecture. "Who is he?" Those three words seemed to rise before my eyes, outlined in the darkness. I felt as though a low, sinister cloud were hanging over me, and I could feel its pressure and was waiting for it to burst any moment. Of recent times I had grown accustomed to a great deal, I had seen a great deal at the Zasiokins'. Their untidiness, the greasy candle-ends, the broken knives and forks, the glum old Vonifaty, the ragged maidservants, the manners of the old Princess herself — all this terrible existence no longer disturbed me. But I could not get accustomed to what I vaguely surmised was occurring in Zinaida now. "She's an adventuress," my mother had once said of her in my presence. An adventuress: my idol, my divinity! That term burned me, I tried to get away from it by burying myself in the pillow; I was indignant. . . . And at the same time what would I not have agreed to, what would I not have given, if I could have been that fortunate one at the fountain!

The blood began to burn and course through my veins. "The garden . . . the fountain," I thought. "I'll go into the garden." I briskly dressed and slipped out of the house. The night was

dark; the trees were only faintly whispering; a gentle cool
fell from the sky, the smell of parsley came from the garden. I
walked along all the paths; the quiet sound of my footsteps both
disconcerted and encouraged me. I halted, waited, and listened
to the heavy and rapid beating of my heart. At last I approached
the fence and leaned on the thin rail. Suddenly — or did I imagine
it? — a woman's figure flitted past a few paces away. I strained
my eyes into the darkness, I held my breath. What was that? Did
I hear footsteps, or was it again my heart beating? "Who is
there?" I stammered almost inaudibly. And what was that? A
suppressed laugh? Or the leaves rustling, or a sigh close to my ear?
I began to feel afraid. "Who is there?" I repeated still more
softly.

The air streamed past me for a moment; a fiery streak glittered
over the sky; a star fell: "Zinaida?" I wanted to ask; but the
words died on my lips. And suddenly everything grew profoundly still all around me, as often happens in the middle of the
night. Even the crickets ceased to chirrup among the trees; only a
window was noisily shut somewhere. I went on standing and
standing for a moment or two longer, then returned to my room,
to my cold bed. I felt a strange agitation, as though I had been to
keep an assignation and had been left waiting alone and had
passed by another's happiness.

¹⁷

Next day I saw Zinaida only for a second: she drove off somewhere in a droshky with her mother. On the other hand I saw
Lushin, who, by the way, hardly deigned to speak to me, and
Malevsky. The young Count smirked and began to talk to me
quite pleasantly. Of all the visitors to the Zasiokins' he alone had
been able to insinuate himself into our house and to find favor
with my mother. My father did not like him and treated him
with insulting courtesy.

"Ah, *monsieur le page*!" Malevsky began. "Very glad to meet
you. What is your excellent queen doing?"

His fresh, handsome face was so repellent to me at that moment, and he looked at me so contemptuously and playfully, that
I made no answer whatever.

"Are you still angry?" he went on. "How absurd! After all, it was not I who called you a page, and pages are usually found in attendance on queens. But allow me to observe that you perform your duties badly."

"Why do I?"

"Pages should be inseparable from their sovereigns; pages should always know what their sovereigns are doing, they should even watch over them"; and he added, lowering his voice: "Day — and night."

"What do you mean?"

"What do I mean? I think I am expressing myself clearly enough. Day — and night. In the daytime it is easy enough; one can see in the daytime and there are people about. But at night — that is the time to expect trouble. I advise you not to sleep at night, but to watch, to watch with all your powers. Remember, in the garden, by the fountain at night — that is where one should be on guard. You'll be grateful to me."

He laughed and turned his back on me. Probably he did not attach any special importance to what he had said: he had the reputation of being fond of mystifying people, and boasted of his ability to take people in at the masquerades — a gift that depended a great deal on the almost unconscious hypocrisy that marked his character. He was only trying to tease me, but every word he said flowed like poison through my veins. The blood rushed to my head. "Ah, so that's it!" I said to myself. "Good! So I did not go into the garden for nothing. But it shall not be!" I exclaimed aloud and beat my breast with my fist, though to tell the truth I had no idea what it was that must not be. "Whether it is Malevsky himself that visits the garden," I thought (possibly he had said too much, and he was capable of such insolence), "or anyone else" (our garden wall was very low, and it was quite easy to climb over it), "it will be a bad lookout for anyone I come across. I don't advise anyone to fall in with me! I shall show all the world and her, the traitress" (so after all I did call her a traitress) "that I can take my revenge!"

I returned to my room, went to my writing-desk and took out a penknife I had recently bought, felt the sharp blades, and, with furrowed brows, with cold and concentrated resolution I thrust it into my pocket, as though such deeds were nothing surprising and my actions nothing new to me. My heart swelled angrily and went numb. I did not relax my displeasure or my compressed lips all that day, and I walked backward and forward with one hand in my pocket, clutching the heated knife and preparing myself for something terrible. These new and unprecedented feelings so greatly occupied and diverted me that, to tell the truth, I thought very little about Zinaida. I was continually thinking of Aleko, the young gypsy: "Whither, my handsome youth?" "Lie down!" And then: "Thou art all spattered with blood; oh, what hast thou done?" . . . "Nothing!" With what a harsh smile did I repeat that word "nothing"! My father was not at home, but my mother, who for some time past had been in a state of almost speechless irritation, noticed my air of doom, and at supper she said to me: "What are you sulking for like a mouse in the groats?" In reply I only smiled at her condescendingly and thought: "If she only knew!" Eleven o'clock struck; I went to my room, but I did not undress. I waited for midnight; at last it, too, struck. "Time!" I whispered between my teeth and, buttoning my coat right up and even rolling up my sleeves, I went out into the garden.

I had already chosen the spot where I would keep guard. At the end of the garden, where the fence separating our domain from that of the Zasiokins' ended in the common wall, grew a single fir; standing beneath its low, thick branches, I could have a good view of all that happened around me, so far as the nocturnal darkness would permit. Here, too, was a little path, which always seemed rather mysterious to me: it crawled like a snake up to the fence, which at this spot showed signs that someone had climbed over it, and led to a circular arbor of dense acacias. I reached the fir, leaned against its trunk, and began to watch.

That night was as still as the night before; but there were fewer clouds in the sky, and I could see the outlines of the bushes, and even the taller flowers, more clearly. Those first few moments of expectation were exhausting, almost frightening. I had not resolved on any step; I only pondered what action I should take. Should I thunder out: "Where are you going? Stop! Confess or die"? Or should I simply strike? Every sound, every rustle and whisper, seemed significant, extraordinary. . . . I made ready. . . . I leaned forward. . . . But half an hour passed; an hour passed; my blood grew still and cool; I began to realize that I was doing all this for nothing, that I was even rather ridiculous, that Malevsky had been making fun of me. I abandoned my ambush and walked right through the garden. As though of intent, not the least sound was to be heard anywhere; everything was at peace; even our dog was asleep, rolled into a ball by the wicket gate. I climbed onto the ruins of the conservatory, and before me I saw the far-stretching plain. I recalled my meeting with Zinaida and was lost in thought.

I started. . . . I thought I heard the creak of a door being opened, then the light crack of a twig snapping. In two bounds I was down from the ruins, and froze still. Swift, light, and cautious steps were clearly to be heard in the garden. They drew near to where I was standing. "Here he comes — here he comes at last!" rushed through my mind. I convulsively drew the knife out of my pocket, convulsively opened it; crimson sparks danced before my eyes, in my fear and anger the hair stirred on my head. The footsteps came straight toward me; I bent down, I strained to meet them. A man appeared. . . . My God! It was my father!

I recognized him at once, though he was wrapped from head to foot in a dark cloak, and his hat was drawn down over his face. He went past me on tiptoe. He did not notice me, though nothing concealed me; but I crouched and cowered so low that I think I must have been level with the ground. The jealous Othello ready to commit murder was suddenly transformed into a school-boy. I was so frightened by my father's unexpected appearance that at first I did not even notice whence he had come or where he went. Only when everything was again still all around me did I straighten up and wonder: "What is father walking in the garden at night for?" In my fright I had dropped my pocketknife in the grass, but I did not even trouble to look for it: I felt deeply ashamed. I cooled down in a moment. But as I returned home, I went to my bench under the elder bush and glanced at the window of Zinaida's bedroom. The small, slightly convex panes showed as dim blue patches in the feeble light coming from the nocturnal sky. Suddenly their color began to change. Behind them — I saw it, I saw it clearly — the white blind was let down cautiously and quietly, was let down to the windowsill, and remained down, motionless.

"What is all this?" I said aloud, almost involuntarily, when I was back in my room once more. "A dream, chance, or — ?" The suppositions that suddenly came to my mind were so new and strange that I did not even dare to give myself over to them.

Next morning I woke with a headache. The agitation of the night before had gone. It was replaced by a dull bewilderment and grief that I had never known before, as though something within me had died.

"What are you looking like a rabbit with half its brain extracted for?" Lushin asked me when we met. At breakfast time I took surreptitious glances first at my father, then at my mother. He was calm, as usual, and she, as usual, was secretly irritable. I waited for him to talk to me in his amiable way, as sometimes he did. But he did not even caress me with his everyday, cold caress. "Shall I tell Zinaida everything?" I thought. " . . . After all, it doesn't matter now, it's all over between us." I went to see her, but not only did I not say anything to her about it, I did not even succeed in saying more than a word to her, much as I wished to. Her brother, a twelve-year-old student in a military school, had arrived from Petersburg for a holiday. Zinaida at once placed him in my charge. "Here you are, my dear Volodya" (it was the first time she had used this diminutive), "here is a companion for you. His name is Volodya too. Please be nice to him; he's still shy, but he has a kind heart. Show him the Nieskuchny Gardens, take him for walks, and take him under your protection. You will do that, won't you? You're kind, too." She graciously laid both hands on my shoulders, and I was completely overcome. This boy's arrival turned me also into a boy. I gazed silently at the lad, who stared at me just as speechlessly. Zinaida burst into laughter and pushed us toward each other. "Now give each other a hug, children." We gave each other a hug.

"Would you like me to take you into the garden?" I asked him.

"If you please," he replied in a hoarse, genuinely cadet voice. Zinaida laughed again. I did manage to observe that never before had she had such a charming color in her cheeks. I went off with the cadet.

In our garden was an old swing. I seated him on the thin board and began to give him a swing. He sat very still in his new little uniform of stout cloth, with broad gold lace galloons, and clung tightly to the rope. "But you should unbutton your collar," I said to him. "It's all right, we're used to it," he said, and cleared his throat. He was like his sister; his eyes especially reminded me of her. I enjoyed doing him a kindness, but meanwhile that same corrosive sorrow was gnawing at my heart. "Now indeed I am a child," I thought; "but yesterday — " I remembered where I had dropped my penknife the night before and went and found it. The boy asked me for it, broke off a stout stem of angelica, carved a pipe from it, and began to pipe. Othello whistled a little, too.

But then how he wept, that very same Othello, in Zinaida's arms, when, seeking him out in a corner of the garden that evening, she asked him why he was so sad. My tears poured down so torrentially that she was alarmed. "What's the matter with you, what's the matter, Volodya?" she asked, and as I did not answer and did not stop crying, she made to kiss my wet cheek. But I turned away from her and whispered through my sobs: "I know everything; why did you play with me? . . . What did you need my love for?"

"I have done you wrong, Volodya," she said. "Ah, I have done you great wrong," she said, and clenched her fists. "How much there is in me that is stupid, dark, sinful! . . . But I am not playing with you now; I love you — you don't even suspect why, or how. . . . But all the same — what do you know?"

What could I say to her? She stood before me and looked at me, and I belonged to her wholly, from my head to my feet, the moment she looked at me. . . . Fifteen minutes later I was running races with her and her brother; I was no longer weeping, I was laughing, though my swollen eyelids dropped tears with my laughter; round my neck Zinaida's ribbon was tied instead of a cravat, and I cried out with joy when I succeeded in catching her by the waist. She did just as she liked with me.

19

I should find it difficult if I were made to tell in detail all that happened to me during the week after my unfortunate nocturnal expedition. It was a strange, feverish time, a kind of chaos in which the most contradictory feelings, thoughts, suspicions, hopes, joys, and sufferings eddied like a whirlwind. I grew afraid to look into myself, if a sixteen-year-old boy can look into himself at all; I grew afraid to take stock of anything; I simply hastened to get through the day till the evening. On the other hand, I slept at night — the child's mental levity helped me there. I did not wish to know whether anyone loved me, and did not wish to confess to myself that no one loved me; I avoided my father, but Zinaida I could not avoid. I burned as though on fire in her presence; but what use was there in my knowing the sort of fire in which I burned and melted? — it was bliss for me to melt and burn so pleasantly. I gave myself over entirely to my sensations, and was cunning with myself, turning my back on my memories, and closing my eyes to what I anticipated ahead of me. . . . Without doubt this drain on me would not have continued for long in any case — a thunderclap ended it all with one stroke and flung me into a new path.

Returning toward dinnertime after a long walk one day, I was amazed to learn that I would be dining alone: my father had driven somewhere, and my mother was not well, did not want anything to eat, and had locked herself in her bedroom. By the servants' faces I guessed that something unusual had occurred. I did not dare to question them, but I had one friend, the young butler, Philip, a passionate lover of verse and an artist on the guitar, and I spoke to him. He told me there had been a terrible scene between my father and mother (and every word was heard in the maids' room; much of the quarrel was in French, but the maid Masha had lived five years with a sempstress from Paris, and she understood everything). My mother had charged my father with infidelity, with intimacy with the young lady next door; at first my father had denied everything, but then he had flared up and in his turn had said something very harsh, "apparently about their ages," at which my mother had burst into tears. My mother had also made mention of a promissory note of the Princess's that had been accepted, and she had spoken very unpleasantly about her and the young lady too. And then my father had used threats to her. "And all the trouble arose," Philip added, "over an anonymous letter; and no one knows who wrote it. Otherwise there would have been no reason for all this affair to come out at all."

"But really was there anything in it?" I said with difficulty, while my hands and feet turned cold and something began to quiver in the very depths of my breast.

Philip winked meaningly. "There was. You can't keep these things quiet, no matter how careful your father was this time.

After all, you have to hire a carriage or something . . . and then you can't manage without the servants."

I sent Philip away and collapsed on my bed. I did not sob, or give way to despair; I did not ask myself when and how all this had happened; I was not astonished that I had not already guessed, long since. I did not even rail against my father. What I had learned was beyond my power to bear: this sudden revelation shattered me. It was all over. All my flowers were torn up in one handful and lay around me, scattered and trampled.

20

Next day Mother announced that she was going back to town. In the morning my father had gone to her bedroom and had sat alone with her for a long time. No one heard what he said to her, but she did not cry any more; she grew calm, and asked for food — but she did not come downstairs and did not change her decision. I remember I wandered about all day; but I did not go into the garden, and did not look once at the Zasiokins' wing. But that evening I was witness of an astonishing incident: my father led Count Malevsky by the arm from the reception room to the lobby and, in our footman's presence, coldly told him: "Several days ago in a certain house Your Excellency was shown the door. I shall not give you any explanation now, but I have the honor to inform you that if you call on me again I shall throw you through the window. I do not like your handwriting." The Count bowed, clenched his teeth, bristled up, and disappeared.

Preparations were put in hand for our return to town, to our house in Arbat Square. In all probability my father himself no longer wished to remain in the country. But evidently he had persuaded Mother not to make a scene; everything was done quietly, unhurriedly; my mother even sent a servant to convey her respects and to express her regret that, as she was not at all well, she would not be seeing the Princess again before our departure. I roamed about as though crazy and only wanted it all to end as soon as possible. One thought never left my head: how could she, a young girl, and a Princess after all, resolve on such conduct, knowing that my father was not free, and when she could have married Belovzorov, for instance? What did she hope for? Why was she not afraid of ruining all her own future? "Yes," I thought, "this is love, this is passion, this is devotion"; and I recalled Lushin's words: to sacrifice oneself for others is sweet. I happened to see a white patch at one of the windows of the wing. "Surely that isn't Zinaida's face?" I thought. . . . Yes, it was her face. I could endure no more. I could not part from her without saying a last good-by to her. I seized a convenient moment and went to her home.

In the reception room the old Princess welcomed me with her usual unpleasant and negligent greeting.

"Why have your people taken flight so soon?" she said, thrusting snuff into both her nostrils. I looked at her and felt relieved. Philip's reference to a "promissory note" had been tormenting me. But she suspected nothing; at least, so it seemed to me then. Zinaida came in from the next room, in a black dress, her face pale, her hair unbound; she silently took me by the hand and led me out of the room.

"I heard your voice and came out at once," she began. "And was it so easy for you to desert us, you wicked boy?"

"I've come to say good-by to you, Princess," I replied, "and probably forever. You have heard that we are going away?"

She gazed at me fixedly.

"Yes, I have heard. Thank you for coming. I had begun to think I would not be seeing you. Don't think badly of me. I tormented you sometimes, but all the same I am not what you imagine me to be."

She turned away and leaned against the window.

"Really I am not. I know you have a bad opinion of me."

"I have?"

"Yes, you have — you have. . . ."

"I have?" I repeated sorrowfully, and my heart began to quiver as of old under the influence of her irresistible, inexpressible enchantment. "I? Believe me, Zinaida Alexandrovna, no matter what you did, no matter how much you tortured me, I would love you and adore you to the end of my days."

She turned swiftly to me and, opening her arms wide, took my head in her hands and impetuously and hotly kissed me. God knows whom that long, farewell kiss was seeking, but I greedily tasted of its sweetness, I knew that it would never be repeated. "Good-by, good-by . . . " I said again.

She tore herself away and went out. And I left the house. I am unable to convey the feeling with which I left. I would never wish it to be repeated, but I would regard myself as unfortunate if I had never known it.

We drove back to town. It took me a long time to cut myself off from the past, it took me a long time to settle down to work. My wound slowly healed; but really there was no bad feeling between my father and me. On the contrary, he seemed to grow even more in my eyes; let psychologists explain this contradiction as they wish. One day as I was walking along the boulevard, to my indescribable joy I ran into Lushin. I liked him for his direct and unhypocritical nature, and, besides, he was dear to me because of the memories he awoke within me. I rushed over to him. "Aha!" he said. "So it's you, young man! Let me have a look at you! You're still rather yellow, but I must say there isn't the former nasty look in your eyes. Now you look like a man, not a lapdog. Well, and what are you doing? Working hard?"

I sighed. I did not want to lie, but I was ashamed to tell the truth.

"Now, don't be afraid," Lushin went on, "don't be shy. The main thing is to live a normal life and not to give yourself over to distractions. For what good will they ever do you? No matter where the wave carries you, it is always bad; but a man may stand on stone so long as he stands on his own feet. I've got a bit of a cough, and Belovzorov — have you heard?"

"No, I haven't. What's happened?"

"Vanished without a trace; they say he's gone off to the Caucasus. There's a lesson for you, young man. And all because they're not capable of getting out in time, of breaking the net. But you appear to have escaped without damage. Now see that you don't get caught again. Good-by."

"I shan't be caught again," I thought. "I shall never see her again." But I was fated to see Zinaida once more.

21

My father went riding every day; he had a magnificent roan and sorrel English thoroughbred, untiring and wicked, with a long, slender neck and long legs; he was called Electric. No one but my father could ride him. One day Father came to me in a good humor — a mood I had not known him to be in for a long time. He was intending to go for a ride and was already wearing spurs. I asked him to take me with him.

"We'd do better at a game of leapfrog," he replied. "On your hack you'll never keep up with me."

"Yes I shall; I'll wear spurs too."

"Come on, then."

We set off. I had a little shaggy raven horse, strong in the legs and quite skittish; true, he had to gallop at full speed when Electric was put into a fast trot, but even so I was not left behind. I have never seen another horseman like my father; he sat his horse so beautifully and with such careless ease that it seemed as though the horse beneath him were conscious of it and proud of him. We rode along all the boulevards, and through the Dvichye Fields, jumped several fences (at first I was afraid to jump, but my father felt contempt for timid people, and I ceased to be afraid), rode twice across the River Moskva, and I was just thinking that now we would be returning home, especially as my father himself had noticed that my horse was tired, when suddenly he turned away in the direction of the Crimean Ford and galloped along the bank. I set off after him. Drawing up to a lofty pile of old beams, he swung himself nimbly out of the saddle, ordered me to dismount, and, giving me his horse's reins, said I was to wait for him here by the beams. Then he turned into a narrow lane and was lost to sight. I began to walk up and down along the bank, leading the horses and swearing at Electric, who would keep throwing up or shaking his head, snorting and neighing. And when I halted he dug his hoofs into the earth one after another, squealed, and bit my mount on the neck; in a word, he behaved like a spoilt thoroughbred. My father did not return. An unpleasant dampness rose from the river; a fine rain fell softly and sprinkled tiny dark spots over the idiotic gray beams, which I now found thoroughly boring as I wandered about in their vicinity. I began to feel anxious, but still my father did not return. Some policeman, a Finn, who was all gray too, and had an enormous shako, like a pot, on his head, and was armed with a halberd (what was a policeman doing on the bank of the River Moskva, I wondered), came along and, turning his elderly, furrowed face in my direction, asked me:

"What are you doing here with those horses, young sir? Give them to me, I'll hold them."

I did not reply; he asked me for some tobacco. In order to get away from him (moreover, I was on tenterhooks with impatience), I went several paces in the direction my father had taken, then walked along the little lane to its end, turned a corner, and stopped short. In a street some forty paces away, outside the open window of a small wooden house, I saw my father. He was standing with his back to me and leaning with his chest against the windowsill. Inside the house, half hidden by the curtain, a woman in a dark dress was sitting, talking to him. The woman was Zinaida.

I was petrified. I confess that I had had not the least expectation of what I saw. My first reaction was to turn and flee. "He will look round," I thought, "and I shall be done for." But a strange feeling, a feeling stronger than curiosity, stronger even than jealousy, stronger than fear, restrained me. I began to watch, I tried to overhear what they were saying. Apparently my father was insisting on something. Zinaida would not agree. I can see her face even now, mournful, serious, beautiful, and with an indescribable impress of devotion, sorrow, love, and a kind of despair — I cannot find another word for it. She spoke in monosyllables, did not raise her eyes, and only smiled, humbly and obstinately. In that smile alone did I recognize my former Zinaida. My father shrugged his shoulders and adjusted the hat on his head: a movement that was always a sign that he was getting impatient. Then I caught the words: "*Vous devez vous séparer de cette . . .*" Zinaida drew herself up and stretched out her hand. . . . Suddenly before my eyes, something unbelievable occurred: my father impetuously raised his whip, with which he had been beating the dust out of the edge of his coat, and I heard a sharp blow on that arm bared to the elbow. I could hardly refrain from crying out. But Zinaida shuddered, gazed silently at my father, and slowly raised her arm to her mouth, then kissed the weal that showed livid across it. He threw his whip away and, running hurriedly up the steps of the veranda, burst into the house. Zinaida turned and, stretching out her arms, throwing back her head, also left the window.

My heart sinking with fear, possessed with a bewildered horror, I flung myself back and, running along the lane, all but letting go of Electric, returned to the riverbank. I could make nothing of what I had seen. I knew that my cold and restrained father sometimes had outbreaks of frenzy, yet I could not realize that I had just witnessed such an attack. But I felt at once that no matter how long I lived, it would never be possible for me to forget that movement, that look, that smile of Zinaida's; I felt that her image, this new image that had suddenly been revealed to me, was imprinted forever in my memory. I stared senselessly at the river and did not notice that tears were running from my eyes. "They beat her," I thought; "they beat her . . . beat her. . . ."

"Now what's the matter with you? Give me my horse!" I heard my father's voice behind me.

I mechanically gave him the rein. He sprang into the saddle. The animal was chilled, and he rose on his hind legs and took one bound of a good ten feet. But Father quickly had him under control; he drove the spurs into his flanks and struck him on the neck with his fist. "Pity I haven't got my whip!" he muttered.

I remembered how that same whip had whistled and the blow it had struck, and shuddered.

"What have you done with it?" I asked after a moment.

He did not reply, but galloped on ahead. I overtook him. I simply had to see his face.

"Have you been bored while I was gone?" he asked through set teeth.

"A little. But where have you dropped your whip?" I asked him again.

He gave me a swift look. "I haven't dropped it," he said; "I threw it away." He was lost in thought and his head sank on his breast. And then, for the first and probably for the last time, I saw how much tenderness and regret could be expressed in his stern features.

He galloped on once more, and this time I could not overtake him: I arrived home fifteen minutes after him.

"Now, that is love," I said to myself again as I sat that evening before my writing-desk, which was now beginning to be littered with exercise books and primers. "That is passion. How could one help revolting, how could one endure a blow from anyone, least of all from the dearest of all hands! But evidently you can, if you really love. . . . Yet I — I imagined . . ."

The past month had aged me considerably, and even to me my love, with all its agitations and sufferings, seemed something petty, and childish, and miserable by comparison with this other, this unknown something, at which I could hardly surmise and which frightened me, like a strange, handsome, but threatening face that one vainly tries to discern in the dusk.

I dreamed a strange and terrible dream that night. I thought I was entering a low, dark room. . . . My father was standing with a whip in his hand and stamping his feet; Zinaida was huddled in one corner, and there was a crimson line, not on her hand, but on her forehead. . . . And behind them both Belovzorov rose covered with blood, grinning with his white teeth and angrily threatening him.

Two months later I entered the university, and six months afterward my father died of a stroke, in Petersburg, to which city we had recently moved. A few days before his death a letter arrived from Moscow that greatly agitated him. . . . He went to ask my mother for something, and they say he even wept — he, my father! On the very morning of the day he had the stroke he began to write a letter to me in French. "My son," he wrote, "fear woman's love; fear that happiness, that poison. . . ." After his death my mother sent quite a large sum of money to Moscow.

22

Four years passed. I had just left the university and still had no real idea what I intended to do with myself, at what door to knock; for the time being, I was loafing about in idleness. One fine evening I met Maidanov at the theater. He had married and gone into the civil service; but I did not notice any change in him. He still went into raptures just as unnecessarily, and grew depressed just as suddenly.

"Do you know," he said to me, in passing, "Madame Dolskaya is here?"

"Which Madame Dolskaya?"

"Why, have you forgotten? The former Princess Zasiokina, whom we were all in love with, including yourself. Do you remember, in the house you had for the summer near the Nieskuchny Gardens?"

"Has she married Dolsky, then?"

"Yes."

"And she is here, in the theater?"

"No, I mean she's in Petersburg. She arrived a day or two ago. She is planning to go abroad."

"What sort of man is her husband?" I asked.

"A splendid fellow, and wealthy. He was a colleague of mine in Moscow. You understand that after that affair — you must know all about it" (he smiled significantly) — "it was not easy for her to make a match; there were consequences. . . . But with her intelligence everything is possible. Go and call on her; she'll be very glad to see you. She has grown even more beautiful."

He gave me Zinaida's address. She was staying in the Hôtel Demuth. Old memories began to quicken within me. . . . I promised myself that I would call on my former "passion" the very next day. But something else came along; a week passed, then another; and when I did at last go to the Hôtel Demuth and ask for Mme Dolskaya, I learned that she had died four days previously, quite suddenly, in childbirth.

Something seemed to strike at my heart. The thought that I could have seen her and did not see her, and now never would see her — that bitter thought pierced me with all the strength of irresistible reproach. "She's dead!" I repeated, staring stupidly at the porter. I slowly made my way into the street and went, not knowing whither. All the past came back and rose before me in a moment. And so that was how it had been resolved, that was what that young, burning, brilliant life, hurrying and agitated, had striven to achieve! As I thought this, I imagined those dear features, those eyes, those curls, in a narrow box, in the damp underground gloom, here, not far from me, who was still alive, and perhaps only a few paces from my father. . . . I thought all this, I strained my imagination; but meanwhile:

> *"From indifferent lips I heard news of her death,*
> *And indifferently listened I to it . . ."*

the words echoed in my soul. O youth! Youth! There seems to be nothing you cannot do, you would seem to have mastery over all the treasures of the universe, even sorrow is a comfort to you, even grief confers added beauty on your face, you are self-confident and audacious; you say: "I alone am alive, look at me." But with you, too, the days speed past and disappear without trace and without number, and everything within you vanishes, like wax in the sun, like snow. . . . And, maybe, all the secret of your charm consists not in the possibility that you can do anything, but in the possibility of thinking that you can do anything, consists just in the circumstance that you cast to the winds strength that you would not know how to use on anything else, in the circumstance that every one of us seriously regards himself as a spendthrift, seriously assumes that he has every right to say: "Oh, what would I have done if I had not wasted my time in vain!"

So too I. . . . How much I hoped for, how much I expected, what a rich future did I anticipate, even when I had only just carried out the momentarily returning apparition of my first love, accompanying it with a single sigh, a single pang of mourning.

But of all that I hoped, what has come to pass? And now that the evening shadows are already beginning to speed over my life, what is left to me more fresh, more precious than the memory of that swiftly passed, vernal thunder of my morn?

But in vain do I upbraid myself. Even then, in that thoughtless, youthful time, I did not remain deaf to the mournful voice that called to me, the solemn sound that reached me from beyond the grave. I remember, a few days after I had learned of Zinaida's death, I was drawn by my own invincible attraction to be present at the deathbed of a poor old woman who lived in our house. Covered with rags, lying on hard boards, with a sack beneath her head, she died painfully and wretchedly. All her life had been passed in one bitter struggle with everyday need; she had never known joy, she had never tasted the honey of happiness; one would have thought that she could not but rejoice at death, at its freedom, its peace. And yet so long as her decrepit body still resisted, so long as her breast still heaved beneath the icy hand that lay on it, so long as her last strength had not departed from her, that old woman went on crossing herself and whispering: "Lord, forgive me my trespasses. . . ." And only with the last spark of consciousness did the expression of fear and terror of her end fade from her eyes. . . . And I remember that there, beside that poor old woman's deathbed, I suddenly felt afraid for Zinaida; and I wanted to pray for her, for my father . . . and for myself.

Ivan Sergeyvich Turgenev was born on October 28, 1818, at Oryol, in central Russia. In 1833 he attended the University of Moscow for a year, but took his degree from the University of Petersburg. He went to Berlin to complete his philosophical education (1838-41). When he returned to Russia in 1841, he had intended to devote himself to a university career; as it did not materialize, he entered the Civil Service, remaining only two years, and after 1845 abandoned all pursuits except literature. From 1845 until his mother's death in 1850, when he came into possession of a considerable fortune, Turgenev lived on his earnings as a literary man. His earliest publications were poetry. Although he contributed one work which has become standard in Russian dramatic repertories, *A Month in the Country*, the majority of his subsequent writing was prose fiction. Besides the seven works collected in the two volumes of *The Vintage Turgenev*, his best-known books are *A Sportsman's Sketches* (1852), *Nest of Gentlefolk* (1859), and *Poems in Prose* (1879-83). Turgenev died in France in 1883.

Harry Stevens, who has made the English translation for the two volumes of *The Vintage Turgenev*, is, under the pseudonym of Stephen Garry, the translator of Mikhail Sholokhov's *The Silent Don*.

The text of this book was set on the Linotype in Janson, a recutting made direct from the type cast from matrices long thought to have been made by Anton Janson, a Dutchman who was a practicing type-founder in Leipzig during the years 1668-1687.

VINTAGE FICTION, POETRY, AND PLAYS

A free catalogue of VINTAGE BOOKS *will be sent at your request. Write to* Vintage Books, 457 Madison Avenue, New York, New York 10022.

VINTAGE BELLES-LETTRES

VINTAGE RUSSIAN LIBRARY

A free catalogue of VINTAGE BOOKS *will be sent at your request. Write to* Vintage Books, 457 Madison Avenue, New York, New York 10022.

VINTAGE HISTORY AND CRITICISM OF
LITERATURE, MUSIC, AND ART

A free catalogue of VINTAGE BOOKS *will be sent at your request. Write to* Vintage Books, 457 Madison Avenue, New York, New York 10022.

VINTAGE BIOGRAPHY AND AUTOBIOGRAPHY

A free catalogue of VINTAGE BOOKS *will be sent at your request. Write to* Vintage Books, 457 Madison Avenue, New York, New York 10022.